The Hungarian Protestant Reformation
In The Sixteenth Century
Under The Ottoman Impact

The Hungarian Protestant Reformation In The Sixteenth Century Under The Ottoman Impact

Essays and Profiles

by

Alexander Sándor Unghváry

Texts and Studies in Religion
Volume 48
The Edwin Mellen Press
Lewiston/Lampeter/Queenston

Library of Congress Cataloging-in-Publication Data

This volume has been registered with the Library of Congress.

> This is volume 48 in the continuing series
> Texts and Studies in Religion
> Volume 48 ISBN 0-88946-837-0
> TSR Series ISBN 0-88946-976-8

A CIP catalog record for this book
is available from the British Library.

© Copyright 1989 The Edwin Mellen Press.

To the memory of

King Uláslzo, ruler of Hungary and Poland,
King Lajos II, ruler of Hungary and Bohemia

Two Archbishops
Five Bishops
the only Protestant Bishop, János Ungváry,
the millions of nameless Hungarian Christians who lost their
lives in the battles against the Muslims, defending Western
Christendom, thus enabling the reforms of Zwingli, Luther, and
Calvin to be realized in the Hungarian Reformation also.

Contents

The Hungarian Protestant Reformation
In The Sixteenth Century
Under The Ottoman Impact

Acknowledgements

The pleasure of research lies in finding ever new sources of evidence. I am therefore indebted to the American Philosophical Society for a Penrose travel grant, to the Curatorium of the Consortium Bernardinum of the University of Utrecht, the Netherlands for their stipend. The latter was matched by gifts of friends who must be named here because without their combined encouragement and help I doubt that my work could have been brought to completion: Hugo Hartenstein, the late Nelly Frey, Otto Mackensen, Anita Jane McCormick, Lászlo Pándy Szekeres, Virgil Seaberry, Dorothee Schuster, Dorothee Siepman van den Berg, Dick and Thea Van Halsema, Patricia M. Vajda, members of the Orthodox Presbyterian Church in Abilene, Texas. These combined efforts opened up many European libraries and their resources. Hungarian sources especially provided me with many references to illumine the past. This was one thing the late John T. McNeill encouraged me to do, saying, "One word of the men themselves is worth more that any description of them."

I often still think in the Hungarian language, therefore I am most thankful to our friend Dorothy Roman who spent many hours reading and where needed reformulating my "Hungarian English", always taking pains to bring my thoughts into words.

Kay Gibson word processed the final draft of the manuscript. In doing so she gave the text an additional proofreading, striving to maintain consistency in style, punctuation and grammar throughout the manuscript. Bonnie Kallweit corrected the final proof. For their contributions I am thankful.

My profound gratitude goes to Mike Downey for his careful preparation of the camera-ready copy.

I thank my friend Lewis B. Smedes of Fuller Theological Seminary for his supportive encouragement throughout the years and his colleague Richard Muller who was so kind to evaluate some chapters.

Finally I express my gratitude to my wife Elizabeth who in research, formulation, and rewriting has had so large a share that this is in a sense as much her book as mine.

Foreword

As a late pilgrim in this country, I have wanted to present a partial history of the Hungarian Protestant Reformation, unfamiliar to my fellow clerics. During my stay at Union Theological Seminary in New York, it was painful for me to learn from my fellow students, that knowledge of East Central European church history was lacking.

The blame for this vacuum should be put on those Hungarians living in the United States*, who have not felt it their intellectual duty to present their ancestors' struggle for religious freedom.

This series of narrative essays and biographical profiles was undertaken in an effort to provide a fully self-explanatory introductory history of the Hungarian Reformation. Since the Reformation has placed responsibilities on the individual, it has been necessary to select some outstanding reformers and present profiles to illustrate how these event-making individuals determined the course of history.

The work on this book was interrupted for decades by pastoral service and teaching at several universities and colleges. On the one hand this had some advantages, because now I have been able to incorporate the latest publications issued by contemporary Hungarian church historians. On the other hand, a discontinuity of style and interpretation became inevitable.

The subject matter is vast and therefore I have attempted to give for a better understanding of the complex issues, a comprehensive history of the Reformation in East Central Europe; a few parallel ecclesiastical developments in Bohemia as well as in Poland have been included.

Because my mentor, the late John T. McNeill, a well-known specialist on Calvinist church history, urged me to share memorable utterances of the unusual and vigorous personalities of the Hungarian reformers, I have endeavored to do so.

I have found it necessary to focus on those sources in which American religious freedom originally rooted. The word 'tolerance' was first coined in

---

*according to the last census ca. 2,000,000.

the midst of the sixteenth century, and interestingly the Hungarian Protestant Reformers were the first to declare religious freedom for Roman Catholic, Lutheran, Calvinist, and Unitarian believers in 1568.

Until now, several blank pages remain in Hungarian church history due to the centuries-long struggle with the intruding Asiatic Ottoman-Muslims, who systematically destroyed the primary sources of historiography. *Ad fontes* research, with few exceptions, was therefore not possible, mainly secondary source materials found in the different archives and libraries in Budapest, Debrecen, Vienna, Geneva, Zurich, Berne, Utrecht, as well as in the British Museum have been employed for this project.

With these limitations I offer this writing as a token of my gratitude for my present freedom and as an overdue document about those faithful men who established the second-largest existing Reformed Church in Europe. This book did not originate in historical nostalgia, but aims to show how the social fabric of Hungary was systematically destroyed by Islamic intolerance on the Eastern frontier of European Christendom. The Hungarian Protestant Reformers started to re-integrate the divided nation into a new framework; their activities made religion a paramount issue in the life of the Hungarian people, thus the former Asiatic Magyars prevented the Islamic conquest of Europe; had they not done so, the history of Western Christendom might well have been very different from what we know today.

The reason that this writer has treated two chapters, that on Melius and the one on Dávid, more extensively, is because both were more than religious dogmatists, they were ecclesiastical statesmen and founders of two distinctive Churches in East Central Europe. It was deemed necessary because contemporary German church historians have forgotten to include these names in the universal history of the Church. In addition, well-known historian Earl Willbur expressed in his last testament that a biography of Francis Dávid, the Unitarian apostle, as well as that of Blandrata, were lacking.

The author is aware that his book is not a definitive work on the rich Hungarian religious history, but only a first step toward a much needed wholeness. He also believes it the right of a biographer to argue with his subject, and not to stand aside in a posture of inhuman detachment.

Chapter I

A Glance at Hungarian Religious History
Before The Conquest of The Danube Basin

The Anthropological Aspect

Lack of knowledge has created blank pages in the religious history of all peoples, including the Hungarians. Careful investigations undertaken by the last generation of Hungarian historians, however, have enabled them to write a meaningful text on some of those empty leaves. These scholars have analyzed Arabic annals, Chinese chronicles, and quite a number of Byzantine sources, and thus they have been able to extend the field of knowledge back to the fourth century A.D., tracing the path of religious and spiritual development of the Hungarian people to the beginning of the Christian era.

Let us marshal some of the significant facts. At the historical moment that a group of people begins to take account of its constituents, these people step into the history of mankind. This new consciousness creates a community which begins to formulate its destiny with specific goals. Among the Magyar tribes this event took place in Asia, when seven tribes elevated Prince Arpád to the rank of ruler.* The late Count, Paul Teleki, made the interesting observation that the Magyars held their first Diet in their saddles on horseback and so established their first federal Constitution, which declared that all constituent members of the confederation had equal rights.

A second law, expressing social considerations, codified the right that all property should be owned and shared equally.

---

*When the seven tribes formed a federation they accepted the name of one tribe, Magyars. In Europe they were called Hungarians.

This forming of a confederation was the first act, a prelude to the conquest of the Carpathian Basin in East Central Europe. The conquest took place in 896 A.D. and the territory was developed into what later was called the Hungarian state. One might compare this conquest with the historical event which took place when Moses with authority and leadership set out to conquer Palestine, as well as with the American Declaration of Independence in 1776, which issued a new nation into the history of mankind.

The Magyars came into Europe as the last people in the *Völkerwanderung*. They closed, as it were, that era and eventually helped to consolidate East Central Europe into Western Christendom. As horseriding nomads of the steppe, the Magyars lived in a multi-lingual, multi-religious, and multi-national empire, which was founded on a voluntary, federative basis. One might say that, metaphysically speaking, these people were living in "cosmic subjugation", and the dignity and authority of their prince was therefore charismatic. Accordingly, his power was theocratic.

When these nomads arrived from the heart of Asia after five hundred years of wandering toward the West, attracted by the Roman Empire and inspired by the *Völkerwanderung*, they joined with the Khazars, becoming a constituent part of the Khazar Empire for nearly three hundred years, "during which they fought all the wars together with the Khazars," as a chronicle reported.

The Khazar federation was situated between Byzantine Christianity and military aggressive Arab Islam in Near East Asia. These Christian and Islamic neighbors tried to impose upon the Khazars their religious as well as their political influence. In fact, the Byzantine mission made such inroads into the ethnically mixed population that in the eighth century a Byzantine episcopacy was established. In attempts to neutralize the influence of both foreign intruders, the pagan Khazar leaders adopted a unique third religious affiliation, state Judaism. Through this politico-religious act, the Christian mission was soon snuffed out.[1] Yet, characteristically, the ruling Turkish Judaizing class granted full liberty of religious practice to all members of the federation.[2] In this way the Khazar religious policy remained free from creedal intolerance. Although there were groups of Christians, Jews, and Muslims among the Khazars, the majority of the population practiced traditional pagan religion combined with an early monotheism.

As members of the Khazar empire, the Magyars assimilated the same religious policy; they basically believed in one God, who was the Heavenly Father, the Spirit who dwelt on high. Because this was not a revealed religion, it had no dogmatic tendencies and could easily display for centuries the same tolerance as the Khazar leaders showed. It is worthy of note that many words with a religious connotation were incorporated in the Magyars' pre-Christian vocabulary, such as sin, God, the Father, forgiveness, saints.

When after several centuries the Magyars finally departed from the Khazar federation and set out to conquer what was to become their father land, *Magyarország*, called Hungary by their European neighbors, three other tribes, the Cabars, joined with the Magyar federation; later they were assimilated into the Magyar ethnical group.

Naturally, during their participation in the conglomerate Khazar empire, the Magyars had accepted ethnical, religious, and even linguistic pluralism, and when they finally settled along the banks of the Danube, they continued to practice this learned tradition. Later, religious syncretism also became the foundation of secular syncretism as was documented centuries later in Transylvania.[3] The majority of the Magyars held strongly to its early monotheistic pagan faith; whereas a minority, consisting of the southern tribes, having established very early contacts with Byzantium, had adopted Orthodox Christianity. A third group, however, had embraced the Judaistic religion during the association with the Khazars, while a fourth group had embraced Islam.

Linguistically, the Magyars belonged to the Finno-Ugric group; there was no relation to any other European language. Racially, the Turkish and East-Baltic ethnical elements constituted the Magyar people.

Another tradition inherited from the Asiatic period also determined the Magyar continuity in the West; namely, in the centuries-long existence on the spacious Asiatic steppes the nomadic tribes had to fight constantly for grazing lands because their million-large herds needed forage and water. They also had to fight off the encroaching neighbors. Accordingly, this way of life demanded and developed strong military policies, disciplines, as well as solidarity with the charismatic chieftains. A military culture was for centuries the inherited form of living, even after the conquest. The fact that the main yearly income tax was based on the number of swords owned by members of the federation illustrates that military priority dominated the

whole organized way of life. One might rightfully call it a military civilization.

Religious Development During the Migration Period

The earliest contact which the Magyars had with Christian missionaries
goes back to the fourth century, when they reached territory under Byzantine influence. According to ecclesiastical sources which are being thoroughly scrutinized by historians, the first missionary work among the Magyars,
who, like the Huns, were ethnically Turkish, was done by Armenian Christians. Nestorian influence has also been registered. The first Apostle known
by name was Gregory the Illuminate, whose apostolate took place about
331 A.D. John Chrysostom also sent missionaries to the Magyar tribes in
398 and 403 A.D. Even the first Bible translator, St. Jerome, wrote in an
epistle that "the Huns learn the Psalter", *Hunni discunt psalterium.*[4] (At
that time, the name Hun was often identical with Magyar, or Onugor.)[5]

There are other records about the Slavic Apostles, Methodius and Cyril,
who met with some Magyars when the apostles went as missionaries to the
Khazars in 861 A.D. They explained the basics of Christian beliefs to these
Magyars, who in return gave them many presents and asked them to pray
to the one God on their behalf.[6]

In the sixth century Byzantine foreign policy used missionary activities to
bring nomad peoples into their political realm. One way was to baptize the
leaders of those people, as for instance was done in 528 A.D. to Gordos,
prince of the Magyars or Mugaris, when he embraced Byzantine Christianity after Emperor Justinian I had agreed to be his godfather, and
Gordos became an honorable patrician of Byzantium. Consequently, Gordos became tied down by double loyalty to the Byzantine interest, and
Orthodox Christianity made strong roots among the Magyar tribes of the
southern wing.[7]

An unbroken chain of reports testifies to the continuity of similar actions
such as that to Gordos. In another tribe Prince Bulcsu also was baptized in
Byzantium in 948, Emperor Konstantinos Porphyrogennetos becoming his
godfather. Another prince, Gyula, embraced Christianity in 952 and brought
to Hungary the priest Hierothos, who later was delegated by the Eastern
Orthodox Church as first bishop to the Magyars.[8]

As a result of the early contacts with Byzantium, the Eastern Orthodox
Church established several monasteries and churches in Hungary after the
completion of the conquest, competing with the Roman Christian mis-

sionaries. The daughter of King Ladislaw of Hungary eventually married Emperor John II and as queen founded one of the most prominent monasteries in Constantinople, the *Pantokraten.*

After the long migration, the Magyars finally established themselves in the more or less empty and unorganized Carpathian Basin. It was empty because the German invasion had forced the Roman Legions to withdraw from Pannonia in the West and from Transylvania or Dacia in the East. After the Roman evacuation, a succession of nomad empires had temporarily been established in the Basin, such as that of the Huns, the Avars, and the Bolgars, who belonged to the Turkish ethnical group. The Slavic elements had earlier been subjugated by the Avars, who brought them as slaves into East Central Europe; when the nomad empires ceased to exist, the Slavs remained in the Carpathian Basin and eventually mixed with the former ruling Turkish people. The Slavic ethnical groups later accepted Christianity and organized themselves into two local tribal associations with Roman connections. These early Christian settlers were soon integrated into the Magyar kingdom having some impact on the process of Hungarian Christianization.[9]

During the occupation of the lands, the Magyar tribes often raided Western countries, such as Germany, Italy, France, Spain, and Switzerland. These military actions had an economic purpose, namely to resettle the needed labor forces from the Western countries. Agricultural workers, artisans, winegrowers were kidnapped in order to serve the former nomads to whom they became economically indispensable. The forced new settlers were often joined by Christian priests and monks, who also helped to Christianize the late pilgrims, the Magyars.

Of course those nations who year after year were visited by the Hungarians collecting sums of ransom in order to keep the peace, developed cosmic fear of the raiders. The raids, however, had a positive impact upon Western civilization in that urbanization and the building of fortifications for self-defense followed.[10] The result was the creation of the so-called Cities of Fear, which eventually became cultural centers in the Western countries. Unfortunately, the Hungarians created understandably an unsympathetic image, and hatred and fear for them was amplified by predictions which prophesied the nearness of the End Time. According to humble monks the End would occur when barbaric people would emerge from the East in about 1000 A.D. Exactly at that time the Magyars rode into Europe and the bishop of Würzburg identified them, proving that they were the Gog and Magog whose arrival had been predicted. The more learned Bishop Abbas disproved, however, that these nomads could be Gog and Magog, but in the end the confusing millenarian prophesy stigmatized the Magyar conquerors for centuries. It was not until the Sixteenth Century when a new Gog and Magog phantom turned up with the Ottoman Muslims that the Hungarian nation was relieved of the stigma, when the then Christian nation repentingly, loudly prayed "From the deep we cry unto our Lord", *De profundis ad te Domine clamavi.*

At a very early time, the former Roman provinces had opened the land for Christianization, and several famous Christian martyrs had found their graves there. Bishop St. Eusebius was martyred by the Romans in 258 A.D. Another martyr, Bishop St. Ireneus, was hanged in 303 A.D.

St. Martin, symbol of compassion, was born in Pannonia, and later became bishop of Tours.

To the religious history of Pannonia belongs also the spread of Arian sectarian belief. Migrating Germans from Asia had settled in Pannonia for a short interval spreading the Arian faith. Their Bishop Ulfius was conse crated there with the Arian rite. Emperor Constantine the Great personally visited neighboring provinces to stem the further spread of Arianism in 322 A.D.[11]

When the Hungarian conquest was finished successfully, and Roman and Byzantine missionaries revisited the land, the Hungarian ruler Géza welcomed them, greatly supporting their missionary activities. For instance, Bishop Pilgrim of Passau reported to Pope Benedict VII in 974 that "the Hungarians obediently put their heads into the yoke of the Lord."[12] It is important to point out that Géza's church policy from the beginning favored non-German missionaries from Gallia, Burgundy, Italy, Ireland, Bohemia, and Poland, to serve his people in the radical transitional period. His intent was to secure his country from the influence of the German emperors, who via German missionaries attempted to establish their influence in East Central Europe among the Czechs, the Polish, as well as among the Hungarians. Thus, the most successful missionary workers among the Hungarians were the Czech St. Adalbert, the Italian Anastasius, the Burgundian St. Astric, the French Bonipart, the Venetian St. Gerard, and the Polish Zoeard and Benedict. Thankful Hungarians sent yearly several casks of wine to the Polish monasteries from which Zoeard and Benedict had come.[13]

During these historical developments, the most important event occurred in the year 1000, when on Christmas Eve, St. Stephen was installed in his Apostolic role as ruler, crowned with a crown sent by Pope Sylvester II. With this sacerdotal act, the Árpád dynasty was inaugurated to rule for more than three hundred years during which they firmly integrated the nation into European Christendom, giving it the mission to defend East Central Europe from the Asiatic invasions. Parallel with Roman Christianization, the Byzantine mission was permitted also until the great Schism of 1054, which separated Rome and Byzantium.

During these missionary efforts, two kinds of western monasticism determined the further developments among the Hungarians. One, the active and serving Benedictines, the other, the rather passive and meditative Cluniac reformers. In the ecclesiastical development which followed, one can observe the culture-creating role of the Christian religion among the former Asiatic nomadic Magyars as they were being integrated into the European culture circle. The conquering people, who as last arrival ended the *Völkerwanderung* from Asia, transformed a desolate European area into a western Christianized, cultural land.

It is a historical fact that all European nations went through a similar transformation; originally all had been conquerors, all had determined the Christian ethos of Europe. In objective, final analysis, all culture had been founded by different conquerors; the Franks had shaped Gallia into the earliest Christian nation, Teutonic tribes had built upon the ruins of Latin Europe a Germanic culture zone ranging over half of the Continent; William the Conqueror had redirected the fate of Albion, and the Anglo-Saxons changed the old America into the new America, giving it specific ethnoreligious contents.

The conquerors with their freedom were responsible, however, for the use and implementation of the historical privilege to rule, and for the realization of values, in order to become respected members of the European commonwealth. The centuries-long contribution of the Hungarians to European Christendom was in time recognized by several Vicars of Christ, who openly stated that "The most faithful member in Christendom was the Hungarian nation, which later became a 'Shield of Christianity and the bulwark' against the Asiatic threat."

Footnotes

1. Mandel, M. *Jozsef Khazar király válaszlevélenek hitelessége.* Pécs, 1929.

2. Dunlop, D. M. The History of the Jewish Khazars. Princeton University Press, 1958. p. 223.

3. Dunlop, D. M. *ibid.*, p. 197.

4. Moravcsik, Gyula. *A honfoglalás elötti magyarság és a kereszténység.* In: St. István Emlekkönyv. Budapest, 1938. p. 186.

5. Németh, Gyula. *A honfoglalo magyarság kialakulása.* Budapest, 1930. pp. 165–171.

6. Király, Péter. *Magyarok emlitése a Konstantine és Method Legendajában.* Budapest, 1974. p. 4, p. 9.

7. Moravcsik, Gyula. *op. cit.* p. 13.

8. Moravcsik, Gyula. Byzantine Christianity and the Magyars in the Period of the Migration. The American Slavic and East European Review, No. 5, 1946. pp. 29–45.

9. Kászonyi, Franz. *Die Rassenverwandtschaft zwischen die Donau Völker.* Geneva, 1931. Publ. League of Nations. Amelthea Verlag.

10. Mittelalterliche Quellen zur Geschichte des Ungarischen Volkes in der Sanktgaller Stiftsbibliothek:

    Die Ungarn in Sankt Gallen. ed. Johannes Duft, Zurich 1957, Verlag der Buchdruckerei, v. Ostheim. AG. p. 48.

11. Archaeology of Roman Pannonia, ed. A. Lengyel and G. T. B. Radan. Lexington University Press, 1980. p. 196.

12. Fejér, Géza. *Codex Diplomaticus Hungariae Ecclesiasticus ac Civilis.* Vol. I. Budapest, 1829. p. 261.

13. Divéky, A. *Magyar és Lengyel egyházi kapcsolatok St. István korábol.* In: St. István Emlékkönyv. Budapest, 1938, Vol. I. p. 474.

Chapter II

Ottoman Encroachment and Hungary's Role in the Defense of Western Christendom

The Influence of Ottoman Imperialism on the Balkan

Through centuries European secular and religious history has been greatly influenced by the invasion of the Islamic Arabs from Asia.

To begin the Iberian countries of Spain and Portugal came under Islamic domination. The occupation took place between 711 and 1492, during which period the conquerors also tried to extend their power into French territories. The French ruler, Karl Martell, however, expelled them in 732 at Tours, and thus saved Western Europe from the Islamic threat.

The Muslim expansion was a far-reaching event in European history, which resulted in a number of interesting changes. For instance, the traffic on the Mediterranean Sea was halted by the Muslims and the economic consequence was that the usual import of wine, corn, papyrus, and oil from Africa had become impossible. One of the cultural-historical results was that the oil used in lamps was no longer available and the lights in the monasteries and churches were no longer burning. This forced the monks to invent the candle as a new means to bring back some light. To secure the continuity of literary work, parchment replaced papyrus. Spices disappeared from the normal diet. Gold was no longer available, and this forced the merchants to strike silver dinari. In political life, the original Mediterranean dominance shifted to the north, and the Popes of Rome lost their influence.[1]

When finally the Christian forces succeeded in reconquering the Iberian peninsula, expelling the Asiatic intruders, Muslim imperialism was moved to a new front. Via Byzantium and the Balkan peninsula, an attack was launched on European Christianity. In this new situation the Hungarian nation had to assume a role similar to that of the French in 732, that is, to defend Christendom, this time on the Eastern front. There the Hungarian nation fought for centuries to rescue themselves as well as western civilization.

The original motive of the conquest of Arab-Turkish Islam

The situation in the over-populated Arab peninsula with its Jewish, Christian, and Islamic believers suddenly exploded. The economic misery and resulting poverty forced the Arabs to lead constant raids on neighboring territories. These raids were in essence nothing else than predatory expeditions. Mohammed, (570–632), once a camel thief, eventually transformed these raids into Jihad or Holy Struggle,* legitimizing them, with the help of Koranic law, as a religious movement. As a prophet he declared and directed a religious crusade against the infidels, "fighting in the way of Allah." For more than a thousand years this Islamic crusade was motivated by a mixture of religious conviction and materialistic greed rather than true and pure religious devotion. The self-appointed prophet Mohammed channelized surplus Arab energy into religio-economic expansion. The movement was sanctified by religious fanaticism: go, conquer, and subdue all infidels on earth. It appears obvious that Mohammedanism has a built-in concept of war which perpetuated itself and thus became an imperialistic force.

In the beginning, the "infidels" were the Arab opponents to the prophet; later the Jewish Arabs and the Christians were included as well. Mohammed's Holy Sword as symbol of Islamic expansion against other religions was in itself a unique religious phenomenon. Of all great historical religions, Islam alone was born with a sword in the hand. Mohammed's religion has always relied on the sword; for thirteen hundred years the mulla, or religious teacher, who read the Friday prayers in the mosque, carried a sword, even if it was made of wood only, as a symbol of his creed.[2]

Historian William Muir, in his book *Life of Mohammed*, observed that "the sword of Mohammed and the Koran are the most fatal enemies of western civilization, liberty, and truth, which the world has yet known."[3]

---

*The character of Jihad, Holy War, changed at this time. It became a continuous struggle.

Author Zwermer also concluded that the symbol of the sword abrogated a whole list of passages in the Koran, all of which taught a measure of leniency towards unbelievers. There are one hundred and ten injunctions commanding the use of Mohammed's sword.[4]

Source of Islamic tradition: the Koran

When a historian turns to the source of Islamic tradition, rooted in the Koran, he finds many dubious dogmas, teachings from other religious as well as oral traditions from which Mohammed composed his "revealed" religion. The paradox of the Koran is that the "Book" never was handed down by the prophet himself. He carved on a variety of materials, such as pieces of bark or palm leaves, notes and reflections and repetitious words; a part of the Koran text was even to be found carved into 9,999 beans. It took Mohammed's successors twenty years to collect and edit the text which allegedly was handed down from above. Textual analysis has proved that many ideas, sayings, and moral instructions were borrowed from Jewish and Christian sources. Mohammed had no direct access to the Torah or the Bible, and his knowledge was derived from hearsay.[5] Unfortunately, whatever Mohammed knew about Christianity he had learned from the contemporary Nestorian-Monotheistic sect, as well as from a Byzantine sectarian monk, Sergius. The latter spread his religious aberration, Monotheism, that is, Christ as god-man had one will.[6] According to Brockelmann, Mohammed's understanding of Judeo-Christian tradition was quite superficial and rich in errors.[7] He sometimes mixed up the name of Mary, mother of Jesus, with Aaron's sister Mirian-Mary. "O sister of Aaron."[8] Among things borrowed was, for instance, the tradition of prayer, which was transplanted from Jewish rituals. Mohammed at times even ordered the Lord's Prayer to be said. Another source of his mixed knowledge may have been his wife, Chadija, who formerly had been a Christian.

It is of interest to note how and why Mohammed changed his sympathy towards Jews and Christians. In the early phase of his religious endeavor, he hoped that either the people of the Old Testament or the Christians would adopt him as their prophet. When he was rebuked, however, he commenced to formulate his own teachings, combining different ideas from other Monotheistic religions. He attempted establishing his priority among these religions by declaring that Abraham was neither Jew nor Christian, but solely a Monotheist Muslim.[9]

He even proved his direct descendance from Abraham via Ishmael, which made him the only legitimate successor of Abraham.[10] In his simplified theology, Mohammed denied the reality of sin, because Allah, the Merciful, had already forgiven the wrongdoing of Abraham.[11] The logical conclusion was therefore to deny the necessity of the Atonement through Christ. The God of Mohammed was more merciful than the punishing God of the Old Testament. The dogma of the Trinity was regarded as nonsense, because it amounted to a new polytheism; according to Mohammed, Jesus was only a prophet and not the divine son of God.

To verify his prophetic ambitions among his illiterate followers, Mohammed several times accused the rabbis and Christian theologians of falsification of Biblical texts, saying that they had left out his name as the last prophet from the original revelation.[12]

Mohammed suffered from epilepsy and in the eyes of his primitive and illiterate fellow Arabs, this affliction was seen as a constant process of receiving revelation.[13]

Mohammed stressed that he was illiterate and only inspired from above; his contemporary opponents, however, accused him, saying that Mohammed each morning and evening wrote down the dictation from his literary helpers. Contrary to the accusation about the alleged textual falsification by the rabbis and Christian theologians, it was Mohammed who edited different religious writings to fit them into the Koran. In this manner he tried to legitimize his prophetic claim.[14] How much was borrowed from a variety of oral and written religious traditions is illustrated by the origin of the name Koran. According to Ignaz Goldzieher, pioneer of Islamic studies, the word was borrowed from Hebrew nomenclature, namely *micra*, which means to read or recite.[15]

Nowadays it is clear that the Islamic religious culture is mainly a constant adoption from different previously existing cultural sources, as Persian, Egyptian, Greek, Roman, and Judeo-Christian. The composition of the Koran received its final form only in the ninth century and after that time more interpretations or additions were no longer allowed. As it was said, "The gate of interpretation has been shut." (Hanafi). Interpretation of the Sacred Law was officially adopted in 767. Islamic religious leaders declared that "the Koran was uncreated and co-eternal with Allah." Calif Ma'mun formulated this as valid dogma, and therefore it became the unchallengeable law of the Muslim state in 827. It spoke for itself and it did not need further clarification. Why dispute about things of which one has no knowledge? "No one knows its interpretation, except Allah."[16] From this affirmation it is obvious that the Islamic religion has nothing to do with reason, and that a true believer should not ask why.

When religious dogma also became state law, it for centuries inspired the Mohammedan warriors to go and fulfill the Koranic aim: to subjugate unbelievers.

Unsolved dilemma: religious tolerance and the Koran

The question of religious tolerance is basically not a religious but rather a philosophical one. The concept of tolerance in itself was unknown until the midst of the sixteenth century. It was born in an age of religious pluralism and had only religious connotation. The word tolerance is not without ambiguity, its disposition being to allow others to have different beliefs, but the torturing question has always been: how long can one tolerate those who are intolerant? The idea of toleration later became conditioned by political, economic, and racial interest as well. A question like this was involved: whom does the inquisition wish to defend when it persecutes infidels and sectarians? The followers of Mohammed naturally answered that they tried to save the concept of the only true God and that they aimed to eliminate any false image. But which God-concept did these Muslims represent? The fatalistic Allah, or the angry Jehovah, or the loving and forgiving God of Christ? These qualitative differences in God-concept colored the meaning of tolerance.

A revealed religion must be absolute, uncompromising, and therefore it becomes exclusive and intolerant. Ecumenical religiosity concerning toleration is therefore a contradiction in itself, although for some cynical observers it means that one believes all other religious dogmas except one's own.

The basic difference between Mohammedan and Christian teachings and practices have been determined by different historical-ecclesiastical situations. For instance: Christianity from the very beginning, that is from the Cross on, suffered intolerance and persecution for centuries, first from Jewish leaders, later from Roman persecutors. Mohammedanism, however, practiced intolerance from its inception, killing off "infidels" with the sword of the prophet. The Ottoman empire was built upon the Koranic law; the obvious result was that the "holy struggle" aimed not only to extend the

Islamic religion but the Ottomanic military civilization as well. Tolerance *per se* was intolerable to the preconditioned Islamic faithful, who lived, worked, and fought under the canonical law of the Koran. The Koran had more definitive influence upon Mohammedanism than the Bible had on Christian Europe. The Koranic law, for instance, accompanied a Muslim from the cradle to the grave; it prescribed exactly all rituals, hygienic ceremonies, dietary customs, etc. Believing individuals were quasi-caged in and, with this subjugation to the law were thus freed from anxiety or religious doubts. The Koran was far more rigorous than the Talmud. For instance, the limitations prohibited a Muslim to seek open social communication with non-Muslim fellow citizens. The non-Muslim believers in turn separated themselves from their Muslim neighbors, if "they met, they met only in vice."

Since in the realm of the Ottoman empire the religion functioned in an absolute determining way, the Islamic world never constituted a nation; members identified themselves with the Koran only, and so Mohammedanism nullified, as it were, nationalities. For instance, when Hungarian Christians were confronted with the Asian conquerors, the confrontation was, in a sense, first with Mohammed and second with the Turks.

When one studies the teaching of the Koran at closer range, and focuses on the prophet's ideas of peaceful coexistence, that is tolerance, one can learn from one of Mohammed's Bedouin followers that "the history of the sword was the history of humanity." The Verse of the Sword in the Koran is loaded with noteworthy remarks:

> "When the sacred months are past, kill those who join other gods with God (the only God) wherever [you] shall find them; seize them, besiege them, and lay in wait for them with every kind of ambush; but if they shall convert, and observe prayer, and pay the obligatory alms (poll tax) then let them go their way, for God is merciful, gracious." (Koran-Sura IX.5).

After Mohammed had established his power in Arabia, he not only oppressed Jewish and Christian Arabs, but with military force attacked three Jewish tribes in 624–625, slaughtering over three hundred men and distributing their women among his followers.[17] The main motive of his anger was that the Jews were reluctant to accept him as their prophet.

The children of the Koran became extremely proud of their only true religion, and declared any other faithfuls as sons of perdition. "Oh believers, take not the Jew or Christian as friend." "Verily, we will inherit the earth and [those] who are upon it." [18] Of course this claim to a universal empire for the Islamic Ottomans was based on the infallible Koranic law. It was the will of Allah, the Merciful, to propagate by force of arms. This holy crusade was called Jihad or Holy Struggle, not war, because war could mean only a temporary *ad hoc* event, but the holy struggle was continuous conquest for *oikoumene*. Consequently, this holy struggle became a canonical obligation to all true believers. The Islamic law slowly divided the earth into a Muslim dominated land of peace, or *Dar Al Islam*, and the other region not conquered yet, or *Dar Al Harb*, (domain of war). Dogmatically there never could be peace between the two parts. It was the duty of a true believer to extend, where he could, *Dar Al Islam* at the expense of *Dar Al Harb*. This holy struggle was always instigated by the religious leader or Imam, because he received one-fifth of the booty taken from the captured infidels.

After the death of Mohammed in 632, the developing Ottoman empire inherited this burden of constant struggle and finally it occupied more or less of three continents: North Africa, parts of Europe and Asia. This new political situation demanded adjustments in the Koranic law, and in the so-called Kanun new legislation by the sultans was incorporated. Theocratic absolutism elevated the sultan to earthly representative of the almighty Allah; the sultan now possessed all earthly property, including the green grass. The dynastic law authorized any sultan, among them Mehmed, the conqueror, to exterminate all male members of his family. The autocratic rulers never felt secure in their realm. The record of sultan Murad IV tells us how he killed off his three brothers, hunting them down on the three continents, in order to secure peace in his empire. Koranic law had already sanctioned this action before his time, saying "Sedition is worse than execution" and "members of the family might become seditious."[19] "And to whomsoever of my sons the Sultanate shall pass, it is fitting that for the order of the world he shall kill his brothers."[20]

The questionable Islamic tolerance subordinated the already subjugated serfs when Calif Omar issued a discriminating law, ordering a dress code in which the infidels had no right to use any color, or form of dress, or a turban, which was used by the Muslims. It was also prohibited to erect cultic buildings, and the dwellings of the infidels had to be painted in a dark color. During his lifetime, Mohammed had already ordered his follower, Abu Bakre, to destroy all tombs in the infidels' cemeteries, because Islamic law prohibited them.

The most severe economic exploitation and punitive taxations eventually forced the Christian *rayas* (poor peasants) to change their religious affiliation, because the Muslim-Christian renegades were exempt from taxations. This economic "tolerance" produced to-be-expected results. After two hundred years the former majority of Christians ceased to exist at the end of the ninth century. The ancient cradle of Christianity was submerged by an Asiatic deluge. Apparently, growing Islamic fanaticism and the alleged Islamic tolerance did not know each other.

Koranic Law Created War Economy

The developing military civilization of the Ottomans was built on war economy, which forced the sultans constantly to territorial extensions with the result that the wars could finance themselves. Mohammed had in his time inaugurated this war economy when his warriors received an annual stipend from his treasury and the necessary capital was secured by institutionalized *razzias*. With this policy followers were now able to devote themselves entirely to Jihad. The sultans' income likewise was based on booty, war proceeds, and over-taxation of the subjected non-Muslim *rayas*. The rayas' poll taxes in return authorized the victims to keep their heads on their shoulders!

The sultan's standing army cost more in peacetime than during military campaigns, which explains why sultans spent more of their time on crusades than in peace at their *seraglio*. Peacetime was furthermore quite risky for the sultans because the janissaries could become restless and a threat to domestic stability. As a sixteenth century observer rightly stated: "To preserve his empire the Turk had to extend it constantly . . . founded on constant conquest, war was its lifeblood."[21] This illustrates, for instance, why Suleiman the Magnificent spent only wintertime in his *seraglio*, for nothing was so alien to him as peace. During his half-century rule, only nine years were spent peacefully in Constantinople.

Pax Ottomanica

This misleading phrase has been coined by a few revisionist historians who have reinterpreted a number of historical sources to question the historical significance of the Byzantine empire.[22]

The Byzantine empire had for more than a thousand years incorporated and defended different countries in the Near East and on the Balkan peninsula, thus playing the role of peacemaker. These territories *qua* religion belonged to the Orthodox Church and they were considered to be the cradle of Christianity. It is a well-known ecclesiastical fact that all basic Christian dogmas, creeds, and synodical traditions were formulated within these realms, which once had been the land of the Apostles, of the Church Fathers, and of the Christian martyrs.

The historical role of *Pax Byzantinica* had been to defend ancient Christian heritage as well as the gate to European civilization. In contrast the so-called *Pax Ottomanica* meant the constant confrontation with one of the other Christian powers.

The origin of the dubious and controversial term of *Pax Ottomanica* has roots in the writing of Lybyer, who summed up his new "objectivity" as follows:

The sultans of the Ottoman Empire "had gathered a chaotic mass of petty states and hostile people into a great and, by comparison, a well-governed and durable empire. In the reign of the great Suleiman no human structure existed which equaled this institution in wealth, splendor, power, simplicity, and rapidity of action and respect at home and abroad."[23]

This dispassionate statement proves eloquently that in the thinking and the writing of arm-chair utopians, statistics do not bleed; in human reality, however, they do and did. In time and space far apart, historians tend to become insensitive to the immense human suffering which is caused by wars, and it becomes impossible for the historical revisionists to conclude that the *Pax Ottomanica* offered a splendid and beneficial solution to the problem of alleged decadence of Byzantium. In line with this explanation, another historical materialist ascertained that the Ottoman conquest brought relief to the indigenous inhabitants when the Turks wiped out the ruling classes, and put an end to feudalistic extortions, thus bringing peace to the liberated serfs. This dubious statement is in itself a contradiction because the alleged *Pax Ottomanica* in practice was the natural outcome of continuous wars, wars to realize the goal which the Koranic law prescribed: to subjugate the infidels who lived in the territories of *Dar Al Harb*. The long-term experience of absorption into the Ottoman empire was a tragedy for East Central Europe. For centuries the conquered Christian people were imprisoned, arresting socio-political evolution. The Turkish occupation robbed the inhabitants not only of their national identity, but in many places of their religious traditions as well. The historical role of Greek, Croatian, and Bulgarian culture-creating-and-sustaining elite was eliminated by brutal deportation. The original national elite was no more, and in their place foreign military feudalism was introduced. Ironically, the new rulers outnumbered the former exploiting class. In Bosnia-Hercegovina, for example, the 85,000 *rayas* population was now ruled by 6000 Beys and Agas, who were the new hungry social parasites.[24]

Advocates of the beneficial policy of *Pax Ottomanica* stress, for instance, how tolerant the Islamic conquerors had been toward the Eastern European Orthodox Church. A closer analysis of this assertion suggests that the words "peace" and "toleration" should be replaced by the word "interest". Since the Pre-Ottoman Islamic movement in the beginning had lacked the necessary institutions and administrative personnel, the highly developed and efficient Byzantine system was adopted by the nomadic new rulers. In Muslim eyes the prestige of Byzantium was immense, and the concept of statecraft of the city greatly affected the Ottoman newcomers. The chief concern of the Islamic rulers was the collection of taxes and an uninterrupted economic activity. The Orthodox Church organization lent itself eminently therefore for administrational support. Because the Christian rayas did not count in the power structure of the state, the Turkish rulers allowed the infidels to organize themselves into Millets. In them they could practice some autonomy and manage their socio-political life, but the concrete task was to collect taxes and secure economic developments. All these Millets were subordinated to the Orthodox Patriarchs who resided in Constantinople. The disciplinary power of the Patriarchate was extended over all the subjugated *rayas*. The poll tax sometimes was increased tenfold, not to mention the different other extortions by Muslim superiors. Of course the serf could not change either his occupation or his residency; they were enslaved for good. Historians who have much sympathy toward this Ottoman form of social consolidation neglect to consider these unpleasant facts in judging the so-called tolerant rule of the Turks. To correct such partiality the revisionists must present facts concerning the roll of the Patriarch. The Orthodox Church leaders, for instance, were very often blamed for not collecting sufficient taxes. Of course the constant wars hindered the productivity of agriculture; hence the taxation had to fall short of the Turkish expectation. The Patriarchs were blamed for income so lost.

The *rayas* were not only overtaxed; the child tribute was another painful and burdensome contribution. In order to be relieved from these molestations, the serfs eventually turned en masse to the Islamic religion and were thus exempt from taxes as well as the child tribute. Such Islamization occurred in Albania, Hercegovina, Montenegro, Serbia, and to a degree in Croatia. In connection with this development historian Arnakis observes, "To the subjects of the sultans in the Balkans, when religion was lost, all was lost; if one became Muslim, he became a Turk."[25]

The average term of a serving Patriarch in office was very short, about one and a half years. During the sixteenth century a Patriarch's time of reign grew shorter and shorter; between 1595–1695 over sixty Patriarchs filled the holy office. In order to receive this position, the aspirant Patriarch had to buy it from the sultan and pay first a yearly subsidy as well as another annual payment, a payment which grew steadily. It even happened that the Pope of Rome furnished the necessary money to pay the sultan in order to keep a Patriarch in office. Out of 159 office-holding Patriarchs, 105 were driven from their seats, and only 21 died a natural death while still in office. Many had died a violent death by hanging, beheading, poisoning or drowning. Cyril Lucarius had suffered the most scandalous treatment. He was dismissed from office several times and finally he was drowned in the Black Sea in 1638, by order of the "tolerant" sultan. His "sin" had been that he had worked together with Western theologians for an ecclesiastical reunion.[26] It was unfortunate that the legate from Holland, with whom he had been in contact, was not in Constantinople at the time to ransom Lucarius. After Lucarius was killed, his printing press, which he had received from England, was also destroyed because Koranic law forbade this infidel practice of printing.[27]

How tolerant the sultans were has been illustrated by these few facts, which contradict the revisionist-apologist who stated, "The Ottoman conquest presented no real challenge to the established way of life."[28] The better informed Greek historian, Trypanis, wrote, "The Greek lands were devastated, its children seized and turned into Mohammedans, one-fifth of its males were for centuries collected every four years *Devshirme*; its women were cast into the harems of Muslim pashas; its churches turned into mosques, and its schools banned."[29] In spite of these quoted facts, Shaw's conclusion was that *Pax Ottomanica* had served a purpose: Through centuries of religious persecution in Europe, it provided an asylum, a refuge.[30]

He fails to explain, however, who those refugees were who profited from the sultan's hospitality.

The pacification by the Turks-Tartars on the ruins of *Pax Byzantinica* meant in reality depopulation and repopulation by Asiatic ethnic elements. Historian Fischer-Galati has correctly stated that this policy of repopulation also involved Spanish Marranos:

> "Toleration of Jewish communities and even encouragement of Jewish migration into the Ottoman empire are a matter of record since the fifteenth century . . . Ottoman policies toward Jews, particularly during the reign of Bayezid II when the massive emigration of Marranos occurred, were the most favorable to the Jews."[31]

Why did the preference for Marranos take place in the Islamic world? During the Ottoman occupation in Spain, the Jewish minority had learned how to collaborate with the conquerors, and therefore they were expelled from the liberated Iberian peninsula. It was then natural for them to settle in the Muslim world. They possessed manifold skills which were in great demand. According to Toynbee, "In Constantinople, since the emigrant Jews from Spain occupied high social positions, they had such privileges as to have printing press as their own,"[32] while in the same territory Muslims were not so privileged. Among the Muslims the first printing press was not established until 1727 by a captured Hungarian theologian, Ibrahim Muteferrika, a Unitarian, who was able to adjust himself to the God-is-One religious society. Muteferrika also studied Islamic law and could so manipulate it to receive a permit for a printing press. He still experienced some difficulties, because Koranic teaching prohibited him from printing books other than the Koran, and he could not use a brush made of pig bristles to clean the types. Eventually "the godless infidel" overcame these hindrances.

Pax Ottomanica's peculiar consequence was the *Devshirme* or child tribute (original meaning is: gatherings). This most inhuman event forced the Christian youth into the service of the Turkish army, called janissary, for administration purposes and also for homosexual use by the janissaries, who were prohibited to marry. This practice slowly diminished the future elite; even more, these youth later had to turn against their own people. On many occasions frightened parents became Muslims in order to save their sons, or they had them marry in early childhood to escape from the "gatherings". *Devshirme* was also one reason why the former Patriarchate from Bulgaria, Serbia, Ochrid, and Pec had disappeared from the ecclesiastical records in the Balkan. Depopulation was the obvious cause.[33]

The final triumph of Islam on the religious level petrified Orthodox Christianity, and the *raya*-Christians were forced into a survival-oriented lethargy. Hellenized Christian Orthodoxy slowly attained a docile attitude and turned toward a contemplative metaphysical way of life.

With regard to *Pax Ottomanica*, the revisionist historians should also report how tolerant the Islam cultural policy was. Mohammedan rule practiced acculturation whenever and wherever the Ottomans extended their influence. When, for instance, the Islamic soldiers invaded Egypt, the famous library of Alexandria, with its half million manuscripts, went up in flames. A similar cultural vandalism occurred after the fall of Constantinople, when Mohammed the Conqueror ordered the large library of the Emperor to be thrown into the Black Sea. After a hundred years a similar attack was led against Christian culture, when Suleiman, the other conqueror, occupied the capital city of Hungary, Buda, and the second largest library in the world, after the Vatican, was destroyed.

Considering these presentations this author finds it difficult to agree with those apologists who have presented *Pax Ottomanica* as a peaceful and tolerant policy. Wherever the conquerors made a desert, revisionists have called it a peaceful development; in reality it was rather a peace of desolation, in which a cultural desert replaced European heritage.

So far, the controversial ideology of *Pax Ottomanica* has been discussed in connection with the nations of the Balkan peninsula mainly. It was a necessary introduction to the Hungarian historical situation concerning the Ottoman imperialistic efforts. The late English historian, Lord Acton, stated that modern European history begins under the stress of the Ottoman conquest, and this is twice-more true of the Hungarian developments.

Pax Hungarica versus Pax Ottomanica

After the fall of Byzantium in 1453, the Asiatic military power besieged for several centuries the Hungarian kingdom as well as its neighboring peoples. Beyond the Ottoman military organization was an enormous human reservoir of human energy and superiority in manpower. The

Hungarian nation was depopulated, bled to death as it were, and yet the resistance of the people against the invaders continued.

At this point it should be stressed that *Pax Ottomanica* as an interpreting, explaining idea, does not apply to the Hungarian people. First of all, the idea of tolerance contradicts the basic teaching of Mohammed, since the Koranic law directly asserted that this part of Europe belonged to *Dar Al Harb* and, therefore, should be conquered by the true Mohammedan believers to extend the Islamic empire. Second, Islamic ideology could not function to pacify and conquer the land of the Danube, because Hungarian nobility fought to uphold their rule, this in contrast to the Balkan dynasties who compromised to keep their power and embraced the Islamic religion. Third, *Pax Ottomanica* did not appeal to the Hungarian serfs either, and they remained loyal to their absentee landlords, paying the yearly tribute to them as well as to the foreign oppressor, ready to carry the double burden of taxation rather than to docilely become Muslims. With this fidelity the peasantry proved that they belonged to European Christianity. Hungarian nobility very often lost all their property and sank into the peasant class, both now together in misery and able to identify with each other. The most influential force which operated against any compromise was the Protestant Reformation. At that critical historical moment, the preacher armed the people with spiritual conscience to fight back the Islamic influence. The Helvetic-Calvinist teaching of *ius resistendi* gave the people the needed ideological tool to resist and not to yield to the oppressor. Fourth, the Muslim rulers with their exploitations and contemptuous attitudes toward the infidels alienated the serfs. Constant raids and arbitrary demands did not make the peasants docile at all; they recognized that the new rulers tolerated them only because where the people are, there are the profits, *ubi populus, ibi obulus*, and what profit could a conquered land offer when the peasants escaped?

In conclusion, Hungary was the *Dar Al Harb*, a constant battlefield, where neither peace nor tolerance could be practiced; neither could it be integrated into an unreliable *Pax Ottomanica*.

Footnotes

1. Pirenne, Henry. Mohammed and Charlemagne. New York: Meridian Books, 6th ed., 1964.

2. Chirol, Valentine. in Foreign Affairs, Vol. I, No. 3.

3. Muir, William. Life of Mohammed, Vol. IV, p. 322. New rev. ed., Weir, Thos., ed. AMS Press reprint of 1932 ed.

4. Zwermer, Samuel. The Sword of Mohammed and Ali. in: Muslim World. 1931. Vol. XXI, p. 109.

5. Becker, C. H. Christianity and Islam. New York: 1909, republished by Burt Franklin, 1974.

6. Bibliander, Theodore. Remarks about Mohammed. In: Consultation and the Monk. p. 14 ff.

7. Brockelmann, Carol. Story of the Islamic People. London: 1950. p. 16.

8. Koran-Sura XIX. 28. Penguin Books, 1956, New York.

9. Koran-Sura. 59, 60. Penguin Books, 1956, New York.

10. Koran-Sura. Penguin Books, 1956, New York.

11. Koran-Sura XX, 20. Penguin Books, 1956, New York.

12. Koran-Sura II. 73. Penguin Books, 1956, New York.

13. Koran, footnote on pg. 21. Penguin Books, 1956, New York.

14. Thomson, Wm. Mohammed, His Life and Person. In: The Muslim World. XXXI, p. 96, 1944.

15. Goldzieher, Ignáz. Mohammedanische Studien, Halle, 1899. Vol. II, p. 40.

16. Koran-Sura III, 59–60 and II, p. 91. Penguin Books, 1956, New York.

17. Watt, W. M. Mohammed in Medina. Oxford: 1956. pp. 208–220.

18. Koran-Sura. V. 57 and Koran-Sura IX, 41. New York: Penguin Books, 1956.

19. Koran-Sura, II, 187.

20. Gibb, A. R. and H. Bowen. Islamic Society and the West. London: Oxford University Press, 1969. p. 36.

21. Cardinal Bessarion. in Patrilogia Series Greeca CLXI cols. 651–653

22. Lybyer, A. H. The Government of the Ottoman Empire in the Time of Suleiman the Magnificent. Harvard, 1913. p. 18.

      Stavrianos, L. L. The Balkans Since 1453. New York: 1958.
      Toynbee, Sir Arnold. A Study of History. London: Oxford University Press, 1934. Vol. III, pp. 27–35.

23. Lybyer, A. H. *op. cit.*, p. 198.

24. Lokwood, W. G. Living Legacy of the Ottoman Empire. In: The Mutual Effects of the Islamic-Christian Worlds: The Eastern European Pattern. New York: Columbia University Press, 1979. p. 214.

25. Anarkis, G. G. The Role of Religion in the Development of Balkan Nationalism. In: The Balkan in Transition. ed. Ch. and B. Jelavich. University of California Press, 1963. p. 120.

26. Kidd, B. J. The Churches of Eastern Christendom. London: 1927.

27. Runciman, S. The Greek Church Under the Ottoman Turks. In: Studies in Church History, Vol. II, pp. 38–59. London: 1965.

28. Shaw, E. K. The Ottoman Aspect of Pax Ottomanica. In: Tolerance and Movements of Religious Dissent in Eastern Europe. ed. Béla K. Király. East European Quarterly, distrib. Columbia University Press, New York, 1975.

29. Trypanis, C. A. quoted from G. Finlay: A History of Greece. Oxford 1877. Vol. V, p. 126.

30. Shaw, E. K. *op. cit.*, p. 181.

31. Fischer-Galati, S. Judeo-Christian Aspects of Pax Ottomanica. In: Tolerance and Movements of Religious Dissent in Eastern Europe. ed. B. K. Király. East European Quarterly, distrib. Columbia University Press, New York, 1975.

32. Toynbee, Sir Arnold *op. cit.*, Vol. VII, p. 164.

33. Anarkis, G. G. *op. cit.*, p. 128.

Chapter III

The Shaping of the Hungarian Religious Ethos

Hungarian religious history points to two radical changes. First, when the Magyars accepted the European Christian legacy in the year 1000 A.D., changing their metaphysical orientation, Christianity went through a simultaneous religious revival known as the Cluniac Reformation. This Cluniac movement shaped the destiny of the Hungarian nation for the next five hundred years. Mission-oriented monks from the West impetuously left their cells for the banks of the Danube to shape the former nomad spirit of the newcomers in East Central Europe. Some western monasteries were completely emptied as the former inhabitants moved to the edge of western Christendom, into Pannonia.

The second radical transformation occurred in the most critical historical moment during the sixteenth century when the Asiatic Mohammedan invasion threatened the sheer existence of the Hungarian people, and the Protestant Reformation offered a hope for a deadly-wounded nation, a defense for the people of Christ. This radical change, inaugurated by the Protestant reformers, helped the Hungarian Christians in their desperate efforts to survive.

When the former horse-riding nomads had settled down in Europe, they had raided the western nations of Spain, France, Italy, and Germany for centuries, always collecting yearly ransoms from the raided people for "peace-sake". No wonder that these actions had created a collective fear on the Continent. No wonder that frightened monks each evening prayed "Save us O God, from the arrows of the Hungarians," *A sagittas Hungarorum libere nos Dei*. The former nomads were now paid in kind.

Looking back to the sixteenth century when the destructive Ottomans invaded Europe, one can imagine what might have happened if the Almighty had responded positively to the monks' prayer requests. Maybe an Islamic Imam would today call the Mohammedans to prayer from the top of St. Peter's Basilica in Rome. As it turned out, it was the historic destiny of Hungary to prevent this from happening. By defending European Christianity for five hundred years, it became possible for Martin Luther and John Calvin to make their reforming impact upon Christianity. A spiritually renewed Europe soon extended its borderline into East Central Europe and into Hungary. As a remarkable result of the religious revolution which evolved in the midst of the political crises, the second largest Reformed Church in Europe was being established in Hungary. How can church historians explain the evolvement of the Hungarian cross-bearing ecclesia in the midst of the cosmic upheaval?

Two historical events prepared the way for the Hungarian Reformed Church. One was the tragic defeat at Mohács in which the leading ecclesiastical prelates, as well as more than ten thousand Roman Catholic Christians, including priests and monks, lost their lives on the battlefield. In addition, many Roman Catholic potentates were slain; consequently, the Roman Catholic Church remained without leadership. A second contributing factor was the systematic Ottoman invasion in which the Islamic military theocracy methodically destroyed most of the existing institutions such as churches, monasteries, schools, and *latifundia*, in addition to which the laity was decimated in a large measure as well.

Chapter IV

The Hungarian Nation as Bulwark
Against the Ottoman-Turkish Conquest of Europe

In springtime, when the grass already grew one inch high, and the Mohammedan gypsy blacksmith commenced horseshoeing the sultan's horses, and when thousands of serfs were forced to dig wells along the highways, it was obvious that the Ottoman-Turks prepared new campaigns against Hungary.

The ancient trade route which ran via the Balkan peninsula from Northern Hungary to Constantinople, suddenly became a military highway. When the intruding Ottomans used this road and occupied the surrounding countryside, the inhabitants saw its five hundred years of cultural traditions come to naught as it was being replaced by an Islamic culture-desert which Western travelers, merchants, and diplomats who crossed the formerly blooming Hungarian territories, often called a "cemetery". Tragic statistical reports support this observation: after one and a half centuries of Ottoman occupation, more than a thousand villages, cities, and other dense settlements had disappeared from the earth.[1] This meant not only the loss of millions of lives and a destroyed Christian civilization, it also meant that the land itself had become a wilderness. This transformation drastically changed even the climate, and the marshy land which developed created special epidemics. A new illness, *Morbus Hungaricus*, Hungarian Death, a morbid fever caused by vapor rising from the marshes, resulted from the constant destructive Islamic activities. The illness eventually spread farther westward, even as far as England. The surviving natives slowly developed immunity, but foreign visitors from the west and from the east quickly perished after a short stay in the country. *Morbus Hungaricus* created

Islamic Mosque

something of a paradox: on the one hand it saved the native population from biological exchange with the intruding Asiatic elements; on the other hand it decimated not only the Hungarians but the Islamic Turks as well. Later in time *Morbus Hungaricus* checked Germanization when the Habsburg rulers tried to colonize the Hungarian reconquered land through forced settlements of inhabitants from Austro-German territories.

Beginning of the Islamic Intrusion

The Islamic intrusion began during the reign of King Louis the Great (1340–1380), who also was ruler of Poland. His military influence at times extended over half of the Balkan peninsula.

Subsequent Hungarian rulers, at the request of the Roman Popes, were constantly involved in religious crusades against the Bogumil heresy as well. This sectarian revolt against Byzantine Orthodox Christianity eventually opened the door for the Islamic political and military interference, and prepared the road for the Ottoman hegemony. In that century the powerful Hungarian nation still could easily expel the Ottoman raiders from its realm (see Chapter III).

King Louis the Great was succeeded by his son-in-law, Sigismund of Luxemburg, who ruled between 1387–1437. Sigismund was educated at the court of Buda, and from the very beginning he was involved in the problem of the Islamic threat. Indeed, during the fifty years of his reign, he spent much of his time crusading against the Ottoman invasions. He and his Hungarian army launched one of the most promising, large scale crusades, together with British, French, German, Bohemian, and Polish military forces, but the battle was lost in 1396 at Nicopolis. One cause of the defeat was the notorious military diplomacy of Venice. According to the planned strategy, the Venetian fleet had the task of blockading the sea, thus preventing the Turkish army from crossing over into the Balkan peninsula. The Venetian army, however, was nowhere to be seen, and King Sigismund and his army were caught by surprise when the Ottoman army unexpectedly confronted the crusaders.

The second cause of the defeat was a confusing event which occurred when the impatient French army unit recklessly started the attack on the Ottoman army before the united army was ready. Although the French attack initially succeeded in scattering the Turkish front, a third event took the victory away from the crusaders. An ambushing Serbian cavalry attacked the combined Christian forces, after which the sultan returned with his men to the battlefield to become victorious through the treacherous Serbian act.[2] King Sigismund barely escaped, but he finally reached Constantinople. There, with Emperor Manual II of Byzantium, he faced the immediate danger of Islam expansion and therefore wrote immediately to the leader of the Knights of the Johannites, Philibert Noiles:

> "We recognize that the city [Constantinople] is in immediate danger and the eventual loss of it would be catastrophic for the whole of Christendom; after my return we will try to mobilize the willing Christendom."[3]

From this immediate action it was obvious that Sigismund's assessment concerning the nature of the Islamic danger was correct, as later events proved. The loss of Constantinople meant the loss of the Balkans and its people. Sigismund also knew that Hungary alone could not possibly defend Europe from the Asiatic deluge. The economic-military forecast stated clearly that the wars were expensive for the western nations and exhausting as far as people were concerned. In contrast, the Ottoman military theocracy could itself support the Islamic wars and sustain the Ottoman army by means of raids on territories not conquered as yet. Because King Sigismund later became involved in many political as well as military actions in western Europe, he was in a sense forced to establish a passive defense policy by building a chain of fortifications in southern Hungary. This stronghold system was built with Nandorfehérvár* as the central axis; more than a hundred fortifications, forming a chain, were supposed to keep the invaders at bay; in short, Nandorfehérvár was to serve as gateway to Hungary. Sigismund, however, soon recognized that this passive defense strategy was not sufficient, because he was constantly being tied down by Turkish charges.[4]

For centuries the Hungarian rulers had been the most faithful supporters of the Holy See, and King Sigismund did not depart either from this tradition. He, as king of Hungary, also became emperor of Germany, and finally also the ruler of Bohemia. In these capacities he soon became involved in ecclesiastical reform policies, in papal schism, as well as in exhausting crusades against the Hussite revolution.

---

*Belgrad

Faithful to his earlier promise to Emperor Manuel II, Sigismund in his function of *Advocatus et Defensor Ecclesiae*, called together a reform- and ecumenical council in Constance from 1414–1418, when John XXIII was Pope, to summon together the western powers for the defense of Constantinople, and to work on the reconciliation of Rome and Eastern Orthodox Christianity, and to neutralize the Hussite religious upheavals.[5]

It was Christmas time, 1414, when King Sigismund and a large court of two thousand members moved into Constance. His entourage included all the Hungarian ecclesiastical and secular potentates, as well as the whole theological faculty of Buda.

Unfortunately, Sigismund arrived later in Constance than John Huss, whom he had given a safe conduct. Pope John XXIII, once himself a highsea pirate, nullified the *salvus conductus* on the basis that it was invalid because Huss was a heretic, and had him thrown into jail. This outraged Sigismund and he became engaged in a hand-to-hand fight, thus aiding the reforming party. There was a moment during a most critical session in which the council of cardinals opposed all reform, that a protonotary demanded to hang a proclamation in favor of the opposition to reform on the door of the meeting hall, Sigismund threatened the protonotary that he would hang the man on the same door himself. On another day of stormy debates, the king stood at the door, preventing opponents from entering by using "his royal fist." No wonder that later one of the participants, Cardinal Fillastre, reported that the opposing cardinals finally acted out of fear for the king. Had they been free, they never would have agreed with him.[6]

At the termination of the Council, Sigismund forced all three Popes to abdicate, and a new Pope, Martin V, was elected. The king also succeeded in forcing the cardinals to recognize the ancient right of patron of the Hungarian kings, to invest and nominate ecclesiastical leaders in Hungary without any papal prerogatives. All the twenty-one cardinals, among whom the future Pope himself, pledged under oath the restoration of the Hungarian *investitura*. A copy of this *Bulla of Constance* was later found in the archives of the royal free-city of Eperjes by historian Béla Iványi. The text proved that the mentioned privilege existed from the time the Hungarian rulers were Apostolic kings, beginning with St. Stephen in 1000 A.D.[7]

This put to rest the controversies regarding this right, which lasted centuries. In fact, King Sigismund had used the kingly apostolic rights in 1404, when he refused to obey Pope Bonifacius IX, reasoning that

"Hungarian Christians live in the neighborhood of unbelievers, as the bulwark and shield of Christendom, for dangerous centuries, and therefore they earned such privilege."[8]

During the duration of the Council, Sigismund had also extended his efforts as peacemaker between the English and French rulers; he visited them personally, asking for reconciliation and their help against the Islamic menace. But all had been in vain. When after four years the Council was closed and the prelates left, the local chronicler noted that "the fat prelates have consumed all the fish from Lake Constance."

Sigismund, as king and emperor, was charged to lead a crusade against the Hussites who rebelled after John Huss was burned at the stake. This crusade became not only a military failure but a church-historical one as well, because during that battle between Hussites and Germans, the religious movement made good inroads into Hungary. In fact, even the first Hungarian language translation of the Bible was the work of Hungarian Hussites (see Chapter V).

The next reform council which took place in Basel from 1431–1438 was called together by Pope Martin V as had been decreed at Constance. The Council agenda was occupied with the Hussite movements. The ruling Bohemian estates as well as the clerical leaders were ready to make concessions; for instance, to permit the use of both kinds, bread and wine, when celebrating the Eucharist with the believers, which had not been allowed before.

Sigismund spent only one-half year in Basel; when things did not move according to his wishes, he became frustrated and often used his flowery Hungarian language to curse the participants loudly, as Aenea Sylvio Piccolomi, the later Pope Pius II, recorded.[9]

The Ottoman threat forced Sigismund to return to Buda, from whence he continued his efforts to reconcile the Pope with the reform-oriented Council. To make his influence more effective, he even planned to transfer the Council from Basel to Buda, and sent a statistic about Buda's capacity to house the participants, such as 4,000 rooms available and place for 4,700 horses. He was even willing to cover the expenses for the invited prelates from the Eastern Orthodox Churches in Constantinople.[10]

The plans could not be realized, because King and Emperor Sigismund died suddenly in 1437. Pope Eugene IV forgot the tradition of *de mortis nill nisi bene* when he bitterly lamented that during the rule of Sigismund the Church was in a worse condition than that of the Jews in Egyptian captivity.[11] Although during Sigismund's rule Buda had become the center of European politics, worldly as well as ecclesiastically, the existential problems of Hungary, the Ottoman threat, did remain unsolved. How large the Islamic danger was may be understood from the fact that only one bishop represented Hungary at the Council in Basel; the Hungarian archbishop had written to Basel, asking to excuse the Hungarians, because they had to mobilize their military forces. "We cannot sleep even at night; others in Europe can snore peacefully."

In summary: King Sigismund had never forgotten his experience at Nicopolis when the imperial Islamic army had massacred the best European youths; therefore during his fifty years of rule it had been his ambition to integrate the western nations in order to rescue Constantinople and European cultural and religious values. All his efforts had been in vain, the rivalry, jealousy, and lack of unity in Christendom had been the best allies of the Ottoman aggressors; only the Roman Popes had offered Sigismund their support, diplomatically as well as financially, and so in half a century the Ottoman empire had added more and more territories for the sultans' resources to use them for new military adventures. The former Hungarian vassals, Serbia, Bosnia, Montenegro, and Moldavia, were time and again incorporated into the Islamic orbit.

The next important event concerning a renewed struggle against the encroachment of Ottoman imperialism took place during the reign of King Ulászlo II from 1440–1444, who also was king of Poland. Ulászlo declared before the coming battle of Varna (Bulgaria) that the Hungarian and Polish borders were common, and that therefore both were being attacked by the barbarian Ottoman Turks: "To the glory of God we have become the wall and shield in the defense of the Christian faith."[12] He followed up this comment by calling up all possible military forces under the military leadership of János Hunyadi. The latter had led a successful campaign on the Balkans in which the brother of Sultan Murad had been captured. This victorious campaign was called the "Long-winter-campaign" (1441–1443). In the meantime, Pope Eugene IV supported the mobilization of Christians and sent a special representative, a *legatus de latere*, Cardinal Julian Cesarini, to Buda. In addition he issued a special Bull in 1443, describing the pitiful situation of their brothers in the faith in the Orient, and asking a tithe of all Church income to finance the planned Turkish crusade.

With Hunyadi's victories, the whole of western Christendom became more willing to support a more ambitious military plan and, as a result, Hungarian, Polish, and Bohemian armies jointly, led by King Ulászlo Hunyadi, and Cardinal Cesarini, moved deeply into Turkish occupied lands. The coordinated strategy again supposedly involved Genoese and Venetian navy participation, which was to block the Ottomans from crossing the Bosporus into European territories, but instead the navies did the opposite and rather ferried the Ottoman army over the strait. Historian Babinger has given a revealing explanation of the treachery of these two maritime participants: "There is good reason to believe that the Genoese and perhaps also the Venetian sea captains gave the sultan decisive help in his undertaking, all the more willingly because he is said to have offered a gold piece for every soldier landed in Europe."[13]

The Hungarian leaders were once more taken by surprise, but Hunyadi's army fought with skill and courage, and the attacking Ottomans were defeated in the first engagement. The Turkish army leader was killed, and the attack led by Hunyadi decided the battle in favor of the crusaders. Unfortunately, King Ulászlo fell from his horse and was killed by a Turk.

With this accident, the whole battle turned into disarray and disaster. When darkness fell on the battlefield, both armies stopped the fight, and the crusaders, panic-stricken, scattered after the death of King Ulászlo and turned homeward. Hunyadi and a relatively small group of crusaders stayed alive; the rest of the armies perished en route home. This first-won and again-lost battle of Varna was to discourage for a long time any other western participation in self-defense actions.

In the Danubian plain, a providential dynasty of Hunyadi succeeded in the second part of the fifteenth century, in repulsing the Turkish assaults, the most celebrated of which was that of Nandorfehérvár (Belgrad) in 1456. János Hunyadi, together with the most devoted monk, St. Capistrano, not only defended the "gate to Hungary", but also totally defeated Sultan Mehmed II. The Ottoman force of about 100,000 armed men and 200 cannons, as well as a large navy on the Danube, was defeated by the skill of Hunyadi and 40,000 enthusiastic but untrained and insufficiently armed men. Sultan Mehmed was wounded when he tried to force his army to hold on. János Hunyadi with his military genius and accomplished victory gave the Christians the badly needed courage to stand up against the seemingly inexhaustible manpower of the Ottoman forces.

In Rome, Pope Calixtus III greeted the good news of the triumph at Nandorfehérvár with enthusiasm, recognizing that not only Hungary was saved, but also the whole of Christendom was relieved. He ordered for all the bells to be tolled on the Continent at noon, in three intervals. This was called "Turkish Bells", and until today these bells toll, but who remembers that their origin was intended as thanksgiving for the deliverance of Nándorfehérvár? The ringing of the bells finally became the mid-day Angelus.[14]

As always, the wars spread disease, and so a few months after the battle was won, János Hunyadi, and soon thereafter St. John Capistrano, fell victim to the plague. Before his death, Capistrano wrote an ode to the memory of Hunyadi in which he expressed the conviction that with Hunyadi's death there was no one left who would face up to the Ottoman threat to Christianity.[15]

János Hunyadi's son Matthias (known as Matthias Corvinus) was elected king in 1458, inheriting the same task his father had undertaken: to contain the Ottoman expansion and to prevent the Koranic command of conquering the lands of the infidels from being carried out. The century-long struggles of the nation had, unfortunately, spent much of the military energy, while the enemy controlled three continents of which the human resources seemed limitless, because more than twelve million families were under the Ottoman hegemony. Hungary's population was at that time not larger than the British of four or five million people. To secure more military forces, King Matthias extended his political influence to Austria, Silesia, Moravia, and later Bohemia, after he had succeeded in pacifying the Hussites there.

King Matthias, like the former King Sigismund, had become involved in the Bohemian controversies; namely, the Holy See asked the king to help dethrone the Czech ruler, George Podjebrad, because contrary to the latter's pledge to the Pope, he had joined the Hussite movement. This request of the Pope demanded a difficult task from an ethical point of view, because Matthias had an alliance with the Bohemian ruler. When earlier in time, Podjebrad had been elected as ruler of Bohemia, there was no bishop in his country who could invest him, and so he had turned to Matthias with the request to lend him some ecclesiastical leaders to perform his inauguration.[16] In the ensuing problem, Pope Sixtus IV, the German Emperor, the Roman Catholics in Bohemia, as well as the Czech estates, all turned to King Matthias for support. Pope Sixtus IV dissolved the alliance between Matthias and Podjebrad on a dogmatic point, reasoning that the alliance had been based on Roman Catholic fidelity. When finally in 1469, the Czech Diet in Olmutz elected Matthias as their ruler, Podjebrad's devoted monk, St. C future was sealed, and his death finally solved the controversy. The remnant of the Hussite forces under leadership of Giskra, were incorporated in Matthias' standing army, and the revamped military force could stand up against the Janissaries. The whole interlude, however, handicapped the king to turn with full force against the spreading Ottoman influence on the Balkan.

The most faithful supporter of King Matthias was Pope Pius II (1458 –1464) "for at this time Hungary was one of the most powerful states of Christendom, and moreover it had every reason to feel directly threatened by the Turkish peril," as historian Babinger has observed.[17]

During his lifetime, King Matthias' father, János Hunyadi, had already identified himself with the Byzantine emperor when Mehmed the Conqueror prepared his attack on Byzantium; Hunyadi had sent a special delegate to the Ottoman sultan, warning him that he, Hunyadi, would not remain neutral if the sultan did not abandon his threat against Byzantium. Hunyadi even proposed to Emperor Constantine XI, that he and his men would defend Constantinople with navy and landed army forces, but the proud emperor and his Council of War had refused the offer at that time, declaring that they intended to defend their fortress with their own forces. Later they regretted this decision.[18]

Pope Pius II himself commenced to organize a crusade, but very soon he faced the unwillingness of the Christian leaders, and it was with bitterness that he "read the gospel" to his contemporaries:

> "Christendom is a body without head . . . Pope and Emperor are merely titles, everyone is a law to himself. Lacking leadership, discipline, and common interest, any force which might be raised to oppose the Turks must fail."[19]

The materialistic, mercantile interest overruled all Christian solidarity. This became clear, for instance, from the policy of Genoa. When Mehmed II besieged Constantinople in 1456, Genoese diplomacy supported the sultan, and Genoese merchants at the same time were helping to defend the city where their merchandise was stored. The chief Genoese and Venetian exports to the Ottomans were weapons, while for good profits the cities also furnished the necessary technicians to serve the sultan's cannons.

King Matthias with his up-to-date standing army often moved into the Balkan territories held by the Ottoman, defeating the occupant forces and recapturing several fortifications, but when he had to return to the distant capitals of Buda or Vienna, the Turkish raiders again invaded the same territories. It is therefore no wonder that the king finally turned to the Holy See to coordinate a general mobilization.

It was during this time that the brother of Sultan Bayezid II, Prince Djem or Cem, escaped to the west, and sent a delegate to King Matthias, asking his support in the removal of Bayezid from the sultanate, and bringing him, Djem, back to Byzantium. Matthias saw a way of using Djem in his crusades, because Djem had large support in Byzantium; therefore the king asked the Holy See to have Djem transferred to Buda. However, there were other powers, like France, Venice, and Egypt, which also claimed the prince. The Egyptian sultan offered four hundred thousand pieces of gold for the unlucky Djem. In the meantime the ruling Sultan Bayezid II was quite content to pay the Holy See a respectable sum of money to be his brother's keeper! Indeed, Renaissance diplomacy used all possible tricks and bribings to get the exiled Ottoman into their hands. Matthias fought desperately for the prince for decades under several popes, and in vain.

King Matthias was a typical Renaissance autocrat, and as such he was pragmatic in his policy, sometimes dictatorial, using threats to reach his ecclesiastical or political goals. One could call him Machiavellian, were it not that the author of *The Prince* formulated his immoral and treacherous political philosophy later, in 1513. Machiavelli's ideal ruler was to be crafty and deceitful. King Matthias had only one goal: to expel the Turks from Europe.

On the request of the Hungarian king, Pope Pius II finally called together a council to coordinate all possible efforts for a crusade. This took place in 1459 in Mantua, where Pope Pius II among others declared that:

> "the Roman Church equally respects all Christian nations, kings, whom we should support without partiality . . . but our beloved son, King Matthias of Hungary, deserves special privilege . . . his great nation over a hundred years . . . serving as a shield for Christianity."[20]

Venice, situated on the crossroad of the Mediterranean, was the most unwilling partner for the proclaimed crusade, because its mercantile interest had developed a special relationship with the Ottoman aggressors. The state of shopkeepers unfortunately knew no moral inhibitions when cooperating with the Islamic conquerors if this meant prosperity. Pope Pius II recognized this duplicity of the Venetian Signoria and admonished their envoy with these words:

"Too much intercourse with the Turks has made you friends of the Mohammedans, and you care no more for (Christian) religion."[21]

The Venetian Council (Signoria) openly bragged "We are first Venetians, and only then Christians."[22]

Recent historical research on the religious indifference of the Venetian Republic brought some clearer understanding. One of the explanations given is that the Venetian Council, in cooperation with the Ottoman sultans, had, for commercial interest, invited the Iberian Marranos (Jewish pseudo-Christians) with their large capital to settle in Venice. In return the Venetian leaders would save the immigrant Jews from persecutions by the notorious Inquisition. Only the cynical agnostic elements among them were investigated. The commercial interactions between the Marranos in Venice and Constantinople apparently had influenced the political diplomacy of the Turcophile Venetians. This new observation partially explains the ambiguous attitude of the Venetian Council toward the suffering Christians.[23] The Jewish merchants who were foremost in trade between the Ottoman empire and Venice, benefited from the common interest of the empire and Venice in maintaining close trade connections.[24]

In the medieval controversies concerning the Judaizing efforts, the positive Jewish role in European history is often forgotten, especially in connection with mercantile benefits. The Jewish minorities apparently soon adjusted to different historical situations, as for instance was shown in 694 A.D., when the king of Iberia, Egira, complained that the Hebrews in his country were collaborating with the invading Muslims.[25]

Jewish traders were indispensable during the Muslim period in the Mediterranean area, and many market days were changed for their benefit, if they happened to fall on a Saturday.[26] On the banks of the Danube they traded salt and captured Hungarians, often exporting the latter as slaves as far as Spain. During this privileged period, Jews and merchants had become synonymous terms.[27]

When a village in Hungary did not have a Jewish trader, it often happened that a delegate was sent to Greece to "bring a Greek to act as Jew," for a Jewish trader had become a status symbol, and if a village had none, it meant that the village was too poor to afford one, because the trader would not be able to exist there.

When Nandorfehérvár became a Turkish military garrison in 1521, there were some Jewish technicians who served as artillery men for the more than six hundred cannons.

Jews, always living in a transient state, as a matter of fact maintained ties with other centers of Jewish life in the east as well as in the west. The information thus gathered was often exchanged; this happened too in Constantinople, where unfortunately information at times was passed on to the Ottomans. Among the few inhabitants of Constantinople who survived the Turkish seizure of the city, were the Jews from the Barlat quarter. In 1454, one of them, Isaac Sarfaty, sent a circular letter to the Jews on the Continent, in which he described with enthusiasm the fortunate conditions of his brothers in the faith under the Crescent. In the years that followed, a massive emigration of Jews to the Turkish paradise took place.[28]

Historian Epstein confirms that the Jews did not oppose the Ottoman conquest; on the contrary, they sometimes helped the Ottomans and were rewarded for this.[29] In two historical events which tragically influenced the fate of Christendom in the Near East and East Central Europe, two sultans issued *ferman* to Jewish leaders for distinguished service. The first sultan, Mehmed II, conqueror of Constantinople, gave a *ferman* to his court physician when the city fell into the orbit of Asiatic savagery. The second sultan, Suleiman II, bestowed a *ferman* on Joseph ben Solomon Ashkenazi following the conquest of Buda, capital city of Hungary, which was occupied not by military action but by Turkish trickery. That two important capitals were lost to Ottoman imperialism were significant events and apparently in both cases Jews had been involved.[30]

The immigrant Jews in the Ottoman empire constituted an autonomous community, which defended its members against Turkish accusations and persecutions.*

---

*For detailed information see Aryeh Shmuelevitz, the Jews of the Ottoman Empire in the Fifteenth and the Sixteenth Century.

Pope Pius II, faithful to his promise, began calling together the European military forces. King Matthias mobilized also and set out with his army for the Balkan, where he waited for the papal fleet. There he received the sad news that Pope Pius II, en route to lead in person the crusade, had died. Cardinal Carjeval, who had been appointed coordinator for the crusade, could do nothing more than send what was left in the treasury to King Matthias, about 40,000 pieces of gold.

The constant Ottoman military actions and the deportation which followed finally forced the population of the Balkans to begin an exodus to Hungary. King Matthias reported to Rome that between 1479 and 1483, more than 200,000 Serbs alone had settled down in his kingdom.[31]

Pope Pius II's successor, Pope Paul II (1464–1471) was immediately contacted by King Matthias who asked the Pope for financial help, otherwise he would not be able to continue alone the rescue operation; between the lines he let it be known that the sultan had again offered an armistice, quite beneficial. He added: "If your Holiness will ask me not to make a temporary peace with the deadly enemy of our faith, you must make it possible for me to lead a new crusade against them."[32] In order to comfort the willing king, Pope Paul sent him a well-decorated cross in which a piece of the original Cross was inserted, as well as fifty thousand pieces of gold. Even more important, a promise was delivered, namely that the Pope was ready to hand over to Buda the long-coveted Prince Djem. Apparently Pope Paul II was ready to please the only European ruler who was ready to continue his service on behalf of the whole of Christendom; in addition he also granted the founding of another university in Hungary, in Pozsony,* now Bratislava. Unfortunately, Pope Paul II, who was willing to support an anti-Ottoman movement, also died, and Pope Sixtus IV, (1471–1484), took over the heavy burden on behalf of the defense of Christianity.

There was no alternative for King Matthias than to continue the costly and deadly crusade against the aggressive Ottomans, so in 1475 he was en route again in an effort to clear the Balkans from the Ottoman raiders. Pope Sixtus had earlier sent envoy after envoy to Buda, asking the king to go and defend the defenseless. Matthias, who had won several battles against the Turkish armies, had in his self-confidence responded: "I do not

---

*See Addendum II.

need encouragement . . . since I was eighteen years old I have fought our common enemy . . . if it is permitted to complain against the Holy See, I could enumerate how little support I have received. Your legate in my camp can tell you that the sum I received from Rome will not suffice even for the yearly payments of ten soldiers. Now, when I continue my fight here I hope that the new promises will be as solid as the words in the Bible: 'Heaven and Earth will pass away, but my words will never pass away'."[33]

It was a fact that the papal financial support often arrived belatedly, and the king then had to finance his standing army himself. Being Matthias Hunyadi, however, he was not afraid to admonish the Pope: "If you Sixtus, will not realize your promises and pledges, I will protest, not only before the world, but before God, Creator of heaven and earth."[34] After another successful victory, when Matthias and his army had freed large territories from the invading Ottomans (Bosnia, etc.), including the stronghold of Szabács, Matthias informed the Pope: "During my campaign I have conquered many fortresses, but not one gave me so many difficulties as this one [Szabács]."[35]

On another occasion, when the king once again had waited in vain for diplomatic and financial support from the Holy See, he wrote: "I have to ask your Holiness, who will serve the Holy See as faithfully as I have if you abandon me?"

The historical background of the lack of papal support was that the Italian City-States, with their egocentric despots, constantly challenged the papal authority and with their petty rivalries the actions of the Holy See.

When the new year arrived, the Vatican sent considerable financial support, but even as it was delivered, the complaining Matthias refused to accept it personally. He asked instead that the money be distributed among the army captains who had fought so successfully against the superior Ottoman forces and had defeated them, in spite of losing the lives of many soldiers. In return for the help, King Matthias sent several captured Ottoman battle standards to Rome to prove his military successes.

Because of the European inner wars among the British, French, German, Italian, and Polish dynasties, King Matthias was never able to win them over for a general offensive to expel the Turks from European lands. In his correspondence with the Pope he finally wrote "I am very tired of begging again and again for support." And although Rome was enthusiastic about the Hungarian victories, the papal legate in Buda, Cardinal Bertalan

Maraschi, had to warn the Vatican: "I ask your Holiness to please honor this king in whom military virtue is linked with a magnanimous soul and deep religious feelings."

In successive years numerous Turkish prisoners of war were sent to the pope instead of banners, to prove that King Matthias kept his pledges. Unfortunately, the relationship between the Vatican and King Matthias was interrupted again when Pope Sixtus IV died. King Matthias immediately greeted the newly elected Pope Innocent VIII (1484–1492) *in medias res*, and pleaded with him to finally send to Buda Prince Djem. To justify his request he told the papal legate that "His Holiness can only succeed against the Ottomans with Hungarian help; he should not trust in the honesty of the Venetian Senate which also wants the Prince. They want only to sell him for good profit to Sultan Bayezid II."[36]

In his claim on Prince Djem, King Matthias could marshall a special and unique argument. He explained that he had the right to the fugitive Prince Djem because the latter was his, Matthias', blood relative. He based this assertion on the fact that, when Islamic raiders had entered Transylvania, the raiders had captured the sister of his grandmother in the eastern province of Hungary where the Hunyadi family ruled. Later, this unfortunate and very attractive victim had married Sultan Mohammed II and Djem was their son. It had been Mohammed's wish that Djem would be his successor, but his half-brother Bayezid had bribed the army leaders and had become sultan.* When Djem allegedly had asked king Matthias' support after his flight, he had promised to accept the Christian faith.[37]

Contemporary and noteworthy historian Babinger still could not explain the whole story about Djem when he wrote with regard to Djem's mother: "We know neither where she came from, nor what became of her."[38]

We know that King Matthias time and again had begged the successive popes to let Prince Djem go to Hungary in order to use him in his crusades; he even had sent a dissident Turk to Rome to prove the willingness of some Ottomans to rebel and to dethrone Bayezid, but none of the Popes

---

*Nota Bene, when Bayezid thus introduced the bakshish system, by bribing the military leaders, he founded deadly corruption also. The bakshish system eventually undermined the whole Ottoman administration and caused the decline of the empire. Pasha Lufti pointed out that bribing among officials in the whole Islamic world was incurable. In 1540 he wrote: "Oh Allah! Save us from the bakshish." Hungarian rayas suffered much from the corrupt system when the military theocracy established it in Ottoman occupied Hungarian territories."[43]

had let Djem, because time was running out, warning the Pope that Djem might commit suicide or that he might be poisoned. He indignantly blamed the Vatican for infidelity, saying that Pope Paul II had promised to send Djem to Buda. The resident papal legate in Buda wrote the Vatican: "I finally succeeded to make from the furious lion a humble lamb again" and added that if Rome should disappoint the Hungarian king, Matthias might invite the Ottoman legate to Buda to make a peace-pact. Pope Innocent sent a conciliatory message after which the king angrily lectured the papal envoy:

> "If I wanted to enumerate all the humiliations I have suffered from Rome, Popes and Cardinals, for my loyalty and services, a whole oxhide [parchment] would not be large enough to write them on."[40]

The next papal envoy brought news of a new development: the French king had finally agreed to let Djem go to Buda. This time the angry Matthias answered:

> "You, ambassador, although I am not born Italian, I also could have made many empty promises and misleading statements. But now it is enough! Your Holy Father can do what he wants with this unfortunate Turk, he now can keep him himself for the next hundred years"[41]

As a matter of fact, Pope Innocent had finally decided to send Djem to Hungary, because only the Hungarian king could use the prince on behalf of Christianity.[42] But when the Pope opened the Continental Assembly in Rome, King Matthias left for his second capital, Vienna, where he died.* When he died, a rumor centered around an alleged remark of the long-agonizing king: "Yes, Rome, I feel your finger in my stomach." Supposedly, the king's painful death came after he had eaten some [poisoned?] figs which he had received as a present from Rome.

In summary: during the many unfortunate diplomatic confrontations between the king of Hungary and the Popes of Rome, only Pope Pius II had recognized the impossibility of a *modus vivendi* between Christianity

---

*Matthias had taken Vienna away from Emperor Fredrick who, being a Turcophil, had constantly intrigued against King Matthias. Emperor Fredrick had gone so far in his sympathy for the Ottomans, that he had offered his daughter, Kunigunda, as a concubine to the sultan.

and the permanent Ottoman offensives. Pius II had said at Mantua, "How can we expect peace from a nation which is thirsty for blood and which already has moved onto a part of Hungary?" Unfortunately, it had been the Venetian merchants who had been ready for a peaceful cooperation with the Turks, in spite of Pius II's clear diagnosis.

When the tired and aging king had written Pope Innocent VIII, he had enumerated his life-long struggle and his services, concluding that:

> "During my several crusades, skirmishes, and besieging of cities, I have sacrificed huge sums of money, many good friends, subjects, and relatives, even my own uncle lost his life. My own body is full of wounds which I received in battles, and now in my old age I feel how much I suffer from those scars . . . . If I had not struggled against the Turks, on my life I tell you, that without Hungarian military help the fate of Italy as well as of the Holy See would have been sealed."[44]

A contemporary of King Matthias, the Franciscan priest and theologian, Osvat Laskai, summed up King Matthias' role: "This powerful nation, whose blood and bones cover valleys and mountains of different European countries, was ordered by God to hold the sword against the Big Turk."[45] Matthias had lived in the age of Renaissance-Humanism, a time in which humanism somehow lost its Christian heritage and contemporary man acted without any moral inhibitions. It was a time in which one man's Christ became another man's Anti-Christ, and in that religious-spiritual chaos man lost direction and goal. The Venetian Republic was a good illustration of the amoral atmosphere. In Venice, the office of the Senate guarded a special locked chest in which a variety of poisons were stored. How and when to use these poisons and against which of their opponents, was the secret decision made by the members of the Senate.[46] The Vatican had failed in organizing a concerted European effort which would have supported the Hungarian struggle in expelling the Ottoman-Turks from European territory, one reason being that Rome was no longer accepted as a regulating, universal force. The developing national awareness, as well as the individual bourgeoisie, and half-pagan humanism continued to undermine the authority of Rome. The efforts of the Vatican to support the Hungarian struggles to rescue the enslaved people in the Balkans had been a historical fact in centuries past, and that these efforts were continued in spite of humanist obstructions is well illustrated by the fact that Pope Julius II, the founder of St. Peter's Basilica (1505) in 1507 transferred to Hungary the sum of money which had been collected to finance the building of the sanctuary.

These efforts on the part of the Vatican stood in stark contrast to the absence of help from the West. When one reads and rereads contemporary sources, one must conclude that there were no signs of solidarity with the suffering populations of East Central Europe coming from western Christianity.

The earlier decisive battles of Nicopolis and Varna had been lost by the Hungarians because the Turks had been able to cross the Bosporus with the help of the Venetian and Genoese fleets. With those crossings in mind, it is of interest to note that an apparent cooperator of the anti-Christian Ottomans was Leonardo da Vinci, the highly regarded humanist, who advocated for instance, that the absolute freedom of man was to abolish all forms of tyranny. In practice, however, Leonardo contradicted this lofty idea by serving notorious tyrants such as Lodovico Sforza and Cesare Borgia. Sforza could not spend a good night if he had not first committed a crime, and Borgia, became the model for Macchiavelli's *The Prince*, the book in which all possible wrongdoings were advocated.

Leonardo da Vinci turned to an even more formidable tyrant, Sultan Bayezid II, and offered his genius to serve him with his military inventions. In a letter addressed to Sultan Bayezid II in 1503 or 1504, dated the third of July, but apparently sent off four months later, and allegedly mailed from Genoa, da Vinci offered the sultan four propositions for the erecting of a bridge, three hundred and fifty meters long, over the Golden Horn, to make military crossing from Asia into Europe easier.

> "I, your slave, [!] have learned that you wish to erect a bridge between Constantinople and Galata, but that you have not been able to proceed because you have no bridge-building specialists. I, your slave, know how to. I will build this bridge with such a high arch, that nobody will be willing to cross it on foot . . . . I will build it thus that a ship with sails up, can pass under it . . . . So God will, you will believe my words and give order with which you will mention your servant who is at your service."[47]

Another of the four proposals was the construction of windmills. In contrast to the help da Vinci offered to Bayezid was his plan for an elaborate defense system of Venice against a possible Ottoman invasion!

Michelangelo was later approached by Sultan Selim I, who was willing to deposit a certain sum into the bank of Gaudi to secure Michelangelo's help.[48]

When after centuries of resistance, Suleiman the Great finally succeeded in invading Hungary, this country became suddenly Europe's central problem. How could that bulwark now protect the divided European nations? The Hungarian defense, which had lasted for a century and more, suddenly collapsed because the nation had been bled to death. It was a catastrophe long foreseen by the nation's leaders. *Pax Christiana* ceased to be Europe's destiny; it was buried together with *Pax Hungarica* at the battle of Mohács in 1526.

1526 - The Battle of Mohács

This most decisive battle took place in Hungary between the Hungarian army and the Ottoman aggressor on the plain of Mohács. Suleiman had pulled together his army from three continents and had a force of more than 100,000 men, much larger than the Hungarian defensive army of 24,000 men. Defeat was therefore unavoidable. King Louis II lost his life on the battlefield as did two archbishops, five bishops, the elite of the nobility, and even members of the University of Pécs, apart from the 20,000 soldiers. It took three months to bury the thousands of victims.

The defeat and its historical significance was equal with the Serbian loss at Cossovo in 1389, and the later battle at White Mountain in Bohemia in 1620. A historian correctly concluded that, wherever the Ottoman occupation was prolonged, that nation never could regain its original greatness; for instance, the Serbian country had to wait five hundred years until it could compose a state of mixed nationalities, mainly from non-ethnical Serbs. A similar development took place in Bohemia, where the Habsburgs had subjugated the people; it was only three hundred years later that it became possible to build up a state in which, however, the Czech ethnic group remained a minority in the Czech-Slovakian-Hungarian-German ethnical combination. Hungary underwent a partial occupation for one hundred and fifty years, although the people never yielded to the oppressor and constantly frustrated the Ottoman-Turks in realizing their goal as prescribed by the Koran, which the revisionist historians have called *Pax Ottomanica.*

In the sixteenth century, Hungary also suffered from the dynastic rivalry between the Habsburg-German Charles V (Spain), his brother Ferdinand I, king of Hungary, and the "most Christian" Francis I, King of France. When the latter lost all his chances against the Habsburgs, he turned to the Ottomans and spent large sums to support Suleiman the Great's attacks on Hungary. In a certain sense one could say that the catastrophe of Mohács was a "present" from the French ruler.[49]

Among the Roman Popes was the truly honorable Adrian II, who asked the "most Christian" king to stop his collaboration with the Asiatic hordes against his Christian neighbors, but Francis I cynically instructed the Holy Father, saying, "I do not want to have the title 'most Christian' in vain . . . but love starts first with self love."

After Mohács, Suleiman moved into Buda, the city which represented at that time the most advanced Renaissance culture in East Central Europe. The dominating cultural influence of the court of Matthias Corvinus had been acknowledged in Poland and Bohemia as the first Renaissance center north of the Alps. Polish historian, Halecki, wrote: "The Renaissance came to Poland, as to all other countries beyond the Alps, from a remote but friendly Italy, in many cases through the intermediary of allied Hungary."[50]

Andrei Oteta, a historian from Rumania, wrote that in the history of European Renaissance, Hungary played a special role. The Renaissance culture had its development in the court of Matthias Corvinus in Buda, and that from Buda, Renaissance culture spread to East Central Europe, fertilizing other nations' cultural development.

This culture center, Buda, was visited by Suleiman. There he fulfilled the Koranic teaching that One Book contained all wisdom and therefore no other books were needed; thus he ordered the destruction of the second largest library in Europe, robbed all treasures, and returned to his seraglio.

The catastrophic outcome of the battle at Mohács had shocked all European nations, and at a number of royal courts divine services were held, even as far as Spain and Oxford in England, for the salvation of the very young new Hungarian ruler. In Venice, however, the Council sent a special envoy to Suleiman to congratulate him on his victory; in fact, they asked the Conqueror to continue his attacks.[51]

The aftereffect of Mohács was that Luther's long-lasting defeatist propaganda stopped (he had dared to identify the Pope with the cruel Turks), and that he made a turnabout and started a campaign of fear against the Turks. This change of mind came too late in connection with the Hungarian crisis; when in 1521, at the Diet of Worms, the Hungarian delegate, Werböczy, had asked support in the war against the Turks, Luther had overshadowed Werböczy's request with his own problem, which was highly unfortunate, because German military aid might have relieved the siege of Nandorfehérvár in the same year, while now the "gate to Hungary" had fallen in Suleiman's hand. Emperor Charles V had suggested to Werböczy that it might be expedient to arrange for an armistice with the sultan, until Charles could put a stop to Luther's defeatist attitude. Many years of indifference followed before Wittenberg started another tune. Lately it has become obvious, though, that the many Hungarian students at the University of Wittenberg did inform Luther of the devastating and constant attacks by the Ottomans. Historian Elert has pointed out this influence: "During the developing Reformation in Hungary, the students in Wittenberg from Hungary, at that time the largest number among the foreign students, definitely altered Luther's historical theology in connection with the Turkish question, as well as his mission theology, both of which he had developed from the theology of the Word."[52] It was characteristic how often Luther failed to see the historical realities. For instance, when Suleiman returned to occupy Vienna in 1529 and suddenly stopped the attacks on the city, Luther immediately called this development *magno Dei miracula*. The fact was that an abnormal rainy season forced the sultan to abandon his project. The city of Nagykörös, which had been declared sultan's city, had the duty to produce saltpeter, basic element to the manufacturing of explosives needed to bring down the walls of Vienna. Usually, this raw material was collected from the normally very arid soil, but in that abnormal rainy year, the saltpeter could not "bloom" from the sandy soil because it was too wet. Therefore the cannons of the Ottomans had to remain silent, and Luther's *magno Dei miracula* occurred, because the saltpeter was lacking. Nagykörös owed its immunity as sultan's city to the fact that it could produce saltpeter, as becomes clear from the pasha of Buda's own words:

"I, bey Olay, pasha Huszein, whose power should be extended. Since the *rayas* [from Nagykörös] from old have produced nitrate, the Magnificent sultan has ordered that they shall not be taxed anymore in any form . . . Sealed by Mustafa, servant of Allah, in Buda."[53]

Suleiman's own chronicler made several comments concerning the extraordinary amount of rainfall that summer in Hungary, and he especially stressed the rainy day of the eleventh of September, the day when the siege of Vienna was halted. He reported also how many horses and cannons were lost in the mud and how finally the rescued cannons were loaded on Danubian boats to bring them back to the depots in Nandorfehérvár, and the gun carriages were burned.[54] One needs to understand the military handicaps in connection with the frequent Ottoman campaigns. The extended distance and the time element constantly limited the military potentiality of the sultan's armies. The armies could not depart from Constantinople earlier than April or May, and it took three months to reach their Hungarian base. To transfer three hundred cannons meant a column of about seven miles length. In addition, the 22,000 camels slowed down the whole progress. All military action had to be concluded on Kaszin day, 28 October, because the camels and the sensitive Arabian horses could not tolerate the cold and the rain, and so there were in reality about three months left for fighting. Austrian historian Hantsch also explained the abandonment of Vienna as due to the weather conditions and the poor Ottoman organization, rather than the Viennese weapons installed on the city's walls.[55] Ottoman historian-secretary, Ferdi, tried to whitewash the sultan's strategy saying that "the Magnificent" had forgiven the children and women of Vienna and that therefore he had left the city intact. This was another legend about Vienna and just as opposite to reality as Luther's explanation had been.

The sultan continued to attack Hungarian land, but he had to face the resisting Hungarian braves in the citadels. Amazingly, sometimes less important fortifications wrecked the Ottoman's ambitions, creating military warfare textbook stories *per se*; for instance, the fortification of Köszeg (Guns) in west Hungary. The resisting defenders stalled Suleiman's military operation for three weeks, and Suleiman finally had to come to a compromise with Captain Jurisich of the fortification: he asked the latter to at least let someone plant a Turkish flag symbolically on the wall in order to save the sultan's face. His army would, however, not enter the city. This was done. Episodes like this occurred several times, helping to delay Suleiman's action against Vienna. Finally, in the time left to the Ottomans before the deadline of October 28, only raids could be performed, and to show how merciful the Koranic command toward the infidels was, the Tatars burned where they went, kidnapped thousands of people, massacred thousands of women who had been violated first. One episode should be mentioned: during the raid on Hainburg, several men had hidden themselves in a chimney; one of them, who appeared sooty from the chimney when the raid was over, became the ancestor of the famous composer Haydn.

In 1541 Sultan Suleiman through treachery was able to occupy Buda, in order to use it as a base of operation against the west. This event alarmed the western nations. King Ferdinand I of Habsburg, who by marriage contract had succeeded to the Hungarian throne, and his brother Emperor Charles V, immediately mobilized a large German rescue army. Under the leadership of General Joachim Brandenburg the army reached Hungary. Luther called the military leader a "woman captain who never saw a bloody sword", and he was not far from the mark. The general was always drunk and he lost in gambling the whole amount of money meant for army expenses. As a result, the unpaid German soldiers looted Hungarian communities and the thirsty ones among them started to revolt because the Hungarian wine was not to their taste. At the wall of Pest the German soldiers refused to attack the fortification because they had not received their attack money.* The end result of the rescue campaign was that Buda remained in Turkish hands. The embittered King Ferdinand complained to his brother Charles V that "the German military commanders had no brains," that "with such an army you never can defeat the Ottomans."[56] In the end, the rescue army was defeated by the *Morbus Hungaricus* and only one-fourth of the military returned to Germany, blaming the climate, the wine, and the food for the disaster. From then on, Hungary was called the "cemetery of Germans." On another occasion, Italian mercenaries also revolted openly when the Emperor wanted to send them to Hungary, because "the wine was not too good."

The restless Suleiman started what was to be his last attack on Hungary and Austria when he was 72 years old. He could no longer ride on horseback and traveled from Constantinople in a carriage, in 1566. His mobilization had begun a year earlier; in all his provinces, all forces had

---

*The military tradition was to give soldiers the so-called attack money before a siege started.

been ordered to ready themselves. Huge depots were ordered stored along the route to be taken, as well as the digging of innumerable wells. All this was financed with borrowed money. When after a slow progress he finally reached Szigetvár on the first of August in 1566, he set up camp there. His army counted more than a hundred thousand men. The fortress of Szigetvár was under the command of Count Miklos Zrinyi, who was one of the most brilliant military strategists, and a member of a well-known Hungarian aristocratic family. The sultan besieged this relatively small fortress for more than two months. When the number of defenders had decreased from eight hundred to a few dozen men and the fortress was in ruins, Count Zrinyi had the burning gate opened. He and his few surviving braves hurled themselves against the Ottoman front, in a final sacrifice. As a religious soldier he had offered himself up on behalf of his country. This concept of pacification with the Creator ruled many contemporary lives. Suffering man became a thinking man, wondering why there fell so much misery on the nation, and his answer became a theological one, "Our fathers sinned and are no more and we bear their iniquities." The preachers were present with the soldiers beyond the walls of fortresses, often even brought from as far as Wittenberg, explaining to the warriors that the Islamic Ottomans were the Anti-Christ, and they were succeeding in their attacks, because God was punishing the Hungarian people. Apart from acting like prophets, and comforting the people, the preachers also incited the men to resist the Anti-Christ by offering themselves up on the walls of the fortification, because God had called them to be a witness there. The preachers' prayers served as a religious display of strength to ready the men for their last fight. János Pannonius, a contemporary Hungarian humanist, observed how exhausted the people in East Central Europe were and prayed: "Our Father, save now your tired Pannonian children . . . ." Count Zrinyi had been one who had manifested this type of metaphysically oriented resistance until his death. This type of heroic attitude created a slogan among the western nations: that the Hungarian destiny was to be a shield, a bulwark, on behalf of Christendom. Aenea Sylvio Piccolomi was the first in humanist literature to formulate this *epitheton ornans*, as if to glorify the nation for its Christian service. French ideologists followed in this trend, and later the Germans also attributed this destiny to the bleeding nation.

In sixteenth century Western literature, the Protestant Reformation and the Ottoman peril were the two most important problems discussed. In

German literature, the Turk became the "Erbfeind", death-enemy, of the Christian faith, while the common German at evening prayed "save us from the Bloodhound". When Germany had learned of Zrinyi's sacrificial death, all of Germany had been plunged into mourning. They too had explained his death as conciliatory sacrifice. The historical irony of the fall of Szigetvár was, that two days earlier Suleiman had died, and he had not been able to hear the victorious cries of his men. The cruel warrior found his grave in the land of the infidels, and "the shadow of Allah", as he had declared himself, was gone once and for all.

Two more facts need to be told: first, that when the defenders of Szigetvár died on the walls of the fortification, the Habsburg army was encamped not far off; however, they did not come to help, but merely watched the fate of Szigetvár; second, when Suleiman the Magnificent prepared for what was to be his last battle, he had to borrow great sums of money to pay for all the preparations, while at the same time in the Asiatic heartland of Anatolia, in the city of Cesme, his faithful followers had nothing but grass to eat![57]

When fortifications like Szigetvár and Köszeg were lost to the Ottomans, the countrysides around the towns, which originally had been protected, were also destroyed and depopulated; in fact, the human settlements often simply vanished from the earth. Maximilian II tried to lessen these senseless destructions, and, according to the Ottoman traveling historian Ibrahim Pecsovi, Maximilian prohibited Sultan Selim at the peace negotiation in Drinapoly (Edirne), from occupying any cities during the armistice. Selim (1566–1574) circumvented this prohibition, and instead of moving into cities, his Tatars burned them down, deporting or killing the population.[58]

Practical Realities of Pax Ottomanica

Some spahis received military feudal land for their military services. Of these new (but often temporary) landowners, some did not want any settlements on "their" land but rather preferred to rent empty prairies as grazing land. Namely, if there was no population, the spahi could avoid paying the yearly tax into the sultan's treasury, which was based on the number of *rayas* and houses on the land.[59] Interestingly, at the peace negotiation of Drinapoly, the Hungarian representative had included a unique demand: those villages which had to pay a yearly tax to the sultan, should also pay tax to the original landowners, now living in non-occupied

Hungary, and both parties could collect only half of the yearly tax. (As a form of protest against the foreign occupants, the serfs already did this on a voluntary basis.)

The occupied Hungarian land suffered a constant exploitation by the ruling pashas, who had received the feudal land as a gift from the sultans. Since these were only temporary donations, depending on the whims of the Vizir, the pashas tried to exploit the *rayas* as much as possible, during their short stays on the land or in the cities. During the 145 years that the Ottomans occupied Buda, ninety-nine Beglerbeys (viceroys) were installed by the sultans. It also happened that before a pasha could establish himself in the feudal property, someone else in Constantinople, by bribing (bakshish), might already have bought the same property from the vizir or the sultan. The average time of service for a pasha was one and a half years. As a result of the exploitations, those Christian *rayas* who could no longer endure the situation had only one option, to escape to non-occupied parts of the Hungarian land. These massive escapes as well as the constant military movements, raids, and the frequent plague epidemics, depopulated the country.

When the Ottomans started to build their own fortifications in occupied territories, the *rayas* from that province were lined up by the thousands for manual service (robot). They were forced to demolish buildings, preferably church buildings, because those provided neatly cut stones which could be installed quickly into a Turkish fortress or a mosque. They would form a human assembly line along which the building materials went from hand to hand. The poor serfs had to remain for weeks on the same location to which they had been ordered. They slept and ate there if the Muslim commander had provisions available.[60]

These destructive processes had a dogmatic foundation in the Koran. Mohammed had prescribed that only one building could be erected, namely the mosque for Allah. Historian Becker, quoting from the Koran, explained why the Islamic intruders methodically destroyed what they could touch. The Koranic teaching stated that the worst use which a believer could make of his money was to build, because each building other than the mosque, would stand to the discredit of its architect on the day of resurrection. No prophet should enter a house adorned with fair decoration. (There were more than 142,000 prophets.)[61]

The fate of the Christian church buildings and other visible arts belong to the tragic chapters of European ecclesiastical history. In the territories of Hungary which were occupied by the Ottomans only four Gothic cathedrals survived. All visual artistic objects such as paintings, sculptures, and frescoes *a priori* were condemned to perish. If any outstanding building remained intact, it was mainly thanks to the need of the sensitive Arabian horses which required protection in winter. Sometimes monumental buildings were used as storage places for explosives. How many of them were destroyed, however, when an accidental explosion occurred? In Buda the pasha had accumulated huge depots of explosives which were detonated when lightning struck, and half the city was in ruins. Countless Hungarians and Ottomans were buried under the rubble. The frightened pasha had János Csanaki, a pastor, arrested and imprisoned, accusing him of secretly praying for this catastrophe. He had spat three times upon the head of Csanaki to show his contempt.[62]

Contemporary sources of church history have registered several similar events of how preachers were punished with great cruelty when the Ottomans lost battles, which they accused the preachers of having brought down upon the Muslims by means of their prayers of intercession.[63] Some cathedrals were transformed into mosques or schools for the Dervishes and therefore were left intact for the time being. A Turkish chronicler reported one occasion of the takeover of a cathedral:

> "During four days, pictures were carried outside, as well as altars, statues, and benches. The remaining frescoes were painted over with whitewash, and after the devilish voices of the infidels were thus silenced, the Mohammedan prayers of thanksgiving were heard."[64]

The Gothic cathedral in Buda, for centuries the place where the Hungarian rulers were crowned, and rich in treasures, also underwent a similar Islamic vandalism; according to the Turkish eyewitness Mustafa Dseialzade,

> "On that day all the Mohammedan soldiers cried loudly and shed tears of joy, when the den of the infidels, which had been filled with pictures, was transformed into a paradise of Djami, where the Koran finally could be read aloud."[65]

Communal buildings were never kept up, instead purposefully neglected, in accordance with Koranic disapproval. Priceless treasures from churches were brought to Byzantium. Even today, the visitor to the Hagia Sophia in

Istanbul can see the huge, six feet high, silver candelabras which came from Buda. The only visual change is that there is now an inscription:

> "Suleiman, ruler of the whole world, who destroyed Buda and burned down all temples, brought these candelabras from that place to bring light into Hagia Sophia."

In addition to such treasures, the robbery included thousands of church bells. The latter were often melted for the fabrication of cannons, which were needed to destroy more sanctuaries in Hungary.[66] A somewhat amusing note in connection with this cultural barbarism is to be found in the archives in Nagykörös. In Nagykörös and Kecskemét the pasha was merciful enough to return one church bell when the *rayas* had saved sufficient *bakshish*. The condition, however, was that the bell would be rung for his salvation on each holy day! In another town, faithful Hungarians bought back their sanctuary three times, from one Islamic ruler after another. When the totally exploited *rayas* had no silver to bribe the Islamic ruler, they held their worship service among the ruined walls of what once had been their sanctuary, just as the Hebrews did at the Wailing Wall. There is an abundance of similar records which easily should convince the modern apologist that the Ottomans sold their "tolerance" only for silver and gold. Not even the appearance of tolerance was involved when the Muslim rulers, keenly aware of the love and loyalty that the *rayas* displayed to their priests or pastors, imprisoned them and held them for large ransoms. An example of this was the imprisonment of the professor and reformed bishop, Dr. Stephen (István) Szegedi Kis, whose books were read in Europe among Protestants and Roman Catholics alike. After John Calvin, he was the most systematic theological thinker, whose *Loci communes*, the first Protestant lexicon, proved this statement. As bishop, Dr. Szegedi Kis was venerated among the *rayas*. Bey Mehmed captured him during a worship service, and kept him imprisoned for two years. During that time, the bishop was frequently led to the marketplace where he was then physically brutalized before his believers. In that manner the Bey hoped to force the people to pay an enormous ransom. When finally a sum of twelve hundred pieces of gold were collected from the whole Hungarian population, Dr. Stephen Szegedi Kis was freed.[67]

Taxation of the Christian *Rayas*

When Suleiman the Conqueror and his armies left Hungary in 1541 to prepare the next attack, another army moved into the occupied territories, the army of tax collectors. That the sultan distrusted his own office holders was documented by the fact that this army was headed by his closest relative, Pasha Halil. It was the latter's duty to compose the *Defter*, a roster of all tax-paying *rayas*. His team went from place to place, including those where only a single *raya* scratched out a meager living, to register all information regarding number of family members, properties, occupations, social status, *et cetera*, and this information was to serve for the next ten years as basis for the amounts levied as tributes to the sultan. In return, the *rayas* were not protected, nor defended, nor did they gain any form of service. The meaning of the word *raya*, relates to their fate: sheep; they were, as it were, fleeced.

A modern historian noted that the greedy and brutal conquerors collected over seventy-three different taxes, fees, and "gifts" from the subjugated Christian serfs in Hungary. This type of economic, social, and physical exploitation could only be called plunder. The *rayas* registered in this manner were from birth 'til the grave hounded by tax collectors. One could not take a step or turn around without having to pay and pay.[68] A sixteenth century observer stated that "The Ottomans moved away everything except millstones and red-hot iron." Although taxation was growing steadily, the occupied part of Hungary never was financially sufficient; about 60% of the budget for the military administration of Buda, for instance, came from Constantinople.[69]

Gustav Bayerle in a recent study has mentioned only fifteen direct taxations; there were, however, numerous so-called gifts as indirect taxes.[70] For example, in the age of unrestricted social life and broken down moral standards, there were plenty of occasions for the Kadi (Judge) to tax the *raya*. If somebody carried out a personal vendetta, he was immediately taxed by the order-loving Kadi. If someone licked some honey, he was taxed that. Even the grass belonged to the Pasha, not to the *rayas*, and so the latter were taxed for it. To illustrate the inequality between Muslim and Christian serf, the follower of Mohammed paid only two Akce, where the Christian *raya* had to pay twenty. Water was not safe for consumption in those days, and wine was therefore a daily drink. Barrel taxation restrained the drinker's thirst. Onion was the most frequently used daily medicine; in consequence, it was easy to detect the use thereof by its smell, and thus the vapor was taxed. If a *raya* had a little garden, the tax officer immediately declared it to be a taxable luxury. Daily bread was taxed twice; first when it was still flour at the mill, the second time at the bakery. When the chimneys smoked in winter, the alert Muslim declared the smoke property of the far-away sultan or the residing pasha, and as there was no way to make the smoke invisible, one had to pay tax on the smoke as well as on the warm room. If the poor *raya* practiced his religion to find some solace, he had to pay for the house of prayer. Did he wish to go to the market? He was greeted by a bridge tax as well as a market fee. Did his cattle go astray? Pay a fee for the undisciplined animals; did he wish to eat one of his chickens? He could not do so without first making some contribution to the Ottoman empire; did he have to slaughter one of his animals? The tax collector again was waiting for a tribute. Cheese and fruits fell under a special taxation. Did the *raya* need a wagon on his farm? He had to pay. When from far away a peasant came on horseback, extra payment was due. The poor peddlers became even poorer when they had the misfortune to meet with a Turk on the road. If a young man fell in love and wanted to get married, there was the bridal tax to be paid; after marriage he was expected to pay bed tax as well. Although the Koranic law prohibited the consumption of pork, the eating thereof was regarded as heresy, in winter the forgetful Muslim demanded head cheese from the *rayas*. In spite of the fact that Muslims are not supposed to drink alcoholic beverages, in practice they must have done well in those days, because when the Ottoman army was about to set out to attack Hungary, the first act was to send ahead army officers whose task it was to close all the wineshops in the to-be-attacked area.

There were instances when *rayas* were overburdened by the military grabbing techniques, and some of them left the settlement for unoccupied parts of Hungary. The clever tax collector, however, forced the still residing *rayas* to pay the share of the escapees. Were they being punished for the fact that they had let their counterparts go? Whatever their reasoning, the Ottomans learned very late the truth of the proverbial saying *ubi populus ibi ubulus*.

In the first phase of the crusades, the sultan ordered many Hungarians to be brought to the Balkan countries as slave laborers; there were several contemporary observers who witnessed these deportations. Envoy Busbecq, homebound in 1554 to Vienna, wrote: "Just as I left Constantinople, I met several wagons with boys and girls who were carried from Hungary to the slave market in Constantinople; this is the commonest kind of Turkish merchandise."[71]

When in 1532, Suleiman had moved toward Vienna in hopes of conquering the city, his raiders had attacked the border town of Sopron in Hungary. After they failed to capture the town, they had devastated the whole of the surrounding rural province, even burning down the five hundred year old monastery. When Suleiman had returned to Constantinople, the city leaders of Sopron petitioned King Ferdinand I for compensation, because only one-fourth of the population had survived.[72]

Another example of the Ottoman practice of extortion, which was common, can be found in the archives of Debrecen. When in 1660, pasha Ahmed Szeidi camped in the vicinity of that city, he invited the twelve magistrates to his camp to enjoy a cup of coffee.* When these citizens, carrying the expected "gifts", greeted the pasha with suspicion, the latter demanded from the city one hundred thousand pieces of gold. To emphasize this order, the pasha pointed to twelve stakes, which were erected in front of his tent, making very clear that those stakes awaited his guests' heads if his demand would not be honored. If the city would pay, Allah would be merciful. All that remained for the senators to do was to rob their own city.

Pax Ottomanica and the Fox Tail

The sultans declared several cities in Hungary as their own, and gave such *hasz*-cities** their special *ferman*, which granted absolute immunity to its citizens. This author is a descendant from one of these cities, Nagykörös. Collective memory of the inhabitants as well as the *Nagykörösi Kronika,*[73] have preserved for posterity an authentic report which shows how such a "privileged" community languished. The protection promised by the almighty sultan was nominal, because the protector lived more than a

---

*Coffee drinking had been introduced in 1541 by the Turks. They called it "black soup", and they served it after a meal. The Hungarians, however, called it Turkish poison.

**hasz - special

thousand miles away in Constantinople; the money-hungry pashas, kadis, raiders, and Janissaries, however, lived in the vicinity.

Nagykörös was founded on sandy hills; it had no river and no fortifications. The open city was therefore quite vulnerable to vagrant Turks. Before the Ottoman occupation, the city had been unimportant, but, as the Ottoman influence spread and raiders started to rob and burn some twenty-six cities and villages in its surroundings, deporting many of the defenseless inhabitants, countless refugees flocked into Nagykörös, trusting in the protection granted by the sultan to the city. Nagykörös slowly incorporated the depopulated territories which nature was transforming into endless prairies. This created a large protective zone of wilderness and swamps around the city, which no highway penetrated, hence travelers could expect to sink into mud. As one foreigner remarked in his memoirs: "The Hungarians put mud upon mud and call it rampart (*lutum luta adponant et hoc vocant "töltés"*). Nagykörös had received its privileged status because the wilderness, the mud, and the marshlands contained chemicals, like saltpeter, needed by the Turkish military as basic material for the production of gunpowder. Interestingly, the Roman historian Plinius, during the Roman occupation of the territory, had already mentioned that Pannonia was rich in saltpeter, but its historical importance became obvious only when the Ottoman warfare had great demand for it. This military need had granted some relative, cultural, as well as social security for the city. How important the saltpeter was for the Ottomans can be read from an order issued by Sultan Mohammed I to the pasha in Temesvár, to speed up the transportation of the "black gunpowder", because it was badly needed in the siege of Crete, a thousand miles from Hungary. So the citizens of Nagykörös unwillingly and indirectly made history with their economical contribution to the military expansion of the Ottoman empire. In return, the citizens were, at least in principle, exempt from any *harac* (extortion). In the city's archives are plenty of *ferman*, issued by sultans; their number alone is proof that these *ferman* were not honored by the Turks. And so, Nagykörös, in spite of its "protected status", finally became another city of fear.

At that time, the main source of economy in the not-occupied, as well as the occupied parts of Hungary, was ranching on the extended prairies. In time of relative peace, sometimes more than ten thousand head of cattle were driven westward to Germany and Italy along the "highway of the butchers", thus bringing as much as six million *florins* into the treasuries of the country. The cattle business, however, became a risky endeavor because the ever-present Turkish raiders after rustling the herds also drove them to the west along the same highway.[74] This rustling also existed for Nagykörös.

Between 1627 and 1665, the magistrates of Nagykörös secured at least fourteen *ferman* from Constantinople to protect the citizens against unjustified bribing by the pasha of Buda. As these letters of protection proved not to be enough, the mayors of the city visited the *Porte* in Constantinople several times, to return with ten more letters of additional protection. One can read such a *ferman* with ironic amusement, because it proves, for instance, that the Ottomans made all efforts to make capital from death. Some contemporary chroniclers remarked that "If any one, in any form, or by any cause, dies, the Turk will produce profit from it." For instance, the sultan issued a letter exempting from taxation the following causes of death: "if someone dies by accident in a fire, or drowns in a river, or falls down from a roof, a cart, or a tree, or when a falling tree hits someone, or a person falls into a well, or when lightning strikes, no pasha, kadi, or tax collector has the right to ask a blood-fee from the surviving family members."[75] There is mention of a case in the records, where a man died of other causes, and the poor widow had to give to the Kadi her only cow as blood-fee, as well as forty florins. The simple excuse for blood-fees was that when somebody died, the sultan lost valuable property. That the extortions were quite arbitrary is shown by the uneven penalties that were claimed. The same Kadi would demand in Buda a hundred Akce as blood-fee; in Nagykörös, however, he would claim forty. It all depended on how hard the victims drove the bargaining.

According to Benjamin Franklin, everyone must die and everyone must pay taxes. The Ottomans already practiced this wisdom, and in the "privileged" city of Nagykörös, seventy-two taxes and fees were levied, although not called by these names. Never-ending complaints were all in vain. A few selected illustrations from Nagykörös' yearly income and spending records follow:[76]

The first direct tax was the tithe of every income for the sultan. The next general contribution was the *robot*, or forced manual labor for the building of fortifications and other projects. Another forced labor was the transportation of wood as well as hay for the sultan's horses. The general taxation began at Christmas time when donations had to be made to the

Christ-denying Muslims. This was followed by quarterly forced "gifts" of 1,000–1,500 florins to Bey Nazar in Buda. In return the bey protected the immunity, but not the city itself. The bey's secretary also "needed the gift" of a cow and her calf, resulting in the fact that the Bey Nazar also required the identical gift. Because the Koran prescribed a ritual washing five times a day, the citizens of Nagykörös had to donate twenty-seven pounds of perfumed soap. To honor protection by the sultan, the city had to express its gratitude with 1,100 pieces of shiny gold, as well as saltpeter in the worth of 120 pieces of gold. Yearly wood payments for the Vizir cost 62 florins. The interpreter, who was so kind as to learn the Hungarian language, received ten wagonfuls of wood. A courier had stomach ache and needed 8 florins for sour cream. The Janissaries extorted 314 florins for the Aga. Another 1200 florins were paid to Bey Nazar. Contribution to the building of the sultan's palace in Constantinople was 70 florins "gift money". "Eleven florins were paid for head cheese to a courier. For the promising New Year, we paid to Bey Nazar 110 florins and 12 fox skins with tails; to his industrious secretary, one fox skin and two knives from Vienna. To the three sub-pashas, also fox skins. To Buda were sent twelve living sheep."

The women of Nagykörös knew special fines: for gossip, for telling a lie, even for widowhood. When a Christian girl refused the approach of an Ottoman, the Kadi adjudicated her to the Muslim; if she left this husband, he had the right to put her in a sack and drown her.[77]

The city's history was made more colorful by arbitrary acts of some pasha who may not have had any jurisdiction in the area, as for instance when the city magistrates were threatened to be impaled if they did not hurry the delivery of: 100 sheep, 400 kila corn, 1000 breads, butter, and 20 cheeses. "If these gifts will not be delivered in the next two days, your heads will dry on the stakes and the milk of your memorable mother will be very bitter in your mouths. I will send 1000 Janissaries and you will be skinned alive in the midst of town."[78] Angry threats and contemptuous letters were addressed to the citizens of the sultan's city, with words as "You disobedient infidels, you swine."

Maybe some sultans had more wisdom to foresee the outcome of the reckless plunder; the greedy subordinates, however, often forced the suffering rayas to enlarge existing foxholes and escape tunnels in order to hide from the Islamic tax collectors. Even when the latter stood at one entrance of the hole, the hiding miserable *raya* still could escape at another end. These foxholes, as well as the coveted and often demanded fox tails, well represent the policies of the alleged *Pax Ottomanica*.

Judicatory System as Another Form of Collecting Tributes

The citizens of Nagykörös had the duty to report to the Turkish *kadi* each judicatory event which took place in the city. However, the city preferred to keep its own legal practice, and therefore it was ready to pay the *Kadi* for every penalty issued to breakers of the law. The amounts to be paid could be quite high; for instance, when in 1636 a horse thief was hanged, it cost Nagykörös 90 florins; on another occasion, the hanging of two murderers cost 199 florins. This tax for executions grew steadily; the hanging of a gypsy-thief cost first 58 florins, but in 1647 this amount had climbed to 130 florins.

Why was Nagykörös so eager to pay for the privilege of hanging its own criminals, instead of leaving this task to the Ottomans? This resistance meant no less than a significant question of Hungarian constitutional continuity. The Turkish military occupation never was acknowledged or accepted, neither by the national leaders, nor by the simple peasants; therefore this independence in judicial proceedings created a unique historical situation. The city's administration, led by simple laymen, was elected yearly by the assembly of magistrates, and ruled by a Hungarian judge and the assembly of twelve. These city-administrators secured the continuity of Hungarian constitutional law. The Ottoman invaders could not prevent this, thus proving that in this one area at least, the Hungarian spirit was indomitable. The historical confrontation which took place in Nagykörös between the Asiatic conquerors and the loyal Hungarian *rayas*, who did not yield, was quite unlike the one experienced with the Balkan people, who were subjugated by the Muslim conquerors.

In other parts of occupied Hungary, the Turkish military were more or less forced to withdraw into the conquered fortifications and cities; and they could not gain the administrative overhand. As a result, the oppressors demanded that village-elders deliver the annual tithes to the fortresses. Yet, with increasing frequency, the *rayas* refused to render the tithe, thus repudiating the Ottoman conquerors. In 1575 there were seventy non-yielding villages in the county of Esztergom alone.[79]

When Sultan Suleiman established military rule in parts of Hungary, he promised the Christian *rayas*:

"Everyone in the Vijalet of Buda must remain where he is, nobody, including children, will be harmed; each property will remain in the possession of the present owner; in case of death, the property will be inherited by relatives."[80]

The obvious goal of this promise was evident: to keep the *rayas* on the land as subjects to be taxed. In practice, however, the promise was never kept by the administrative officeholders, and the *Kadi* immediately shared a good portion of the meager inheritance of a deceased *raya*'s relatives.

By 1568,[81] the sultans had to yield to Hungarian pressure and permitted that the Christian *rayas* in occupied territories could pay dues to their absentee landlord; paradoxically, they contributed thus to the resisting Hungarian nobility their share to defend the freedom which they themselves had no longer. At the same time, the sultans permitted also that criminals should be handed over to Hungarian authorities for punitive action.[82]

In summary: Although the sultan inherited from the Koran the order for warfare, it proved to be an economically unsound enterprise. In Hungary for instance, the yearly tax collection brought in between six and eight million Akces. The upkeep of the military rule in that country cost, however, 23 million. This meant that the sultan had to subsidize each year about ten million Akces, which was then equal to 300,000 pieces of gold. All that for a questionable power-play.

Ottoman Military Policy

The continuing military struggle between the Cross and the Crescent resulted in a radical demographical transformation, not only among the people of the Balkans, but also in Hungary. When a large number of the Balkan people in a sense rescued themselves by accepting the Muslim politico-religion, they were freed from all otherwise obligatory services, and the landowners lost their work forces in that way. The *rayas*, thus lost as laborers, were soon replaced with people from Hungarian territories, through the notorious raids of the Ghazis or Akindjis, who were a kind of militia recruited from Tatar, Slav, and Rumanian homeless people. The sole reason for the existence of the Ghazis was the perpetration of raids, by day or by night, against the settled Hungarian population. With complete disregard of any treaty, their duty was to invade and practice a scorched-earth policy, stealing whatever they could as their reward.

Basically, they were criminals, but instead of being imprisoned, they were "forgiven" by the sultans and sent out to continue such atrocities as their nature dictated.

The re-interpretation of the past often can be misleading. For instance, one can understand from a revisionist interpretation of historical truth that "The Ottomans followed the traditional Islamic policy of tolerance toward the people of the Book", whether Christians or Jews, who had the right to protection of their lives, property, and religions, as long as they accepted the Muslim rule, and paid the special head tax.[83] Historian Paret, however, contends that the Ottoman fiscal policy in an indirect way forced millions of Christians in their territory to become Muslims.[84] The extent of forcible conversions to Islam varied with the circumstances of the Turkish conquest.

On the other hand if a Muslim gave help in any way to the religion of the *dhimmi*, he was to be summoned thrice to repent, and then, if obdurate, was to be put to death.[85]

Ottoman historian Evliya Cselebi was a world traveler, whose *Narratives of Travel in Europe*[86] between 1660–1664 were found in Uskodar. Cselebi (whose name meant friend of saints) was born in Constantinople, probably in 1611. His father, in the company of Sultan Suleiman, was present in 1541 when Buda was occupied by trick, and he also witnessed the death of Suleiman at Szigetvár. Evliya had learned Latin and Greek, as well as other languages, among them Hungarian. As a youth he had asked Allah to give him luck in his travels and faith in his old age.

Evliya Cselebi joined the raiding Turkish army and vividly described what happened to the native Hungarian people when the Ghazis invaded their homeland. From his accounts one can understand how much, or rather how little, those Ghazis contributed to the *Pax Ottomanica* notion of humanity, peace, and tolerance. Let Cselebi speak:

> "When pasha Mehmed Kucsuk arrived with his foot soldiers in the city of Fogaras, he brought along 61,000 Hungarians who had been taken prisoner. In another neighboring prison camp already three thousand men had been chained from neck to neck."[87]

> " . . . seven thousand prisoners taken; their heads [pierced] on the spears looked like a huge moving forest."[88]

> "Our army was sent into the different valleys, hunting for Hungarian men."[89]

"A big cathedral stood in Várhely, but the Vizir ordered it burned down . . . afterwards he gave his soldiers two days to go looting."[90]

[The cathedral was apparently not incorporated into the so-called religious tolerance.]

"At evening all the prisoners were tied together and they had to remain in that position until morning; suddenly, however, we heard a strange noise at the other end of the valley, and therefore we slaughtered all the prisoners, to avoid the possibility of two fronts. The next morning it turned out that some grazing cows had made those alarming noises; so we went out and captured more prisoners 'again'" (quotation marks mine).[91]

"As we continued our journey, the Tatars joined us; they brought to our camp more than ten thousand prisoners. We continued our journey, burning villages, cities, and taking prisoners. We looted a lot."[92]

"The Tatar Ghazis returned at night, and brought again about twenty thousand prisoners. In the following days the price of prisoners on the market went down, only a few piastres were paid for a man . . . ."[93]

"Szamosujvár was a strong castle and blooming city; we burned it down. We found a tomb of a former Hungarian king, filled with treasures, so we emptied it . . . . The Tatars went after more prisoners and finally their number was twice that of the Tatars. The Vizir ordered again to kill many of the prisoners. When I asked him why that was necessary, he told me that he was afraid of a Hungarian attack, and then the prisoners might revolt also. The next morning we learned, however, that the infidels had left the valley, and we had reason to be sad for such a loss of money."[94]

"At the time when this army left Transylvania-Hungary in 1664, more than a hundred thousand prisoners were registered in the sultan's records. Prisoners could be released upon payment of ransom by relatives; the income from such a transaction went to the sultan's treasury. On one day, for instance, six hundred *Kisze* [a wallet containing five hundred piastres] were earned; in comparison the yearly tribute to the sultan, paid in Transylvania, amounted to ca. 2,000 *Kisze*."[95]

"We also took the city of Sebes, and a thousand prisoners, but that community was very poor; when the mayor paid only seventy *Kisze*, the pasha had him beheaded, and nominated another mayor, who paid one hundred *Kisze*."[96]

Many similar reports illustrate that the only purpose of the Islamic Turks-Tatars was to rob the land and to make quick cash from prisoners, unconcerned as they were with the simple economic law not to kill the hen if you want some eggs. How much was robbed is also told by Cselebi: "When our army entered Hungary at the Danube River, we had only three hundred carloads of belongings, but when we moved out, we had 18,000 carloads, as well as a hundred thousand prisoners and innumerable animals. Because the pasha had ordered everything burned, there were not enough provisions and during three days, 5,000 of the prisoners died and also many animals, but I, Evliya, with my thirteen prisoners, luckily survived."[97]

He also told of another gruesome act: maybe it was too expensive to take living *raya*-prisoners to faraway slave markets; the men were beheaded and their heads presented to the sultan who paid ready cash for each. This presentation of heads became the basis for the donation of feudal Hungarian lands as reward to the spahis.

The peaceful, tolerant Muslims also introduced into military history of Europe the cutting off of noses and ears of prisoners as well as of fallen Hungarians, as proof of their valiant fights. Is it a wonder that the century-long continuing Islamic religious fanaticism inspired aggressive wars in which both sides were taught to be brutal? Voivod Pajazit, for instance, allowed the ears of twenty *rayas* to be nailed to trees because he wanted to extract more tax from them. During the resistance of the city Szeged in 1552, three thousand ears were sent to the sultan. The unfortunate victims whose arms, hands and/or legs were cut off received some pension from the Hungarian kings.[98]

In spite of all this, Stanford J. Shaw writes that there was no Ottoman misrule of their subjects in the true sense of the word.[99]

It is known that similar cruel practices took place during the siege of Szigetvár. When Count Zrinyi died with his warriors, the noses and ears of the dead were cut off and sent to Constantinople to the new sultan to comfort him that his father had not died in vain at Szigetvár.[100] Pasha

Szeidi sent at one time 3,000 skinned heads to Constantinople as a loyal gift to his sultan.[101]

Ottoman chronicles reveal more details of the continuing depopulation. Over the river Drava, which formed the southern border of Hungary, a new bridge was built in 1603; in the first year after its completion, 80,000 prisoners were led over it to the Ottoman slave-markets.[102] In the year 1663 more than one hundred thousand prisoners left Hungary via the same route.[103]

Historian Joseph von Hammer published a report written by the Austrian envoy, Gerlach, who was an eyewitness. According to this report, the Ghazis captured more than fifteen thousand Hungarians at the southern front of Hungary in 1574.[104]

It happened again and again that, when the sultan sent his rewarded spahi to Hungary to be feudal lords in the conquered land, the *Sancak**** was totally devastated, only a few villages continuing to vegetate here and there. The money-hungry Turk would first send a friendly request to his Hungarian neighbor to hand over to him some cities and villages which still belonged to the free part of Hungary. For instance:

> "I, officer Ibrahim, in Szolnok in 1555, send my gracious letter to the Hungarian captain who owns some fortifications, like Korpona. I greet with charming style Captain János Krusich and ask that he hand-over land, which the sultan in Constantinople has promised me. I also suggest that he endorse the names of the communities, as well as of the people, into the sultan's book. Do it peacefully, otherwise you will never live in peace any more. I tell this request now as your benevolent good neighbor.
>
> Ibrahim, chous, [officer], who will live in Buda.
> P.S. You can never defend those people, we can carry them away any time."

Captain Krusich's short response on the impertinent letter reads:

> "Magnificent warrior, good neighbor, I received your bizarre letter, and as you told me that you are my friend, yes you could be one, as long as you will not do anything which contradicts my honor. I was astonished when reading your letter; you must be a queer fish,

Sancak - military district.

because we have a peace treaty, signed by my ruler and the Shadow of Allah. Do you want to start a war? Please, do not use paper in vain, because as long as God is my help, I will not honor your foolish demand. Take notice: if you try to occupy my land, I will visit yours in return, and you will never hear the crowing of a rooster on that land. That is all. Korpona, 1555. János Krusich.[105]

Another letter, dated 1691, this time from Bey Mehmed, illustrates how desperate and under pressure a Turkish leader could be when thirty-six villages had been deserted by Christian *rayas*. In this letter, sent to the Hungarian, that is, unoccupied part of the country, the Bey begged the rayas to return and stay under his authority in the district of Gyula.

"My God may keep you all. I, the mighty commander of fort Gyula, together with my comrades, have learned about your tremendous suffering; therefore we really pity you, and to all of you who ran away and want to return, adults as well as little children, we send you this letter under oath.

We swear on our Turkish faith, on our one God, Allah, on the great Mohammed as well as on our Koran, on our weapons, and on our mother's milk, on our souls and our lives, that we will take all of you under our protection; we will lessen your taxes as well. . . . May God remain with all of you, and may He lead you back to your dwellings. We have written this letter in the fortress of Gyula, 1691."

From a cultural-historical point of view, the city of Gyula is remembered as the town from which an ancestor of the great artist Albrecht Dürer wandered out to Germany. Antal Ajtosi Száraz was himself a famous artist, a goldsmith, member of a noble family, who also fell victim to the Asiatic barbarians as one of multitudes.

The letter from Bey Mehmed confirms the devastating results of the exploitation of the Hungarian population. The empty *Sancak* and the burned down cities and villages were ample proof of the practical results of the *Pax Ottomanica*. Even if Cselebi's witness reports were not accurate in statistical figures, one still can read beyond them the abhorrent policies of the Ottoman intruders. The depopulation is proof in itself. As earlier mentioned, at the beginning of the sixteenth century the Hungarian population was between four and five million people. By natural multiplication this could have been fifteen million toward the end of the seventeenth century instead of the actual three million. The Hungarian nation lost at least ten million souls, either killed, enslaved, or unborn.

The country roads were at times crowded with wandering Christian *rayas*, wearing chains around their necks, in their hands a small paper certificate. as well as a beggar-staff. These were the prisoners of the Turks, who sometimes temporarily were set free when other good-hearted Christians would sit in prison for them as hostage. Then the begging *rayas* could set out and try to collect from other miserable compatriots the demanded ransom. They were the tragic figures of Koranic inhumanity, wandering in the shadow of *Pax Ottomanica*.

ADDENDUM I

The following excerpts of two letters belonging to the secret correspondence between the sultans of Constantinople and subordinate pashas in Buda, throw clear light on the exploitation practiced by the Ottomans in occupied territories. They also give the reader an understanding of the plight and endurance of the *rayas*, who, in spite of frequent inhuman treatment, managed to survive. The two letters in question focus on the demands of the sultans that the pashas honor the privileges which were granted the city of Nagykörös because of its importance to the needs of Turkish forces.

From Sultan Ahmed to Pasha Ali in Buda. August 27, 1614.

"On arrival of this my imperial letter, may it be known that the citizens of my hasz city (Kamara possession) Nagykörös have escaped to the Hungarian Christian-held land because of the constant exploitations and humiliations; now, due to our sweet promises and guarantees, those who have dared to return to their former places, are re-assuming the production of saltpeter day and night in my imperial boilerhouses, producing the badly needed nitrate. Let nobody dare to billet in the homes of these people either, nor take away their belongings. Those who have come back from the Christian-held land shall be protected, otherwise there may be another exodus. Therefore: memorize my imperial decrees and deliver this letter immediately to István Tollas, who is the Lord Mayor of Nagykörös, and fearfully obey my signature."[106]

Apparently the plundering troops did not respect this imperial order for it was shortly thereafter followed by another edict issued to Nagykörös, this time by Sultan Murad IV, whose letter was addressed also to the pasha of Buda.

"When this highest majestic letter reaches you, mark well that in the fortified city of Buda a gunpowder factory is in operation and that the badly needed nitrate is being produced by the people of the city Nagykörös, who are supposed to be under your protection. Because they render these services they are to be exempt from all other forms of service."[107]

This letter, addressed to the pasha in Buda, was delivered to István Török, mayor of Nagykörös, in May 1635.

All was in vain, for the following year, another warning was sent to the pasha in Buda.

ADDENDUM II

While in the midst of his perpetual warfare, King Matthias Corvinus Hunyadi as humanist Renaissance ruler, also took time to enhance cultural programs. One of his projects was to establish a second university, the University of Pozsony.[108] In Rome, the king had an envoy supported by Cardinal Bessarion who, together with him, aimed to incorporate several Greek refugee scholars into the faculty. Bessarion represented the continuity of the Greek tradition; he even convinced the German Regiomontanus who was in Rome, to learn the Greek language before joining the faculty in Pozsony. Regiomontanus was a famous astronomer who declared some fifty years before Copernicus that the earth was moving around its axis.

Since the Hungarian crusade led by King Endre II in 1214 against the Muslims in the Holy Land, Byzantium had been incorporated into the foreign policies of the successive rulers and King Matthias' most far-reaching diplomatic plan was to reconquer Byzantium and reunite Constantinople with western Christendom. That is why his plan for the University of Pozsony was to reintroduce the Greek language and Greek literature, because since the Great Schism Greek had been forbidden by Rome, Latin by Byzantium, and as a result the Greek culture had fallen into oblivion in the West. No wonder then that there was great interest in King Matthias' cultural policy among leading Humanists like Ficino, Lorenzo de Medici, Bessarion, and Bonfini, as well as among the Humanist Popes. They saw the king as a new Hercules, who would rescue European cultural heritage and fight off Ottoman barbarism. Matthias invited to his court in Buda Neo-Platonists and Christian humanists and thus created an intellectual circle. The first printing press was established in the king's residence, and more than thirty copyists worked in his constantly growing library, transcribing manuscripts. This library, which served as a first "public" library in Europe, was unfortunately completely destroyed by the Ottomans in 1526.

Footnotes

1. Révész, Lászlo. *Beitrage zur Kenntis Südeuropas und das Südeuropa unter dem Halbmond.* München, 1975. N.O. XVI, Bd. p, 218.

2. Kling, G. *Die Schlacht bei Nicopolis im Jahre 1396.* Berlin, 1900, Nauck. p. 101.

3. Barker, J. W. *Manuel II Paleologus, 1391–1425.* A Study in Byzantine Statesmanship. New Brunswick, N.J. 1969. p. 482.

4. Silberschmidt, M. *Das Orientalische Problem zur Zeit der Erstähung des Türkischen Reichs.* Berlin, 1923. p. 97.

5. Finke, H. *Acta Constanciensis. Vol. I. Akten zur Vorgeschichte des Konstanzer Konzils.* Münster, 1896. p. 401.

6. Finke, H. *ibid.,* Vol. II, Paderborn, 1899, p. 144.

7. Constanzer Bulla. found by historian Béla Iványi in the Archives of the royal free-city of Eperjes. Published in Szeged in 1931 in: *Acta literarum ac Scienciarum regis universi tatus Hung.* Francisco Josephine. Vol, I, p. 71.

8. Finke, H. *op. cit.,* p. 96.

9. Beliczy, Angela. *Confessio,* Vol. III, p. 46. Budapest, 1983.

10. Fraknoi, Vilmos. *Magyarország Egyházi és Politikai összeköttetései a Romai Szentszékel.* Budapest, 1902. Vol. II, p. 25.

11. Fraknoi, Vilmos. *ibid.,* p. 27.

12. Benda, Kálmán. *Magyar Nemzeti hivatástudat.* Budapest, 1937. p. 25.

13. Babinger, F. Mehmed the Conqueror and His Time. Princeton University Press, 1978. p. 37.

14. History Today, London, 1966. No. III, Vol. XVI, p. 174–183.

15. *Theologia Szemle,* 1984. No. 4, p. 237.

16. Theiner, A. *Vetera monumenta historiae Hungariae sacram illustrantia maxima parte nondum edita ex tabularis Vaticanis.* Romae, 1860. Vol. II. p. 405.

17. Babinger, F. *op. cit.,* p. 99.

18. Babinger, F. *ibid.,* p. 100–101.

19. Anea Sylvii Opera. Baslea, 1551. p. 656.

20. Fraknoi, Vilmos. *op. cit.,* Vol. II, p. 115.

21. Migna, J. B. Cardinal Bessarion; in Patrologia series. Graeca CXXI. col. 651–653.

22. Rázso, Gyula. *Buda, Bécs, és Velence: Az Europai Törökviszony.* In: *Hadtörténeti Közleméyek.* Budapest, 1973. Vol. XX, p. 662.

23. Pullan, Brian. The Jews of Europe and the Inquisition of Venice, 1550–1670. Totowa, N. J. Barnes & Noble. 1983.

24. Shmuelevitz, Aryeh. The Jews of the Ottoman Empire in the Late Fifteenth and the Sixteenth Centuries. Leiden, 1984. E. J. Brill. p. 165.

25. Pirenne, H. Mohammed and Charlemagne. Meridian Books, New York. 1961. 6th ed. p. 155.

26. Weitz, H. *Deutsche Verfassungsgeschichte.* 1885. Vol. IV, 2nd ed. p. 47.

27. Pirenne, H. *op. cit.,* p. 257.

28. Babinger, F. *op. cit.,* p. 107.

29. Epstein, Mark Alan. The Ottoman Jewish Communities and Their Role in the Fifteenth and Sixteenth Centuries. Freiburg, 1980. IU, Vol. 56, p. 34–43.

30. Shmuelevitz, Aryeh. *op. cit.,* p. 92, 93.

31. Apponyi, Albert. Lectures on the Peace Program and the Constitutional Growth in Hungary. Budapest, 1911.

    see also: E. Albrecht. *Das Türkenbild in der Ragusanisch-Dalmatischen Literatur des 16en Jahrhunderts.* In: *Slavische Beitragen.* 15. München, 1965.

32. Fraknoi, Vilmos. *op. cit.,* Vol. II, p. 135.

33. Fraknoi, Vilmos. *op. cit.,* p. 150.

34. Fraknoi, Vilmos. *op. cit.,* p. 150.

35. Fraknoi, Vilmos. *op. cit.,* p. 150.

36. Fraknoi, Vilmos. *op. cit.,* p. 193.

37. Joo, Tibor. *Mátyás és Birodalma.* Budapest, 1938. Atheneum Publ. p. 86.

38. Babinger, F. *op. cit.,* p. 427.

39. *Mátyás Király Külügyi* Budapest, 1893-'94. Vol. II. p. 244–248. *Levelei.*

40. Fraknoi, Vilmos. *op. cit.,* p. 202.

41. Fraknoi, Vilmos. *op. cit.,* p. 215.

42. Thuasne, L. *Djem, Fils de Mohammed II.* Paris, 1892. p. 265.

43. Babinger, Franz. *Zwei diplomatische Zwischenspiele im Deutsch-Ozmanischen Staatsverkehr unter Bayezid II. Westöstliche Abhandlungen.* Wiesbaden, 1954. p. 315.

44. Joo, Tibor. *op. cit.,* p. 89.

45. Joo, Tibor. *ibid.,* p. 136.

46. Joo, Tibor. *ibid.,* p. 47.

47. Babinger, Franz. *Vier Bauvorschläge Leonardo da Vinci's an Sultan Bayezid II. (1503).* In: *Nachrichten der Akademie der Wissenschaften in Göttingen.* 1. Phil. Hist. Klasse.

48. Babinger, Franz. *ibid.,* p. 11.

49. Buchholz, F. B. *Geschichte der Regierung Ferdinand der Erste.* Bd. V. Wien, 1834, p. 196.

50. Halecki, O. *The Cambridge History of Poland.* Cambridge U. Press, 1950. p. 273.

51. *Magyar Tudományos Akadémia Történeti Bizottságának Oklevél Másolata--.* ed. Lajos Ováry. Budapest, 1890-1894. Vol. II, p. 6.

52. Elert, W. *Morphology des Luthertums.* Vol. I. München, 1952. p. 336–344.

53. Majlát, Jolán. *Egy Alföldi civis város kialakulása.* Budapest, 1943. p. 43.

54. Káldy-Nagy, Gyula. *Szuleiman.* Budapest, 1974. Gondolat Publ. p. 192.

55. Hantsch, Hugo. *Die Geschichte Österreichs.* Vol. I, Graz, 1959. p. 231.

56. Bors, János. *Hadtörténeti Közlöny.* Budapest, 1895. p. 97.

57. Káldy-Nagy, Gyula. *op. cit.,* p. 210.

58. Mérey, Klára. *Szigetvári Emlékkönyv.* Budapest, Akadémia Kiadó. p. 166.

59. Salamon, Ferenc. *Török világ Magyarországon.* Pest, 1864. p. 221.

60. Nagy, Lajos. *Emlékkönyv.* Káposvar, 1899. p. 63.

61. Becker, C. H. *Christianity and Islam.* Burt Franklin Reprint. New York, 1909–1974. p. 56.

62. *Studia et Acta Ecclesiastica.* Vol. III. Budapest, 1973. p. 928.

63. Thuri, Pál. *Idea Christianorum Ungarorum Sub Tyranide Turcica.* Oppenheim (Germany), Typus Hieronymi Gallery. 1616. p. 69.

64. Chalife, Mehmaed. *Tarichja. Hadtörténeti Közlemények.* Budapest, 1925. p. 423.

65. Thury, János. *Török Történetirok.* Budapest, 1911. Vol. II, p. 231.

66. Salamon, Ferenc. *op. cit.,* p. 442.

67. Akadémia Kiadó. Budapest, 1974. p. 132.

68. Juhász, Kálmán. *Laien im Dienst der Seelsorge während der Türken - herrschaft in Ungarn.* Münster, Westfalen, 1960. Aschendorfischer Verlag. p. 11.

69. Fekete-Nagy. *Rechnungsbücher türkischer Finanzstellen in Buda.* 1550-1580. *Türkischer Text.* Budapest, 1962. p. 772.

70. Bayerle, Gustav. Ottoman Tributes in Hungary. The Hague, 1973. Mouton Publ. p. 22–24.

71. Busbecq, Ogier Ch. de. Life and Letters. ed, Forster and Daniel. London, 1881. p. 162.

72. Payer, Sándor. *Soproni Evangélikus Egyházközség Története.* Vol. I. Sopron, 1917. p. 64.

73. Nagykörösi Kronika. Gergely Balla ed. Kecskemét. 1856.

74. *Festschrift Herman Wiesdlecker, zum sechzigsten Geburtstag.* A. Novotny Publ. Graz. 1973.

75. Salamon, Ferenc. *Magyarország a Török Hodultság Korában.* Gustav Heckenast ed. Budapest, 1864. p. 298.

76. Archives of Nagykörös, Hungary.

77. Salamon, Ferenc. *op. cit.,* p. 280.

78. Májlat, Jolán. *op. cit.,* p. 40.

79. Bayerle, Gustav. *op. cit.,* p. 11.

80. Révész, Lászlo. *op. cit.,* p. 216.

81. Bayerle, Gustav. Ottoman Diplomacy in Hungary. Bloomington, Ind., Indiana University Press, 1972. p. 4.

82. Salamon, Ferenc. *op. cit.,* p. 305.

83. Shaw, Stanford J. History of the Ottoman Empire and Modern Turkey. Vol. I. Cambridge University Press, 1977. p. 19.

84. Paret, Rudi. *Toleranz und Intoleranz im Islam.* Seculum, 1970. XXI.4, p. 361.

85. Tritton, A. S. The Caliphs and Their Non-Muslim Subjects. London, 1930. p. 232.

86. Cselebi, Evliya. Narrative of Travels in Europe between 1660–1664. Translated into Hungarian and ed. by Emerich Karácsony. Budapest, 1904. Magyar Tudományos Akadémia Kiadás. Manuscript found in the library of Pasha Petrev in Uskodar.

87. Cselebi, Evliya. *ibid.*, Vol. IV, p. 144.

88. Cselebi, Evliya. *ibid.*, p. 137.

89. Cselebi, Evliya. *ibid.*, p. 136. (Year 1661).

90. Cselebi, Evliya. *ibid.*, p. 67.

91. Cselebi, Evliya. *ibid.*, p. 72.

92. Cselebi, Evliya. *ibid.*, p. 76.

93. Cselebi, Evliya. *ibid.*, p. 77.

94. Cselebi, Evliya. *ibid.*, p. 83.

95. Cselebi, Evliya. *ibid.*, p. 154.

96. Cselebi, Evliya. *ibid.*, p. 72.

97. Cselebi, Evliya. *ibid.*, p. 155.

98. Takáts, Sándor. *Rajzok a Török Világból*. Vol. I, Budapest, 1916. p. 382.

99. Shaw, Stanford J. The Ottoman Millet System: An Evaluation. In: Tolerance and Movements of Religious Dissent in Eastern Europe. Béla Király ed. New York 1975. Columbia Univ. Press. p. 168, 184.

100. *Császári és Királyi Állami Turcica*. Vienna.

101. Szabo, István. *Magyar Népesség életrajza*. Vol. XIII. Budapest, 1941. Magyar Történeti Társaság. p. 87.

102. Ottoman Chronicles. A. Refik. ed. Vol. I. Istanbul, 1928. p. 300.

103. Acsádi, Ignáz. *Magyarország Buda visszafoglalása után*. Budapest, 1909. p. 23.

104. Hammer, von J. *Geschichte des Osmanischen Reichs*. Buda(pest) 1827–1835.

105. *Hadtörténeti Okmánytár*. Budapest, 1910. Vol. XV.

106. Sziládi-Szilágyi. *Török-Magyarkori Oklevéltár*. Vol. I. p. 9. Pest, 1863.

107. Sziládi-Szilágyi. *ibid.*, p. 42.

108. Astrik, Gabriel. The Medieval Universities of Pécs and Pozsony. Frankfurt am Main, 1969. p. 42–43.

Chapter V

The Sectarian Movements
and Early Hungarian Translations of the Bible

The world's best known book is the Bible. "A strange book," wrote Mereskovsky. "It is impossible to get enough of it; no matter how much you read it, you always feel you have not read enough . . . ." There is nothing one can say or think that could surpass the Gospel; there is nothing in the world to which it can be compared. Yet, for a thousand years this extraordinary book was not universally read because it could not reach the people for whom it was written. For the real dissemination of the Bible, it was necessary to introduce printing. It is significant that Gutenberg began his activities, incalculably important for cultural history, by printing the Bible. The Bible had already been translated and printed in most European languages in the period just before the Reformation.

What the Reformation accomplished by translating the Bible in the sixteenth century can be with justice called the beginning of Biblical literature.

The Roman Catholic church was very much aware of the role the teaching of the Bible played in shaping society, and this awareness contributed to the many sharp controversies that arose over the translations of the Gospel. These disputes centered around the question: Who would interpret the Bible, the historical church or the lay people?

The Bible in the hands of laymen presented the great danger that people would begin to interpret it in their own way, rather than deferring to the Church. The sects were especially prone to giving distorted interpretations, since their biases strongly influenced their interpretations. Very early, already in the second millennium, the Middle East and East Central Europe witness distortions spread by the heretical movements.

The sects as pioneers of the lay Bible

"Ferre nulla est terra, in qua haec secte non sit," or "There is no land without sects." Apologists for the sects often quote St. Augustine when, speaking from experience, he said: "The leaders of the sects emerged from the ranks of great men."

The Bogomil, Cathari, and Patarene sects of Bulgarian-Bosnian origin illustrate the divergences from the Church. These sects preached that only the "pure ones" who belonged to them would enter heaven. Later the Picards, who originated in France, and the Czech Hussites or Taborites tried "to bring heaven to earth," after first doing away with the nobility and the "sinful cities."[1]

Hungary's geographical position and distribution of races must have contributed to the fact that, since its conversion to Christianity (1,000 A.D.), Hungary was the constant point of contact or conflict for the various sectarian movements. It is worthy of note that no heretical movement originated in that country. This was perhaps due to the fact that the founder of the Hungarian Christian state used violence to impose his "apostolic commitment" on Hungarians who refused to give up the pagan faith. Under such circumstances it is understandable that in Hungary the sects collided with both the ancient pagan faith and the new Christian religion. The king and the Church mounted a concerted campaign against the pagans and the sects which were infiltrating the country. But it is also probable that the protest against the dynamic royal power which was forging the Hungarian people into a national state did not need heretical movements.

During the first centuries of the Hungarian Christian kingdom, the Patarene sect penetrated Hungary from the south, from the Balkan peninsula. This sect was a variation on Bogomilism. The latter, as "Ecclesia Bulgaria", became the national religion of the Bulgarian people.

To this day, church historians have not been able to provide a clear explanation of the origin of Bogomilism. One conception is that a mystical Bulgarian priest, Bogomil, only reinterpreted the Manichean-Gnosticism teaching for his people in order to oppose the ossified Byzantine Orthodox church.[2] Later church historians tend to accept the interpretation that the historical figure, pope* Bogomil, was not the founder of this religious or political movement, but only one of its organizers.[3] A third school of thought denies any such role to Bogomil: "The alleged use of pope Bogomil's name is unlikely."[4] George Wild bases his contention on the Greek custom whereby educated Greeks did not trace the name of the sect back to its supposed founder, but rather, using the principle of name analysis, deduced the name from the contents of the religious phenomenon.[5]

Nam Bogomil slavice est Deo carus . . . according to the Latin name designation, the name *Bogumil* is of Slavic origin and has the same meaning as *Theophylon* in Greek, *Gott Lieben* in German, or Lover of God in English. According to Wild, this name expresses the religious concept of the sect. Similarly, the Western representatives of Bogomilism, the Cathari, used the name, Friends of God. There is no doubt that this concept originated in the New Testament.

Various etymologies attempt to explain the origin of the name of the Bogomil-Patarenes who filtered into Hungary. One of these traces its origin back to travelling merchants, called "Patari," who brought the sect to the city of Milan.[6] According to other interpretations, *patera*, the Latin word for chalice, would account for the meaning of the name, since the sect received Holy Communion in both kinds. This name was already known in the 11th century and was used among Milan's laity.[7]

The Albigenses, as church historians know them, drifted westward from Italy. They spread quickly, their numbers swelled by returning Crusaders.[8]

Another theory is that the emigration of the Bogomils to the north and west was provoked by conditions in Bulgaria. The Byzantine Emperor, Basil, "The Bulgarian Killer," conquered Bulgaria in 1018, forcing the sect to flee to foreign lands, including Hungary where they served as soldiers.[9]

Bogomilism was the religious movement of the Slavic peoples of the Balkans. This sect was the third Church in addition to the Eastern Orthodox and Roman Catholic Churches, and spread from Byzantium into countries of Western Europe. The two historical Churches fought Bogomilism for four hundred years. Crusades, missions, and finally inquisitions tried to wipe out these "half Christians."

---

*Greek Orthodox priest

The Popes of Rome tried to persuade the rulers of Hungary and the feudal lords of the northern parts of the Balkan peninsula to crush these religious movements by means of military force. For more than three hundred years, the Hungarian kings acceded to Rome's demands. Yet the Holy See could not profit from military victories. The Croation historian, Jiracek, wrote:

> "King Louis, ruler of Hungary, pacified Bulgaria in 1365. He asked Rome to send him 2,000 missionaries to reconvert the people of that country to the Roman faith. But only eight Bosnian monks arrived."[10]

When the Hungarian king, Kálmán, at the urging of Pope Gregory II, occupied Bosnia, Dalmatia, Croatia, and Bulgaria, the heretics left. The Hungarian military victories, however, were not especially significant because, for example, in Bosnia, not a single Roman Catholic church was left, since the fanatic followers of the sect had destroyed every church building and institution. The Roman Catholics had neither believers nor institutions nor revenue left. King Kálmán and the Pope relinquished the revenue of the Hungarian churches, and placed Bosnia under the authority of the Hungarian archbishop so that he would take care of material and defensive needs. Neither Church nor King could take advantage of the military successes, however, because the two orders, Dominican and Franciscan, could not agree on who would direct the Inquisition in Bosnia.[11] The missionary work carried out among the Balkan people by a handful of Minorite monks was not successful; neither did it avail in southern Hungary where the sects slowly penetrated. Religious-political factors, such as the reaction of the Slavic peoples of the Balkans against the Hellenized Byzantine ruling house, contributed to the successes of the sects. The latter ultimately adopted the conquering Turkish Muslim system whereby Turkish sultans took advantage of the dissatisfaction of the Slavic peasants and shepherds, recruiting them as soldiers, and thus obtaining a virtually inexhaustible supply of human resources in the wars to conquer the West.[12]

Diplomatic correspondence between Hungarian King Sigismund, later Holy Roman Emperor, and the Holy See, often mentioned the Patarenes of Bosnia, who fought side by side with the Turks.[13]

Today, Marxist historians judge the heretical movements as if they had essentially induced social class struggle in addition to the religious conflict.

These movements, however, as historical phenomena, were outside the Church and tried expressly to destroy the Christian Mother Church's world view and spiritual power. The heretical movements preached absolute dualism and Gnosticism, which can never be reconciled with the essence of Christianity.[14]

The above analysis again proves that where the historical Church loses its role, political catastrophe is inevitable. It testifies that religion is an historical reality that creates cultures and societies. The historical role of the "half-Christian" sects had far-reaching effects, greatly contributing to the sinking of the ship of the early Christian church in the Balkan peninsula beneath the Asian flood.[15]

Parallel with the Patarenes, the Waldensians, having earlier made important inroads into Austria and Germany with their theological teachings, then came from Austria, Bohemia, and Poland and infiltrated the religious and social life of the Hungarian Christians. To them are ascribed early German translations of the Bible.[16]

These Waldensians first settled in Hungarian cities, then tried to transform the religious thinking of the emerging bourgeoisie. These refugees that came from the west were generally leaders of the sect, many of whom were learned theologians aptly called "priest-proletarians" because of their poverty.[17]

Recently, Marxist ideologists have studied intensively the history of the sects, giving rise to the publication of new sources. Of course, many obstacles lie in the path of research, because the Inquisition destroyed both the sects and their documents. Consequently, the temptation is great to fill in the missing material with ideological formulas.[18]

From 1327 to 1395, the Inquisition pursued the Waldensians who escaped to Hungary. Most of the refugee sects were of German origin. For example, in 1401 among the German and Hungarian population of the city of Sopron, many of the men and women asking for forgiveness were mainly of German descent. The houses where they had held their meetings were demolished, their dead were exhumed and burned.[19]

The records of the Inquisition demonstrate that there were not many dogmatic differences between the Waldensians and the Hussites who later merged with them. This is corroborated by the fact that they were called pseudo-Hussites.[20]

This lay religious movement flaunted its complete knowledge of the Bible, and its illiterate members quoted *de verbum ad verbum* from the Scriptures and floundered in the outdated legalisms of Moses. The records of the Inquisition inform us that former priests of the Roman Catholic Church, called rectors, were found among them, but the dynamic leaders were mostly artisans. Other sect officials were *Fratres*, believed to be chosen by the Creator Himself, who represented the prophets or at least played the role of apostles. They rejected the saints, then Purgatory, then oath-taking, then the host and finally excommunication. As a result of the Inquisition's persecution, they became crypto-Christians and either returned to the Roman Catholic Church or became absorbed into one of the similar sects. Their teachings, however, do not reveal the ideology of class struggle which would have made them precursors of later Marxist movements.

By accepting martyrdom, they were not preparing to take power in this world. Their world view and theology was Biblical, which demonstrates that the culture of the Waldensians must have been on a higher level than that of pure peasant ideology.[21]

The report of the legate dealing with the Patarenes hiding in Hungary is worthy of note. He considered them to be Waldensians: *qui ipse sunt Waldenses*. The report states that the difference between the Waldensians living in Buda and other sects was minimal. They fought on a common foundation against the secularized church leaders. They held worship services in common and went so far as to anathematize the Pope and his Hungarian bishops.[22]

Church historians have inferred from the lawsuits brought against the Waldensians that they were quite widespread in Hungary in the 14th and 15th centuries. This is corroborated by the fact that the number of Waldensian rectors in Hungary was roughly the equivalent to the number working in Bohemia, Austria, and Poland.[23]

Since the Waldensians were of German origin, they moved near their German-speaking relatives who had settled earlier in Hungary. Their missionary work among the Hungarian population was strongly hampered by the fact that they did not speak the language of the people. This explains, at least in part, why they did not leave more historical source material behind.

We have already mentioned that the Waldensians were known by their opponents either as pseudo-Hussites or half Christians, similar to the Patarenes in their beliefs. Both lacked a systematic theological concept, everyone believing more or less according to his capacity, *Credentes pro suis capacitatibus plus et minus,*[24] but both basically confessing the dualistic teaching, which was the legacy of the vanished Manicheans: The world is both good and evil; that is, the world was created by both God and Satan.

Dualism took two forms: one, absolute dualism, according to which Evil, as the creation of Satan, existed from time eternal; the second, relative dualism, which ascribed the origin of Evil and matter to the first son of God, who defied Him. The second son, Jesus Christ, redeemed man on earth.

The sect introduced Holy Communion in both kinds. Members carried the wine needed for this in leather bags hung around their necks. They left their homes in cities that had become dangerous for them and resettled in wine-growing regions of Hungary, where they met and held religious services in wine cellars.

Essentially these religious movements replaced the laws of the feudal churches with Biblical laws; consequently, it became necessary to translate the Bible. So that it would serve the interest of the people, the Bible was adapted to socio-political conditions.

If confronted by the Inquisition, members of the sects pretended to be faithful to the Church. They could survive only by this deceit. If they fell into the hands of the Inquisition, they often shammed conversion, were trained in the theology of the Church, and as official priests served their own secret purposes.[25]

When social conditions were safer, they worked to eliminate the difference between clerics and laity, and introduced their Bible-centered concepts to the faithful.

To counteract the influence of the sects, the missionary Church itself translated parts of the Bible into the vernacular, and in so doing, helped spread lay interpretation. The Franciscans were particularly outstanding, for they virtually identified themselves with the heretics and played a role in the people's revolutions.[26]

To show how early the Balkan heretical movement became a cause of war, we can quote from the work of St. Gellért,[27] entitled *Deliberatio*, which demonstrates how Bogumilism affected the very recently converted Hungarian people. Bishop St. Gellért also worked in the southern part of the country, where he came into direct contact with the Slavic peoples of the Balkans. He noted: "From the Balkans, where the people never have lived without false doctrines, a new heresy is raising its head." He listed the radical doctrines of the heretics: for example, they denied the resurrection of the body, which would shake the foundations of the dualist creation theory of the Bogumils which included the Satanic origin of the body, *"Omnes uno simul ore carnis negant resurrectionem,"*[28] or, all of them almost unanimously denied the resurrection of the body. Furthermore, since God did not create water (it is not specifically emphasized in Genesis), they believed that after the Last Judgment, the Creator would remove water from the world, thereby increasing the land area eight-fold. Logically, they rejected baptism, since the devil created even water.

St. Gellért's writings confirm that the Bogumil sect had a much earlier influence on church life in the Middle East and Europe than was formerly believed.[29] The *Deliberatio* was probably written around 1046. Moreover, many sects moved west from Hungary. The Bishop attributed their successes to the fact that they carried out intensive missionary work among the recently converted Hungarians. The heretical movements were also spread in Hungary by the many Bulgarian refugees who settled in the south.[30]

At the time of the Magyar conquest of Hungary in 896 A.D., a situation of pluralistic religiosity had prevailed. In addition to the original pagan religion, the Byzantine Orthodox Christian faith, Jewish faith, and Mohammedanism had been present. As a result, an unusual attitude of religious tolerance had come into being. The customs of the earlier pagan faith were often "christianized", thus assuring survival. From this syncretic practice, religious tolerance had already evolved in the first centuries of Christianity. Ultimately, the Roman Catholic Church, that had grown in strength, began its missionary work in this region too. But the sects did not submit easily. The question arose: why not?

One reason clearly lay in the psychological attitude of martyrdom, the joyful acceptance of persecution. According to the dogmatic belief of the sects, the only obstacle to salvation or union with God was the body. To die for one's faith was therefore a joyful event for the "pure ones." They went to the stake dancing. With similar dogmatism, they forbade marriage so that the newly born would not come under the domination of the devil because of his corporeality; on the other hand they practiced homosexuality *(Masculorum concubitoribus)*.[31]

The members of the heretic's society never laughed. They hastily muttered their short prayers. Anna Comnena, Greek princess and theologian, wrote: "If you meet someone with lowered head and eyes, muttering softly, you will know that he is a Bogomil."[32]

In one of his treatises (*Hic Sunt*), the Slavic historian Racki describes a dialogue between a Franciscan missionary and a Bogomil:

> Bogomil: Why do you not persecute the pagans and leave us in peace?
>
> Monk Cseri (Franciscan): Nobody, not even the pagans, say that they were created by the devil as you declare about yourselves, and we must persecute the sons of the devil.
>
> Bogomil: Beware, you persecutors. If you destroy the last devil from the world, you will render yourselves superfluous and unemployed . . . .[33]

Even from the social point of view, the sects very often took over distorted concepts and gave false interpretations of the Bible. For example, they used the saying "Do not worry about tomorrow . . . " to avoid regular work. In many cases, they would wander through villages, supporting themselves by begging, but also by stealing. Dollinger, an historian who studied them, called them, not without foundation, the anarchists of the Middle Ages.[34]

Every sect had its day. The Patarenes slowly discredited themselves, exhausted in their negatives. The "last Cathari" were burned in 1324 in France,[35] thus opening the way for a much more positive religious lifestyle, which historians call the Hussite movement.

The establishment of the first Hungarian university to combat the sects.

When, in 1367, Louis the Great, King of Hungary and Poland, had spread his reign over many Balkan peoples at the urging of the Holy See, he clashed with the heretic church there. By means of many successful military campaigns, he pacified these peoples; however, from the religious standpoint, his campaigns had not reached their goal. Louis the Great asked Rome for more missionaries. His plan was to build many fortress-like monasteries on the country's southern borders to stop the invading sects.[36]

The king realized that he had to use similar methods against the religious-spiritual movements. He wanted to establish a university in Hungary to this end. At that time, it was the prerogative of the teaching church to establish such institutions; he asked the approval and support of the Pope. To justify the request, he wrote: "It could serve as the border fortress of science and faith on the frontier of East Central Europe threatened in its faith."[37]

He thought that the threatening Patarene-Waldensian movement could be isolated by training the intellectual leaders at the new Hungarian university. He also hoped that the institution would attract young people thirsty for knowledge away from the heretics. The ruler was of the opinion: "Real knowledge would deprive the heretics of their strength."[38] The king, who founded the university, was able to plan and create dimensions appropriate to his bold ideas. In 1660, the Turkish world traveller, Evlia Cselebi, wrote:

> "Among others, in the inner court of the godly Apollo was a scientific college which had no fewer than seventy halls of royal dimensions . . . its walls were covered with paintings of Plato and other Greek subjects . . . ."[39]

The king, not without reason, chose Pécs, which was known in medieval historiography as *"Quinque Basilicae."* The former Roman city was already the capital of Pannonia in the 11th century. Its cultural importance can be traced back to the first centuries of Hungarian Christianity. In 1020, the Bishop of Pécs, Bonipertus, asked Fulbert, Bishop of Chartres, to send him the *Priscian-codex.* This codex was used as a Latin grammar in Western schools.

Pope Urban V, one of the Popes of Avignon, gave permission to establish the University of Pécs, which opened in 1367, notwithstanding the fact that earlier Popes had refused to give permission to establish new universities.*

What could have brought about such radical change? Perhaps one reason was the fact that in East Central Europe, the spreading of lay sects

---

*Pope Urban had already given permission for the universities opening in Vienna in 1364 and in Cracow in 1365.

endangered general culture. The Holy See wanted to control the development of Europe's religious culture by means of strong centralization, and the universities seemed the best means to accomplish this.

A further reason was the new spirit which induced the teaching church to play a greater role in lay education.

The establishment of the first university coincided with early humanism in Hungary. The Pope had not been able to give permission to create a theological faculty. The reader must remember that the Papacy was in a difficult situation, because it lived in "Babylonian captivity" in Avignon, France, and hence was under dominance of the French king. As a result, the Sorbonne in Paris, and the theology which it taught, became the exclusive authority in church matters. In consequence the Popes were unable to grant theological faculties to other universities, including the one in Pécs, whose model was the university of Bologna, rather than the Sorbonne. Thus, Hungarian youth who wished to study theology were forced to go to the universities of Paris or Prague.

Pécs emphasized law, particularly ecclesiastical law, important in defending the dominion of the Church. In spite of this, university education there very quickly became secular.

The prohibition to establish a faculty of theology at Pécs University gave rise to a paradoxical situation. Where the university was mainly a missionary university called on to fight the heretical movements, Hungarian theological students in Prague soon came under the influence of another sect, namely the Hussites. Thus, these students who were trained to counteract the Balkan sects brought the Hussite movement into synthesis with the Patarene and Waldensian movements. (Already in 1367, in Prague, we find Hungarian students among those matriculating. Over a period of twenty years, more than one hundred students were registered.)[40]

The pedagogical program of the University of Pécs clearly reflected the so-called "Speeches of Pécs University" containing the lectures of former university professors.[41] In these the professors dealt at length with the Patarenes and Waldensians. They directed their words at disproving the "false doctrines of the heretics", and as antidotes, they proposed St. Augustine's formulas concerning the "well-ordered community" (*"Ordinatio concordia"*). Remarkably enough, however, these speeches also criticized the social conditions of the period.

1. They sharply critiqued the Hungarian nobility: They demanded not a ruling but a serving nobility, which would fit the new concept of *virtus* and would be useful to the new society.

2. The speeches also treated the concept of human dignity. They projected the humanist social concept into the existential questions of the age and analyzed them penetratingly.

They wanted to answer the question of what should rule over the souls of people: the primitive pedantry of heresy, the piety of their false peace, or classical traditional religion?

The declarations were an early proof that they had already envisioned the ideal of Renaissance citizen yet to be born. Thus the approaching end of the Middle Ages was intimated and a new human ideal was born, that of ethical commitment to social responsibility.

The concept of *Imitatio Christi*, the Divine Friendship, became the subject of a new and dynamic religious and social movement, the *Devotio Moderna*, whose basis was formed by the great changes in the older mode of living which took place in the 14th and 15th centuries. This transformation could not be called a crisis, but belonged to the constant rhythm of birth and death.[42] The societies of East Central Europe (Austria, Bohemia, and Poland) were faced with problems similar to those of the Hungarian state and church. The literature of all these countries as well as the writings of historians of the period provide ample analyses of the problems.

The *Devotio Moderna*, commonly called Devotio, was a lay-movement, inspired by monks and originated by religious innovations of the Dutch Geert Groote.* It spread quickly throughout Europe, one after another new monasteries (Augustinian and Carthusian) emerged in East Central Europe. Twenty-four Augustinian monasteries were active in Austria alone.[43]

The Devotio, however, differed according to whether it was practiced in Czech or Moravian parts of the country. It clashed with the Waldensians, because the members of the Devotio remained within the Church. Both Czech and German members of the movement translated the Bible into their own tongues in defiance of King Charles IV's prohibition of 1366. Czech and German national consciousness accompanied this religious movement in Bohemia, which ultimately led to the development of a separate German and Czech Devotio.[44] Both the Austrian and Czech

---

*See Albert Hyma *The Christian Renaissance* (1924).

founders came from the ranks of the rulers, the church leaders, and the nobility. The court intelligentsia saw the Devotio as a way to renew the Church. In Czech and Moravian lands, more than twenty monasteries were established.

The *Devotio Moderna* movement became the subject of and was presented in the "Speeches of Pécs University". The speeches also condemned the unworthy priests and the secularized hierarchy. The critical pronouncements pointed toward the approaching Reformation. It was not the priestly office which gave dignity to the clergy, but just the opposite. These and other theological debates resounded in the halls of Pécs as well as in Prague. The topics were also preached from the Hussite pulpits.

The Devotio in Hungary was based in part on the Carthusian order established earlier, but a broad foundation was provided by the Hungarian Order of St. Paul, the White Monks,[45] founded by Canon Eusebius.

The universities founded in East Central Europe all joined the *Devotio Moderna* movement. Thus, the "Speeches of Pécs University" preached principles resulting in those of *theologia affectus* or emotional theology.[46] The Hungarian believer not only gave evidence of Dutch but also of Italian influences, which can be attributed to the fact that the university of Pécs had adopted the system of the university of Bologna, many of whose professors came to Pécs.

The original missionary role of Pécs university changed in important ways. A folk religious movement developed from three directions. From the south, the still virulent Patarenes, from the west the Waldensians, and finally from the north, the teachings of the Hussites made their inroads. Around the university the walls between lay and clerical elements fell. Celibacy was abolished. Simon, the provost of the city of Pécs, drove out the Papal inquisitor Jacobus. The Gospel, the Psalms, and the Pater Noster were translated into vernacular Hungarian. This was justified by simple folk logic: Why should the Bible not be translated into the language of the people? After all, it was first translated into the language of the pagan Latins.

At the same time, the situation at the Polish university of Cracow was the reverse; innovations were resisted. Foreign students who came to study there had to sign an oath against Hussite teachings.[47]

The successor of the Hungarian-Polish king, Louis the Great, who had founded the university of Pécs, was Sigismund, Holy Roman Emperor, Czech-Hungarian king, and son of Charles IV (1368–1437). He continued the church policies of his predecessor, fighting heretics and Turkish Muslims who supported them. This was a serious enterprise because according to the logic of religious ideals for those who had once rejected the traditional dogma and taken a critical stance, there was no stopping. A new literary genre appeared in this period, a literature of religious controversies, Biblical criticism, which led to radicalization.

Thus, Jerome of Prague, who later became John Huss' companion at the stake, soon appeared at the court of King Sigismund in Buda and campaigned openly for the new dogma. He was imprisoned quickly, but was released shortly thereafter. He went to Poland and continued his controversial polemics at the University of Cracow. Jerome was Polish, that is, Slavic; he preached among his brothers that the Czech Hussites were the people of the Old Testament.[48]

Among the Hungarian students who returned from the agitated atmosphere of Prague were Thomas Pécsi and Bálint Ujlaki. The already well-known master Simon Tessovai conferred the title of master on the latter. Tessovai represented the Hussite tendency in Prague. Combining Wycliffe's teachings and previously disseminated Waldensian dogmas, the two Hungarian seminarians preached among the Hungarian people. One of the reasons for their success was the fact that the Waldensians had already organized many Biblical communities, which simplified the church rites. Thomas Pécsi and Bálint Ujlaki carried out similar pioneer work. At that time John Huss was still a loyal member of the German priesthood and preached the Gospel in the Bethlen chapel in Prague.

The Hussite movement, which at the beginning was an exclusively religious reform movement in Hungary, was turned into an extremist socio-theological direction. The two Hussite propagators, Pécsi and Ujlaki, were often helped by the Franciscan missionaries, including many who hoped that John Huss would accomplish the renewal of their Church. Many others among them anticipated that freedom of conscience and free inquiry would invigorate religious life at the twilight of the Middle Ages. One after another, enlightened Franciscans left their monasteries and, as well-trained theologians, directed the lay religious revolution. There are data that

Franciscan monks who escaped from Poland joined the Hussite heretic movement.

While King and Emperor Sigismund was occupied with the Hussite wars and reformation of the Church, he convened two reform councils. Although in Constance and Basel he removed and appointed Popes, he was incapable of coping with the sectarian movement in his own empire. Thus, peasant rebellions with religious overtones broke out in no fewer than five episcopates, and laity demanded that the conditions of the people be changed.

Finally, Pope Eugene IV was forced to take action to keep the situation from deteriorating any further. He sent the famous inquisitor of the time, Jacobus de Marchia, to put a halt to the heretic movements.

Thanks to Jacobus' knowledge of the Hungarian language, he could exert wide-ranging influence on the eager and neglected people, of whom, as he reported, he returned 25,000 to the bosom of the Church.

One of the Hungarian church leaders sent this appraisal of Jacobus' work in a report to the Holy See:

"Our Holy Father and Lord, after kissing your blessed feet, we report to your Holiness: The reverend father, Brother Jacobus Marchia, vicar of Bosnia, of the Minorite Order, whom Your Holiness sent to Hungary to eradicate the evil heresies, wandered through the country at physical danger to himself. With the help of God, he brought a rich harvest to God's Holy Church in the parishes of Kalocsa and Bács. He suppressed many heretic priests and laymen, whose numbers have increased in the border lands . . . . He investigated them sedulously, and the heretics voluntarily confessed that they had defamed the sacraments, some in forests, some in cellars, others in mills, even in mountain caves, and pits dug into the earth. They have been receiving communion in two kinds for a long time, they even carried the blood of our Lord Jesus Christ in bags lined with tar and hung around their necks. They carried it to their accursed hiding places. In the silence of night, many went to these unholy places, alas, and they spilled our Lord Jesus Christ's blood on themselves, so that it poured down even to their sandals . . . . Obviously, he exposed many other not minor deviations committed against the Catholic faith. If Your Holiness had not taken steps quickly to deal with the situation

through Master Jacobus, the heretics would have taken arms to
wipe out the prelates along with the priests, as they did in Bohemia
. . . ."[49]

Another letter from a contemporary describes Jacobus as follows: "He
spoke to our Hungarian people so effectively, it was as if the apostle Paul
stood next to him."[50]

Jacobus used the methods of the Inquisition with full force at the city
of Kamence (in the southern region of Hungary, bordering the Balkans),
the center of Hungarian Hussites. Pécsi and Ujlaki lived in that city. Master
Jacobus burned the archdeacons and priests of the Church at the stake;
indeed, he did not even spare the bones of the dead, whereupon the
leaders of the heretics disappeared. By the time the investigation was over,
the populations of about sixty villages and cities had fled their homeland to
Moldavia, (part of Rumania today), under leadership of Pécsi and Ujlaki.
This exodus was no small task. Ujlaki, who finally surfaced in
Constantinople, continued his missionary work among the Turkish Muslims
so effectively that the Sultan himself sat in judgment on him, and giving
evidence of Islam's religious tolerance, had him flayed alive; he was accused
of wanting to nullify the holy laws of the Koran.[51]

Although Master Jacobus visited and examined all regions of Hungary
affected by the heretic movements and mercilessly suppressed them, he did
not attain his goal. His savage methods were so excessive that the members
of his own Order turned against him. The provost of Pécs expelled him.
Others took offense at his openly rebuking the immorality of the monks,
thus exposing them to the judgment of the faithful. The monks of the
Franciscan monastery of Zeng simply closed the door to him and even
threatened him physically.

The Hungarian Hussites brought not only religious and social reform,
but also an early form of nationalism. This nationalism was awakened when
the German citizens of several cities, using their legal privileges, refused to
allow Hungarians to settle in their cities. At the time of the wars with the
Turks, they refused even to give asylum to the Hungarians, on pretext of
heresy. This justifiably outraged Hungarian national feeling.

A similar phenomenon occurred in Prague where the German patricians
oppressed the Czech plebeians, arousing their Slavic pride. The Czech

Hussite movement grew not only into religious and social trends, but also into a national folk revolution.

The class solidarity of the Hungarian plebeian and peasant social strata appeared for the first time in a protest against payment of tithes, because they considered the attitudes and behavior of the priests incompatible with the priesthood, not because of dogma. The inquisitor himself acknowledged that the clergy was negligent and that it had contributed to the diffusion of the sects. In an admonition (Secret Speech to the Clergy) Jacobus wrote:

> "They have taken up the priesthood not because they were driven by the Holy Ghost, but for reasons of simony, money, and nepotism. They do not care about saving souls; all they care about is filling their purses. This is the reason for the falling away of the faithful. Ignorant and dissolute persons enjoy emoluments, and pure and learned priests go hungry. Daily I am urged to preach to the people to encourage them to pay the tithe. When I was in a city accompanied by a priest true to his faith, many fellow priests urged him to ask me to speak about paying the tithe. Whereupon the upright priest answered: 'How can I ask him when you do not say the breviary, you do not care about the Church or the altar? You spend your days gambling, hunting, horseback riding, fornicating, and everyone is outraged at your morals'."[52]

It is no wonder therefore that Master Jacobus asked the expulsion of more than twenty seminarians and monks, many of whom joined the sectarian rebels. In another episcopal district, he demanded that forty seminarians be expelled. As a result, there was a shortage of priests in those regions.

Jacobus wanted to eradicate the heresies by reforming the leaders of the Church itself. He was not successful, however. The priests of Pécs, for example, continued to live openly with their wives.

The Papal legate was an over-zealous enthusiast of God's laws similar to his opponent, John Huss, who ridiculed his fellow priests in the Bethlen chapel of Prague. Both were believers and fanatics and had the same goal: spiritual and moral regeneration, but how different their methods and their worlds!

Pope Eugene IV and Emperor-King Sigismund moved every worldly and churchly power to support Jacobus, but the intellectual atmosphere, the lay social movement, and the bitterness of the lower priesthood prevented them from reaching their goals. So intense was the spiritual need for renewal, that the revolution of the next century brought victory to the Hungarian Reformation precisely in those regions where Jacobus had burned alive the spiritual mediators of the searching souls.

In 1439 Jacobus returned to Rome and prepared a detailed report for the Holy See. The archives of the Vatican kept his report, which scholars discovered only at the beginning of the 20th century. The dusty papers buried for centuries became sensations of church history. The report was clarified, and a *terra incognito* disappeared from the map of Roman Catholic church history. Publications connected with the report shed light on the up-to-now untouched medieval world in Hungary.

Jacobus not only described in detail the essence of the religious problems of East-Central Europe, but also made an excellent diagnosis of them. He summarized the Wycliffe-Hussite dogmas in sixty-four articles. He noted that these religious dogmas showed close kinship with the teaching of similar sects of neighboring countries.

It appears from the paragraphs which follow that the Hungarian Hussite leaders were not following in the footsteps of the moderate Calixtines, but that they wanted to remedy the religious and social dissension with the ideology of the radical Taborites. The main features of Jacobus' paragraphs are:

> Paragraphs 1–5 reject the over-developed, outworn forms of the feudal world which caused the corruption of the priesthood. These were replaced by the order of lay preachers and Holy Communion in both kinds.

> Tenets 6–9 evoke a renewed pre-feudal social order with its pure life style. They reject human dispositions that go beyond the Bible. Under the cloak of Christianity, "feudal schemers" smuggled these into church organizations, dogmas, and laws. Paragraph 10 protests the Inquisition, citing the command "Thou shalt not kill."

> 16–20, 31–33, 36–44 analyze the contradictions of religious life. They point out that the Church has not been carrying out its mission and is not fulfilling its teaching vocation. It has not brought people out of darkness.

64.4 reflects the characteristic puritanism of the peasant lay movements, in contrast with the immorality and materialism of the ruling classes.

Jacobus states that the absurdity of the sect's faith showed in their declaration that John Huss is the only saint and prophet.[53]

(A complete summary of the main features are provided in an appendix).

The first Hungarian translation of the Bible

We have presented an overview of the lay religious movements, because only through them could we receive an answer to the question of why and how the first Hungarian translation of the Bible appeared in the fifteenth century.

There are many controversies surrounding this question and, to this day, a whole series of literary and religious questions has not been answered. One of these unanswered queries is: Who were the first translators of the Bible? The Protestant writers believe that the first translations were made by the revolutionary Hungarian Hussites. The historians of the materialist school try to prove this, too. According to this theory, Pécsi and Ujlaki, the former seminarians of Prague were the Hussite Bible translators. However, the theologians of the Roman Catholic Church maintain that, without a doubt, the translations were done by traditional monks. In the monasteries of Pannonia, monks dedicated their entire lives to translating the Holy Scriptures.

These anonymous translators were pioneers from the standpoint of both religious history and of literature. They had to create new words, expressions, indeed a whole new religious language to meet the linguistic demands of the Bible, virtually without any previous models. Based on contextual analysis of the text, some scholars suspect the presence of certain Patarene theological principles. For example, religious suicide, *endura*, customary only among the Patarenes, is included. We see this when the translator-commentator considered the body to be created by the devil, thus something to be despised. Furthermore, omitted parts of the Bible reflect the religious ideas and attitudes of the sects; such as, for example, the slighting of St. John the Baptist in their translations. According to them, John the Baptist was only a creature of the devil, forced to confess faith to

Jesus. The Patarenes also used the first parts of St. John's gospel in their ritual, thereby trying to confirm Jesus' lack of a body. In their view, Jesus must have been a spiritual phenomenon.

Many similar oddities, misconstruction, and false exegeses of the text could form the basis for the alleged Patarene-Hussite authorship. The controversy surrounding these issues is complicated by the fact that scholars have been unable to find the original Latin text which the translators must have used. Only three fragments have survived of the first Hungarian translations of the Bible from the fifteenth century.

The first part of the so-called *Révai-codex* containing parts of the Old Testament is presently in the archives of Vienna. The second is the *Jászay-codex* of the Gospels in the archives of Munich. The third, the *Apor-codex*, containing the psalms of David was in the Székely Museum in Székelyudvarhely in Transylvania and was destroyed in World War II.

The writers of the Roman Catholic Church have substantial reasons for their point of view. The question then arises how the *Apor-codex* came into the possession of a Premonstrant convent as a liturgical book if its authors were revolutionary heretics. Historians can prove that, beginning with the Fifteenth Century, parts of the Bible were read in convents in the Hungarian vernacular. They ascribe this to the *Devotio Moderna* lay movement.[54]

There are further objections to the authorship of Bálint Ujlaki and Thomas Pécsi, such as the discrepancies in their ages and the date of the translation. The chronicle designates the translators as *duo literari et duo clerici*, in other words they were still seminarians. But at the time of the alleged Hussite Bible translation, Pécsi and Ujlaki were about sixty years old. Pécsi studied in Prague in 1399, Ujlaki in 1411 when he was fifty-five years old. He must have at least reached the rank of parish priest. Furthermore, when Pécsi was student at Prague, John Huss was still a faithful and official council speaker.

The Patarene leaders who wanted to justify the innovations with the old teachings necessarily identified themselves with the teachings of the Old Testament. The old texts, however, contain such unwelcome comments as, for example: "The prophets of the people tell fortunes for money." Such statements were promptly omitted for they were irreconcilable with sectarian teaching. The prophet Amos' statement (4:4) "Bring your sacrifices every morning, your tithes every three years," was also left out of the text, for the Patarenes preached the denial of the tithe in order to incite the people against the established church. These omissions in translation in the Fifteenth Century give an idea of the sectarian adjustments in the pre-Protestant Biblical translation. The date is also uncertain. Most probably it was begun in 1439, and by that time the Prague students in question had already emigrated to Moldavia.

There is no doubt that laymen wanted to restore the feudal church in Hungary to the Gospel of Christ. Among others, they preached a community of wealth between rich and poor, which naturally served social revolution. They needed translations of the Bible that would justify their movement. The Dominican Butler opposed a similar Bible translation when, contrary to John Wycliffe's followers, he reasoned thus: "The people should not read but listen to the message of the Bible, for otherwise it will lead to misconceptions, unbelief, and finally revolution."[55]

The Roman Catholic Church did not always prohibit access to the Holy Scriptures for laymen, but strict regulations always surrounded it. Roman Catholic translations of the Bible predated Protestant ones by centuries. Thus, for example:

In France translations were made in the fourteenth century and were printed in their entirety already in 1487.

In England the entire Bible had been translated before Wycliffe.

In Germany before Luther a long series of vernacular translations were read by laymen.

In Italy the Bible was translated in the fourteenth century and printed in 1471.

In Spain the entire Bible was translated and published in 1478.

In Poland the complete Bible was published in the fifteenth century. It had been previously translated into the vernacular Polish in 1390 at the request of King Louis the Great's daughter, Jadwige. This "Polish" Bible could once have been found in Sárospatak in Hungary.[56] Its present location is unknown.

In Russia there is a known Russian translation from the fifteenth century. It was published in Novgorod. The translation was done with the help of rabbis who knew Hebrew; as a result, it tended to be Antitrinitarian.

In Lithuania, a Bible translation appeared in Wilno in 1525 to 1528.

Furthermore, vernacular translations appeared among the people of the Balkans. HVAL Christianus translated the Scriptures into a Slavic language in 1464.[57] Earlier, around 1248, Pope Innocent IV allowed Bishop Segni to introduce the liturgy in Slavic.[58] In broad outline the history of Hungarian translations follows:

Since the Roman Catholic Church in Hungary was a missionary church, the Bible was quickly published in Hungarian. An Italian church writer, Jacopo Passavanti (ca. 1345), complained about the obscurity and awkwardness of the German, Hungarian, and English Bible translations.[59]

In addition to the "Hussite" translation described above, there is a Bible translation in the so-called *Jordánsky-codex* was copied for generations, the last time in 1519. The language used here is much more advanced and colorful than that of the earlier "Hussite" Bible. In his preface the translator wrote:

> "We have to write, speak, and read the Holy Gospel . . . . Read, listen, and learn the Word of God in which lies . . . sacred knowledge."[60]

Furthermore, toward the end of the fifteenth century, a new Biblical work containing both Old and New Testaments was completed whose author was Lászlo Báthory, a monk of the Pauline Order. This Bible was in the Corvina, the library of King Matthias, enormous even by European standards, which had about 2000 books and many manuscripts. During the age of Hungarian humanism, this huge collection was a kind of public library, similar to the library in Florence.* Tradition has it that the humanist Matthias asked Rome to allow the Bible to be published in Hungarian, but that his request was rejected. According to legend, Matthias responded by choosing two monks and keeping them prisoners until they finished the translation.

---

*The Corvina library was later destroyed by the Turks. It had been the second largest library in Europe, the Vatican library being number one. *Századok* 1975. No I p.196.

This conduct is characteristic of this Renaissance autocrat who in a similar way claimed the right of the advowson which originated with the first Hungarian "apostolic king" in opposition to the Holy See. This apostolic right of the advowson recognized the right of the reigning Hungarian king to appoint the bishops of the country whose names he simply sent to the Pope to inform him of their appointment. Rome was reluctant to acknowledge absolutely this right. In vain, King Matthias referred to the fact that the Hungarian church had been a national church from the beginning. It must be mentioned here that what the archbishop of Esztergom had as a born Papal legatee (*Legatus natus*), i.e., a permanent legation to the Holy See, other churches could not obtain for a long time. Matthias tried to warn the Holy Father that, if he wanted to excommunicate him, he, Matthias, was not afraid, because he could exchange the Hungarian royal apostolic double cross for a triple cross at any time: in other words, he could adopt the Greek Orthodox Church. And he renewed his alliance with the Russian Czar, Ivan III.

Matthias' father-in-law was the King of Naples, in whose court Lorenzo Valla wrote in 1440 his famous critique about the spuriousness of the *Donation of Constantine*. No matter how finely written in humanistic style, this critique was unmistakably anti-papal. All evidence indicates that Matthias knew his work very well. Diplomatic correspondence with the popes shows that anti-church spirit prevailed in his court as it did in the court of the King of Naples. Matthias was the Renaissance ruler par excellence, whose permanent army, "the black army", was composed of Hussite mercenaries. He left hardly any doubt about his own lay religious tendencies. In this respect he preceded Erasmus by far.

The reformational and lay piety of King Matthias manifested itself in other things also. For example, when his subjects from Transylvania asked for the restoration of their former rights in 1476, i.e., the use of the formulas of baptism, marriage, the eucharist, etc., in Hungarian, he gave his assent. At the same time Matthias ordered the Báthory Bible to be displayed in his Corvina library. Then he had the *Breviary of Esztergom* printed to facilitate the liturgical service of the priests and the participation of the faithful at worship services.[61]

King Matthias, similar to Machiavelli, of a civic cast of mind, viewed religion as a means for serving the state and society. He tried to establish a national church, independent from Rome, like French Gallicanism and

English Anglicanism, and to include the masses of believers in his plans. The king took further steps to bring both the church and the society under his personal rule. Since his power spread throughout East Central Europe, he wanted to combine and use the forces of his territory in the wars of liberation waged against the Turks, who were conquering the Balkans. His state church with its considerable material resources became an instrument in his policies defending Europe. When Pope Paul II did not back Matthias' church policies, Matthias was ready to use any form of power against the Holy See. Citing the ancient right of the advowson of Hungarian kings, he opposed the changing policies of the Popes. We quote the following from one of his letters which is characteristic in both style and content:

> "We would not have expected Your Holiness to violate our royal prerogatives in which we have been secure for a long time and which we have exercised at the example of our predecessors. Your Holiness knows or could at least know from the speeches of others the spirit and character of my Hungarians, who would rather leave the Catholic faith for the third time and join the camp of the unbelievers than allow the revenues of the country to be paid to the Holy See in disregard of the royal election and presentation. This conflict should not give occasion for more trouble or scandal. I have been informed of what some have attempted through your Holiness to violate my right and the ancient liberty of my country. I chose the Reverend Antal Zárai, confessor of my beloved wife, Her Highness the Queen, for the above-named church of Modrus. As a worthy, moral, and learned man, I introduce him to Your Holiness for your confirmation . . . . Do not try to put up obstacles, no matter who asks you to. Your Holiness can be sure that no matter who tries, no one will ever succeed in gaining that church, even if it means leaving it without a pastor."[62]

After Matthias had spread his rule to Austria and the countries of Bohemia and Moravia, he established his rights advowson; indeed, he imprisoned without restraint, the archbishop, and bishops of his country and one after the other, forced the church princes to resign if they were reluctant to accept or acknowledge his absolute rule.

He established a broad popular base for his policies. Matthias combined the lay Hussite and humanist religious and cultural movements, thereby creating a synthesis that led to the pre-Reformation. With all these measures and reform policies, the king brought his countries into that wider European reform movement which from the Thirteenth to the Sixteenth Century spread through Europe. This reform period drew the state church's attention to the principles of the Gospel and tried to restrict worldly ambitions. This explains the rapid revolutionary Protestant development which Martin Luther's activities initiated in Hungary too. Only secondarily can the tragic situation that befell the Hungarian Roman Catholic Church be attributed to the loss in death of Roman Catholic princes on the battlefield at Mohács, two archbishops and five bishops having lost their lives in the battle fought there against the Turks in 1526.

These political and religious events account for early Hungarian translations. In addition to the translations mentioned, other vernacular manuscripts have survived which are known under the name of "codex-literature". This "codex-literature" was something of a paradox in the age of the printing press. One source was the enlivened intellectual life of the recently reformed Franciscan and Dominican monasteries. The other source was the influence of the spreading heresies and worldly humanism. Buda became the center of this new literature. The nuns themselves asked for religious literature in Hungarian, instead of in Latin. The emerging manuscript literature was promoted and popularized by the hand copying of inexpensive books printed by the press. (Before, it had been difficult for copyists to obtain the expensive and rare books).[63]

It should not be forgotten, however, that even during the Latin period the preaching monks constantly had translated selections from the Bible for worship service; in fact, the custom survived into the beginning of the Reformation, because there were not enough translations in the vernacular. Even if there had been, the aggressive representatives of Habsburg Catholicism would have burned them.

Today, it is hard to appreciate the obstacles in the way of translating the Bible in those centuries. During the early period, there were not enough dictionaries, and translators had to create hundreds of new nouns, idioms, expressions, even verbs. Luther introduced expressions that were equivalent to Hebrew theological concepts from the vernacular. These strenuous efforts were really creative work. Under circumstances in which reading and writing were considered a science, translation was a difficult task. Many an anonymous translator had to translate the elements, metaphysical abstractions, common sayings, etc., of Hebrew and Greek religious cultures into a language that had not yet developed adequate religious concepts and vocabulary. It could not have been easy to render the Bible from the medieval *lingua sancta hebraica*, through the mediation of the Latin texts into the logic of the Hungarian language. Only priests who were highly cultured in language and literature and formally trained, and who could dedicate their entire lives to the *stuba scriptoria* could accomplish the task.

Through this translating, which was about equivalent to doing penance, religious thought descended from the heights where it had soared for centuries to the level of earthly man. Thus, abstract religious life and its concepts increased in value socially, too. These belated translations came to the aid of the churches that were weary of their missionary work and that strove to enliven the teaching of Jesus. In periods of religious-spiritual crises, the translator-priest saw the alarming social facts and proclaimed them through the words of the prophets. Naturally, in doing so, he searched for religious-moral causes at the root of the crisis. In other words, the writer-translator found an historical dimension for his people in the Holy Scriptures. He drew a parallel with the fate of the Old Testament people of Israel, erring and distraught by inner conflicts.

The work that Tauler, Eckhardt, and Luther carried out among the Germans, Dante among the Italians, the anonymous translators had to do in Hungary. The monks in the *stuba scriptoria* were replaced by the preachers who often became martyrs. They created new tools for the church-to-be-renewed so that it could accomplish its mission.

Footnotes

1. Aeneas Sylvius, *Dialogus Contra Bohemos et Taboritas*. Opera. Ballileae, 662.

2. Hodinka, Antal. *Egyházunk küzdelmei a boszniai Bogumil Eretnekekkel*. Budapest, 1887. p.21.

3. Schmaus, Alois. *Der Neumanichaismus auf dem Balkan*. Saeculum, Band 2, Jhrg. 1951. Heft 1, München, p. 271–298.

4. Wild, Georg. *Bogumili als Ausdruck des Selbstverständnisses der mittelalterischen Sektenkirche*. In: *Kirche im Osten*, Bd. 6, 1963. p. 16–33. Verlag Vandenlock, Gottingen.
   " . . . dass sie gelehrten Griechen den Namen der Sekte nicht von seinem Gründer ableiten, sondern in der Beurteilung dieses religionsgeschichtlichen Phänomens von der Namensanalyse ausgehen."

5. *In Svaevian et Italiam Borealem Saepe Intrant Eorum Mercantores* . . .
   Horum Etiam Ex Hungaria an Nos Pervenerunt . . . Petrovice B**o**zsi**d**a:
   Cerkva bosanska i Krszt jani. In: Bosnyak egyház és a keresztyénség. p. 100
   fnt.i.2. Zagreb, 1867.

6. Runciman, Steven. *The Medieval Manichec.* The Viking Press, New
   York, 1961. p. 103

7. Runciman, Steven. *ibid.*

8. Hodinka, Antal. *op. cit.*, p. 26.

9. Racki, Ferdinand. *Bogumil i Patarini,* in Rad VII.III. Slavic Review

10. Jiracek, C. J. *Geschichte der Bulgaren.* p. 327. Prag, 1876

11. Hodinka, Antal. *op. cit.*, p. 92

12. Sadnik, Linda. *Religiöse und soziale Reformbewegungen bei den slavischen
    Völkern. I. Das Bogumilentum in Bulgarien.* in *Der Blick nach Osten.* 1.
    1948. Heft 3–4, p. 46–54.

13. Hodinka, Antal. *op.cit.*, p. 104

14. Hodinka, Antal. *ibid.*, p. 88

15. Hodinka, Antal. *ibid.*, p. 93

16. Hajdu, Heinrich. *Lesen und Schreiben im Spätmittelalter* Pécs, 1931, p. 19

17. Lea, H. *Geschichte der Inquisitionen im Mittelalter.* Übersetzt von
    Deutsch. Bern, 1909, p. 37–41.

18. Werner, Ernst. *Nachrichten über Spätmittelalterische Ketzer aus
    Bohemischen Archiven und Bibliotheken.* In: *Beilage zur Wissensch.
    Zeitschrift der Karl Marx Universität Leipzig.* Gesl. Reihe
    12.1963.H.I.p. 242

19. Haupt, H. *Waldenstum und Inquisition im Südlichen Deutschland.*
    Freiburg 1890. p. 78
    also: Székely György: *Tanulmányok a parasztság történetéhez
    Magyarországon a 14–ik században.* Budapest, 1953. p. 375.

20. Ernyei, Jenö. *Régi cseh telepitések hazánkban.* In: *Föld és Ember.*
    Budapest. 1923, p. 75

21. Erbstosser, M. *Socioreligiöse Strömungen im späten Mittelalter.* Berlin,
    1970. p. 137.

22. Bod, Péter. *Historia Hungarorum Ecclesiastica. Bd. I Lugduni–Batavorum.*
    1888. p.130.

23. Hamman, Gustav. *Waldenser in Ungarn, Siebenbürgen.* in: *Zeitschrift für
    Ostforschung,* 20 Jhg, 1971. Marburg/Lahn p.437.

24. Dollinger, Ing. von. *Beitrage zur Sektengeschichte des Mittelalters.* München, 1896. BndI p. 242–243, Bnd II, p.297.

25. Dollinger, Ing. von. *ibid.*, Bnd II, p. 330.

26. Harnack, Adolf, von. *Dogmen Geschichte*, Tübingen, 1922, p.374–378.

27. *Deliberatio Gerardi Moresanae Eccl. Episc. supra Hymnun Trium Puertorum ad Insigrimum Liberalem.* p.98–99.

28. Battyányi, Ed. *Sancti Gerardi Episc. Chanadiensis Scripta et Acta Alba–Caro*, MDCCXC.

29. Hodinka, Antal. *op. cit.*, p. 27.

30. Szekfü, Lászlo. *Eretnekség és Tirannizmus.* In: *Irodalmi Tört.Köz.* Budapest, 1968. LXXXII.V. p. 501–515.

31. *Deliberatio* . . . 284. Comp. I. Tome 1, p. 9–11.

32. Buckler, Georgia. Anna Comnena. Oxford University Press, London, 1925. p.53.

33. Racki, Ferdinand. *Hic Sunt Starine*, Vol. I. p. 109–140. Slavic Review.

34. Dollinger, Ing. von. *Kirche und Kirchen.* Wien, 1891. p.51.

35. Heer, Friedrich. The medieval world. Wien, 1956. p. 201–204.

36. Denifle, H. *Die Entstehung der Universitäten des Mittelalters bis 1400.* Berlin, 1885. p. 415.

37. Csizmadia, Andor. *A Pécsi Egytem Történetéböl* Pécs, 1967. Vol. I, II, III.

38. Kardos, Tibor. *A laikus mozgalom magyar Bibliája.* Pécs, Minerva, p.55, 1931.
    A huszita Biblia keletkezése. MTA. I. Oszt. Koz.3.kot. 1952. 1/2.

39. Karácsony, István. *Evlia Cselebi török világutazo magyarhoni utazásai.* 1660–64. Vol. III, p. 198–200.

40. Frantisek, Kraus. The Crisis of the Middle Ages and the Hussites. The Reform in Medieval Perspective. ed. St. F. Ozment, Quadrangle Books, Chicago, 1971.
    Quotation: *Monumenta historiae Univ. Carolo Ferdinandae. Pragensis.* I.II. Prague 1830.

41. *Sermones compilate in studio generali Quinque ecclesiensi in Regno Ungariae. Bayerische Staatsbibliothek,* München CIM.22363. fol.67.recto.

42. Winter, Eduard. *Frühhumanismus, seine Entwicklung in Böhmen und deren europäischen Bedeutung für die Kirchenreformbestrebungen im 14.Jahrhundert.* Berlin, 1964.

43. Winter, Eduard. *ibid.*, p. 89.

44. Winter, Eduard. *ibid.*, p. 92.

45. Hermann, Egyed. *A katholikus egyház története.* München, Aurora, 1973. p.150.

46. Majusz, Elemér. *A pálos rend a középkor végen. Egyháztörténet*, 3.1945. p.1–53.

47. Toth Szabo, Pál. *Cseh–Huszita mozgalmak*, Budapest, 1917. p. 144.

48. Toth Szabo, Pál. *ibid.*, p. 102.

49. Fejér, Géza. *Codex diplomaticus Hungariae ecclesiasticus et civilis.* Budae, 1844. 7–810.

50. Szalkai, Bálint. *Ferences barát Cronica Minorum.* Vol. II, p. 241.
    Eusebius Fermendzin: Acta Bosniae, Zagrabiae. 1892. p. 173.

51. Codex Fermendzin, *Acta Bosniae.* Vol. I. 77. Zagrabiae, 1892. p. 40.

52. Lukcsics, Pál. *A Pápák Oklevelei a XV–ik században.* Budapest, 1938. No. 586. 614.5 ol.

53. Lukcsics, Pál. Vatican Lat. 7307.P.No.15 Budapest. 1938 (see Appendix)

54. Timár, Károlyi. *A szegedi premontrei apácák magyar nyelvü emlékei. Szegedi Egyetem Füzet.* Vol. I 1934, p. 195.
    Forradalmi munka e a legrégibb bibliaforditásunk Magyar Kultura, 1930.I szam.

55. Butler, S. Determination: *Consulendum est vulgari populo in Scripturam Sacram legere cupiant.* In M. Deaneslely: The Lollard Bible and other medieval biblical versions. Cambridge, 1920. Appendix II. 402–15.

56. Harsányi, István. *A sárospataki lengyel Biblia, Magyar Könyv szemle*, 1909. XVIII, p. 117.

57. Hodinka, Antal. *op. cit.*, p. 451.

58. Hodinka, Antal. *op. cit.*, p. 133.

59. Passavanti, Jacopo. Ed. D.L. Polidori, Florence, 1863, p. 288.

60. *A Jordánszky kodex bibliai forditása.* Budapest, 1888. p. 349.h. Régi Magyar Nyelv, 5.

61. Abel–Hegedüs. *Analecta Nova.* Budapest, 1903. p. 291.

62. *Vatikáni okmánytár. No. 124, 125. sz.levelek.* In: *Monumenta Vaticana.* Vol. I–VI. Budapest, 1891.

63. Szerb, Antal. *Magyar Irodalom Története.* Budapest, 1943. p. 43–45

APPENDIX

Propositions and statements of Hungarian Hussites in 1435, were reported by Jacob Marchiai to the Pope. After several centuries this report was found in the Vatican archives: Codex Vat. Lat. 7307. The report was published by Pál Lukcsics as *15th Century Letters of Popes* in Budapest, 1938. Akadémia Kiadó.

1. Holy Communion must be served in two kinds, bread and wine.
2. During the worship service the Gospels ought to be read. Services may be held in a cave, barn, or a house. Both sexes are allowed to sing the Psalms. Laymen are allowed to serve Holy Communion.
3. A chalice made of wood may be used to serve the wine during Holy Communion; it needs to be consecrated first.
4. Christ's body dwells in the Communion bread and the wine is his blood.
5. The name of saints must be abolished from worship services.
6. Neither the Virgin Mary, nor the Saints, can help; God alone is our Helper.
7. Do not bow down before Mary, but for God only.
8. Nobody shall fast on a vigil before holy days.
9. Because the Commandment prohibits killing, even criminals cannot be killed.
10. Keep only the Sunday holy; other feasts are man's invention.
11. Do not honor images; they are the work of the devil. This habit only makes man ridiculous.
12. Do not make either images or crosses.
13. Do not make the sign of the cross.
14. To adore images is in vain; they are made for profit only.
15. The Pope does not have more authority than a simple monk.
16. A pilgrimage is not authentic; the Pope has no authority to proclaim one.
17. Do not take it seriously when the Pope absolves sins.
18. Since we are equal in Christ, neither the Pope nor the ruler is more important than anyone else.
19. Neither the Pope, nor the Ruler, has the right or the power to make laws; it is enough that one keeps God's law holy.
20. Holy water, oil, or unction do not have any effect.

21. The Baptismal font is a human invention; Christ was baptized in a river.
22. Only the preacher should pray the Lord's Prayer.
23. Every layman or laywoman may hear confession.
24. The priest, as well as the layman, can be custodian of the host.
25. Offerings on behalf of the dead have no effect.
26. The picture of the Virgin Mary is worthless.
27. There is no such thing as Purgatory.
28. Do not believe in revelations of saints; believe only in the teaching of the Bible.
29. The poor Christ rode on a donkey; the Pope and the ruler ride a pompous horse.
30. They (Hussites) depict the Pope when he celebrates Mass as ministered by the devil and surrounded by demons.
31. Ignore excommunication by the Pope; what he curses, God has blessed.
32. The bishops allegedly can marry virgins, but priesthood and canonry are only inventions of the devil.
33. Do not contribute anything to an altar, like candles, because this is a form of simony.
34. A priest cannot absolve a deadly sin.
35. Ecclesiastics who make worldly fortunes are the devil's brothers.
36. Church princes who excommunicate the believers are members of the devil and anti–Christ.
37. Those priests who collect worldly goods are enemies of Christ.
38. An arrogant vicar of Christ is not worthy to be a babysitter of a child.
39. Those priests who collect tithes or other worldly goods are heretics.
40. The Roman Catholic Church is the Synagogue of Satan, invented by man, and is the mother of the curse and the source of all wrong.
41. Those who want absolution for their sins go to Rome with a full purse to have all their sins expiated.
42. The greedy priest, like a bird of prey, is happy when someone dies.
43. Do not take an oath; it is prohibited.
44. The Pope by his authority demands respect for the laws of the Church, rather than the laws of the Old and New Testaments.
45. The laws of the Church are contemptible, hairsplitting and without any reason.

46. Church laws are fabrications; the Pope has no authority because he is corrupt.

47. Those who are loyal to the Pope are faithless wolves and subverters.

48. Priests let themselves be worshipped like gods, although St. Peter did not permit Cornelius to worship him. Priests ought to be hung together with Haman.

49. Tax collection for the Pope is a simonian heresy and pretends to look like a pious act.

50. All ecclesiastical offices like patriarchs, bishops, and deacons have been invented because of a simonian inclination; they only serve the devil.

51. Clerical leaders like expensive horses and women; they even sleep with married women.

52. There are in the court of Rome no shepherds, only predatory persons.

53. Priests are pastors of benefices, not of souls.

54. Low–ranking priests are servants of the bishops.

55. The Roman Church has become a den of robbers; she does not hold services for the people but for the money.

56. The princes of the Church proclaim the virtue of obedience in the name of Christ. In effect, however, they preach in the name of devils.

57. Everyone can preach, even a child.

58. One does not need man–made laws to be saved; the law of Christ suffices.

59. He who adores images is an idolator.

60. The blood of Christ is carried secretly in a leather bag to their Holy Communion.

61. Those who assembled at the Synod of Prague in 1420 swore to keep the following propositions:

    a. Any priest is allowed to preach without special permission of the bishop.

    b. Every layman is allowed to preach, and serve Holy Communion in both kinds, including to children. To serve a wafer only is a human invention.

    c. All properties must be taken away from the clergy, forcing them to return to the original status of simplicity.

d. Dreadful sins like simony or heresy must not take place in the Church. Anyone who does anything wrong against the Holy John Huss will be punished because he is a false Christian.

The Hussite, puritan peasant movement, proposed just the opposite of what the feudalistic Church, which led a secular–materialistic life, was doing.

CHAPTER VI

Diminishing Roman Catholicism
Under The Ottoman Occupation

In many places the Protestant Reformation began in different ways and forms. In Zurich, Switzerland, for instance, citizens began to eat sausage on Friday instead of fish. In Kolozsvár, Transylvania, it commenced when the burghers decided to lead the "fat monks" out of the city. In Hungary the transformation from Roman Catholicism to Protestantism took place rather smoothly, without too much confrontation. This moderation may be explained by the fact that the first reform–generation was made up mainly of Franciscan and Paulinian theologians and clericals. Earlier the Roman Catholics had in many places already started their own spiritual reformation, predominantly by ardent Franciscans. In Western Europe the Hungarian Franciscans represented about thirty percent of the total priesthood and the number of their monasteries made up approximately thirty–four percent of all cloisters. This meant that between 1500 and 1700 Franciscan monks were incorporated into the *Vicaria Hungariae*.

The Hungarian Franciscan order, bent on reform, had returned to the originally intended simple way of monastic life at the beginning of the sixteenth century. In 1518, they resigned from earthly goods and were commonly called the Observants, because they observed the tradition of Francis of Assisi. These were the men who as chaplains, without hesitance confronted the intruding Muslim Turks on the battlefield as well as on the walls of the *végvárs*, the fortifications in no man's land.

How puritan the order had become may be judged from a petition sent by a seventy–year–old abbot to the Holy See. He humbly asked permission to eat meat three times a week, except on holy days, because of his ailments; he also asked permission to wear a heavy coat lined with fox fur because in the cold season the Midnight Vigil was very cold. He assured the Holy See that his fellow priests would not see the fur lining . . . .[1]

The *Devotio Moderna** also made an impact upon the pre-Reformation renewal. The Franciscan and Paulinian** orders had developed among the laity a new religiosity, and the popular religious movement introduced, among other things, the native tongue in worship service, which in conjunction with the use of church Latin, created a bilingual literature as well. In education a pedagogical synthesis had taken place between ecclesiastical and mundane elements, so that more and more worldly activities were stressed, thus renewing society. All these religious and social innovations advanced the coming of the Protestant Reformation.

Catholic restoration developed an ascetic lifestyle, and asceticism usually practiced criticism on the secular–oriented spiritual life in the mundane world and attempted to reintroduce a puritan way of life. As Hungarian orders began to resign from their worldly possessions and to practice once again contemplative lives, denying themselves the former pleasantries, they also helped shape the surrounding worldly society. This puritanic and other–worldly outlook enabled Roman Catholic intellectuals including clergy to accept the Protestant religious and social renewal. This development in turn helped to create for the Hungarians a common spiritual homeland in which they knew no borders in the divided nation.

In the same period Hungarian theological students were returning from western Protestant universities, well prepared to be future leaders of the Reformation in Hungary. It was to be their task to help integrate their fellow–countrymen into the western spiritual as well as intellectual world, in attempts to prevent the isolation which might have been caused by the Islam interference in the Christian way of life.

Since many former Roman Catholic believers joined with the more dynamic and renewed religious movement, the only alternative for the priests and monks was to unite also with the Protestant Reformation. Thus they could help to rebuild the Church as well as the society. Former Roman Catholic theologians and priests such as Mathias Dévai Biró, who became

---

Devotio Moderna, a puritan, ascetic religious movement based upon the teaching of the Dutch Geert (Gerard) Groote, 1340–1380, Brothers of the Common Life.

**Paulinian order originated in Hungary.

Luther's beloved pupil, as well as Mihály Sztárai, András Sz. Horvát, Imre Ozorai, Ferenc Dávid, István Szegedi Kis, and Péter Juhász Melius, originally were students in Cracow, Wittenberg, or Vienna. In Wittenberg they first learned Lutheran teachings, then later at the Universities of Zurich and Geneva they were exposed to Helvetic–Calvinist theological doctrines, and armed with this knowledge, they successively built the Hungarian Reformed Church.

In the West the Roman Catholic church awakened to its own reform movements, but this came only thirty years later. When Pope Paul III finally called together a reform council in Trent in 1545, he declared in his opening message:

> "We lost Hungary to the Turks. Germany was in danger and the whole world in fear and grief."[2]

The close interrelationship between the Hungarian rulers and the Vatican concerning the defense of European Christianity has been discussed. Hence it is understandable that Pope Paul III was deeply touched when he had to admit the tragic loss of the Hungarian people to the Roman Catholic Church. However, the indifference toward this historical loss on the part of the prelates of the Roman Church was illustrated by the hesitancy and unwillingness they demonstrated when they had to assemble for the Council in Trent. They deplored Trent's uncomfortable site and its poor climate. More than eighty cardinals and bishops chose to linger in the Eternal City Rome, instead of serving their flocks in far–away bishoprics. Pope Paul had to admonish them several times to attend the Council, but in the end only nine prelates were present at the opening! When after many days the assembly finally could come together to hear the Pope's sad admission of loss, the attendants soon hurried to the luxurious dining hall for a banquet, given by the host, Cardinal Madruzzo. The banquet, at which seventy–two different gourmet dishes were served, lasted over three hours. The hundred–year–old wine which was served to the concerned princes of the Church matched in a sense their own ages. In order to cajole the reluctant clergy to Trent, Hungarian King Ferdinand I earlier had to pledge to the Council a whole herd of cattle from Hungary. Was the Lucullan feast a funeral repast for the lost member of Eternal Rome? Exactly one hundred years earlier the Hungarian king, Ulászlo II and János Hunyadi led their desperate crusades on the Balkans for the safety of the future hungry patriarchs.[3]

Pope Paul was not the only one who expressed his sadness about the loss of Hungary. Erasmus of Rotterdam, a former pacifist humanist, also aired his depressed feelings about the debacle:

> "I learned about the tragic news of the downfall of Hungary, the misfortune at Mohács. That defeat was the shameful product of the European rulers and not the fault of Hungary. The rivalries between the rulers within Christianity have brought this catastrophe to the Hungarian people . . . the poor Hungarians are now under the Ottomans' bloody wolf and they now ask help from western Christians."[4]

Since in occupied parts of Hungary the Ottomans demolished all the monasteries and with them all the records and documents pertaining to church and monastic life, historians have to turn to the Vatican library where some reports concerning Hungary are intact. There is, for instance, a report from the Franciscan Bishop Mate Benlich, pertinent to the time between 1659 and 1664. He gave an account of his sufferings. Often imprisoned, he suffered many mistreatments from the hands of the Turks, physical abuses which slowly had worn him down. When not in prison, he could travel only at night in deep darkness. From the sanctuaries under his jurisdiction only a few remained intact; therefore, he had built several portable altars to be used during worship under the open sky. He reported, though, that many of the believers did not dare to attend the celebration of the Eucharist because the Tatar–Turkish raiders often visited these open air places of worship, carrying both priest and members of the congregation off to be sold into captivity. Benlich's report preserves some statistical data as well. During visitations to ten former bishoprics over a period of five years, he could confirm only 3,292 believers in a territory where once two million Christians had lived.[5] When suspicious Turks finally accused Benlich of smuggling money to Rome, the elderly bishop had to postpone his visit to the Eternal City.

Another bishop, Bentlich, was imprisoned, put in chains in 1564. Condemned as a spy, he was sentenced to be beheaded; however, when the poor *rayas* collected four hundred pieces of gold as ransom, Bentlich was freed.[6]

It was this bishop who proposed to the Holy See not to send missionaries overseas, but rather to send them to the occupied part of Hungary which fell under his jurisdiction, because there were plenty of "savages" living under Ottoman rule. He added that he had found many unbaptized grown–up lads who were sporting mustaches.

An objection on the part of the Ottomans was that the Roman Catholic Church had far too many holy days—exactly one–third of the year was so designated; in consequence the *rayas* could not produce enough for the pashas.

Proponents of the idea of Islamic religious tolerance would do well to read the correspondence between the offices of Roman Catholic bishops and local congregations. When loyal Catholic believers petitioned for a serving priest, the pre–condition was this: "If the Turks will imprison the clergy, the parish must agree to pay the demanded ransom."[7] Or was the "tolerance" illustrated by the report of a Hungarian contemporary observer that sometimes a Muslim would visit a Roman Catholic sanctuary in order to light his pipe from the eternally burning light on the altar?

The extent of the catastrophic results of the Ottoman occupation of parts of Hungary can be visualized in a statistical report. In 1526 there had been 1500 Franciscan monks; in 1606 only five monasteries remained with a total of thirty monks.[8] There had been twelve bishoprics in Hungary, but when Tridentine–Reformed Catholicism attempted to regain their influence in the lost Hungarian territory, only two or three bishoprics were still under papal authority as a result of the Ottoman conquest. When in 1586 one of the cardinals searched for a qualified cleric to fill the office of bishop in the third bishopric, he could not find one. The one who might have been available refused the nomination because of the financial insecurity of the Church.

Footnotes

1. Májusz, Elemér. *Egyházi társádalom a középkori Magyarországon.* Budapest, Akadémiai Kiadó, 1971. p. 218.

2. Heer, Fridrich. *Die Dritte Kraft.* Frankfurt a. Main, Fischer Verlag, 1960. p. 82.

3. Jedin, Herbert. A History of the Council of Trent. St. Louis, MO., Herder Book Co., 1957. Vol, I, p. 533.

4. Jedin, Herbert. *ibid.,* p. 722.

5. Ványo, Tihamér. *A hazai hodoltság a vaticáni források tükrében.* In: Vigilia. Budapest, 1973. February. p. 91.

6. Ványo, Tihamér. *ibid.*, p. 92.

7. Balogh, Joseph. *Existenz und Rechtslage der Katholische Kirche in Ungarn zur Zeit der Türkenherrschaft.* Rome. In: Studia Salesiana, subtitle Dei Libro. p. 27.

8. Hermann, Egyed. *A Katholikus Egyház Története Magyarországon 1914–IG.* München, 1973. Aurora Publ. p. 213.

9. Hermann, Egyed. *ibid.*, p.211.

CHAPTER VII

Ottoman Preference For Roman Catholicism Or Protestantism?

The question which group, Roman Catholics or Protestants, the Ottoman administration preferred, was for a long time a point of disagreement between the respective theologians. In historical perspective the objective answer to the question must be: neither-nor. It has been indicated that Koranic law ordered the subjugation and enslavement of the infidel rayas, and this order was practiced policy from the beginning of the occupation of Hungarian territory. Historian Kissling's conclusion on the answer to the question of preference is convincing. He declared Islamic tolerance *a priori* non-existent.

> "That herein one has to do with primary, real tolerance, can be considered even less because there are enough other Islamic regulations which contradict this idea."

When, according to Islamic constitutional concept, the inhabited world is fundamentally divided in the so-called Islamic general territory (*Dar Al Islam*) and the to-be-conquered land (*Dar Al Harb*), then the Islamic claim to world dominance is clear and the non-Muslim is automatically marked as the opposition, and, in consequence, primary tolerance is already contested. As a matter of fact, it may be said that the minority rights of the *rayas* completely contradicted a true tolerance."[1]

The question of preference became more actual when sultan Suleiman extended the Ottoman invasion after the battle of Mohács. At that moment he attempted to establish some form of collaboration (as had been done among the people of the Balkans) among the Hungarian leading groups. His first suggestion to the nobility was to call together a political Diet of the estates to work out a *modus vivendi*. The response was that more than ten thousand Hungarians left the occupied territories, declaring that the Ottomans were "the natural enemies of the nation."[2]

After that rebuke the sultan turned toward the clergy, Roman Catholic as well as Protestant, in an effort to win their cooperation. Among the people of the Balkans this effort successfully had brought the enslaved Orthodox people under the sultan's thumb. In Hungary, the purpose of the sultan's effort was the same: to keep the despised rayas in their place. In general the Roman Catholic clergy in Hungary was regarded by the Ottomans as the natural agent of the Habsburg dynasty, but at that time the Roman Church and her membership were diminishing rapidly, and their historical role became limited.

When the Ottoman administrators slowly realized that neither religious group was willing to serve them, they showed no preference for either side.

In order to illustrate that the only motive which directed the Muslim overlord in connection with church-related events was the exploitation of the rayas, some sample cases will be presented which may illustrate that if in some case a preference was shown by the administration, it actually was only a tactical move.

For instance, the French envoy from Constantinople reported to his ruler that a special prayer was recited in Hagia Sophia, asking Allah's interference to keep the Western unbelievers divided through dogmatic controversies.

It happened that a dispute developed between Roman Catholic and Protestant leaders around the question of who should have the use of the sanctuary. At first, the buildings had been divided for different worship services, but when the rapidly growing Protestant congregations needed more space, the contest began in earnest, and the Kadi or the Mufti became involved. This meant immediately that special fees had to be paid in addition to the yearly church tax. In the *hasz* city Kecskemét, the Kadi decided on behalf of the Protestants because they formed the majority. This favorable decision cost the Protestants forty cows, two bulls, and, for the temporarily imprisoned preacher, the ransom of one hundred seventy florins.[3]

In another case, a dispute took place between Lutheran and Reformed pastors who both could use the one and only standing building in the community. The question became: Who must pay the preacher? The wise

Aga declared a Draconian rule: "Preachers, if you wish to keep your infidel heads on your shoulders, make peace among yourselves. If not, your heads will roll in the mud like pumpkins."[4]

In the two-thousand-year-old city Pécs, the Roman Catholic congregation was divided when agitating Jesuits introduced the Gregorian calendar. The believers preferred the use of the old calendar. Finally, Bey Mehmed imprisoned all the Jesuits and called together a Council, which included Protestant clergy. He blamed the Jesuits, calling them spies, accusing them of worshiping three gods, also of painting pictures of Gods on panels, and in conclusion he condemned them all to be impaled. Of course the end of this burlesque trial was that the frightened believers offered ransom for the priests. The price was set at three thousand florins, and because Allah was merciful, the sultan was satisfied with pocketing one thousand florins. And the calendar? No record . . . .[5]

Nagyharsány, a reformed town which possessed an ancient Gothic church, was suddenly invaded by horse-riding Ottoman Turks. The purpose of the surprise visit apparently was to make a quick cash profit. The invaders herded together from the neighboring area all the rayas as spectators to the following Hollywood scenario. The invaders ordered the city council to bring twenty yoked oxen. These were tied with chains to the inside pillars of the church building, obviously in order to pull down the old house of prayer. It was the invaders' commission to procure building materials needed to fortify a military outpost which had to help keep up the Ottoman peace. As expected, the frightened as well as indignant members of the Reformed congregation commenced the customary bargaining and bickering. Finally the *rayas* had to empty their pockets as well as the treasury to continue their prayers in "eccentric" tradition.[6]

In 1630, the Turks aimed to build a windmill in the city of Mezotur. The mill was to grind wheat. This would secure a monopoly for the Turks, since the daily bread was subject to tax without limitation. For the construction of the mill, strong cut stones were needed which were easily found in the walls of the Cathedral. The poor members of the church were forced by the Ottoman soldiers to demolish the building and to transfer the stones to the waterfront, a task which was performed with tears in the eyes and murder in the hearts.[7] Contemporary readers can easily visualize that Christian churches thus could become profitable Islam enterprises.

The *hasz* city Nagykörös offers an example of the corruption indulged by the pasha of Buda at the time of the re-catholization of Hungary, begun by the Habsburgs. In 1674, the Habsburg Inquisition subpoenaed all Protestant pastors in Hungary to appear before the Roman Catholic Court. The preachers first had to buy from the pasha in Buda a *salvus conductus*, which proved to be an excellent opportunity to exploit the travelers. The pasha also offered the pastors asylum, for good payment, of course. At the same time, he began secret negotiations with the inquisitors to hand over the pastors who sought asylum, again for remuneration. Only when the ruler of Transylvania threatened the pasha with military intervention did he abandon his policy. One of these pastors was Bishop Gergely Ungváry, Church leader in central Hungary. With his family he fled to Buda, trusting a friendly contact he earlier had had with Bey Ali, the intimate counselor of the sultan. During his absence from his congregation, the pulpit had been filled, against Ungváry's objections, by another pastor, who also was persecuted by the Habsburg inquisitors. In this painful situation, Gergely Ungváry, by the consent of his elders, excommunicated the congregation. At that time, this meant that the entire city population was excommunicated. The result was that no baptisms, no weddings, no funerals could be performed, because Ungváry had informed the Debrecen theological seminary about the situation, asking them not to support his disobedient flock with a teacher or cantor. This intermezzo shows two characteristic features: first, the "protecting" pasha was ready to sell out the Protestant clergy to the Habsburg Inquisition for money. Second, after a century of Reformation, the Reformed bishop sustained the Roman Catholic tradition of excommunication.[8] It should be noted here that more than three hundred Protestant pastors were expelled from their own territories and a large number of them were sold as galley slaves. Turkish actions like these could hardly be called sympathetic toward Protestants.

In Szeged, the demands for a church building, coveted by both the diminishing Roman Catholic congregation and the increasing number of Protestants, led to a rather ridiculous as well as sad Turkish decision. Only a few priests were still serving a small Roman Catholic flock, and the Protestant pastors therefore thought to claim the church building for their large congregation. The Kadi first ordered that an open disputation of creeds be held to clarify which denomination had the right teaching. In the midst of the dispute, a kitchen boy, dressed in a soiled apron, suddenly burst into the assembly, asking a Protestant preacher "Tell me, how many Evangelists were there?" When the puzzled pastor began to enumerate the four, the Roman Catholic kitchen boy interrupted him, saying: "You are wrong, there were five," naming an unknown Muslim as fifth evangelist, upon which the Kadi declared the Roman Catholic religion as winner. Therefore, the priests kept the right to the use of their church building, even though it echoed in its emptiness.[9]

Another interesting feature was recorded which revealed that some Janissaries often visited the Protestant worship service, leaving only when the Lord's Supper was being served. During their long stay in Hungary, they had begun to learn enough of the Hungarian language to follow the worship service. Maybe the service broke through the boredom of their otherwise dull lives. On one occasion, the pastor began to read from Paul's letters to the Corinthians and Thessalonians, when a Muslim stood up, telling the pastor in no uncertain terms to leave those cities alone because they belonged to the almighty sultan, "Talk about your own city Kiskocsord!"

In the early years of the Hungarian Reformation, frequently what appeared to be encouraging news was being published in western Protestant circles such as Zurich and Wittenberg. This was possible because some optimistic Hungarians would spread their wishful thinking by writing to Bullinger and Melanchthon letters praising the tolerance of the Turks, who allegedly not only permitted but even supported the Reformation movement. In consequence, Melanchthon, unaware of the true situation, spread this false news, emphasizing the cruel persecutions of Hungarian reformers by the Habsburg Inquisition (which was true), and suggesting the alleged tolerant behavior of the Ottomans. Hence the West showed no inclination to know that the Ottomans traded religious support as common merchandise, selling tolerance to the highest bidder. It has to be stressed again that in practice any ecclesiastical lawsuit was won only by the Kadi or Mufti, because to win a case one first had to pay the expected bribes, then the winner also had to pay the expenses of the trial, and finally, the one who lost had to pay fees as punishment. In the end the Protestants and the Roman Catholics lost while the traders of "justice" made their profits.

In 1616, Paul Thuri, rector of the Reformed College in Tolna, sent out a circular letter to inform all Hungarians in the divided country about his experience with the Ottomans, who had established local administration in the merchant city Tolna. This letter, *The Life of Hungarians Under the Rule of the Turk*, was, fortunately for history, published as a document in Germany by the well-known Hungarian scholar, Albert Szenci Molnár, who used the letter to comfort those exiled Huguenots who complained about their bitter existence and persecution for their Reformed conviction.[11]

Thuri described how the Muslim system conquered the land step by step. In the first phase of occupation, they acted with caution and lenience in order to subordinate the rayas slowly to the Turkish interest. The by now well-known second step was the over-taxation of the population, squeezing more and more punitive fines from their pockets, and undermining the morale as well as the moral basis of the Christian society. By means of false accusations citizens were forced to face capital punishment through death at the stakes, and the only way out was to allow circumcision according to Muslim tradition. The Kadi would often address an unsuspecting *raya*, asking "What is your opinion about Mohammed, or the Koran?" If the answer was polite and indirect, the *raya* was cornered by another question in Socratic fashion: "Why do you then not become a Muslim?" When the *raya* did not follow up his answer with the deed, he faced the death penalty for refusing to recognize the truth of the Koran.

Thuri also narrated the following: When an epidemic struck the community, every citizen had to kill a dog, because god wanted a blood-sacrifice. This nomadic Asiatic belief was incorporated into the Mohammedan metaphysics. If someone did not have a dog, he had to buy one and kill it. The result was, of course, that the city was littered with innumerable dead dogs, causing another plague to descend upon the people.

Another matter discussed was the fact that when a *raya* defended himself against a drunk(!) Muslim, the *raya's* hand was cut off; if he shook a finger in warning to a troublemaking Turk, the finger was cut off.

During the repeated burning down of Tolna, the church building had also been ruined. Because the Christians were unable to rebuild the church, they erected a hut out of reed which served as a house of prayer. There remained no bells, no towers, no clocks, for the three thousand inhabitants of the city. When an unfortunate citizen was forced to become a Muslim, his first act to prove his faith was to gather stones, then proceed to the reed-hut of prayer, spit on it, and throw the collected stones against its walls. When the Turks discovered a dead body in the vicinity of Tolna, the citizens had to pay a blood-fee of four hundred florins. When this happened again and again, the suspicion arose that the corpses were planted by the Turks in order to obtain quick cash.

Through Tolna ran the military highway. When the Turkish army lost a battle, the pastor of the city was punished immediately, accused either of being a spy or of praying malediction upon the faithful warriors of Allah . . . . "I tell you, there was not one pastor who was not brutalized by them (Ottomans), the feet of many were so beaten that they were unable to walk." "The main Ottoman ambition is to destroy our congregations, our schools, where I have several hundred students, because, as long as we teach them, they will never become Muslims. I proclaim that we are living in constant danger, it is dangerous to speak out, but maybe it is even more dangerous to remain silent . . . ."[12]

This document gives us quite a different picture of Hungarian life under Ottoman occupation than the information which Melanchthon had received and spread. To rescue the remnant of Christian civilization in Hungary, Thuri and his co-workers attempted to build a new Protestant Christianity. The fate of the citizens of Tolna under Asiatic despotism was not an isolated historical event; thousands of Hungarians faced similar experiences. A contemporary saying summed the overall situation up in a short question: "Who wishes to be mayor?", which reflected the existential hopelessness of the time. In the town of Dobrony the people were so over-taxed that they simply were unable to pay the *harac*, extortion sum, to the pasha. Therefore pasha Mustapha Hadzsi imprisoned the mayor, sending this laconic message to the citizens: "I will not free your mayor, even if he will rot in his cell," concluding "I will soon document to all of you how your homes smell when they burn."[13]

These types of constant threats explain why the people of any community became unwilling to assume the leadership under the Ottoman reign of terror. This common unwillingness created a bizarre legislation which by itself was contrary to normal social life. In the city Miskolc this ordinance was issued: "If any citizen dares to refuse to be an elected officeholder, he must pay the punitive fine of two hundred florins to the city's treasury." In spite of this severe municipal law, Miskolc was unable to secure a mayor. Whoever might have been available to be elected rather paid the fine and avoided becoming either a hero or a victim of *Pax Ottomanica*. The universality of Islamic inhumanity was well illustrated by the actions of Miskolc's citizens as well as by the fear which dwelt in other cities as well.

Viewing these many examples of the nature and acts of *Pax Ottomanica*, one may ask which psychological aberrations dictated such antisocial and inhuman behavior on the part of the occupying Islam forces. The ethos of a nation is always reflected in its judicatory system and the kinds of punishment it metes out. A criminal code not only unmasks, but also accuses the accuser. The always present sadistic atrocities, as the skinning alive of missionary Bálint in the presence of the sultan, or the hurling into the ocean of Francis of Assisi, under another sultan, the burning alive or the piecemeal slicing up of living persons, or the cutting out of tongues of the sultan's secretaries, making them "the mute ones", in order that the sultan's secrets might be kept, the massacring of populations, as happened in Hungary, all these atrocities were not the result of the actions of demented individuals; they were the result of an institutionalized sadism. Similar atrocities run through Islamic history, indicating grave aberrations in spiritual values of the Koranic teachings. One wonders which expression would best denote the true nature of Islamic policy: *Pax Ottomanica* or *Holocaustum Ottomanicum*?

History knows no final verdicts, therefore this author appeals to the supporters of *Pax Ottomanica* to review the facts for the sake of a better informed future generation.

Footnotes

1. Kissling, Hans Joachim. *Einiges über den Türkischen Hintergrund zur Zeit der Slovenischen Reformation.* In: *Abhandlungen über die Slovenische Reformations Geschichte, Kultur, und Geisteswelt der Slovenen.* Vol. I. München, 1968. p. 61.

2. Szakály, Ferenc. *Török uralom és a reformácio Magyarországon a 16.szádad közepén.* Világosság, 1984, Januar XXV. p. 58.

3. Földváry, Antal. *A magyar református egyház és a török uralom.* Budapest, 1940. p. 97.

4. Thury, Ettele. *A Dunántuli Református Egyház Története.* Pápá, 1908. p. 135.

5. Földváry, Antal. *op. cit.,* p. 95.

6. Földváry, Antal. *ibid.,* p. 140.

7. Farago, Bálint. *A mezötun református egyház Története.* Mezötur, 1927. p. 20.

8. Földváry, Lászlo. *Adalékok a dunámelléki evangélikus református egyház egyházkerület történetéhez.* Budapest, 1898. Vol. I, p. 201–207.

9. Földváry, Antal. *op. cit.*, p. 93.

10. Földváry, Antal. *ibid.*, p. 173.

11. Thuri, Paulus. *Idea Christianorum Hungarorum in et sub turcismo.* Published by Albert Szenci Molnár in Hannau, Germany, 1616. Republished and interpreted by Géza Káthona. Akadémia Kiadó. Budapest, 1974. p. 66–70.

12. Thuri, Paulus. *ibid.*, p. 66–70.

13. Hegyi, Klára. *Egy világbirodalom végidéken.* Budapest, 1976. Gondolat Publ., p. 219.

CHAPTER VIII

Early Period of the Reformation in Hungary

Hungarian Christianity as well as the state itself were rooted in the Roman Christian tradition. Therefore, the history of the nation was for centuries in essence ecclesiastical history. In the sixteenth century, church history also recorded what happened in the nation, because the religious events determined the course of history in Hungary.

After battles which lasted one hundred years, Hungary finally was occupied and divided into three separate spheres of interest. One part on the western edge of the country belonged to the Habsburg dynasty. This dynasty represented what is called Habsburg Catholicism, which no longer was universal Roman in its aspects; it could be equated with religious Germanization of the ethnical groups which constituted the small state of Austria.

A second part of the divided Hungarian nation was Transylvania in east Hungary. It became semi-independent under Ottoman influence. Out of political necessity the ruler of Transylvania acknowledged, with the help of religious leaders, four religious denominations: Roman Catholic, Lutheran, Helvetic Reformed, and Unitarian. For the first time in European church history, the Diet of the Estates declared in 1568 these denominations as free and equal. This occurred under the threat of the Ottoman peril, when King János Sigismund (Zsigmond), disgusted with the decades of bitter confrontations between competing theologians, declared: "Enough of theology!"

The third and largest part of the nation came under Ottoman occupation. From the very beginning, the Muslims tried there a practice of *divide et impere* religious policy. In the first phase of the occupation the Ottoman rulers welcomed the developing Protestant Reformation and openly favored Protestant congregations in judicial and administrative cases. It was clear that this religious policy was directed by the sultan's office in Constantinople. In the second phase of occupation the Ottomans observed how quickly the Roman hierarchy was diminishing between 1546 and 1559, (the number of serving priests had declined by 68 percent), and their antagonism toward Roman Catholicism lessened. At one point in a dispute between two opposing religious leaders, a wise pasha declared: "I was not sent from Constantinople to Hungary to reconcile two 'idiotic' (*quotation marks mine*) religious factions, but to consolidate our power, and force upon the *rayas* military peace." This rare warning should have lessened the religious disputes, but unfortunately this did not happen.

To unite the divided nation at least spiritually, and to establish a form of cooperation among the separated parts, a new type of missionary activity had to be inaugurated. Human history has demonstrated that when religious leaders assumed historical roles, a nation could be born or reborn. The religious developments in the sixteenth century proved this assertion once again. New missionaries arrived suddenly on the banks of the Danube to give different direction to the struggling nation. They were the Protestant preachers who with vigor represented the renewed Christian consciousness. Their sermons still show us how the people could change their cosmic orientation, and, how in Old Testament sense, the "non-people" again became "a people".

As the Protestant Reformation spread into the divided Hungarian territories, the pulpit became a national Mount Carmel from where the preacher-prophet addressed the whole nation in spite of the physical borders. The reformers called the rulers as well as the ruled to repentance. These preachers truly were dramatic personalities in a dramatic age. Without exception they were frequently imprisoned, they suffered persecution, either by the Ottoman or the Habsburg oppressor, they "lived between two pagans." Nobody knew precisely where they were born or when they died, and their graves, like that of Calvin, remain unknown and hidden.

All leading Hungarian theologians and preachers studied first at foreign universities in Cracow, Vienna, Wittenberg, Geneva, or Padua, and prepared themselves there for a life of commitment. After completing their studies they returned home from the peaceful universities to step right into a bitter struggle. Prison became often a preparation for their life mission.

The spiritual activity of the reformers was awesome; they frequently participated in the Synods, they worked out doctrinal-theological problems, they organized churches, they issued laws and decrees upon which a new, coherent society could be built, always with disregard of their own danger and suffering. In addition they were totally committed to the development of a new school system, with free education for all, as well as the establishment of twenty-nine printing presses which were to provide the literary works of the Reformation. Some of them even found time and energy to work on Bible translations. With all this activity they were successful in creating not only a large public readers' forum, but also a well-prepared Protestant leadership among laymen. In reaction to this development, Ferdinand I of Habsburg before long issued a deadly legislation against the printers: printer-preachers were to be drowned! The Habsburg mentality matched here to some degree that of Sultan Bayezid II, who in 1483 already had prohibited the use of a printing press, the only difference being that he ordered the cutting off of hands of any person who violated his decree.

Because of these prohibitions, several hidden printing presses worked secretly in two parts of Hungary. There were even so-called wandering presses. The preachers who were printers as well even became at times book salesmen with an "instant pulpit".

During these times of persecution the front page of the book was born; it included title, name of author, year of publication, as well as the place of issue. In this manner the Habsburgs attempted to control the publishing process. However, in the illegal publications which saw the light, the printers, for reason of self-preservation, falsified data which created in later times immense difficulties in finding out accurate authorship, as well as the printing location of many opera. A safer process was to have works printed abroad and to smuggle them back in book-caskets or barrels as merchandise.

A positive result of the printing press literature was that it introduced the native language, replacing the Latin texts. Thus a uniform Hungarian literature was created, with standard grammar. In final outcome the style and grammar used in Gáspar Károlyi's Bible translation standardized secular literature. The Protestant Reformation and the ensuing religion were indeed the result of the printed Word.

The historical task of the Protestant theologians, preachers, and writers was to develop a unifying religious attitude, not unlike that of the Jews in the Old Testament, as a framework for living. Only a unified religious fellowship could unite the divided nation. The first experience with Lutheranism did not produce the needed framework; neither did its political ideology fit to the nation's struggle for survival. Before long, however, a second alternative, the Helvetic-Calvinist religious tenets, offered a more promising solution. The Hungarian people, surrounded by Germanic, Slavic, and Ottoman ethnical neighbors, found in the supernational HelveticCalvinistic religious experience a national saving and serving pattern for the integration of the divided generations of Magyars. The Helvetic *ius resistendi* concept gave them a doctrinal basis to say "No" to the Ottoman and Habsburg-German challenges. The Helvetic religious orientation in time was characterized by neighboring people as *Magyar Vallás*, Hungarian religion.

Influence of the Lutheran Reformation in Hungary

The Lutheran Reformation reached the Hungarians at an early period. Luther's ninety-five theses were being read in the German speaking cities of Hungary in 1518. In 1522 the Roman Catholic archbishop denounced from pulpits in Hungary the spreading of Luther's innovations. In the same year several Hungarian students studied in Wittenberg under Martin Luther, and in 1523 a reform-Franciscan monk preached Luther's exhortations to a large audience in Sopron. Also in 1523 the Hungarian Diet acted and demanded that Lutherans should be burned (*Lutherani . . . comburantur*). In reality this demand was not so much an ecclesiastical as a sheer political utterance, partially inspired by anti-German considerations, because the first advocates of Luther's reforms were to be found among the German speaking city people. Another motivation for the radical recommendation may have been to secure more papal support against the Ottoman threat. As it was, the flames of the stakes advocated by the legislators of the Diet never caused smoke because the jurisdiction of the Diet ended on the battlefield of Mohács in 1526.

In the western part of Hungary, the ruling Habsburg Ferdinand I ordered punitive action against the Zwinglian "pestilence" in 1534. This proves that parallel with the Lutheran innovations, Helvetic teaching was present also among the Hungarians.[1]

In the further advancement of the Hungarian Reformation the western influence definitely determined dogmatic and church pronouncements. For instance, Luther's teaching concerning the Eucharist became one of the most determining factors in directing the Hungarian Reformation away from Wittenberg. In 1539, one of the Hungarian magnates, Ferenc Révay, a leading feudal politician, wrote Martin Luther, asking the Reformer to clarify his teaching with regards to Holy Communion. Luther's answer that "not the understanding, but the simple belief grants salvation", did not satisfy Révay. In essence, Luther returned in this answer to the early scholastic teaching of *credo quia absurdum*, believe because it is absurd. In this period of theological assertions Luther even called inquiring reason a harlot. Luther and Révay exchanged several letters, but not convinced, the latter finally left the Lutheran camp.[2]

In Luther's theology concerning the Eucharist the interpretation of its meaning displeased many believers who saw it as a sheer exegetical process. How should the words of Christ "This is my body" be interpreted? Was the believer eating the real body and drinking the real blood of the Redeemer? Embittered theological controversies like this robbed the Lutheran movement from universal appeal and in the end delimited it. When Luther reintroduced the medieval magical salvation concept which he first had refused, and, agreeing with the Roman Catholic Church, stated, "I rather confess with the Pope that the blood is real."[3]

These endless and time-consuming disputes gave Luther no time to scrutinize other, non–theological, but determining factors which endangered the universality of his purification of the Christian religion. Thus his reform became a nearly exclusive Germanic Christianity. In consequence, a new religious map of the Continent emerged.

After Luther's death, simplistic followers reduced Luther's well–intended spiritual renewal to a simplified Wittenberg Credo. This will be discussed in a following chapter.

Influence of the Helvetic Reformation in Hungary

After Luther's death his moderate successor, Philip Melanchthon, and Heinrich Bullinger in Zurich greatly influenced the outcome of the Hungarian Reformation. When Melanchthon in Wittenberg lost his irenic

theological leadership to the radicals, and the Hungarian students were
expelled from the university for their crypto–Calvinist sympathy, the
Hungarian Reformation was led toward the camp of Calvin and Bullinger.
Bullinger had great sympathy for the fighting Hungarian nation. Whatever
news he could collect from his Hungarian students and friends he
immediately shared with other reformers in the West. In contrast to the
hairsplitting Lutheran theologians in Wittenberg, Bullinger and Calvin
unified the two theological teachings concerning the Eucharist between
1549 and 1551 in the so–called Consensus of Zurich (*Consensus Tigurinus*).
The dividing factor was thus abolished. Very soon thereafter Bullinger
formulated the *Second Helvetic Confession*, which in 1566 was adopted by
the Hungarian Reformers at the Synod of Debrecen. In addition to this
Confession the *Heidelberg Catechism* also served as basic teaching for the
developing Reformed Church of Hungary under the able leadership of
Péter Juhász, called Melius.

Church historian Máyusz in his excellent study of church society in
medieval Hungary, has pointed out that the Franciscan order was closely
associated with the Italian spiritual tradition and did not allow any German
tradition into monastic life. The *Vicaria Hungariae* belonged to the Italian
Cismontan and not to the German Ultramontan organization.[4] This is
noteworthy, because until recently the alliance has been a neglected aspect
when explaining Hungary's preference for the Helvetic Confession. Could
it be that traditional Hungarian Latinity was a determining factor in the
choice? After all, Hungarian cultural and religious traditions had been
based upon those of the Sorbonne in Paris, of Italian universities, and of
those domestic monasteries which were connected with a Latin heritage.
There are several records available which reveal how and why monasteries
in Hungary prohibited membership of Germans in their orders. The Latin
undercurrent in the spiritual influence of the first generation of Franciscan
Protestant theologians and preachers may also have been involved in the
choice between Lutheranism and Helvetic–Calvinism.[5]

A non–theological development conducive to the reformation process
was new membership in the feudal aristocracy. At Mohács many members
of the leading hereditary aristocracy had died on the battlefield, and they
were being replaced by energetic and newly–orientated members of
aristocratic society. Many church–princes also had lost their lives at Mohács
and the huge feudalistic lands which had belonged to them had fallen

vacant. Now these lands were donated to the new aristocrats, often for military purposes. When one of the reformers succeeded in converting a new magnate to Protestantism, suddenly large territories were opened to the Reformation. The new patrons established in their fortified properties new centers of culture. The symbol of this new aristocracy was *Arte et Marte*, serve with culture as well as with the sword.

The new Protestant feudal lords had the military and political power to grant immunity to the reformers. The latter could then have printing presses in safe places which produced, as has been mentioned, the necessary new Protestant literature. This protection also provided the means for the translation of the Bible and for the establishment of modern schools. Because the Habsburg rulers needed the support of these lords, they did not interfere in these developments at that particular time. Thus, the life of the Protestant Church could radiate from the protected centers, reaching large segments of the population.

In the history of Christendom, believers have formed different concepts of Christ. His role in Church and society has been seen in accordance with the immediate spiritual needs of the people. During the Hungarian Reformation, Christ was presented as the Suffering Redeemer. This view, based on the Biblical text in the Acts of the Apostles, (IV, v.12),[6] offered the desperate, struggling, and diminishing nation the meaning of redemptive history. In this manner the previous secular–humanist historiography was replaced by a Biblical orientation. In the Christ–centered theodicy of Mohács, Christ was the Lord of all human events, including human suffering. The defeat at Mohács was explained as a providential act of logical punishment for the unfaithfulness of the Hungarian people. Suffering now had an educational purpose: If the people would return to the cross–bearing Christ, their suffering would diminish, and the dispersed people would return from their captivity. The Reformed theologians offered, in Old Testament tradition, an optimistic formula for national salvation, and this explanation prepared the downtrodden nation to face the Muslim threat.

In the Ottoman–held territories, Protestant Church organization was slowed down by constant atrocities committed by the occupant forces, and only slowly the best form of adjustment to the unpredictable Ottomans was discovered. The first step was to involve the still available Hungarian population in decentralized congregations constituting the new Protestant

Church. As has been explained, the Lutheran form of church government did not appeal as an example to be copied because in the hierarchical system the Princes carried the authority. The second step therefore was to involve church members as much as possible in the life of the congregations on the basis of voluntary commitment. The Helvetic form of church government, laymen and pastor together, offered a viable alternative. An additional advantage of this system was that it was possible to make leadership less visible to the Ottomans, who always were out on some pretext to collect bribes, and who made therefore the preachers responsible for the conduct of their flocks.

The laicized Reformed Church became more effective because she associated with the developing burgher–plebeian working population. The Protestant congregations recognized a new work ethic which helped to reorganize the dissolute social life unprotected by the state. Daily work became a form of worship; labor was recognized as honorable. For the first time in Church history, common workers were incorporated as equal members in the *Res Publica Christiana*, in which the native language proclaimed the Good News to the thirsty souls.

Footnotes

1. Kissling, Hans Joachim. *Protestáns Szemle.* Budapest 1913, p. 518.
2. Karácsonyi, J. *Egyházitörténeti Emlékek*, Budapest, 1903. Vol. III. p. 386–389.
3. Luther, Martin. W. A. Weimar ed. 26.432.
4. Máyusz, Elemér. *Egyházi társádalom a középkori Magyarországon.* Budapest, Akadémiai Kiadó, 1971. p. 293.
5. Máyusz, Elemér. *ibid.*, p. 277–287.
6. Acts of the Apostles, IV, v. 12. "Salvation is found in no one else, for there is no other name under heaven given to men by which we must be saved."

Chapter IX

Mathias Dévai Biró, The Hungarian Luther?

In the early decades of the sixteenth century, the picture of ecclesiastical life in Hungary was undergoing a rapid change. Humanists and diplomats like Szalkai, who for years was Primate of Hungary without having been ordained, or, Count d'Este, who had been appointed archbishop when he was seven years old, entirely disappeared from the stage. With them, the medieval *fratres*, who had been sitting in their *stuba scriptoria* copying old manuscripts, vanished, and in their place the wandering preachers entered the scene. These preachers translated the Word of God into the vernacular; they wrote, printed, and published books, even selling them in order to spread the comforting Word for which the Hungarians thirsted. These new authors would throw themselves into raging disputes and more than once their lives were at stake because the losers often would pay with their lives.

Hungarian Protestantism produced not a single conspicuous figure who was not subject to torture and at least one term in prison. Most of the reformers were unable to avoid persecution; they constantly had to avoid captivity, fleeing from Roman Catholic prelates and aristocrats.

Always on the move, they hurried from one end of the country to another in order to attend religious disputes. As soon as a new theological book was published, preachers would put their heads together to discuss and weigh its new points of view. Practically all of them had attended universities abroad for years. Coming home they faced struggle and danger, and often they were forced to flee to the freedom of foreign countries. They truly burned with an ineffable fever of the soul.

The religious dialectics of the age created a situation where those reformers who once had repudiated certain dogmas and had placed themselves in the realm of free critical choice, could no longer find a fixed point on which to take their stand. Hungarian Protestantism therefore had to go through many stages before it became what it is today. Whereas the strength of Roman Catholicism rooted in its stability and resistance to historical evolution, the strength of Protestantism was in the dynamics of its development. This historical and psychological phenomenon helps to account for the extraordinary theological tension which was found in Hungarian Protestantism in the second half of the sixteenth century. The great theological discussions of that epoch did not take place between Roman Catholic and Protestant opponents, but between Protestants of varying persuasions.

It was mainly the Protestant preacher as writer and disputant, living in a feudal society, who observed and boldly exposed the alarming social conditions which surrounded him. He not only revealed the ills but also through social and historical analysis searched for the moral causes behind them. The pastor-confessor sought a new yardstick with which to measure mankind, especially his own compatriots. He found it in Scripture, predominantly in the Old Testament, which abounds in historical crises. The Old Testament atmosphere invaded the souls of the Hungarian people, causing them to develop a deep sense of guilt. It also invaded the literature, and one of the characteristic features of Protestant literature was that it came close to a public, common confession of ethical culpability. It sought a common absolution of sin, because the great historical tragedy common to all had swept the whole nation into one community of sufferers. Apart from Protestant literature, the sermon became the most characteristic genre of the age, inasmuch as the Protestant religion depended entirely on the preaching of the Gospel. The old belief in authority was discarded, and the faith of newly awakened men no longer was dictated by the authority of Rome, but rather by their personal convictions. One of the first representatives of these men was Mathias Devái Biró, who by his contemporaries was called "*Lutherus Hungaricus*", "The Hungarian Luther."[1]

Place and time of birth of Devái Biró are as little known as the time and circumstances of his death. He entered the scene in 1523, when he had just returned from the University of Cracow. He was then still active as a Franciscan monk, but in 1529 he already was sitting at the feet of Luther, becoming an ardent disciple. The reformer became also a friend to whom Devái Biró returned more than once in the course of his life. With Luther's letter of introduction, he returned to Buda where he became a preacher, and not long thereafter an author as well.

In 1531 Devái Biró was to be sentenced by the Primate of Hungary for his activities and was transferred to Vienna to be investigated by Faber (Fabri), bishop of Vienna, who was an agent of the Habsburg Inquisition. Devái Biró was imprisoned in Vienna between 1531 and 1533. In the end, his former flock helped him to escape. Interestingly, later the Lutheran Bishop Péter Bornemissza was imprisoned in the same place after facing inquisitor Faber, and he also managed to escape.

Back in Buda, Devái Biró continued to preach the Gospel; however, Buda changed masters. Ferdinand I lost the capital, and the rival King John had Devái Biró imprisoned for preaching reform in "an all too original form."

Imprisoned from 1534 to 1535, upon being freed he showed alarming symptoms of approaching blindness, which prompted him to go to Germany in hopes of a cure. It was not long before he was challenged to attend a disputation the subject of which was the new book by a Hungarian Franciscan, a former professor at the Sorbonne University, Fr. Dr. Szegedi, *Censurae in propositiones erroneas Mathiae Devái Biró*,[2] which had been published in Vienna in 1535. The theological significance of this book was that it comprised the first Roman Catholic polemics in Hungary, and as such it probably started the Counter-Reformation.

To publish a book which Devái Biró had written in prison, he departed for Nürnberg in 1536, still hoping to find healing for his ailments. From Nürnberg he once more set out for Wittenberg in 1537, where his beloved teacher Philip Melanchthon supported him and wrote a letter of recommendation to the German prince Georg Brandenburg asking for financial support for Devái Biró. It is known that the latter also lived in Basel where he published *A Discussion on the State of Souls After Death and Before the Day of Judgment*. Melanchthon had written the introduction for this work. Devái Biró's teaching on life after death was a hotly disputed topic at the time, and he faithfully followed Paulinian teachings. The second part of his book contained fifty-two theses which he offered as basis for his Reformation theology; the third part described Devái Biró's prison life in Vienna.

In 1538 he continued his activities as a reformer, but in 1541 another Roman Catholic bishop had him persecuted and his work was once again interrupted. This time, however, he had learned to outwit his persecutors, and he left for Wittenberg, where he wrote a fundamental Hungarian grammar, *Orthographia Hungarica*,[3] which was published in Cracow where once he had been a student. Devái Biró's reason for writing the grammar was that it was "the gate", as he expressed it, to the reading and understanding of the Holy Writ, which he saw as the number one duty of true believers. He disclosed his new socio-philosophical opinions, writing that the ancient Christians knew only few holy days, and that they worked hard to glorify their Creator.

In a short span of time Devái Biró translated and modified Luther's Short Catechism, as well as translating several parts of the Bible, putting his new grammatical style to use. In 1538 he also published in Cracow the first theological textbook in the framework of an *Explanation of the Ten Commandments*.[4]

As soon as these two books had left the press, making deep inroads in the growing Protestant movement, Hungary was stirred by a new conflagration. This time, King John allied himself with the Pope and as a result, the presses of the heretics went up in flames. Devái Biró, who was one of the most visible leaders of the Hungarian Reformation, had to escape again to Wittenberg, where he lived in Melanchthon's home.

Both Luther and Melanchthon showed their Hungarian disciples great friendship, although Melanchthon, with a more flexible nature, found the shorter way to the hearts of the Hungarians. Szlávik wrote:

> "He [Melanchthon] showed a warm interest in Hungary and he preached for them [Hungarians] every Saturday afternoon with particular regularity. Perhaps they owed this to Melanchthon's warm feelings for his first teacher back in Bretten, Johannes Hungarus, of whom he used to speak later with the highest appreciation."[5]

In spite of his repeated persecutions and imprisonments, and in spite of his failing eyesight, Devái Biró proved to be successful in his reformational activities. For an open disputation to be held around 1544, he prepared the articles of his *Dogmatics*, and people flocked from all points of the country to hear them. When the disputation was terminated in 1549, the first Synod was held at Erdöd in the same year. All twenty-two preachers who attended adopted the pure Lutheran doctrines which had been prepared by Devái Biró, who had already died, probably in 1545.

The first article prepared by him and subscribed to by the Synod of Erdöd concerned Holy Scripture; it was entirely orthodox in its wording and rejected Antitrinitarianism.

The second article dealt with the Son of God, the sole intercessor; it eliminated the intercession of saints.

The third article dealt with salvation; good works were declared to be of no avail.

The fourth article focused on the question of what kind of saving faith men should have.

The fifth article showed to what use good works still might be put.

The sixth article defined the essence of the two sacraments. In the Lord's Supper men were partaking of the body and blood of the Lord Jesus Christ. This had not been Devái's final standpoint, however. The article contained protests against those who called the Lutheran Lord's Supper the "Devil's Mass".

It is interesting to note that confession of sins was still retained; he who had not confessed was not permitted to partake of the Lord's Supper.

Last but not least it was strongly stressed that the participants stood upon the premises of the Augustana Confession; thereby they probably wished or hoped to shield themselves against being suspected of Helvetic "heresy".

To work from a different premise was of course unthinkable for this first Synod, because those attending were without exception disciples and students of Luther. They had made their pilgrimage to Wittenberg to receive from him their ordination; at home they were allowed to exercise their sacerdotal functions only after showing ordination papers received in Wittenberg.

In spite of the deep loyalty Devái Biró and his companions felt toward Luther, even Devái himself could not escape accusations of orthodox Lutherans in the Saxon cities of upper Hungary, who brought charges against him in Wittenberg. These Saxons observed a jealous vigilance over Luther's doctrine of the Lord's Supper. They accused Devái of seeking a middle position between Zwingli and Luther.

The core of the question had really more to do with Melanchthon, who, in his endeavor to mediate between extremes, went so far as to subscribe to the Augustana Variata Confession, whereby he became a man of the middle road. Luther wrote in this connection:

"By the way, what you have written me of Mathias Devái I greatly
admire, because with us too he has so good a reputation that it is
hard for me to even speak of it. Be this as it may, it is certainly
not from us that he received the doctrine of the sacraments. We
steadily fight such doctrine, publicly as well as privately, and there
is here no suspicion or slightest sign of that abomination. Therefore
you may stand firm and not doubt that, unless God makes me
insane, I will ever agree with the adversaries of the Sacrament,
neither will I ever tolerate that abomination in the Church
entrusted to me, or if, which God may avert, I were to do
otherwise, you may confidently call me insane and damned . . . .
Magister Philip I do not suspect at all, nor do I suspect any of our
men. Given at Wittenberg, 1544."[6]

According to this letter, Luther himself was surprised to learn of the
Saxon accusations, declaring that he had no suspicion whatsoever regarding
Devái's faithfulness to his teachings. Nevertheless, he did point out that the
doctrines regarding the sacraments were Calvinistic, an idea which Devái
could not have learned in Wittenberg, and that he, Luther, would continue
to fight. Was there any truth in the accusations raised against Devái? In
general his fidelity to Lutheran theology was above suspicion; however, the
fact was that he had lived at one time in Switzerland and had had ample
opportunity to familiarize himself with Calvinistic doctrines. It was also true
that Devái stood for the conciliatory spirit called *"Variata"* which
Melanchthon represented. The Synod of Erdöd dealt among other matters
with this Augustana Variata Confession.[7]

Devái Biró's own writings, however, must have the last word; church
historians have never been able to find in them one single sentence
deviating ever so slightly from the Wittenberg line. On the other hand, he
was not the kind of man who would slavishly reproduce the Lutheran
doctrines on the Lord's Supper. The difference in motivations of Luther
and of Devái should now be pointed out. When Luther as monk had
stepped out of his cell, his initial argument was directed against the Roman
misuse of the Church. His reasoning was socio-political as well as economic.
According to him the sale of indulgences made Germany a cow to be
milked by Rome. In contrast, the central question of salvation was Devái's
beginning of spiritual reformation. He warned his followers not to trust in
the intercession of saints for their salvation, although the confused priests
and monks in that time had offered the immensely suffering people as

consolation nothing but the intercession of saints and the doing of good works. Against this cheap idea of salvation, Devái reintroduced Christ, the only Redeemer, into the Christian life, stressing that men were sinful and that the Holy Spirit accused all creatures. Nobody but Christ could lift the misery from a repenting nation. He explained that the saints once had been sinners too, and therefore they would not be in a position to bring spiritual renewal.

At one time, Devái as existential theologian had written about the status of the sleeping saints and Mary replacing Christ as Redeemer, taking to task the Roman Catholic thesis which he called misleading. According to Devái, the saints were sleeping somewhere. Therefore they could not know the existing human predicament, peoples' lives and sins. Hence they could not mediate before the Creator, neither could they bring the Good News.

Apparently Devái Bíró presented with this argument a unique theological idea, because, after his death, the Roman Catholic theologian, Martin Chemnitz, in his book *Examen Concilii Tridentini* (1565–1573)[8] argued against Devái's treatise in great detail. Devái Bíró, however, was the only one who had presented alternatives on this theological problem. He had advocated to forget the dead saints, and rather to pay attention to the living ones. Luther had been ambiguous on this topic; when one of his Hungarian students had asked him once whether the intercession of saints helped or not, Luther's answer had been that it was permitted to pray to them *"Permittamus illos orare."*

In the midst of persecution Devái had searched for a safe place and had settled down on the land of a most influential Hungarian magnate, Baron Péter Perényi, who was deeply involved in the Lutheran Reformation. Baron Perényi was steeped in Luther's controversial teaching of Eucharistic theology. The immediate cause of sharp discussions between Perényi and Devái therefore was when will the simple bread become a sacrament– while it is being carried into the sanctuary or only after it has been closed into the ciborium? Devái, who could not bear such hairsplitting, because he leaned more to Melanchthon's formula *media sententia*, soon left his protector.

Devái had in fact pioneered a special formula for the Lord's Supper. In his understanding bread and wine were not only outward signs, as Zwingli had taught, but they also brought the believers into the presence of Christ. The two elements were not identical to human body and blood. They were the glorified body and blood of the crucified Christ. However, they carried *Sole Fide* the Promise, without any transformation taking place, and thus the believers by faith took in Christ, the Redeemer.[9] He stressed though that only the true believer was able to join thus with Christ during this religious act, the unbeliever receiving only the simple bread and wine, no more.

The Hungarian disposition toward the mystical-transcendental theological tendencies made them watchful as became clear from the correspondence between Count Révay and Martin Luther. Révay had to refuse the medieval magical approach to the sacraments.

As stated, Devái Biró in general remained in the camp of Luther, but on this very sensitive question of the Lord's Supper, he preferred the irenic approach. His followers did not challenge the Zwinglian thesis, but rather tried to reconcile it with the conciliatory efforts of Melanchthon. For the Hungarian spiritual climate, Devái Biró presented less complicated theological concepts, as he explained how the overburdened soul could meet with Christ in the Holy Communion, and so restore the lost *Imago Dei*, God's real image, but he could not escape from the negative effects of the Eucharistic controversy, neither could he offer a final answer.

According to ecclesiastical sources, Devái Biró was inclined toward the Bucer-Melanchthon irenic concept when he returned from Wittenberg for the third time. Maybe "Hungarian Melanchthon" would be a more correct epitaph than "Hungarian Luther", because it would signify better the vigorous intellectual transformation of Devái's religious dynamism. His theology and his well balanced, reformational social commitments kept their value for successive generations. His contemporaries were impressed by his heroism which won him the epitaph "Hungarian Luther". Devái Biró wrote the principles of his theology not only in his books but in his life as well, when he summed up his reformed convictions:

> "Every man is bound before God, by eternal salvation or eternal damnation, to bear witness of, and confess to men and angels his faith; therefore they who, under whatever pretext, conceal or suppress the truth they have recognized, also deny Christ, and they who deny Him are thrown under Satan's fist and sent to eternal damnation."

This confession of Luther's disciple breathes a spirit of resolution, of profound knowledge of his Master.

Luther told the following anecdote about Devái:

> "Once in Buda the Turk wished to set up an ordeal to decide between the defenders of the old and the new Faith or perhaps

only to put both on their mettle by having them sit down on a powder barrel about to be exploded. Devái sat down on his barrel with equanimity, whereas the Catholic priest bolted."[10]

Devái was an "existential" theologian in the true sense of the word. His activities stirred up the whole country, his books and disputes helped to formulate the first theses of Protestantism. In addition, he organized religious communities all over the country. Now as voluntary traveler, now as refugee, he shuttled to and fro among the spiritual centers of Europe, keeping pace with the intellectual developments of the Continent. Because he was strong in faith, he could also be tolerant, and so became the consoler and prophet of a nation fallen into despair.

Then, suddenly, Devái was lost to sight; the assiduous searching of church historians so far has been in vain. Perhaps Devái died during one of his voyages abroad of which there is no report. In his destiny somehow a whole epoch is described. Born out of the religious longings of centuries in travail, the fame of his deep-seated faith has been preserved by his late descendants in another century of pain and sorrow.

Footnotes

1. Schesaeus, Keresztély. In: *Ruinae Pannonicae Libri*, 1585 RMK. Vol. III. 613. Budapest.

2. Fr. Dr. Szegedi, Gergely. In: *Rabus, Historien der Martyrer.* Strassbourg, 1566–1572. Vol. II, RMK, Vol. III, 309.

3. Devái Biró, Mathias. *Orthographica Hungarica.* RMK, Vol. I, p. 20.

4. Devái Biró, Mathias. Explanation of the Ten Commandments. RMK, Vol. I, p. 353.

5. Szlávik, Mathias. *Die Reformation in Ungarn.* Halle, 1884. p. 11.

6. Ribini, J. *Memorabilia Augustanae Confessionis.* 1781. Vol. I, p. 60.

7. Révész, Imre. A Magyar Református Egyház Története. Debrecen, 1938. p. 6.

8. Chemnitz, Martin. *Examen Concilii Tridentini.* Frankfurt, 1585. Tertia pars p. 129.

9. Horváth, János. *A Reformácio Jegyében,* Budapest. Gondolat P. 1957. p. 170.

10. Luther, Martin. *Wittenberger Tischreden.* Weimar, 1883. 6.6516.

Stephen Kis of Szeged

Chapter X

Stephen Kis of Szeged, Hungarian Reformer during the Ottoman Occupation
1505 –1572

At the beginning of any significant historical event always stands an extraordinary figure, whose name becomes a symbol for a new age. In the history of the Protestant Reformation, Martin Luther and John Calvin were such giants. In Hungarian church history it has been Stephen Kis of Szeged, also called Szegedi, whose genius in the end determined the development of the Reformed movement in the Ottoman occupied part of Hungary.

As *Pater Patriae*, Szegedi incorporated in his lifework the fate of the suffering Hungarian people. The missionary events of his life, the frequent humiliations, imprisonments, and physical suffering, in one way symbolize the destiny of his religious followers. In another way his life experience was close to that of St. Paul, finding final victory. "Not I, but Christ working in me."

The never-ending persecutions which Szegedi endured, first on the part of the Habsburg Catholic Inquisition, then by the Islamic Ottomans, increased Szegedi's popularity among Protestants as well as among Hungarian Catholics. That the impact which Szegedi made upon the Hungarian Reformation was important may be illustrated by the fact that Karl Barth, contemporary Swiss theologian, when preparing lectures on the history of the Hungarian Reformation, first asked for the scholarly theological works of Szegedi. These works had been published after Szegedi's death in Geneva, Zurich, Basel, and London, where he was well-known.

Szegedi was born in 1505 in Szeged, a city which took pride in its seventeen cathedrals and other sanctuaries. When Szeged was later occupied by the Ottomans, these sanctuaries, with few exceptions, were destroyed.

An early record, characteristic of young Szegedi, narrates his unquenchable thirst for knowledge. After finishing preparations at Hungarian schools, he joined those peregrine students who by the thousands visited European universities, because the Hungarian universities of Pécs and Pozsony ceased to exist after the Turkish invasion. In 1535 Szegedi first attended the university of Vienna, where several Hungarian scholars with humanist inclinations were lecturing. After Vienna, he studied in Cracow, another center of humanistic intellectual life. At this Polish university, a thousand Hungarian students prepared themselves for future intellectual leadership. At that time Cracow became the center of reformation ideas. Church historian Révész has suggested that the first Protestant initiatives reached Hungary from Cracow and not from Wittenberg. It is an historical fact that Szegedi's fellow students from Cracow later became prominent Hungarian reform leaders such as Imre Ozorai, Mathias Dévai Biró, and István Gálszéchi.

Into the intellectually fermenting atmosphere of Cracow, Szegedi arrived in 1537. He must have been an outstanding student, for he mastered the Latin, Greek, and possibly also Hebrew languages. In 1540, he was entrusted with teaching the Latin classics.

His fellow students undoubtedly exerted religious influence upon Szegedi. Before long his inquisitive mind turned *ad fontes*, to the sources of the sixteenth century's spiritual revolution.

From 1543 on, at the age of 38, he studied in Wittenberg under Luther, Melanchthon, Crucinger, and Maior. He became a favored student of Luther and spent several years in Wittenberg. Later, when Szegedi wrote *Assertio vera ad Trinitate*, circa 1573, published by Beza in Switzerland, he may have been instrumental in involving Maior in the bitter disputes with the Antitrinitarian (Unitarian) spokesman, Ferenc Dávid.

After completing his studies in Wittenberg with a doctorate of theology, Szegedi returned to Hungary and as pedagogue-theologian began to prepare a new religious generation, constantly sending the future elite to study abroad in order to arm them with high level academic knowledge in facing the challenges from Roman Catholic as well as from Ottoman sides. During the strenuous labor between "water and fire" to establish a spiritual Israel among the Hungarian people, Szegedi went through several humiliating experiences. In Catholic-ruled Hungarian territory, the bishop-governor, who already was losing the religious battle with the Protestant Reformation, ordered Szegedi to be physically tortured, to be robbed of his precious and large library as well as of other property.

Barely recovered from his physical mistreatments, Szegedi moved to the territory occupied by the Ottomans and there began his educational and ecclesiastical services, only to face new abuses. A controversy developed during one of his worship services, as a result of which the Ottoman bey had him imprisoned, accusing Szegedi—among other allegations—of being a spy. The latter conclusion was drawn from Szegedi's activities as chaplain to the defending militia of the *Végvár* in no-man's land, which forced him to travel much. This chaplaincy had come to him because he was becoming a well-known pastor, a moderate preacher. It has already been recorded how Szegedi was dragged from prison by the Turks, who humiliated him before his fellow Christians, and how he finally was freed in 1562 after the whole Hungarian Christian population had gathered together the demanded ransom in gold.

Szegedi's private family life was also filled with pain and sorrow; the recurring plague took the lives of two of his wives and seven of his children. It is known that he married three times.

These happenings were characteristic of those days in which wars disrupted sanitary services and monastic hospitals were burned down by the Islamic invaders. *Morbus Hungaricus*, raging at times as an epidemic, killed the inhabitants of whole settlements. As far as is known only one son of Szegedi survived; he became a student at Basel university and later became instrumental in the publication of his father's formidable literary works.

History shows clearly that to be a prominent leader, or a renowned scholar, or a city mayor in those days was never without danger; threats to life were always around the corner. The Ottomans attempted to eliminate visible leaders, knowing full well that in beating the shepherds the herd would be scattered.

The central problem for any leader in Ottoman domain was to bring order, neutralizing the destabilizing efforts of the Muslims. In the process of renewal, the Church's most important task was to restore authority, which in turn would lead to order. The source of order was to be found in the Gospel, hence the ecclesiastical workers' twofold task became to build the *Imago Dei* into the souls of their flock and to reestablish a society built upon the Gospel. In this manner regenerated men would practice God's order. In the end the Bible became the overriding authority.

Szegedi as Teacher and Church Organizer

Szegedi's pedagogical task was to bring order into the life of society. During his entire lifetime he remained a peripatetic pedagogue. As professor, he kept in constant contact with educational institutes by visiting them. His goal was to further the building up of the schools to the level of high academics. His modern pedagogical system was based mainly on the teaching concepts of Luther first, later on those of Calvin. His plan for Christian education aimed to motivate students to act as Christ's militant pupils. Disciplined and of puritanistic orientation, they were to become the elite which was lacking, because they had either died on the battlefield or had landed in slave markets in Constantinople. In a sense his plan brought forth a pedagogical democratization in which the needed leaders were recruited from the lower classes. Indeed, Szegedi's "classroom" did not have walls; it was as far extended as the ethnical borderlines.

As *Pater Patriae* Szegedi was a man in a hurry, he had no patience in sustaining the outdated and complicated Aristotelian scholastic system. He respected the values of tradition as long as they presented valid truth; however, they should not be propagated any longer just because they were antique. Szegedi introduced practical methods of learning in his text book *Loci communes* as well as in his theological presentations, offering a system of tabulating and dividing resulting in a systematic outline of contents. A student was thus enabled to present his thesis briefly and come to a clear and logical conclusion. This method proved to be quite useful and practical, not only for students, but also for pastors in the preparation of sermons. These encyclopedical forms made Szegedi's works quite popular in theological circles at home as well as abroad.

Szegedi was an existential teacher and academician *per se*; always before his eyes was the practical goal of building "a mighty fortress" on systematic Reformed theology. In this process it can be observed how challenge and response were at work, shaping the outcome of his endeavor. He did not work in isolation but visited contemporary reformers such as Bishop Melius of Debrecen, seeking coordination for his national rescue operation. He also often re-visited the Protestant centers in the west to keep up-to-date with new Protestant tendencies.

It was Szegedi's ambition to reduce theological controversies, since the Tridentine recatholization and the extending Ottoman menace exerted much pressure on the Protestant movement. The worsening historical situation forced this conscious church leader to identify with the mediating, that is irenic, theological school in order to prevent the reform movement from splitting on the grounds of dogmatic intolerance. All his theological works show eclectic tendencies, proving that he was not dominated by any special theological trend and that pluralism was his specialty. His close relationship with Theodore Beza prevented Szegedi from eyeing deviations such as the Anabaptist and Antitrinitarian movements. Beza's declaration on them had been short and to the point:

> "This devilish freedom has filled Poland and Transylvania with many pestilential sectarians who would be tolerated nowhere else."[1]

Szegedi's biographer, his former student Skaricza,[2] has pointed out that Szegedi carefully avoided religious confrontations whenever this was possible. Maybe his self-controlled ecclesiastical policy was rooted in Biblical faith rather than in antagonistic creedal convictions. He was not afraid to communicate the balanced view that Protestant and Catholic believers were brethren and sisters; that the continuation of their animosities would lead to a cultural and historical suicide. This he ventured in a passionate, partisan, and narrow-minded age. Even in his widely read and often republished work, *Speculum romanorum pontificum*, which dealt with the spiritual and ethical shortcomings of popes, Szegedi's clear intention was to restore Christian oneness in a form of ecclesiastical federalism which would be constituted of equals in common virtues, not in common sin.

It was a historical turning point in Hungarian church history when Szegedi assumed the role of church leader, because it meant the elimination of the Constantine form of state-church. The Caesaro-Papal tradition was replaced by the self-governing Reformed Church, developing a democratic system built upon pastor-layman participation. In embryonic form the first Presbyterian congregation was already at work.

Why Szegedi so long postponed his ordination has long been discussed and scrutinized. When he returned from Wittenberg, he had assumed

mainly an educational role. Was it his experience with the Constitution of
the Lutheran Church which held him back, seeing how the landed autocrats
as new princes subjugated for their own interest the local communities? He
did become reluctant to accept serving a church in order to be manipulated
by those new "princes". Moreover, the Gospel seemed to become the
monopoly of the new subservient priesthood; this was exactly against
Luther's original concept. He had advocated that the layman should first
become a priest himself, then to his fellow man. The concept of universal
priesthood fitted the ecclesiastical needs of East Central Europe better.
When Szegedi finally became bishop in the Helvetic-Calvinist Church, he
was immediately faced with the dilemma of relating authority to the
freedom proclaimed by the Gospel. He assumed the task of organizing the
Church of Christ and needed, of course, authority to secure order and
stability within the Church as well as within the developing society. He also
had to ensure a degree of freedom for the members of society in order that
they remain morally responsible. Only Paulinian theology could solve the
dilemma; therefore Szegedi introduced the Gospel as the only source of
authority. This in one sense freed man from bondage, in another made man
a servant of the Redeemer when he accepted Christ's teachings as absolute.
In short, Szegedi did not yield authority either to any human organization
or to the clergy, reserving authority exclusively for the Gospel.

Apart from organizing and leading the Church, Szegedi wrote extensively
the necessary Reformed literature, thus educating his fellow pastors, ac-
quainting them with theological writings from the West as well.

In his role of pastor, Szegedi always preached conciliatory sermons, quite
different from those of his fellow Bishop Sztárai, who with his fervent
antagonism alienated not only his own congregation, but also frequently
sowed hatred among Hungarians who espoused different religious persuasions. As theologian and pedagogue, Szegedi preached Christ also "via
his pen", as his biographer Skaricza pointed out when he explained
Szegedi's concentrated efforts of bringing Christ to the populace as well as
to his fellow theologians and pastors.

It was an apocalyptic age when Szegedi entered into Hungarian Christian
Church life. He and his coworkers had to eliminate much of what had
become worthless in the Church of the past before they could begin with
building anew. The renewed Church was to become once again a teaching
as well as a serving Church.

Szegedi, who was foremost a theologian and a writer, was able to avoid the road on which faith becomes reduced to a sheer intellectual exercise creating only dogmatic poverty. He became a theological bridge-builder who considered of less importance, for instance,the overdisputed topic of how to apply the concept of predestination to the daily life of the Hungarian Church. His Eucharistic theology revealed also his moderation, removing him far from those theologians who in their disputes regarding the Eucharist pursued each other as it were around the Lord's Table.

In Western Europe the spread of the Reformation began at universities and urban societies. In Ottoman occupied Hungary, however, Szegedi had to deal with an overwhelmingly rural population, only in limited numbers with burgher-plebeian elements. This was due to the fact that the once important cultural centers had been destroyed during the ongoing wars. In the remaining few towns, the more educated mobile merchants were the most helpful, financially as well as in spreading the Good News. Because feudal society ceased to exist in Szegedi's territory due to the Turkish occupation, and since the Lutheran principle of *cuius regio eius religio* was not applicable in Ottoman-held land, he never had to face the feudalistic controversies. The feudalistic landlords who might have practiced Luther's principle were no more. This situation enabled Szegedi to build a Christian brotherhood from the bottom upward.

As theologian, academician, and pastor-bishop, Szegedi was not only a rational man, but also a creative genius as well; more than that, he had a natural instinct for identifying with the yearnings of his compatriots. He somehow embodied the developing religious patriotism, being able to create, as it were, a psychological community based upon a common knowledge of the Christian past, always present by virtue of memory. His people had lived for centuries on a metaphysical level. The same metaphysics directed and determined their ethos for the future as well, even though it was temporarily submerged in a non-Christian, Islam environment.

Szegedi not only recognized the obvious spiritual immunity, he tried to revitalize this subconscious heritage in order to initiate a new religiosity as had been manifested in the Helvetic Confession. When he succeeded in reviving the common heritage, he brought his fellow man into the realm of cosmic freedom and to a spiritual home in Christ, the Redeemer, who would lead his followers into the Age of Redemptive History.

Within this framework, Szegedi reached his pedagogical goal and saw the emerging of individual personalities, so typical of the Protestant Reformation. His church members began to act with self-reliance, becoming able to be conscious witnesses in challenging situations. This new attitude was like that of Galileo, objected to by the Inquisitor during the trial in Rome:

> "Do you think that we are like the Protestants of whom everyone thinks according to his own mind?"

Szegedi's educational system purposefully had cultivated individualistic personalities which became visible during Szegedi's lifetime, and the remarkable aspect of his system was that in the post-feudalistic age, individuals now on a voluntary basis helped to shape the Reformed Church as well as the society.

When Szegedi assumed the responsible office of bishop, he declared immediately that he could not serve God without also serving His people. He remained as bishop always *primus inter pares*, and under his leadership reformed preachers gradually replaced the missing oligarchy with a serving spiritual aristocracy.

In 1572 the overworked *Pater Patriae* died. His co-reformer, Theodore Beza, in Geneva, reflected on Szegedi's death:

> "I firmly believe that all Christian Churches in Hungary suffered very deep wounds when those old soldiers and athletes worthy of eternal memory, Dominus Szegedi and Dominus Melius, were snatched away by death. Nevertheless through the goodness of God, lie will finally surrender to truth through those who succeed Szegedi and Melius in their labors."[3]

In final analysis, contemporary theologians should recognize Szegedi's success in re-integrating part of the Hungarian nation into the *Respublica Christiana*.

Szegedi's Theological Heritage

Szegedi is regarded by contemporary historians as the most scholarly of the Hungarian reformers. He was a prolific writer. Yet, after his death, his works were lost to posterity for a long time; it was as if he were buried deep under the books which he had issued. Amazingly, his works appear to have been gathering dust for centuries; only recently have they drawn the attention once again of scholars in Hungary.

It is difficult to explain why this negligence occurred, because in his own time he was highly regarded. Was one of the reasons that after his death a more rational Protestantism became dominant, replacing Szegedi's evangelical Biblicism after all the dogmatic disputes had ended? Or was it the voices of the Enlightenment, attempting to discredit classic Protestant writings? That was, after all, the time in which Voltaire became the exclusive voice of the new paganism, declaring that "God was needed only as a club over the heads of the masses: *'Ecraséz l'infame'* ". Of course, the Roman Catholic Index also helped to eliminate the works of the Reformers.

In connection with Szegedi's spiritual pilgrimage, it should be mentioned again that many of his books could not be published during his lifetime in Ottoman-held territory, because the invader did not allow a printing press to exist in Szegedi's bishopric. It was only after his death that Western theologians paid homage to the Hungarian reformer, publishing all his writings.

In general, Szegedi's works became quite useful to students at home as well as abroad. They could be used as practical textbooks because they offered in a simple, lucid way systematic treatments of the too scholarly and therefore too complicated theological works by other authors. Szegedi outlined a number of controversial theological books, resulting in compact editions which covered Christian ethics, religious as well as judicial and social subjects. It would demand intensive concentration on the part of modern readers to assess the importance of these condensed writings and gather rewarding contents from the still countless pages and thereby make the religious atmosphere of the sixteenth century come alive.

Since in those days the spiritual desires for nourishment were quite intense in East Central Europe, Szegedi made great efforts to furnish the necessary reformation literature by means of which he as national pedagogue intended to shape the spiritual and intellectual life of his generation.

Because Szegedi once had been called *Pater Patriae*, a small number of Hungarian theologians have begun in recent times to reintroduce Szegedi's original ideas, making them come alive as a living heritage, undergirding modern uncertain morals.[4]

Szegedi's first existential composition was born out of the Antitrinitarian (later called Unitarian) controversy. (See Chapter XIX on Ferenc Dávid.)

At the time, the Protestant Reformers attempted to reformulate the Christological doctrine, which earlier had been attacked by Erasmus and his followers and now was being distorted by the Humanist ideologists. The latter not only discredited the basic tradition of the divinity of Christ, but also attempted to divide even further the already atomized nation as the Islam infiltration was spreading. Bishop Szegedi observed how the Ottoman administrators favored the Turcophile Unitarians in his bishopric.

In 1567, Theodore Beza observed with great concern the Hungarian struggle among the Unitarian innovators, sending a circular letter to support Szegedi and Bishop Melius of Debrecen in their efforts to arrest the further development of the Unitarian movement. In addition, Beza published Szegedi's *Assertio vera de Trinitate*, which dealt with the Antitrinitarian debates. Máté Skaricza, a student of Szegedi, brought the manuscript to Geneva after Szegedi's death.

The *Assertio vera de Trinitate*, Verification of the Trinity, contained all Biblical *loci* with which the veracity of the concept of Holy Trinity could be proved. Using an apologetic approach, Szegedi first exposed the advocate of Antitrinitarian teaching, the Spanish humanist Michael Servetus, who on the basis of non-existence in Scripture of the term Trinity, concluded that the concept of Trinity was therefore highly unlikely and hence unacceptable. To show the absurdity of Servetus' argument, Szegedi pointed out that the words sacrament and *liberum arbitrium* were also non-existent in the Biblical text, yet nobody wished to get rid of them.

The original literary sources from which Servetus had borrowed his innovations from the University of Padua, where Arab-Aristotelian, Islamic, and Hebrew syncretic philosophy had replaced the Orthodox Christian dogmas, resulting in a confusing theistic dogmatism. A momentous paradox could be found in the combining of all these conflicting metaphysical ideas into a new religious universalism.

A second essay, *Confessio vera fidei de uno vero Deo*, contained a collection of scriptural texts serving as only authoritative sources of Christological theology. During the theological polemics, Szegedi had proved his talent for clear, exact definitions of religious terms. This gift he skillfully applied to his *Confessio*, first published in Basel in 1588, after which several reprints followed. With this essay, Szegedi not only showed his knowledge of Scripture, but also his exegetical skill as well. He succeeded in disproving Servetus' *loci*, which at that time were the sources of inspiration for Ferenc

Dávid, although he still held a moderate view. However, eventually Dávid reached the point where he began advocating his *nonadoramus* thesis which denied the divinity of Christ. Szegedi was successful in reducing the ambiguous terminology of Dávid and his patron, Blandrata, who intentionally made cryptic the questions to be debated.

Szegedi's *Speculum romanorum pontificum* was published in Basel in 1584. This writing may have been inspired by two events. First, the antipapal crusade led by Luther, which influenced the spiritual climate of Wittenberg, especially when Luther narrowed down the Reformation to only one problem: that of the Pope being the anti-Christ. This dark view of Rome spread over the Continent. The second event may have been the reassessment of the papal role in Western Christendom. It was expedient to point out some of the gross mistakes made by the Vicars of Christ. It was also necessary to expose Habsburg Catholicism for the harsh persecutions of Hungarian Reformers. Szegedi intended to give the persecutors a mirror, *Speculum*, which would reflect what the Roman hierarchy was doing or had done in the name of Christ.

The book was divided into four parts, two of which will be discussed here. The first part dealt with church-historical events. The dubious origin of Roman supremacy was well illustrated. Papal decrees which had been accumulating for centuries constantly exposed conflicting issues and thus discredited the authority claimed by the Holy See.

The second part of the work explained the origin of the moral and spiritual failures of the Vicars of Christ within the framework of organized religion. There was a time when several Popes were competing with one another. Szegedi depicted that in Christian domain many church as well as worldly princes had acted as anti-Christ, and that therefore Luther's stand, holding only the Popes responsible, was unacceptable. As example, Szegedi mentioned a German archbishop whose only visit to his cathedral had been when he was laid out in a coffin. Another illustration given was that of King Matthias Hunyadi (Corvinus), who had forced the Pope to give the archbishopric of Esztergom to a seven-year-old relative, who arrived in Esztergom in the company of his wet nurse.

In 1584 *Speculum romanorum pontificum* was published in Basel, in an enlarged form also as *Spiegel des weltlichen römischen Bapsttum*. Because the papal *Index* threatened even the printing companies in Protestant Basel, the name of the publisher as well as place of publication were omitted.

Szegedi had used available authentic ecclesiastical sources, be it without due criticism, and so legendary materials were included in his writing. Exposing materialistic egoism as the source of many aberrations and obvious immorality of the Renaissance Popes, he charged potential faithful Christian readers to correct the baseless papal tradition of universal power, not only in spiritual but also in worldly realms. How could the Vatican return to Christ's teachings, abolish empty ceremonies, including the medieval magical concept of the Eucharist, and omit several of the seven sacraments?

Szegedi, from a critical viewpoint narrated all the obvious historical errors of the Roman Church, attempting to explain the insidious human frailties. In the end he saw only one simple cause, that of thirst for power. Later in history Lord Acton convincingly stated that power intends to corrupt man, that absolute power absolutely corrupts him.

When Szegedi analyzed the private lives and acts of several Vicars of Christ, he observed their total lack of moral inhibition. This led the rulers of the Church to worldly power struggles; they became warriors, destructive forces, and they could never heal the antagonism existing in Christendom.

Some Popes had remained faithful to Christian ideals, as Szegedi pointed out in a quote from Pope Gregory I (604 A.D.), who complained that there was a too rapid increase in the number of saints. For instance, it was enough for a prince to become a saint if he died on Good Friday. (Before Gregory, Pope Damasus already possessed a catalog of all saints buried in secret places in the catacombs.)

Szegedi's treatment of papal history was not done in time sequence; instead he grouped together those who had common characteristics and profiles. He introduced psycho-historical explanations to mitigate the inner motives of behavior of those on the throne of St. Peter. In total his treatment was not the customary denunciation; he often used irony to expose the vanity of the Church princes.

During the sixteenth century, the Protestant controversy demanded endless rebukes, disputes, creedal confrontations in cathedrals and classrooms, in market places and in blacksmith workshops, as well as in the bars. This meant that in the literary works a constant search for an alternative had to be incorporated with improvement of a discredited Christendom in mind.

After the Tridentine Council, the Roman Catholic reformers became more aggressive; this forced the Protestant leaders to clarify their theological convictions, which eventually led to the separation of the Lutheran and Helvetic branches of Protestantism in Hungary.

Among other works of Szegedi the most noteworthy is his *Theologiae sincere loci communes de Deo et homine*, (Unadulterated theological common topics), published in Basel in 1585, later published five more times in Western theological circles.

In the preface the author explained why he called it unadulterated; his whole presentation was based exclusively on Biblical sources. He included in *Loci communes*, as it is commonly referred to, all the commonly discussed and studied theological and ecclesiastical topics of the Reformation. Philip Melanchthon, the *preceptor Germaniae*, had introduced this new literary genre in 1521 when he published his *Loci*.

Szegedi's didactical purpose, like Melanchthon's, was to produce a textbook in which all Protestant theological, church organizational, as well as ethical and social subjects were to be incorporated. When Szegedi finally finished this work, it comprised close to five hundred folio pages. The book became a Reformed encyclopedia in the hands of Hungarian as well as foreign students. The readers could discover how the industrious author systematically collected the discussed topics from the most important sources written by other Reformed theologians. The difference between Melanchthon's and Szegedi's *Loci* was that the latter had to furnish a more elaborate didactical textbook fitting Hungarian needs. Because of the vivid, understandable style, *Loci* was also made easier reading for the church laymen, who could use the book to gain information about the new religious developments.

Loci communes was divided into two principal parts. The first included theological definitions, explanations, and theories about the nature of God and His attributes; the qualitative difference between the image of God in the Old and the New Testament. In the Old Testament, God was seen as an angry, jealous, and punitive warrior; in the New His image was that of a merciful, loving, and forgiving God and as Triune God. Szegedi presented an elaborate concept of the Creator and Sustainer, probably the more so because he was deeply involved in the Antitrinitarian controversy, defending with two books the integrity of the Reformed tradition.

The second part dealt with the nature of man, his origin, destiny, his sinful inclinations, never able to redeem himself by his own will. Szegedi discussed the cultural anthropological aspect of man as co-worker in the created universe. He depicted man as one who could not know himself as long as he could not relate to his Creator, in other words, as long as he could not regain in life the *Imago Dei* which he lost in the Fall.

In his encyclopedia, the author presented all discussed subjects in *tabulae*, giving exact definition of the topics and verifying them through Biblical explanations. Thus student-readers could gain a quick overview of theological material and master the complicated topics for their examinations.

The sources which Szegedi used for *Loci communes* and from which he systematized his work included mainly the writings by Swiss reformers. His method was to quote several opinions from different authors, combining their teachings in parallel texts. Thus the reader became informed about a number of views on the subject and had the free choice to select what fitted his intellectual need; he also would be well versed in Reformed theology.

Szegedi treated the Helvetic-Calvinist authors impartially as he selected parts of their works, showing all possible options regarding the subject under discussion. The theologians whose writings were incorporated were: Wolfgang Musculus, professor in Berne, who like Szegedi was a balanced, middle-of-the-road Reformer. He had written a *Compendium*, based more or less on the thoughts of Beza regarding reform, in the meantime keeping in touch with Wittenberg. Also included were the successors of Zwingli; Heinrich Bullinger; Theodore Beza, co-worker of John Calvin; Petrus Martyr Vermigli, an Italian exulent, then at Oxford; and Philip Melanchthon of Wittenberg, a man of broad human understanding. It was natural for Szegedi to include the latter, his former inspirer. Both had begun as Roman Catholics, with the same humanistic understanding of self, and now had reached their spiritual-religious maturity in Reformed theology.

With his universal ecclesiastical knowledge and theological understanding, Szegedi was well qualified to select the topics and compile the encyclopedia for his generation in Hungary, giving the Christians a basic foundation, guiding them to a balanced stance.

When Szegedi formulated his theological views, the Protestant Reformation in Europe was not yet divided by dogmatic niggardliness and the Roman invitation to Reformers to attend the Tridentine Council still offered some hope; unfortunately the Protestants passed up this opportunity for conciliation.

When reading *Loci communes,* one is struck by the close parallels and nearly identical quotations which Szegedi compiled. One should keep in mind that this did not mean plagiary. Reformers happened to reach the same conclusion about the same topic; not surprisingly, really, because most of them had studied in Wittenberg and were there nourished and inspired by the same theological concepts.

Predestination

In *Loci* Szegedi was now forced to discuss the most controversial problem of predestination. He presented the theses of Calvin, Beza, Musculus, and Vermigli, upon which Geneva had built Reformed dogmatism. Their views were closely interwoven, yet the wordings were in conflict and obscured the identical end-conclusion, which was that in predestination good works did not count, because if they had merits they would neutralize the concept of universal sin, and no one would deserve mercy. Only God's infinite goodness and limitless love made election logical and possible via the redemptive act of Christ.

Prayer

Concerning prayer the Reformers agreed that it could take place at any time and at any place because God was omnipresent and would hear honest, unselfish petitions. The only premise was that prayer, in order to be effective, had to be offered in the name of Christ. Adversity in life was seen as an indication that the Creator warned the individual to examine his shortcomings and to repent so that mercy could be extended to him. Some specific instructions were: not to pray for the response of the dead; neither to pray with pagans, Muslims, or Jews, but rather with brethren in the faith; not to approach God with petitions to punish personal enemies, because the latter would contradict God's eternal goodness and love.

Eucharist

Focusing on the celebration of the Eucharist, Szegedi gave numerous quotations from parallel theses, describing the many sacraments which had been adopted in Old Testament times by the Temple cults; pointing out that the renewed man, growing in the knowledge of God's will, kept only two sacraments, Holy Communion and Baptism. The Reformed standpoint was that only those persons would receive the promised blessing who participated with true faith in the Lord's Supper; unbelievers would profit nothing. Szegedi explained that when Christ took bread and broke it, He symbolized that only by His grace man could be redeemed. Christ did not create an obscure ceremony; one was to eat and drink the elements in unsophisticated manner at all times and in all places of the world. Interestingly, Szegedi finally worked out his own conviction regarding the celebration and meaning of the Eucharist, as well as its role in the Reformed Church. He presented his view in the essay *Quaestiones de verbis Coenae Domini*, which was published in Zurich in 1584. In essence it was a comparative study of Lutheran and Helvetic-Calvinist concepts of the Lord's Supper, and in one hundred pages gave a thorough explanation of the original Christological roots of pre-Lutheran and post-Lutheran treatments of the topic.

When Szegedi adopted his view on Holy Communion from fellow reformers he followed in an indirect way Calvin's Eucharistic tradition, in which bread, wine, and the Rite together made valid the Reformed Holy Communion.

Baptism

The second sacrament, Baptism, was viewed as a universal offering in which Christ called the whole of mankind to Himself, to be baptized in the name of the Father, and of the Son and of the Holy Spirit. Szegedi stated that Christ did not baptize in the name of Abraham and Jacob, which would have limited the act to the Jewish tribes.

Beza had had an important Calvinistic influence upon the Reformation-theology of Szegedi and Melius. At the same time, however, Bullinger made deep inroads with his words, which were less exclusive from a dogmatic point of view. Bullinger's momentous correspondence with Hungarian and other reformers, more than twelve thousand letters, circulated among the theologians and helped them to clarify some of the over-disputed religious problems. Bullinger's goal, like that of Szegedi, was not dogmatic impurity, but Christ's Church functioning as a serving body.

Calvin had had only limited personal connections with the Hungarian Reformers, but he made a theological impact on the second generation of church leaders after Albert Szenci Molnár in 1624 published Calvin's *Institutio*.

Among several of Szegedi's short essays still worth mentioning is *Tractatus brevis de traditionibus quibusdam pontificum romanorum*, which was published in Basel in 1584. Written in dialogue, using a question and answer form, it focused on such problematical topics as purgatory, the essence of the Church of Christ, history of the popes, the papal Mass, and many other actual and popular subjects of discourse. It did not help the confused spirits of man in the post-humanistic age, as they were searching for clear answers and irenic forms of reconciliation.

The books which have been discussed here contain scholarly material which Szegedi in his capacity as professor and theologian used in teaching the younger generation. They give us a good idea of the level on which Hungarian youth of those days were being prepared to take their turn in propagating the Gospel. What was most characteristic of Szegedi was his global view and his gift of grasping with crystal clear logic the profound theological problems of the Reformation, simplifying them, so that they formed one coherent body. There was no one-sidedness in Szegedi.

When, after his death, Szegedi's works were published in the West, they succeeded in bringing his Hungarian generation closer to other religious thinkers, mainly in Switzerland and England, where his books were read.

Szegedi's final victory became reality not by worldly power or force, in spite of Habsburg Catholic and Ottoman oppression, but through intellectual excellence and deep rooted faith. Only recently it has become obvious that it was not worldly imposition through which Szegedi brought the Reformation in the life of the Hungarian people. He and his co-workers represented a special Hungarian, strongly eclectic and traditionalist variety of Reformed theological thinking, which was influenced by the special Hungarian circumstances.

Footnotes

1. Beza, Theodore. *Epistolorum Theologiarum liber unus*. Genevae, 1573. p. 21.

2. Skaricza, Máté. *Stephani Szegedini Vita*. ed. by Géza Kathona. In: *Humanizmus és Reformáció*. Akadémia Kiadó, Budapest, 1974. p. 90–144.

3. Lampe, Adolphus. *Historia Ecclesiae in Hungaria*. Utrecht, 1728. p. 262.

4. See:
Kathona, Géza. *Fejezetek A Török Hodoltsági Reformácio Történetböl.* Budapest, 1974. Akadémia Kiadó. p. 145–189.

Toth, William. Stephen Kis of Szeged, Hungarian Reformer. *Archiv für Reformationsgeschichte, Jhg 44.* 1953. Heft. I, p. 86–102.

Bucsay, Mihály. *Szegedi Kis István. Speculuma.* In: *Studia et Acta Ecclesiastica.* Budapest, 1973. Vol. III. p. 103.

Chapter XI

Gáspár Károlyi
"The Godly Old Man"
± 1520–1591

In the sixteenth century, which was truly the century of the revolution caused by that "strange" book, many new translations came into being during the years of the Reformation in Hungary. Of these, the work of Gáspár Károlyi, the "godly old man", as he was called, was the most important.

Preceding him, Benedek Komjáthy, court priest, had translated the letters of St. Paul, which became the first book printed in Hungarian. Komjáthy was a Hungarian of strong Catholic faith, who fled the Turks and found refuge in castles which, at that time, took in persecuted scholars of various nations. One of these, Paulus Ruthenus, professor at the Polish University of Cracow, described how these castles became meeting places for humanist followers of Erasmus. The lady of the castle of Nyaláb supported Komjáthy while he studied in Vienna where his book was published in 1533. Komjáthy based his work on the text of Erasmus, which he cross-checked with the Vulgate. Like a good Catholic, he finished his translation on "The evening of St. George's Day, at the pealing of bells for high-Mass."

Naturally, Komjáthy also used earlier Hungarian translations, from which he developed a single compilation. As a translator, he wrote: "I read and followed many holy doctors." His translations were strongly influenced by and became urgent because of the continual conquests of the Turks and their violent proselytizing. According to Komjáthy, God had "sent the pagans with topknots to punish us for our sins." He wanted to console the suffering Hungarian people with the Holy Scriptures. This reason for translating the Bible was unique in Europe, yet it was very real, because the master of the castle of Nyaláb himself had lost his life fighting the Turks in the battle of Mohács.

After Komjáthy's compilation, many new and revised translations of the Scriptures were published by Protestant presses. These included the outstanding New Testament one by János Szilveszter, professor of Hebrew at the University of Vienna; those of the Unitarian minister Gáspár Heltai; and the Protestant Péter Melius Juhász. Heltai's translation was not popular, because he had been in turn Catholic, Lutheran, Calvinist, and finally Unitarian. Although Melius' translation was the most original, he could not finish it, because as a Bishop, he was wholly occupied with the organization of the church. Furthermore, he died young in 1572. After several attempts to publish a complete Bible, Gáspár Károlyi finally succeeded. Only after long and arduous decades spent organizing the church could this "godly old man" take the time to achieve the great goal of his life.

The struggle to produce the Hungarian Bible went on in the clamorous search for God that lasted the entire sixteenth century. This bitter religious struggle was ended by Gáspár Károlyi, then Reformed superintendent. His character fitted him for the role he played in church history. He could view the struggles of his time from the perspective of centuries, and rising far above the embittering conflict of dogmas, he could leave them behind to interpret the eternal word for his people. Hungary is indeed indebted to Károlyi for making the Bible truly a book of the people.

Hungarian Protestantism has its carefully preserved memories in the area of historic relations between Poland and Hungary. Many theologians went to Cracow in the first decades of Hungarian Protestantism. The Hungarian religious reform did not start out from Wittenberg, but from the north, in the humanist reforms of Poland. Only when Martin Luther's dramatic struggle radicalized religious reform did Hungarian students go to Wittenberg in great numbers.

Luther was undoubtedly Europe's most successful translator of the Bible; he based his religious and cultural system entirely on the Holy Scriptures. As a reformer, he established a school to which generations of Bible translators flocked from the entire Protestant world.

The Hungarians, however, modified the tradition of Luther. In contrast to Luther, who based his work on the Hebrew text and on the German language, the Hungarian reformers included the Latin text in their textual analysis. The works based on Latin sources were prepared with the highly developed methods of humanist philology, and enjoyed great prestige in the debates with Bible translators of various denominations.

Károlyi's rendition of the entire Bible was made possible by the fact that Bishop Péter Melius Juhász consolidated the Calvinistic (Helvetic) Church in northeastern Hungary. The theological trends, previously in a state of transition, slowly crystallized, and the dogmas took on their final forms. As a result, the reformed religion of the One Book could become an established system. The translation became official, backed by theological authority.

Preliminaries: Luther's Battle with the Hebraists

In order to understand the background of Károlyi's Bible translation later on, one has to look at the Wittenberg tradition which Luther began. In the beginning, Luther had based his Biblical literary work on the writings and teachings of the rabbinical experts in Hebrew. When he grew in knowledge, however, he became acquainted with the authentic text of the Bible and the correct interpretation of the cultural terms in the Scriptures, realizing that the Hebraists were giving a false interpretation. The post-Biblical Hebrew literature itself was rampant with anti-Christian interpretations which the German scholar, Räuchlin, who was otherwise pro-Semitic, scornfully called "Patched up Jesus."

Earlier, Nicolaus de Lyra, on whose *Disputatio contra perfidiam Judaeorum* Luther had relied, had emphatically pointed out that many heretical or anti-Christian views were included in the Hebrew writing. For this reason, Lyra considered the rabbinical commentaries harmful from a theological point of view. They proclaimed the Christian teachings of the Holy Trinity, the pre-existing Redeemer, and the doctrine of original sin, among others, to be absurd.

The Jewish religious leaders of the time were well aware of Luther's revolutionary significance; so at first they rushed to support and influence him. As a result, dubious Hebrew interpretations had slipped into Luther's exegesis. The Hebraists' previous attempts at undermining the credibility of the Vulgate were self-evident. They considered Luther's appearance on the scene a good opportunity; thus, they hastened to disseminate Luther's writings in every territory of the Church, including Jerusalem.[1]

Parallel to this, the Marranos, Spanish and Portuguese Jews converted to Roman Catholicism, infiltrated the Christian churches and transformed the churches' dogmas with their own new interpretations. The Spanish Marranos who were living in Amsterdam gave huge amounts of money to send Luther's writings to Spain. Their goal was to undermine the Catholic hierarchy that had once driven them out.[2]

It slowly dawned on Luther that this support of dubious value led to similar distortions to which leaders of the older Hussite sect must have succumbed. During the acrimonious disputes the question arose: Who had tampered with the old Hebrew texts that the translators of Alexandria had used, and when did this happen? During these disputes, Luther accused his opponents outright of trying to distort the texts of the Scriptures for the second time.[3] Then he summed up his bitter accusations: "Those Hebraists made gossip out of the Holy Scriptures."[4] "I will write a new introduction to the Bible in which I am going to warn readers not to believe the rabbis, for they are blind."[5] "These rabbis by and large falsified the Biblical texts with their marginal notes and glosses . . . . This is rubbish! Accordingly, we simply throw it out . . . ."[6]

Károlyi's Background

Like most reformers, who frequently came from a privileged class, Gáspár Károlyi was a member of a Hungarian noble family. He was born in Nagykároly around 1520. He studied for some time at the University of Cracow in Poland,*before going to Wittenberg, where he studied under Philip Melanchthon. Later, he continued his wide-ranging studies at universities in Switzerland as well as at the University of Strasbourg. He proved exceptionally adept at foreign languages. He learned Hebrew and German in addition to the classical languages.

His first teacher of Hebrew was Johannes Forster (±1558), who introduced a new method of teaching grammar and who compiled a new Biblical dictionary. Using this dictionary, he eliminated from Christian religious literature the tendentious distortions which had crept in when rabbis had

---

* Already in the fifteenth century, one fourth of the student body at the University of Cracow, that is, 2300 students, were Hungarian

helped Luther with translations of Scriptures. By the time Károlyi arrived in Wittenberg, the battle over the translation of the Bible had ceased.

Károlyi's Ecclesiastical Policy

After the death of Forster in 1558, Paul Eber, linguist from Wittenberg, became the greatest scholarly influence on Károlyi. In addition to Eber's knowledge of Hebrew, his historical view, based on the Bible, decisively influenced Károlyi's world view. On returning to Hungary after his years of study, Károlyi vividly recalled the literary debates that took place in Wittenberg. Soon his own experiences convinced him that the tendentious rabbinical explanations and post-Biblical Hebrew codices were two of the sources of the Reformation's inner conflicts. For this reason, but perhaps also to avoid Luther's mistakes in exegesis, he used, in addition to the Greek and Hebrew texts, various Latin translations, including the Vulgate.

When Károlyi returned from his studies in western universities he stepped into the middle of Hungary's chaotic life of war and domestic conflict. He was driven by the Turks into the city of Szatmár, which had been under siege for a long time. With the help of the defender of the castle, he escaped from Szatmár in 1562 and went to the city of Gönc in northeast Hungary to take up his duties as pastor.

During the second half of the sixteenth century, the Hungarian nobility, one after another, left the Roman Catholic Church, and by taking the Protestant preachers under their wings, they decisively helped to spread the Reformation. They opened the way for Gáspár Károlyi to begin and extend his missionary work throughout a large part of the country.

Károlyi belonged to the second reformed generation. To these fell the task of consolidating the framework and results of the Reformation and systematizing the new creed.

In this period the religious ideas and theological trends in conflict with each other were still in ferment, but slowly the Helvetic tenet replaced the doctrines of Luther and Zwingli. Before he had left Wittenberg, Károlyi had clarified his own fundamental principles and had adopted eclectically from the Helvetic teaching. Under the leadership of Károlyi as superintendent, the council convoked at Tarcal promulgated the religious doctrines of Calvin and Beza. Relying on these doctrines, he reorganized in 1562 the church district that extended through the area of three former Catholic bishoprics.

From then on, Károlyi was in such constant feverish activity that he no longer had time for a private life. As superintendent of his church district, as writer creating the literature of religious disputes, as leader of the council debates, and as apologist fighting Antitrinitarians, he lived at an almost superhuman pace, devoting his whole life to his calling. His work as church organizer was no longer hampered by the former Roman Catholic leaders, but by marauding Turkish troops who constantly broke into the church districts, often destroying what he had built with such enthusiastic devotion. One after another, the Turks captured the newly organized congregations and their pastors, and demanded crushing ransoms. The surviving populations of the impoverished cities and villages often had to suffer the loss of their loved ones, for they could not pay the demanded sums. One day, the Turks took Károlyi's brother-in-law, hoping in this way to regain the pay lost to them by the embezzlement of corrupt Turkish military leaders. Károlyi was unable to fulfill their demands and had to ask his landlord for a loan.*

While he was expanding his church in the northeast region, he built up his own congregation in Göncz. The population of Göncz was made up largely of refugees from the Turkish invasion, similar to Calvin's Geneva whose population was tripled by Western Protestant refugees, who had arrived en masse. City government was also similar to that of Geneva. Thus the lay city leaders and the servants of the church acted in the city's social and church life as equals. His growing congregation slowly became an example akin to the democratic system of the Old Testament. This history-making dynamism definitely assured the future of Protestantism in Hungary. In that dangerous century, the pastor had to merge with his congregation if he wanted to keep and protect his flock.

As a reformer, Karolyi had to assume the duties of the State, which was no longer functioning. Consequently, he had to institute a new cultural policy including a school system through which a new generation would be raised that would further promote Protestantism. Károlyi sent his schoolmasters to foreign universities, thereby later providing Hungary with scholars thinking in European patterns. It was from these that he subsequently selected the assistants he needed to translate the Bible.

---

*Sometimes a whole congregation was deported by Turkish raiders and sold in the slave market of Constantinople (Istanbul).

Károlyi's Personal Life

Facts concerning Károlyi's personal life are scarce since he left no diaries, no journals,* and because his constant public work limited his private pursuits. The little information we have recounts a succession of family tragedies. His activities as church leader were often interrupted by the death of his loved ones. The epidemics of the century that struck again and again took six of his children and two of his wives. He married three times. (It is interesting to note that his contemporaries married an average of three times.) Ever present death and tribulation can be attributed to the havoc wreaked by the burning of cities and villages, by movement of soldiers, by the interruption in the training of doctors, by the destruction of the monastery hospitals, above all by the prevalence of black plague and cholera, as well as *Morbus Hungaricus.*

Every piece of information on the life of Károlyi indicates that he lived an austere, conscientious, and intrepid life as pastor, church-organizer, reformer, and head of his family. He was a humble believer. In his faith and his lifestyle, he resembled the great reformer of Geneva, Calvin. An interesting disciplinary procedure demonstrates how brave and uncompromising he was.

In one of the cities belonging to the church district, the leaders of the city brought a very mild judgment on a murderer, even though canon law punished murder by death. (Public life, brutalized by the wars, made this merciless severity necessary.) When the city leaders ignored Károlyi's warning, he excluded them from the sacraments. When even this proved futile, he put the entire city under interdiction. For months, the bells did not call the faithful to service, did not warn them to repent. Thereupon, the stubborn city officials turned to the king with their complaints. The Catholic Habsburg monarch began to inquire by what right this heretic superintendent passed judgment in his royal domain. The problem was solved by the murderer's unexpected death. The banning itself reflected the barely dimmed traditions of the Roman Catholic Church. We have numerous records of similar cases in the early Protestant period.

The hectic, wearying lifestyle of the sixteenth century soon undermined Károly's energy, producing the characteristic description "the godly old man." Many biographical data indicate that life of most preachers came to

---

*As far as is known.

an unexpected, often premature end. Church history cannot always account
for how and when their lives closed, whether by persecution, Turkish
captivity, or plagues.

Károlyi's character was tempered by that tragic period. He became an
authentic example for succeeding generations: he suffered for his faith; he
was persecuted because he served the people in the anarchy of the feudal
period, times that "turned the hair of the young grey."

It may be noted that the life story and personalities of most of the
Hungarian reformers who preceded him were incomparably more interesting than their literary legacies.

There was a kind of daring vitality reminiscent of the knights of old in
these reformers. As they returned from the foreign scenes of their student
days, from Wittenberg and Geneva, preaching the new creed that was
causing such an upheaval, they fought, like the Greeks at Marathon, hoping
against hope, against what Hungarian chroniclers of the time called two
pagans, the Moslem Turks and the Habsburg Catholics.

These preachers were not bound to a single congregation. They were at
home everywhere they could preach the Word. Prison was a kind of
preparation for them. These tireless men incarnated the new human ideal
of the sixteenth century. It was no longer an empty respect for authority
that kept these souls to their faith, but personal conviction. They knew from
experience that even if they should lose everything, they still had what was
of greatest value, autonomy in faith.

Károlyi's Writings

Károlyi gave this self-preserving value to the people by making the Bible
a popular book.

As long as the cathedral-building medieval Catholic church restricted
itself to preaching the living Word, the people remained a passive audience.
The reformers changed this with the vernacular Bible, whose text was
constant and universal, and which the people could read for themselves. In
reading this Book, everyone could be a minister to himself and to his fellow
men.

There were a relatively large number of printed books in Károlyi's
Hungary. More than once, the Bible was ordered from foreign presses in
tens of thousands of copies. The dissemination of ideals was not the

exclusive province of the Roman Catholic hierarchy; the faithful had to acquire personal faith in their own way in order to obtain salvation. This universal spiritual need was one of the causes that led to Károlyi's translation of the entire Bible. This work had the greatest effect on the intellectual and spiritual life of Hungary in the sixteenth century. His translation helped bring about the religious synthesis between Western Protestants and the Hungarian people of East Central Europe.

The "strange Book" was the main literature of the century, and any literature outside of it was only an instrument to serve the faith. New in this literature was a social outlook. Thus, lay religiosity was expressed in various ways, and the Word preached to the people resounded through Protestant literature. It produced the historical principle of popular Puritanism that shaped morals and reconstructed society.

Károlyi's confessions indicate that, as apologist and church organizer, he always sensed the transience of his work, and felt the need for a Hungarian translation of the complete Bible. While working to save the souls of his flock, he realized that the Eternal Word was the only answer to earthly despair. In identifying the fate of his own countrymen with the persecuted of the Old Testament, he discovered that the fate of the Hungarians paralleled the tragic history of the Jews. From the Scriptures, he gathered the message for his own age: repentance and humility before God. In his prose writings, notably his two-volume philosophy of history, *Two Books (Két Könyv)*, this Christian consciousness of guilt deepened into an historical view.[7]

The *First Book* is the justification of God in history, a *theodicea*. It demonstrates that the deterioration of the country and the presence of evil was not God's will, but punishment for idol-worship and the sins of many. Following the tradition of the Protestant apocalyptic literature, the *Second Book* tells of the approaching end of the world.

These books of historical philosophy speak of the period's Turkish problem: God punishes the idol-worshipping Christians by inflicting the infidel Turks on them. Accordingly, history is not blind, but is directed by God. The philosophy of the books is defined by Biblical truth. God armed the Turks against the Hungarians; thus, the sultan is the instrument of God's punishment.

Károlyi listed the sins that had aroused God's wrath. God did not give a country to a people, not even to the Jews, to be theirs forever, no matter how they lived. Every king should read God's Book and act accordingly. At his coronation, the king should be given a Bible. The clergy should warn him when he erred, for God gave the people into his hands to be looked after. Károlyi admonished the ruler:

> "There is no end to the great cruelty, to the plunder, to the spilling of innocent blood. The poor are skinned . . . like cattle led to slaughter. If you want gold, you open your mouth before the poor . . . . If you build a house or castle, you build it with the blood of the poor . . . there is no end to your music-making, singing, dancing, and feasting."[8]

The open proclamation of this sense of social responsibility in the age of aristocrats, sunk in the anarchy of feudalism, served the cause of social justice. Gáspár Károlyi was not propagating class warfare; he was preaching the prerequisites based on God's Word for healing the human and social ills of the age. In his books one finds an insight into his incomparably vast knowledge of the Bible and his mastery of the Bible's style, and can understand that these books were written by one who would later become the celebrated Bible translator.

Károlyi saw historiography not as an end in itself, but as a means to serve theology. This concept descends from St. Augustine's historical teachings. In this view, the interpretation of the Turk as the scourge of God, *Turca Dei Flagellum*, was logically incorporated. Károlyi, the prophet proclaiming the rigorous consistency of God's universal order, openly rebuked the Hungarians for their sins and announced the menacing truth:

> "For the nation or kingdom that will not serve you will perish; it will be utterly ruined." (Isaiah 60:12)

This Biblical quotation constituted the essence of the theodicy of history, that the punishment of church and lay authorities who trampled on the law was inevitable.

Károlyi's prophecy was spoken to Hungarians: Behind the tragedy of Mohács was the profaned God and His violated law. From this view flowed an optimistic summary, "The Turks may rage, but they cannot rule the conquered peoples of East Central Europe for long if the souls convert to the reformed spirit. The Turk's punitive mission will end soon, because the

Gospel will be propagated by the Reformation. Thus, the Turk is not so much an enemy as a tool, as a teacher to the disobedient people."

His hopeful warning was: "Hungarians are solely responsible for God's inflicting the pagans on us. If we had been penitent, God would have spared us His wrath."

It is necessary to bring in this brief commentary on *Two Books* because this text became the historical and world view of the Sixteenth Century Hungarian Reformers. Their psychology and national mission would be incomprehensible without it.

While organizing the church, and carrying on religious polemics, Károlyi recognized the historical phenomenon that, after undergoing long and bitter struggles and chaos, every generation longs for a peaceful life and spiritual shelter from which authority bans the doubts of the age. Consequently, he retired from the noisy world and "built a mighty fortress" by effecting the complete and up-to-date translation of the Bible. He wrote with puritan modesty:

> "As God and my clear conscience are my witness, my only purpose in accomplishing this work was to respect God and build His house. Everyone is allowed to brings gifts to God's house. Others can bring gold or silver; I bring what I have: the complete Bible in Hungarian."

(in Introduction to the Bible)

His patrons were filled with a similar spirit of humility; they did not allow him to mention their names in the introduction in exchange for their material support. What a contrast to the pomp and vanity of the Catholic humanists, to whom fame was the central concern! A few decades earlier, this same attitude was reflected in the role of numerous "lame-souled humanists." Károlyi stated in the preface to his work: "I wrote this translation for three years, expending every effort and wrote at great haste, often sighing: If only God would give me the strength and spiritual health to finish this work."

The Bible of Vizsoly

His plea was heard, and the completed work was printed in 1590 in Vizsoly.

He accomplished the great undertaking with few co-workers, scholars and preachers all, who were living within his jurisdiction. Károlyi translated the New Testament himself, but, for the Old Testament received help in preparing the notes, writing the glosses, and chiefly in solving technical problems.

Once translated, the Book had to be published and defended. Many highranking aristocratic families helped him in this. He wrote joyfully that these families had constantly urged the publication of his work. Respecting the solemn nature of the printing, the type was ordered from Germany with great care; this was neither simple, nor easy, nor lacking in danger. The Habsburgs prohibited the importation of Bibles, and the Roman Catholic authorities forbade their publication. To circumvent these prohibitions, one of the Hungarian Protestant nobles had constructed next to an old church a separate building where the press and the publications were hidden.

At this time, the Counter-Reformation of Trent had begun. The Tridentine Council asked the Catholic Habsburg monarch to forbid the operation of all presses in Hungary. Exception was made only for those supervised by the Jesuits. However, in northeastern Hungary where Károlyi's church district was located, the Protestant nobles could protect his activities, even if it meant openly opposing Habsburg power.

It must be mentioned that due to the feverish haste in which the work was done there were flagrant omissions, particularly in the New Testament. The marginal notes, for example, were not printed. One of the reasons for this could have been the threat from royal power, but another reason must have been that overwork and constant tension wore Károlyi out and affected his accomplishment. His colleagues often must have heard him praying to his Creator to give him the time and strength to finish his undertaking. The year after the Bible was published in Vizsoly, he died.

The Bible, divided into three parts, left the presses in folio size. The first two contained the Old Testament, the third the New. In these not only the authorized, but the apocryphal books were also included, in verse form. Each individual part was preceded by a brief summary of contents. Explanation of the words and meanings could be found on the margins.

The translator also listed the basic texts he had used. Naturally, he was already acquainted with the previous Hungarian partial translations; he compared them with the original texts, having in his grasp Hebrew, Greek, and Latin. In addition to the official Vulgate of the Roman Catholic Church, he used contemporary Latin translations of the Dominican Santes Paganinus (d. 1541), the Septuagint; the explanatory text of the Parisian

Professor, Franciscus Vatablus (d. 1552); the translations of the Hebraists, Sebastian Műnster (d. 1552); and the Latin Bible of the converted Jew, Immanuel Tremellius, professor of Heidelberg; and many Latin-Greek translations of Calvin's successor, Theodore Beza, whom a critic considered to be the best Protestant translator of the Bible. English theologians also considered Beza to be the greatest church thinker of the age.

Remarkably enough, Károlyi left out the German translations of Luther. Perhaps, he remembered the disputes between Luther and the Hebraists and thus relied exclusively on the original texts. On the whole, modern criticism considers his translation to be on the general level of the linguistic and exegetical scholarship of the age. His work is not free from linguistic mistakes and at times, the language is strange due to the influence of Latin. But with respect to the most essential thing, fidelity to the text, there are no conspicuous deficiencies.

Tremellius had a particularly strong influence on Károlyi's translation of the Old Testament. The summaries preceding the books indicate this. Theodore Beza's Greek and Latin translations must have influenced Károlyi's New Testament. During the Reformation, Beza's renditions exerted a great influence on the French Bible (1588) as well as on the English Authorized Version published in 1611. In this manner, Károlyi's Hungarian Bible was connected through Beza to Western Bible publications.

This "godly old man", committed to a faithful, clear, and easy-to-understand interpretation of the texts, instinctively turned to the language of the people. He used their expressions and sayings liberally, influencing later secular literature. Without being made official by his Church as Luther's Bible was, Károlyi's was in common use, not only among the Helvetic, Lutheran, Unitarian creeds, but also among later Protestant ones. Its quick dissemination led to the publication of a new edition in 1596, but this had to be done abroad due to the prohibitions in Hungary; it was also published in 1608 in a revised edition.

To this day, it is the most popular book in Hungary. It has reached three hundred editions. The living Hungarian language, the developing literature, and the modern way of thinking owe much to the life work of the faithful translator.[9]

The mistakes in translation did not spring from an inadequate knowledge of Hebrew, but from insufficient knowledge of cultural history. In the sixteenth century, Bible translators of the West struggled with this, too; even Beza was no exception.

Károlyi's rendition was strongly influenced by his Christological conceptions. Thus, references to Christ, both in the Old and New Testament, were included in the marginal notes, confirming the coming of the Redeemer and the fulfillment of the prophecies. At the same time, he recognized the difference between the Old and the New Testament, and the corruption of the text due to carelessness. Károlyi cited St. Jerome's confessions concerning his own mistakes in the Vulgate. Learning from this, he adhered with the utmost precision to his ancient text, the Masserata. One can note that in terms of accuracy, he excelled Jerome's translation.

He was, moreover, driven by the religious-educational goal of giving in his translation scriptural proofs to the children of the Reformation. He wanted to teach and build and not dissertate on angelology, but give direction to the new congregations that had just been converted and were on their way to becoming literate. He said that there were customs and ceremonies in the Old Testament which were no longer binding on the people of the New. Károlyi often illustrated the complex theological, Biblical, and religious questions with easy-to-understand examples, and since Bible translation was not a literary problem but primarily a theological one, his very translation was in itself a kind of reformation. His exegetical evaluation, the summaries, and thousands of marginal notes, are undoubtedly on a very high scholarly level.[10]

The Hungarians of the sixteenth century who accepted the Bible realized that their history merging with that of Europe coincided exactly with the history of the Old Testament.

Continually a persecuted minority, the Hungarian Protestant Church went through frequent self-revisions, always inspired by the Bible. Every generation had to achieve something of Christ's teachings; this inspired and promoted a constant demand for dynamic development. Where else could the Hungarian people, non-European in origin, turn in their geographical and racial solitude during those blood-soaked centuries, if not to the source of Eternal Life?

Neighboring peoples were less infused with the revolutionary spirit of Protestantism that transformed society and culture. Some kept faith with Greek-Eastern Orthodoxy where there was no Bible-centered tradition. Others, the northern and western neighboring peoples, withdrew from the

Reformation and returned to the Roman Catholic Church. As a result, the Bible did not become a popular book to the same extent as it did with Hungarians, possibly, at least in part, because of the policy of persecution by Habsburg Catholicism. (This policy eventually forced Károlyi's Bible to be published abroad, it had to be smuggled in,[11] and there was always danger of confiscation.)

But the Hungarians rejected all these influences, relied wholly on the Word of God.

We should not be surprised then, when, even today, according to the statistics of comparative Bible translations, the British Bible Society printed and distributed (since the Society's inception) 4,5000000 copies of the Bible in Hungary.

All of these were in a revised Károlyi translation. As a result of his old style and use of the Hungarian language, his rendition became identified with the Word. Currently, the number of copies put into circulation every year exceeds 60,000. The original Károlyi Bible was re-issued in Hungary in two volumes in 1981. This edition, satisfying the most demanding taste of bibliophiles in terms of technique and bookbinding, created a sensation and was almost sold out by pre-publication orders. To this very day, the demand for Bibles among Protestants in Hungary far exceeds that of neighboring countries.[12]

The Fate of the Hungarian Bibles

Catholicism defended itself against the spirit and religious aspirations of the new age "as against cattle-plague or black plague," by completely closing down the borders. Indeed, Habsburg Catholics printed an Index (list of forbidden books). This, too, was soon put on index, because if it were to become widely known, the people of the Empire would realize which books were worth reading. The severity of the persecution was illustrated by the fact that up to the middle of the nineteenth century, sixty percent of three hundred editions of the Bible were published in foreign countries, chiefly the Netherlands and England. The foreign publishers frequently fared badly with their Bible publications, for their consignments were often confiscated.

That the Bible became a rare and valuable possession is demonstrated by this council decree:

"At a meeting of the council in the Year of Our Lord 1629, the church fathers ordered that every pastor has to have his Bible. If he has a *suba** and no Bible, he must sell his *suba* and buy a Bible. If he has neither *suba* nor Bible, he can no longer remain a pastor."[13]

But even more typical of the age is the secret report to the Pope, (before the Counter-Reformation took place), in which the author was forced to acknowledge: "In Hungary, there is only one Roman Catholic for every one thousand Protestants." Thus, the prohibition, burning, and confiscation of Scriptures had to become the main concern of the Holy See.

Naturally, the "other pagan", the Muslim Turk, joined the Bible-destroying campaign. When four thousand copies of Károlyi's Bible were printed in the city of Nagyvárad, Turkish troops seized them and together with the press, destroyed the translation, of which ten thousand copies had been planned.[14]

Another example is found in the following: The city of Debrecen, called the "Calvinist Rome", ordered five thousand copies of the Bible from the Netherlands. The printing was accomplished in two years (1717–1719). The Bibles were sent in casks as if they were wine. They travelled around Germany a year until they reached the Polish-Hungarian border. The Austrian customs officials discovered the secret of the casks; they immediately notified the Viennese authorities and locked up the unique shipment.

When the city of Debrecen found out about it, referring to the laws of the country, they asked that the goods be released and sent on their way. The chancellery asked the bishop of that border region to investigate. The bishop, however, delegated the right of examination to Jesuit theologians. This took ten years. After a very thorough exegetical examination, the Jesuit theologians asked that the Scriptures be confiscated for the following reasons:

1) This translation did not contain the apocryphal books.
2) The formula of baptism was not the same as that in the Roman Catholic text (Matthew 28:19).

The original formula of baptism was "In the name of the Father and of the Son and of the Holy Spirit." In the Dutch edition, the formula said: "*to*

---

*Suba - a wide sheep-skin coat reaching the heels.

the name of the Father and the Son and the Holy Spirit." Consequently, the examiners asked:

> "Let His Majesty, the Habsburg ruler, order the burning of these books, dangerous in every way, subversive to the State, the ruling house, the Roman Catholic Church, to public morals, to social order and peace."[15]

The Bishop of Eger did not even wait for permission, but burned most of the Bibles.

The city of Debrecen and the leaders of Western Protestant countries protested this Bible-burning malevolence to the government in Vienna. The people of Debrecen explained to Vienna why they were forced to have Hungarian Bibles published abroad, asserting that only a single mistake had been made by Dutch printers, who could not speak Hungarian, namely using "baptizing *to* the name of the Father and of the Son and of the Holy Spirit," instead of *in*. (Matthew 28:19)

Debrecen promised to correct the errors when they received the books, whereupon the royal chancellery allowed the unburned Bibles to be shipped to Debrecen with the warning that insofar as this correction was not done, those who ordered the Bible would be beheaded and their property confiscated.

Yet the Bishop of Eger refused to hand the books over to Debrecen. He called together the priests, nuns, and lay congregations of his diocese and solemnly burned the remaining Bibles in their presence. He justified his action by saying:

> "I would rather pay the expenses, but I will not tolerate heretical writings in this country."

The wrangling over this case lasted until 1754, or thirty-six years, in a period which Habsburg-Catholic historians proudly called the age of Enlightenment.

Károlyi's Death

What happened to the ashes of Gáspár Károlyi, the "godly old man'? When in 1591, his body returned to dust, and his soul to his Creator, his body was buried in the crypt of Vizsoly. During the Counter-Reformation, his consecrated workshop was seized and his grave disappeared. Even in this, he suffered a fate similar to that of John Calvin, whose remains rest in an unmarked grave.

When Károlyi's spirit "returned to the Chief Shepherd of saintly souls," his lifework continued, because his translation, in a million copies, taught the merciful love of God. Thus, he helped bring peace and beauty to his sorrow-filled nation. Even during his lifetime, the "godly old man" was called the "living Bible." After his death, this became really true.

Károlyi's significance in church history is that, through that "strange book," the Eternal God speaks to Hungarians in their own language.

Footnotes

1. Lewin, R. *Luthers Stellung zu den Juden*. Leipzig, 1911. pp. 18,19.

2. Brieger, T. *Aleander und Luther*. 1521. *Quellen und Forschungen zur Geschichte der Reformation*. Gotha, 1884. p.h25, p. 80.

3. Lewin, R. *op. cit.*, p. 57 ff.

4. Newman, L. I. Jewish Influence on Christian Reform Movements. New York: AMS Press, 1966.

5. Luther, Martin. Concerning the Jews and Their Lies. in *Werke*. 1542. Weimar Ausgabe, 1883 cf.

6. Luther, Martin. Concerning the Ineffable Name. 1543. *Werke*, WA 53. p. 417. Table Talk, English translation, Vol. 54. Philadelphia: Fortress Press, 1967.

7. Károlyi, Gáspár. *Két Könyv*, Debrecen, 1563. RMK. Magyar Nemzeti Museum, Budapest. p. 77.

8. Károlyi, Gáspár. *ibid.*, p. 105.

9. Dán, Robert. *Humanizmus, Reformácio, Antitrinitárizmus és a héber nyelv Magyarországon*. Budapest: Akadémia Kiadó, 1973. p. 65.

10. Kallay, K. *A vizsolyi Biblia otestamentumi részeinek exagetikai értéke Károlyi Emlékkönyv*. ed. B. Vasady. Budapest, 1941. p. 91.

11. Czegledi, S. *A Bibliafordítás kellékei és feltételei*, RMK. p. 164.

12. Farrar, W. F. History of Interpretation. London: 1886. p. 505.

13. Zsilinszky, M. *Magyar Protestáns Egyház története*. Budapest, 1907. p. 505.

14. Révész-Biró-Bucsay. *A Magyar Református Egyház Története*. Budapest, 1949. p. 149.

15. Révész-Biró-Bucsay. *ibid.*, p. 164.

Chapter XII

The Reformation Among the Saxons in Hungary

It is a fact that the Saxons dwelling in Hungary were the first to be awakened to the significance of the religious events which were taking place. This was inevitable because their language was German and ties with Germany existed. The names of the first two students who managed to go to Wittenberg were Baumhaeckel, a Saxon, and Cziraky, a Hungarian. In 1522 both were studying under Martin Luther.

Thus the Saxons were the ones who opened a path for the new religious development in Hungary. They also provided the first martyr, Andrew Fischer, whom an intolerant Catholic nobleman hurled down from a fortress wall. (Later it became clear that Fischer had not been a Lutheran, but an Anabaptist!)

Among the Reformers of upper Hungary was Johann Stoeckel, a follower of Melanchthon, who was given by the Saxons no less proud a name than that of *Praeceptor Hungariae*. He was also a disciple of Leonard Cox, who came to settle in Hungary and established a school there. By 1530, Stoeckel was studying in Wittenberg. He had spent seven years there before he was called back to his fatherland where he established his own school, which was also to be the subject of his first book, *Leges scholae Barthphensis*. Stoeckel's educational system was built upon the leading humanist principles of teaching then prevailing in Hungarian schools, but he enlivened them by adding the new pedagogical ideas of Protestantism. In Stoeckel's College, where the everyday language was Latin, Hungarian, German, and Greek languages and literatures were taught. Disputations were the order of the day.

This modern educator was the first to formulate the creed of the Saxons, which was called *Confessio Pentapolitana* (Confession of the Five [Saxon] Cities). In 1548 it was followed by the *Confessio Heptapolitana*, adopted by the leaders of the new religious movement in all the seven Saxon cities of upper Hungary.[1] These creeds faithfully interpreted Luther and Melanchthon, as we may read from the introductory sentence:

> "Those articles of the Christian Faith ought to be observed and taught that are contained in the Augustana Confession and those that in the Commonplaces of Philip are proposed and added, in the same form and order as they are to be found here."[2]

When King Ferdinand I, prodded by the Archbishop, finally asked the Saxon cities for declarations about their Protestant faith, they answered merely by quoting the Augustana Confession, which had been acknowledged as legal by the Diet of Augsburg in 1555, presided over by King Ferdinand I. The Saxons made clear that they wanted nothing else but what was believed and confessed by their German brothers in the faith.

During the sixteenth century the Saxon cities did not actually suffer much from the Habsburg Court which was trying to win them over as allies against the Hungarians propagating the Helvetic faith. When occasionally the Catholic Primate of Hungary attempted to bring them back to his flock, they defied him so that the Primate no longer had a private army.

In his *Church History*, Borbis describes the situation of the Saxons as follows:

> "We should not assume that the Catholic clergy always kept its bitter enmity against those confessors of the Lutheran doctrine; we are told that up to the year 1552, [the year in which the Saxons overwhelmingly adopted the Lutheran faith] there existed a fraternity of both Catholic priests and Lutheran pastors the Senior of which fraternity was elected now from among Catholics, then from Lutherans, provided these latter remained faithful to the Augustana Confession, and did not let themselves be seduced by the doctrines of the hated Sacramentarians—Zwingli and Calvin. Thus in the years 1558 and 1560 the Archbishop of Gran, Primate of Hungary, Nicolaus Olahus-Olah, himself agreed to the Augustana Confession."[3]

That suggests that if some Saxons became martyrs, they very probably came from those groups who deviated toward the Helvetic or Anabaptist tendencies.

Church historian Révész has tried to explain this fact as follows:

"A serious gulf of political difference began to open between the Lutheran Germans of Hungary and the pure Hungarian elements. The former, and that both in the northern districts and in Transylvania, identified themselves, out of ethnical sympathies, with the cause of the Habsburg dynasty, thus securing for themselves, for some time at least, freedom from relentless religious persecution on their part."[4]

Whereas in the beginning the Saxons participated actively in the spiritual struggles of Hungarian Protestantism, their participation grew less and less, because with the adoption of the Lutheran tendency they had reached their highest aim—ecclesiastical autonomy. The Reform of Wittenberg thus meant for them their political renaissance as well.

The development of the Saxons who dwelt in Transylvania may be said to be in general analogous to that of their brothers of the same tongue in Upper Hungary.

In 1542 the Ottomans approached Buda, the capital, and thereby cut off Transylvania, which from that year on was to live an autonomous national life under elected princes. This geographical and political event had a decisive influence on the ecclesiastical life of the Saxons of Transylvania who previously for approximately three hundred years had lived under the control of the Primate of Hungary. From now on they could consider themselves autonomous. The man who brought this about was John Honterus, himself a Reformer fed on the humanism of Erasmus.

In the first year of Transylvanian autonomy, 1542, Honterus hastened to formulate his views on ecclesiastical policies, on a Lutheran basis. He wrote "Formula reformationis . . . " where his views were set forth in nineteen articles. He sent the book to Wittenberg through Heltai, the Hungarian translator of Scripture, who was just to depart thither. Melanchthon hurried it through the press, and Luther endorsed its principles. The era of Protestantism was thus opened for the Saxons of Transylvania. The Formula was to become their catechism, and in 1547 they published it in their national,

German, tongue: *"Kirchenordnung aller Deutschen in Siebenbürgen."* ("Church order of all Germans in Transylvania").

The monasteries situated in the Saxon cities were immediately secularized. The monks who were not inclined toward the Lutheran faith had to leave the cities, but most of them gladly married, and, having become faithful Lutherans, participated actively in the life of Protestantism. Saxon literature could succeed in the wholesale copying of Lutheran writings only because the Saxons had gone into the religious revolution as a united group and had thereby avoided the multitudinous centrifugal tendencies in the religious and intellectual fields. In the beginning, the Saxons as middlemen were able to exercise a deep influence on the Lutheranism of the Transylvanian Hungarians. Because of them, Gyalui Torda, leader of the Hungarian Lutherans, could write Melanchthon in 1545 that the whole of Transylvania had embraced Protestantism.[6]

The autonomous political life of Transylvania was developed by three "nations" (so-called in the Transylvanian Constitution): the Hungarian, the Székler, and the Saxon. In their Constituent Assembly, these three "nations" regulated their common affairs in the most correct parliamentary manner. This was also true so far as religious problems were concerned. When the Saxon Reformers were invited to attend the Assembly, they discovered to their great astonishment that their ecclesiastical autonomy had been written into law. Only one point was debated, fasting; but the presiding Voivode John Sigismund remarked that the new religion was a city affair only, and so he passed on to the order of the day.

The Assembly of 1550 granted the Lutheran Church her constitution without any restrictions. The Transylvanian declaration thus came five years before the Peace of Augsburg, where only a temporary agreement regarding Lutheranism was achieved, granting "liberty", which later was made illusory under the principle of *"cuius regio eius religio"*. Transylvania never admitted that principle, not even in the midst of its bitterest struggles over religious doctrines.

It is worth mentioning that the Saxons of Transylvania exercised early a proselytizing activity among the Rumanian agricultural peoples who surrounded the Saxons' homes. For this purpose they translated and published Luther's Catechism into the Rumanian language (1544).[7] The missionary zeal of Honterus was continued by his successor, Valentine Wagner, who translated the same Cathechism even into the language of the Greek merchants who as immigrants had settled Transylvanian cities.

The next significant step in Church policies was taken when the Saxon bishopric was established. There was a practical reason for taking this step. Before this, all candidates of divinity had to go to Wittenberg for ordination, but inasmuch as the voyage was costly, the Saxon leaders wished to establish their own bishopric. This they did in 1555, and at the same time a new ecclesiastical statute containing six articles was promulgated.[8] When one looks at this statute today, one must admit that not too much was demanded of a future bishop. Among other things, he had to know Luther's Catechism and be able to defend it on Biblical grounds; he had to speak German; he had to be able to enumerate the books of Scripture. Before long the new Saxon bishops began functioning and ordained one Saxon pastor after another.

When the Helvetic tendency reached Transylvania, the leaders of the Saxon Church immediately established censorship over the new Western literature, lest "opinions drawn from them without good judgment should contaminate the Saxon people." To the statute *Reformatio ecclesiarum Saxonicarum in Transylvania*, which had been written by Melanchthon, articles were added which were directed against the Helvetic deviators.[9]

The Saxons thus succeeded in building up their ecclesiastic and political cadres virtually without resistance, but their leadership remained with the pastors who were obliged to supervise the private lives of their flocks as well. Outside the cities there was decentralization, for the pastor was not appointed by the bishop but elected by the parishioners.

The most impressive personality of the Saxon Reformers, who was also the first in time, was John Honterus, who had studied in Cracow and Basel. When he returned to his country his first act was to set up a printing press. He was in steady correspondence with Luther and Melanchthon. The latter esteemed Honterus very highly, both as reformer and as humanist. The printing press of Honterus worked without interruption. It was he who translated many works of Martin Luther out of Latin, more than one into Hungarian. He further prepared a very incisive plan for the organization of schools, *Constitutio Scholae Coronensis*, (Constitution for the School of Brasso-Kronstadt). It is a clear illustration of how the schools of that epoch were organized in imitation of German schools.

The Saxons of Hungary, including those of Transylvania, did not create any special theological tendency, deeply aware as they were of the fact that their Reformation had actually taken place in Wittenberg. In their local Reformation, that of Wittenberg was simply a further efflorescence.

When toward the end of the sixteenth century, the Melanchthon tendency toward moderation succumbed, pure orthodoxy was established among the Saxons too.

Footnotes

1. Ember, Pál. D. (Lampe) *Historia Ecclesiae Reformatae in Hungaria et Transylvania.* Trajecti ad Rhenum (Utrecht), 1728. p. 76.

2. Ribini, Johannes. *Memorabilia Ecclesiae Augustanae Confessionis in Regno Hungariae.* Pozsony (Presburg), 1787–1789. p. 67.

3. Borbis, Johann. *Die evangelisch-Lutherische Kirche Ungarns in ihrer geschichtlichen Entwicklung.* Nordlingen, 1861. p. 17.

4. Révész, Imre. *Geschichte des ungarländischen Protestantismus.* Budapest, 1925. p. 4.

5. Honterus, Johannes. *Corpus Reformatorum.* Braunschweig, Vol. V. p. 172.

6. Egyházitörténeti Emlékek. *A Magyarországi Hitujitás Korából.* Budapest, 1902–1912. Vol. II. p. 452.

7. RMK. Vol. II. No. 35 1877–1930

8. Teutsch, G. D. *Urkundenbuch der Evangelische Landeskirche A.B. in Siebenbürgen.* Hermannstad 1862–83. Vol. II. p. 3.

9. Révész, Imre. *A magyar református egyház története.* Debrecen, 1939. p. 83.

Chapter XIII

The Reformed Mission Among the Eastern Orthodox Rumanians in Hungary

Since the early period of Christendom, a tension existed between the Greek- and Latin-speaking Churches. This division had begun when Rome proclaimed that "Rome has spoken, the case is closed", *Roma locuta est, causa finita est*. It was the Greek Orthodox Church and its theological considerations which controlled the religious, spiritual life in East Central Europe.

With the duality in Christendom in mind, it seems logical that the Protestant opponents of Rome during the Reformation began to express interest in and sympathy toward the Eastern Orthodox Church. The translation of the Augsburg Confession into Greek, for example, indicated a growing interest.[1] Martin Luther was the first to represent this tendency. In his view the Church of Christ was much wider than just the Roman Communion. With the translation of the Augsburg Confession, the road was opened for a new recognition of the role of Eastern Orthodoxy which had been neglected in the Western Christian world, and with the recognition the way was opened for ecumenical historical writings.

When Luther's pioneering work ended, it was Phillip Melanchthon who played an important part in building up a closer connection with the Orthodoxy of the East. According to historian Benz, Melanchthon paid more respect to the authority of the Founding Fathers.[2] Because of his humanistic education, Melanchthon had extensive knowledge of the Greek Fathers. From this greater respect there grew among the Protestants the conviction that the Balkan people, who were under Muslim domination, needed a Protestant mission, the more so because theologians described Eastern Orthodoxy as superstitious. They were inclined to suggest that it should be liberated from its present idolatry in order that the static Eastern Church could experience its own Reformation.

From these considerations sprouted a mission in the Balkans among the wandering Rumanian people who, forced by the Muslim threat, *en masse* took flight into the Hungarian territory. This non-theological factor of the Islamic expansion warned the Christian leaders that it was no longer possible for East and West to ignore each other.

As Christian leader, Melanchthon did his best to win the sympathy of the Eastern Orthodox Church, in order for her to become a fellow-reformer in Hungary. The Patriarch of Constantinople, however, being under Turkish control, could never overcome his suspicion and he even forgot to answer Melanchthon's letter. Furthermore, the Protestant Reformation was a logical offspring of a secularized Roman Christianity, which in essence opposed spiritual, mystical, Eastern Orthodoxy.

In the *Reformed Mission* among the Rumanians in South Hungary and Transylvania, two distinguishable epochs can be recognized. The first was started by Lutheran Saxons in Transylvania, who were inspired by Wittenberg's theologians. Through local and individual efforts, they gave the illiterate wandering and semi-settled Rumanians as well as their semiliterate priests the much-needed religious literature. The Catechism, parts of the Bible, as well as the psalmody, were translated into native Rumanian and traditional Greek tongues. The end result, however, was very meager because the suspicious and superstitious people were led by semi-literate clergy who used to perform their religious services in a foreign language, Slavic, which they had memorized because they could not read the Slavic texts; this resulted in empty rituals.

The second epoch, which commenced and continued for one hundred and fifty years, was initiated by the Hungarian Elector* of Transylvania and the Reformed Synods. During this epoch a corporate endeavor organized Rumanian Eastern Orthodox bishoprics, nominated Orthodox bishops, educated the clergy, established printing presses, published Christian literature in the native Rumanian language, and organized several Rumanian schools.

Lutheran and Reformed translations into the Rumanian language were the first printed literary materials according to Rumanian historian G. Bog-

---

*Elector, Prince, Voivod, King, are the titles used for the Transylvanian rulers. They changed from one to another during constitutional developments.

dan Duica: "They gave to us Rumanian books, Rumanian preachers, Rumanian students . . . They not only fought against our old religions but against our old and primitive superstitions as well . . . furthermore, we received from them also our first ecclesiastical organizations."[3]

The Protestant missionaries aimed to restore to men the religion of the Book. The premise for acceptance of the spiritual revolution was a well educated elite, and where a well-taught class was present the Protestant mission had been able to make inroads, while where a literate elite was lacking the Reformation as an integrating force of European Christianity could not penetrate. With this obvious historical understanding commenced the *Reformed Mission* among the Rumanian pastoral people in sixteenth century Hungary.

The Rumanian Motive for Reformation

The spiritual genesis of Rumanian Reformation did not stem from an anti-denominational bias. It stemmed from a special concept of witnessing which belonged to the Reformation of the sixteenth century. The Reformation had brought a great re-discovery of the Gospel in the history of Western Christendom. To promote God's glory was the central experience, a *bonum magnum*.

When one searches the history of the Rumanian Reformation of the sixteenth and seventeenth centuries, one finds this concept of religious totality as the main motive behind the actions of those men who participated in the movement.

The Reformation did not grow through a step-by-step converting of individuals or groups of sects, but through corporate actions, either from the Diet of the nobility and magistrates or from the decrees of the Elector of Transylvania. It is remarkable to observe how much the Reformed literature was occupied with the influence and the responsibility of the magistrate. One finds the expressed opinion that the first duty of a magistrate should be to guard the Gospel and religious matters. Calvin had formulated this in his *Institutes* thus: "As long as we live in this world, the civil government is designed to cherish and support the external worship of God, to preserve the pure doctrine of religion, to defend the constitution of the Church."[4]

The Second Helvetic Confession as it was introduced in 1566 had the same emphasis: "We teach that the main duty of a magistrate is to control the religion. Consequently the officials keep the fate of the Gospel in their hands and do not permit any false propaganda."[5]

The best known Hungarian preacher of those days, Péter Bornemissza, expressed it thus:

> "The princes are the 'nurses' of the Church and schools; they order the people to glorify God and to demolish the idols, to secure free proclamation of the Gospel."[6]

With these views in mind this author has attempted to illustrate the theological background of an age in which the people lived under the "compulsion of God", an age which demanded a total participation of everyone in the religious movement, including the political office holders and the Electors. Their intention was to secure spiritual welfare for every individual, because the Electors regarded themselves as the stewards for God.

In order of time, John Sigismund was the first Elector in the East part of Hungary, later called Transylvania. He spent long days in leading religious disputes among his theological advocates: Lutherans, Calvinists, and Antitrinitarians. At one time he closed a religious dispute with the confession:

> "Since we are, by the grace of God, the ruler in this part of the earth, our duty is not only to defend physical wholeness of our people, but to secure spiritual goods for them and to defend them against the Anti-Christ."[7]

The action for a Rumanian Reformation was generated by similar pious concepts of Christian princes. It was the same atmosphere which dictated the following decrees at the Diet of Torda in 1566:

> "We guarantee the free proclamation of the pure Gospel among all 'nations' in our territory; we do not permit blasphemy of God's glory by ignorance, so we decree to do away with all idols which have been kept among our people, and to preach the Gospel, especially among the Rumanians whose pastors are blind, leading a blinded people."[8]

The Religious and Spiritual Situation of the Rumanian People

The first confessed motive of the Rumanian Reformation was a religious consciousness; that is, nobody was permitted either to offend God's glory through religious illiteracy or to obstruct growth of the Kingdom of God in Transylvania. From this religious conviction the Diet acted logically in warning the Rumanian Eastern Orthodox priests who were "blind, leading a blinded people."

What was the historical situation of which this condemnation was only a reflection? Antonio Possevino, a Jesuit theologian, wrote in 1583 in a report on Transylvania: "The Protestant and Roman Catholic propaganda remained fruitless among the Eastern Orthodox Rumanians because of their complete illiteracy."[9]

The published documents of the Diets and archives of the magistrates, the general description of the Rumanians in the sixteenth century, picture the Rumanians as serfs who lived unsettled lives as nomad-shepherds, wandering from one corner of the country to another. They could not pay a regular income tax but instead gave a fiftieth, the *quinquagesia ovium* from their herds. The clergy had originally been exempted from paying the fiftieth in 1578, but in a later decree the Diet limited the number of popas (priests) to two per village because it had become customary among the shepherds to buy an ordination from their superiors in order to avoid taxation. During the sixteenth century some wandering bishops from outside the Electorate visited the mountainous nomad-shepherds and they ordained many of them to pastoral service. The Diet often objected to this procedure, because it usually involved a bribe. Rumanian historian Stefan Metes described it thus:

> "The ordination of Rumanian clericals was a very easy matter if you had the wish and the necessary money; peasant boys with little literary knowledge could achieve it."[10]

The *caluger* or *popa* lived among the shepherds and did manual labor. The only thing which distinguished him from the other people was his uncut hair.

The continuous invasion of the Ottoman Turks in South Eastern Europe brought a radical change in the demography. The Balkan people moved towards the north. The Rumanians, among others, sought refuge in Transylvania. From the records of the Diet of Transylvania it is known already that in the seventeenth century about one-third of the total population of Transylvania was Rumanian.

The nomadic shepherd's mode of life created moral laxness and the Diet drew up drastic laws to bring the Rumanian people, who often had arrived without ethical regulations from Muslim-occupied territories, under control.

The most authentic source which has preserved many facts about the Rumanian people is the *Codex Sturzanus*, which contains the writings of Popa Grigore in the sixteenth century. Grigore collected all kinds of popular religious beliefs and legends that lived in the memories of the Rumanian wanderers. According to the Rumanian historian Hasdeu, who published the *Codex Sturzanus*, the legends and religious beliefs were the products of the Bogomils, a thirteenth century sect of Manichean descent. In the Balkans the Rumanian popular religion had kept up those beliefs of heretic character.[11] These Bogomil influences in time made it difficult for the Rumanian Eastern Orthodox people to be changed through Western influence. The Gospel preaching did not reach the ears of these simple people. The Reformed Synods and the few well-educated popas were engaged in endless struggles to ban the popular superstitions. Historian Iorga has admitted in his evaluation of the sixteenth and seventeenth centuries that though the Rumanian people had a numerous clergy, the people nevertheless believed in all kinds of primitive superstitions.[12]

An organized Eastern Orthodox Church in Transylvania did not exist until the arrival of the Protestant Reformation in the sixteenth century. The Diet of 1566 authorized Bishop Grigore as Rumanian Superintendent to organize the Rumanian Eastern Orthodox Church in Transylvania. Earlier the Hungarian Roman Catholic Church and the Apostolic King had not permitted the existence of any Eastern Orthodox bishopric in Hungarian territory. It had happened though that sometimes a refugee bishop would arrive from Turkish occupied areas who would try to serve his flock.

In summary, it may be said that one cannot historically speak of an established or accepted continuity of the Rumanian Eastern Orthodox Church. The decrees of the Diet proved this, for example, when it nullified the consecration of shepherds as clergy and declared such a consecration illegal, because it was bought from an unauthorized bishop.[13]

A German observer, the Jesuit Andreas Freyberg, wrote:

> "Everyone can be consecrated to the clerical profession, even without knowledge of the Lord's Prayer and the number of sacraments, as long as one pays the fee which is asked by the bishop."[14]

A Protestant pastor, Albert Wurmloch, who translated and published the Rumanian Catechism in 1546, wrote to Germany that the Rumanian clergy read the Gospel in a foreign language called Slavic, which nobody could understand.[15]

This information gives some kind of picture of the spiritual and religious life of the Rumanian Eastern Orthodox people in the pre-Reformation period. Their Church, using a foreign liturgical language not understood by its members and even clergy, could not fulfill her original destiny, that is to be a teaching Church.

One may only conclude that there was some sporadic clerical work in an unorganized church, in which a faintly-known Gospel was seldom preached.

The sixteenth century was a critical age in the history of the Rumanian Eastern Orthodox Church. The Protestant Reformers clearly saw that the stagnation in this church was due to historical reasons and that the Church was petrified and not life-giving. Its ethos did not intend to reshape the world according to the principles of faith; it rather wished to fight the world and escape from it. That was the primary reason for the passive mood of Eastern Orthodox piety. Contrary to this oriental passivity, the crucial point in the Reformation Church is that God speaks anew to every age of history, and that the Christians must obey Him within that concrete situation.

The Literary Preparation in the Rumanian Language toward Reformation

In the early period of the *Reformed Mission*, the catechism was a popular way to teach the newly interpreted Christian dogmas. Among the first writings published for propagation of Reformed teachings among the Rumanian Eastern Orthodox people was a catechism.* Hurmuzaki cites that in the Saxon city Szeben, according to an order of the nobility, two florins were given in 1544 to Philip Picor, a Saxon printer, for the publication of the Rumanian Catechism.[16] Rumanian historian Sulica states that this Catechism was translated from a Hungarian text and that the nobility mentioned by Hurmuzaki belonged to those former Rumanians who had become Hungarian nobility; it was they who sponsored the educational

---

*In 1550, the Saxon Balint Wagner, a student of Melanchthon, had already published a Catechism but, only in the Greek language.

efforts to bring the Rumanian shepherd and peasant to a reformed Eastern Orthodoxy.[17]

According to Hurmuzaki, some people and popas were enthusiastic about the Catechism, but many threw it away in horror.[18]

In 1564, another Hungarian nobleman, Miklós Forro, financed in the city of Brasso another Hungarian publication by printer Coresi, namely a collection of sermons and a book of Eastern Orthodox rituals. Only one copy of this manuscript has been preserved; the others were destroyed by the Eastern Orthodox clergy.

The chief gain of the publication of the Catechism was that it opened the way for the much-needed church literature as the Decalogue, the Lord's Prayer, and the Gospels in the Rumanian language. It was characteristic that the publishers mentioned in their foreword the name of the Eastern Orthodox priest Sava in order to secure authority for the whole mission. The publishers' main purpose was to instruct the illiterate people to know their sins, to learn where they could receive forgiveness after repentance and to live according to the Gospel. In this manner no one would have to put his salvation into the hands of illiterate priests but into the hands of the Mediator.[19]

The *Reformed Mission* among the Rumanians did not plan to proselytize the shepherd people; the missionaries simply offered the Gospel to replace the demonology, which occupied the people as one sermon illustrates: "It is a lie brethren that the devil has been born from the souls of the dead. The blinded popas tell such stories to frighten and exploit the people."[20]

Simion Stephan, a dedicated Rumanian Orthodox Reformer, became the translator of the New Testament, receiving authorization from Elector George (György) Rákoczi, who financed the printing. Stephan, who had already translated the Psalms into Rumanian, was the pioneer who created a unified Rumanian literary language.[21]

The Rumanian Reformed Episcopacy

The Rumanian reformation effort, led by the Electors and the Diet, lasted over one hundred and fifty years. During that period a second step was taken after the long preparation in the literary field, namely to inaugurate a new church policy in connection with the Eastern Orthodox Church. To this purpose the Diet and the Elector appointed Popa Grigore as bishop (1566), who then became the head of the Eastern Orthodox church in Transylvania.[22]

From the repeated Electoral decrees we can gain the impression that Bishop Grigore met with strong opposition in his effort toward unification. The Elector, John Sigismund, ordered every popa to obey Bishop Grigore. The latter called together several Synods to lay down a church policy, but the popas simply did not attend. Many objected to the use of Rumanian language in church services, the complaint being that they wanted to praise God in Slavic only.

Bishop Grigore renewed his request for further support from the Elector; however, he soon disappeared from the scene and it is unknown what became of him. The reformation effort, however, continued and many results were permanent, among which was the use of the Rumanian vernacular.

Grigore was succeeded by Bishop Paul Tordási, whose missionary task and the conditions under which he was to labor were described in a letter of confirmation by the Elector. The two most important tasks were: to spread the Gospel, and to reform the sacraments according to the teachings of Christ.

Electoral Religious Policy

In the history of Transylvania, the Rumanian elements did not play an important political or ecclesiastical part until the seventeenth century because until then their number was small in proportion to the three "nations", that is, the three dominant ethnic groups. These three nations with four allowed religions, Roman Catholicism, Lutheranism, Calvinism, and Unitarianism, constituted the Electorate as they were called under the law of the land.[23]

Prince Bocskay, after waging a successful war against Habsburg Catholicism, secured for the first time in the history of Hungarian Protestantism the freedom for the poor peasants who were serfs of the Roman Catholic nobility, to make their own choice of faith. In his peace treaty with Vienna in 1608 Bocskay refused the concept of *cuius regio eius religio* and thus opened a new chapter in church history: that of the personal freedom in religious matters. This occurred forty years before a similar European decision was taken at the Westphalia Peace Treaty.

Prince Bocskay regulated the ecclesiastical relationship between the state and Rumanian Eastern Orthodoxy in a similar broad sense of religious liberty. To realize this he nominated the bishop or *vladica* Spieidon as *episcopus et supremus superintendens* over the Rumanians in his country.[24]

Bocskay confirmed the guiding principles of the religious policy of the Electorate by stating that the tradition of the "three nations" that were living in Transylvania was that the different peoples should be represented by their own clergy. The Elector wanted to follow a similar policy concerning the Rumanian Eastern Orthodox Church of which one part exclusively used the Greek liturgical language, because he was conscious of his duty to defend all his people and their religions. The view that the God-given order to hold these traditions unchanged was rooted in the sixteenth century concept of magistrates, was in Bocskay's time already was called tradition.

In this case it was the Elector himself who directed in his first *Conditions* what kind of ecclesiastical life would have to be established among the Rumanian subjects. It was to be through Rumanian bishops who would have to serve the Electoral church policy.[25]

The politically-influenced tolerant policy of the Electors finally stabilized the status of Rumanian Orthodoxy, as can be understood from the Electoral decree at the Diet of Alba Julia in 1609:

> "The Elector, prompted by the miserable situation of the Rumanian clergy who follow the 'Greek sect' [that is those adhering to the Greek liturgical language], and out of respect for God's glory, has felt himself forced to exempt the Rumanian clergy from serfhood."[26]

This meant that the clergy was free to move from one place to another, though only with permission from their bishop. A second provision was the exemption from taxes which the clergy while being serfs had been obliged to pay. This liberating policy represented some advance in comparison with the situation in neighboring countries, as Eastern Orthodox historian Benedek Jancso has pointed out:

> "From the Slavic document it was clear that rural popas in the Balkan countries were serfs; Bulgarian Czar Simon in his time initiated a tradition in that he 'donated' Popa Todor and his family to the Rilski monastery."[27]

With this Electoral church policy the Rumanian Eastern Orthodox Church slowly crystallized her status and gained social privileges for her clergy.

The next important Elector who was concerned about the Rumanian interest was Gábor Bethlen, who was Prince of Transylvania from 1613–1629. He quite soon made known his decree in which he described his intention:

> "Our goal is to have no vacant Rumanian Orthodox bishoprics but to fill them with ardent and talented bishops, who will edify their clergy with redeeming dogmas, through which they can save the Church from all aberrations."[28]

With this intention Bethlen installed Bishop Theophysus Praesopli in 1615. The whole tendency of Electoral church policy in this age was contrary to proselytizing; it aimed only at voluntary, self-reforming development within Rumanian circles.

Prince George Rákoczi, who ruled from 1629–1648, brought constitutional security for the Rumanian Orthodox Church. In 1643 the Prince regulated her constitutional rights at the Diet. For centuries the Rumanian Eastern Orthodox Church had belonged to the category of "tolerated" Churches, but now, through Rákoczi's action at the Diet, Eastern Orthodoxy was declared constitutional.

The tolerant spirit was partially influenced by an outward action which nowadays may be called ecumenicity. The concept of a closer Christian cooperation between Eastern Orthodoxy and Protestantism, as presented by the Englishman Jacob Dury (Duraeus), reached the Elector's court. Reformed Bishop Gelei, who was in contact with Dury, outlined the ideas and conditions. He suggested a union between the Hungarian Reformed Church and the "to be reformed" Rumanian Eastern Orthodox Church. He thought of a loose alliance with a broad autonomy.[29]

Though Gelei did not over-emphasize the differences in dogmas, he misjudged the importance of Eastern Orthodox liturgy and ceremony which represented the strength of Eastern Orthodoxy.

The following superstitions were finally condemned in 1675 by the Rumanian Eastern Orthodox Synod, which shows how deeply rooted they were among the clergy.

1. Use only water for baptism, discontinue the use of fire and smoke.
2. Do not pray for human bones or for clothes of dead relatives.
3. Do not swing chickens and kids over a corpse in order to immunize them against phantoms.
4. Do not wash the feet of animals with holy water to ward off hoof-and-mouth disease.
5. Do not burn candles before the heads of bulls.
6. Do not throw bread and money in a grave during a funeral.
7. Do not pray for the return of lost animals.
8. Prohibit the conjuration of spirits on Maundy Thursday and do not bring food to the deceased in the cemetery.

Gelei saw the problem of the deep-rooted superstitions among Rumanian Eastern Orthodox laity, but he assumed that teaching would overcome this problem and that the Rumanian Eastern Orthodox Church then could be restored to her original evangelical character.

Outside the Church realm, on the social level, a definite improvement came about. More and more Rumanian popas were elevated to the rank of nobility, and with that their historical role was growing for the first time in the history of Transylvania.[30]

That these Rumanian leaders were equalized with the Hungarians meant that the Elector's policy was based on a solid foundation. The latter explained his actions on behalf of the Rumanians thus:

"Life of man is a constant struggle, . . . the most important is the one which we fight on the bastion of salvation. Among the militant citizens we must mention the clergy, who are defending Christ's sheep. We now offer the title of nobility to Popa Peter, who lives a pious and faithful life among his Rumanian believers."[31]

The last Transylvanian prince, Apafi, still needed to warn his bishops to enforce the Rumanian liturgy and language in church services: "if they, [the clergy] will not learn the tongue in a set time, they must be dismissed from the clerical status."

The End of the Reformed Mission Among the Rumanians

The Rumanian mission broke down suddenly when the political situation changed. Transylvania lost its independence and a new chapter was opened in the church history of Transylvania. What the Protestant leaders had not been able to do, the Roman Catholics did now under the Habsburg rule: they imposed their Church system upon the people. The Rumanian Eastern Orthodox Church accepted Roman Catholicism and gained thus higher status and recognition. An overwhelming majority of the Rumanian clergy accepted union with Rome. In Transylvania, as in Poland, the Reformation and its mission had prepared the way back to Rome.

In evaluating the Reformed Mission in Transylvania, Rumanian historian Baritiu wrote: "The historian who is occupied with the essence of the Reformation feels uneasy about one question: how and why did it happen that between 1566 and 1670 not one Rumanian Orthodox stood up firmly for his religious convictions, for dogmas, sacrificing even his life, or why one cannot find even one who could stand fast for the new religious beliefs, like a hero in the Western lands . . . ."[32]

Alexander Grama, Rumanian specialist on Rumanian church history during the sixteenth and seventeenth centuries, has made the remarkable statement that in a deeper sense the Rumanian Reformation has no history. History exists only where there is struggle, resistance, victory or defeat, and these elements were lacking in the Rumanian Eastern Orthodoxy. This meant that the Reformation never became a part of the Rumanian soul.[33]

In this historical evaluation of the missionary endeavor among the Rumanian people during one hundred and fifty years, one must look at the final results. Outwardly, it was a complete failure. To explain this one must keep in mind the differences between Western and Eastern Christendom. The Protestant Reformation was a rational spirito-religious product of Western Christianity, and it would have been quite impossible to suppose that it could have grown on the spiritual soil of Greek Orthodoxy. In consequence, a Lutheran or Calvinistic ecclesiastical movement never could have happened in Eastern Christendom, because the conditions were absent in the Eastern spiritual life. Western religious life stressed the rational, individualistic cult, whereas the Eastern spiritual climate nursed an impersonal mysticism. In another realm Eastern Christians had developed a more or less passive attitude toward the secular world, whereas the Western Christians advocated a passionate and active participation in the politico-social life, thus representing a *semper reformare* view of life. As a result, the Western believer had become a convinced missionary, in order to change his milieu. The Eastern Christian, however, remained for long centuries abeyant and passive.

These two kinds of Christian perspective were confronted in East Central Europe during the sixteenth and seventeenth centuries when the Protestant Reformers started their missions, not recognizing the deeply different human attitudes toward the same religion. The reformers belonged to a well-educated class and they could not understand the Rumanian folk religion with its mystical, irrational content. It is evident that the missionaries wanted to abolish all those superstitions which were in their opinion the 'only' obstacle for the spreading of a rationalistic religion of the Bible. The religion of the Book demanded a literary and cultural standard which was lacking among the Rumanian nomads and illiterate settlers of Transylvania. It is significant that from the whole missionary endeavor only the cultural service was accepted by the Rumanian Eastern Orthodox people, who continued their former religious tradition. Rumanian historian Lupas expressed it so: "The greatest and undeniable result of the Protestant Reformation was that it introduced into the liturgy our own native language and that it developed our Rumanian literature. In the later historical development, this greatly helped to build our national consciousness and solidarity of the nation."[34]

The paradox of the Reformed Mission, which stemmed from a deepfelt transcendental religious responsibility of the Hungarian Reformed toward their fellow Rumanians resulted in the fact that Rumanian Orthodox people remained outside of the realm of Western Christianity. Basically, the whole Reformed Mission among the Rumanians in Hungary was reduced to a language struggle: Should the backward Rumanian Orthodox people be educated in the Slavic, the Greek, or their native tongue? Nicolae Iorga has condemned the Rumanian Eastern Orthodox clergy saying that the habit of the use of the Slavic language was abandoned very late. Until 1590 not one Rumanian sentence had been written down among the Rumanians themselves, although the Slavic letters could not be read without laughing. How could any education take place when a foreign language was used, a language which nobody could understand?[35]

The discussion of the development into the seventeenth century was deemed necessary in order to show that the Hungarian Reformed Church was from the very beginning a missionary Church, and that the mission was not in vain when seen in perspective, because it had forced the Rumanians to develop their mother-tongue as a literary language.

Footnotes

1. Benz, Ernst. *Wittenberg und Byzanz*. Marburg, 1947. p. 68.

2. Benz, Ernst. *Die Ostkirche*. Munchen, 1952. p. 3.

3. Duica, Bogdan A. as quoted by Marianne Székely in: The Influence of the Protestant Transylvanian Princes on the Rumanian Cultural Developments. Debrecen, 1935. p. 28.

4. Calvin, John. Institutes, transl. John Allen, 7th Amer. ed. Vol. II. Philadelphia, 1936. p. 772.

5. Second Helvetic Confession. III. Debrecen, 1907. p. 113.

6. Bornemissza, Péter. *Predikáciok*. Detrekö, 1584, p. 40.

7. Szentmártoni, Kálmán. *János Zsigmond*. Székelykeresztur, 1934. p. 344.

8. Szilágy, Sándor. *Monumenta comitiala regni Transyl vaniae*. II. Budapest, 1880. p. 326.

9. Veress, Andreiu. *Documenta privitoare la Istoria Ardealului*. II. Bucuresti, 1929. p. 274.

10. Metes, Stefan. *Istoria Bisericii si a vietii religioase a Romanilor din Transylvania sü Ungaria*. Nagyszeben, 1935. Vol. I, p. 458.

11. Hasdeu, P. B. *Cuvente din Bantrani*, I, II. Bucuresti, 1879.

12. Iorga, Nicolae. *Sate di preoti din Ardeal*. Bucuresti, 1902. p. 129.

13. Teutsch, Gustav D. *Geschichte der Siebenbürger Sachsen*. Nagyszeben, 1925. 4e Auflage. p. 256.

14. Dobrescu, Nicolae. *Fragmente privitoare la Bisericii Romane*. Budapest, 1905. p. 61.

15. Wittstock, Henrich. *Beitrage zur Reformationsgeschichte des Nosnergaues*. Wien, 1858. p. 58.

16. Hurmuzaki, E. *Documente privitoare la Istoria Romanilor*. Bucuresti. IV. p. 84.

17. Sulica, Nicolae. *Annuarul licelului de baieto al Papiu Harian din Targu-Mures, pe amlui 1932–35*. Publicat de Dimitriu Marlinas.

18. Hurmuzaki, E. *op. cit.* XI. p. 861.

19. Bianu-Hodos. *Bibliografia Romaneasca Veche*. 1508-1830. Bucuresti, 1903. p. 51.

20. Iorga, Nicolae. *Geschichte des rumanischen Volkes, II*. Gotha, 1905. p. 117.

21. Bianu-Hodos. *op. cit.* pp. 165–170.

22. Metes, Stefan. *op. cit.* p. 81.

23. Knight, George. History of the Hungarian Reformed Church. Washington, 1956. p. 42.

24. Szilágy, Sándor. *op. cit.* Vol. V. p. 304.

25. Révész, Imre. *Magyar Református Egyház.* Debrecen, 1938. p. 350.

26. Gyulafehérvári Libri Regii. XIX, 36 b.

27. Jancsó, Benedek. *A Román Nemzetiségi Törekvések.* I. Budapest, 1896. p. 512.

28. Dobrescu, Nicolae. *Fragmente privitoare la Istoria Bisericii Romanae.* Budapest, 1905.

29. Bitay, Árpád. *Az Erdélyi Románok a Protestáns Fejedelnek alatt.* Discsö, 1925. p. 83.

30. Gyulafehérvári Libri Regii. XV. p. 90.

31. *ibid.* XXXV, pp. 99–101.

32. Baritiu, Georgiu. *Catechismulu Calvinescu impusu cleriilui si poporului Romanescu sub domnia Principiloru Georgiu Rakoczy.* Nagyszeben, 1879.

33. Grama, Alexander. *Institutiile Calvinesta in Biserica Romaneasca din Ardeal.* Balázsfalva, 1895. p. 5.

34. Lupas, Joan. *Istoria Bisericeasca a Romanilor ardelui.* Nagyszeben, 1918.

35. Iorga, Nicolae. *Istoria Romanilor in Chipuri si Icoane.* Bucuresti, 1908. p. 143 ff.

Chapter XIV

Albert Szenci Molnár
East Central Europe's Wandering Reformer
1574–1634

Europe reached a spiritual and intellectual peak in the sixteenth century. The social dynamics of the Reformation encouraged people to abandon their provincialism. The population of the Continent, chiefly the young people, took to the road to broaden their intellectual horizons. This wandering differed in many respects from earlier pilgrimages, which had been motivated chiefly by piety. Previously, when a wandering monk set out trotting on his donkey, he pulled his cowl over his head to shut out the world and read the biography of a saint. Monasteries had built their windows facing inside courtyards in order that nothing from the world could penetrate.

The new traveler, in contrast, marveled at the beauties of nature, kept a diary and with his passion for learning sought a role in regenerating the world. "A new Holy Sepulchre whose name was free religious inquiry was moved to Europe." Liberated by the Reformation, man left home for the sake of traveling itself. But he also had a rational goal: to learn, to become acquainted with scholars, and to prepare himself for some special usefulness. Traveling became a kind of science.

Along with the new traveling was born a new literary genre, the travel diary. Justus Lipsius, a Dutchman, was the father of these intellectual tourists, and his 1586 diary was called *Epistole de peregrinatione italica*.[1] Lipsius had a young Hungarian traveling companion named Mihály Forgács. Twenty-year-old Forgács lectured at Wittenberg in 1587 where he quoted

Albert Szenci Molnár

the advice of his master: "Use any trick, any stratagem to break into the company of famous scholars."[2] He admonished his young contemporaries studying in Europe not to fear the perils of travel and to be better than "pigs wallowing in their familiar pens." The purpose of travel must be fought for, he said, with the triple goals of wisdom, knowledge, and ethics. Many followed this advice. They were like the wandering student who, having reached his host in Holland, "put away his only shirt and his prayerbook."

In 1644, a Hungarian writer, Dávid Fröhlich, compiled a two-volume travel manual which was the most popular book of the time in Europe. *Bibliotheca seu Cynosura peregrinatium* was its title.

So these young men of the sixteenth century made it their aim to see what was beautiful, to make friends with great men, and to read otherwise inaccessible books. They were Protestant descendants of the wandering Abraham, intent on building a bridge of faith between Western and Eastern Europe. Many, driven by a tragic misunderstanding of life and never finding a spiritual home, shivered in the Asian climate of Islam which the Turks had spread from Buda to Vienna.

The island country of England also sent its sons to the Continent, on the so-called "Grand Tour," so that they could polish their manners, learn social graces, and perhaps acquire new languages also. There were colorful stories to be read of what happened to these traveling, wandering, sometimes vagabond youth of Europe. Younger students traveled often with a tutor, and it happened that when the latter ran out of money, he would force his students to beg or even steal. A tutor might send his student to take a few geese from the goose farm, telling him that it was the custom of the region to give gifts to wandering students. Of course the ingenious youth was astonished when the farmer, who did not share that view, gave him a thorough thrashing. There was a case when the tutor returned a youth (to whom he had promised to teach Latin), and the boy proved to be eloquent in Slovak instead. Meanwhile, the tutor had vanished like a donkey in a November fog.[3]

In this generation of wandering students one of the most outstanding figures was Albert Szenci Molnár. He was the son of a Calvinist miller and vintner who quickly had adapted to the emerging capitalist life style. As Molnár noted in his diary, he was born in 1574 in the city of Szenc in the western part of Hungary. His mother died while he was young, and his father, in the custom of the time, entrusted his son's education to an older wandering tutor. Albert Molnár was barely twelve when he and nine others began moving from city to city, visiting the famous educational institutions of Hungary.[4]

Albert's father could not have known that with this educational method he had decisively determined his son's career. In the course of the grand tour of Hungary, young Molnár visited the Protestant printing press in Göncz. The mysterious art of printing so captured his fancy that he spent some time in 1590 as a printer's apprentice while Gáspár Károlyi printed the first complete Hungarian Bible. Molnár could never get printing out of his system. He eventually became acquainted with almost every printing press in Europe. The Biblical life style, the theological atmosphere, and the knowledge of printing followed him throughout his entire career. In the next forty years, Molnár wrote, translated, and printed his private library which grew to twenty volumes.

Filled with his impressions of Göncz, Molnár enrolled in the Reformed College of Debrecen in Hungary, one of the first colleges in Europe to teach Calvinist theology. Many students there had returned from abroad with colorful stories and firsthand knowledge of Heidelberg, Wittenberg, and Geneva. In his journal written in Debrecen, Molnár relates his attempts to write poetry, his intense desire to read, and complains that his Hungarian books were taken from him because Latin was the compulsory language of scholarship. Students caught speaking their mother tongue were deprived of a day's food or a weekend liberty.

Molnár's thirst for firsthand knowledge and his hunger for Western culture set him off on the dusty roads of Europe again at the age of sixteen. He did not know that by wandering these roads to cities and universities he would walk himself into Europe's Protestant history. The statistics of his ceaseless travels show us that he lived in more than five hundred cities. Everywhere he gathered knowledge necessary to create a European religious-spiritual synthesis.

While most wandering students started out on their travels with money and letters of recommendation, Molnár had neither of these. He trusted the loving solidarity of Protestant society. He trusted in God's Providence and that Providence predestined him to endure days of hunger, danger, and humiliation in the years that followed. How many times he wrote in his diary: *"Deus bone, quantas hic molestias devoravi"*. (Good God, how many humiliations have I endured!) Like Saint Paul, Molnár had no possessions other than his staff. And yet this most persistent Hungarian traveler of the sixteenth-seventeenth century had Someone who helped him through many wretched days in the course of his wanderings.

When Molnár left Debrecen in 1590, he went through Vienna, which had been destroyed by an earthquake. There was no place to lodge. When he finally reached Wittenberg, some six hundred mountainous miles to the north, he met a compatriot, András Ungvári, who led him to the Bursa, the association of Hungarian students of which Ungvári was Rector. "At once I felt at home," wrote Molnár in his journal.

In 1591 Molnár registered at the theological faculty of Wittenberg University, which preserved the legacy of Luther and Melanchthon. From there he soon went on to Heidelberg, the oldest German university, founded in 1388, and also the first to represent the teachings of John Calvin. A year later, Molnár was in Strassbourg, where he stayed until 1596 and earned his baccalaureate degree.

At that time, Strasbourg University was Europe's most outstanding. It had more than a thousand students, many from the Continent's aristocracy. Johann Sturm, the most well-known pedagogue of the time, had raised the university to a high level. He was a Calvinist, however, and the Lutheran ministers forced him to resign. Religious controversy soon paralyzed the institution. The university was seized with religious polemics, "the mania of the century," which was also a sort of safety valve. Every tension, every religious, social, and political blindness of the sixteenth century vented itself in the name of polemics. Now that anyone could read the Bible for himself because it was translated into the vernacular, he could forge his weapons and go to battle with quotations from the Holy Scripture for "his truth." Formerly such disputes had raged among monks in solitary cells, and a neurotic monk might defend Scripture with Scripture by throwing a Bible at his opponent's head in the heat of the argument.

Molnár's reasons for going to Strasbourg are interesting. He wrote in his letter of application to the university, "I had to leave my own country, because at home the dreadful Turk was wreaking destruction and the educational institutions were closed. Moreover, what my teachers in Germany wrote about me is all true, and you will hear more and greater things about me."

The Hungarian King and German Emperor, Maximilian II, made the school in Strasbourg a university in 1566, and it became one of the first universities to enact the law that students older than sixteen could no longer be caned. Such progressive thinking resembled the laws of London which forbade husbands to beat their wives after nine o'clock at night.

In Strasbourg Molnár took Holy Communion as the Calvinists did, so on one occasion the Lutheran president of the university expelled him. His professors, however, gave the outstanding student warm letters of recommendation when he left Strasbourg. In the last worship service Molnár attended in the Lutheran church in Strasbourg, the fiery pastor spoke of love and forgiveness, based on Psalm 120: "I am a man of peace; but when I speak, they are for war." Lightning struck the church during the sermon and Molnár expressed in his journal his relief, for he had difficulty harmonizing the "peace" of the sermon with the intolerance of the university. And so the peripatetic student, disliked for his Calvinism, set off again as penniless as before.

One of Molnár's Strasbourg professors had made a deep impression on Molnár when he had shown him a Bible and dictionaries in his home and had asked Molnár whether there were such in his country. Shamefacedly, he had had to confess that there was not even one dictionary in his language. After that conversation, Molnár had made a vow to compile a Hungarian dictionary and offer it to his people.

Was it to compensate for criticism he had suffered in Lutheran Strasbourg or as balm for his homelessness that Molnár traveled now to Switzerland, heartland of Calvinism? He was received warmly there because at that time Hungary was ninety percent Protestant and predominantly Calvinist. In Zurich when he arrived, there was a council being held after the synthesis of Bullinger's and Calvin's emphases. A harmonizing spirit prevailed; neither Geneva nor Zurich dominated. Molnár was welcomed to the meeting and the president asked the stranger to say a few words.

Molnár spoke as a theologian representing the "syncretic view" and made a good impression. His presentation was so good that the council not only welcomed him to attend the meetings, but also gave him some much needed material support as well.

In Geneva, the real destination of Molnár's Swiss trip, old Theodore Beza, Calvin's heir and translator, offered him "white wine and bread." He asked for news of Hungary in his conversation. He affirmed with tears in his eyes, "Calvin did become my father in Christ." He wrote in Molnár's diary, quoting some words of St. Augustine on the subject of free will. To young Molnár Beza's study seemed filled with the spirit of God's eternal word as the saintly seventy-seven-year-old Beza and he spoke together.

And then, amazingly, Molnár was off to Rome. The emissary of the Spanish king in Zurich asked for his company "so I may have someone to have intelligent discussions with on the way." In Rome, city of museums, Molnár's Hungarian compatriots showed him many churches, but "there were too many relics and letters of indulgence" he noted later in his diary. The students of the Collegium Hungaricum even took Molnár to see Pope Clement VIII, who was in his summer palace in Mount Caballi.* The solitary Calvinist sat at the papal table, little knowing that this pope would begin the recatholization of Hungary by the sword and other violent means, and unaware that Pope Clement was also revising the outdated Catholic Vulgate Bible to fight Protestant Biblicism and to reclaim authority for Rome. (*Roma locuta est, causa finita est.*)

In 1596, upon his return from Rome, Albert registered again at the University of Heidelberg. It was strangely to his advantage that many students, cooks, and professors had fled the city to escape the plague. Molnár stepped into a place left vacant and escaped starvation. But as students returned, he lost his free board and was forced to sell his books in order to eat. In addition to that, he also caught a peculiar facial rash which a doctor tried to treat with dog's milk. As a reaction, his whole face swelled so that he could not open his mouth to eat.

He recorded another misfortune concerning an unpaid wine bill. One day as Molnár was reading the Luke 38 account of the Gadarene demoniac, the servant of the innkeeper came to collect the money for wine which Molnár had drunk with three friends when they were accepted into the medical faculty. After all, Molnár reasoned with himself, had not a professor encouraged them to remember Paul's admonition to Timothy: "Stop drinking only water, and use a little wine because of your stomach and your frequent illnesses." Did not water often cause sickness and death?** But

---

*Fui conviva summi pontificis Clement VIII in palacio ad montem Caballi, as Molnár wrote in his diary.

**Water was often not potable in those days.

how was the bill to be paid? Molnár the pauper vowed that from then on he would no longer drink wine. Instead, he reverted to an old custom of his, he sang psalms, in German, Latin, and Hungarian, to take his mind off food and drink. (Journal, p.492).

Meanwhile, letters from home urged him to return to Hungary, promising good jobs. Molnár was admonished "not to study everything indiscriminately, but only the subjects that you will need at home." Still penniless and homesick, Molnár left Heidelberg for war-torn Hungary. After the long journey, the reunion was short-lived. He embraced his brothers and set out to find a Hungarian benefactor. From village to city, from city to castle Molnár went, but his purse remained empty. So back to Germany he went. He worked for minimal wages in various printing shops, consoling himself that the great Melanchthon had done the same for seven long years. At that time, some printers had a way of exploiting the talents of scholars and writers. Erasmus was apparently the only author who managed to support himself only by writing, and he "begged disgracefully" from everyone, for which his English friend Colet sharply rebuked him. Even Luther received only a few copies of his books from the publisher as compensation for all his work.

Dictionary

So, Albert Szenci Molnár, veteran traveler aged thirty, settled down to join the ranks of poor authors. He lived in the little German town of Altdorf, where the university gave him free room and board. True to his vow, he began to compile a Latin-Hungarian, as well as a Hungarian-Latin dictionary for his people. It was a pioneering work. He wrote the dictionaries from memory, completing them in six months.

The Hungarian people were linguistically isolated in Europe. Molnár attempted to build a bridge somehow to other nations so they would become acquainted with the Hungarian language. His dictionary served this purpose.

At that time, dictionaries took two forms: a smaller one that only provided a brief explanation of the words; and a larger one in which the etymology and quality of the word was analyzed and explained in detail. These were, however, just in one language. Later, the classical bilingual, Greek-Latin, dictionaries became the models for bilingual ones of the national languages. Molnár's pioneering work continued this line of development; like an encyclopedia it included proverbs and explanations.

He did not yet draw a line between dictionary and encyclopedia. With this system, Molnár incorporated into his literature the emerging city bourgeoisie who were able to read and write. So a new level of vernacular linguistic development was reached.

By clinging to the elements of folk-language and original Magyar words, Albert unconsciously preserved the autonomy of the Hungarian language. According to linguistic studies of modern Hungarian, only twenty percent of the words in this language are borrowed from other languages, Latin, German, or Slavic, over the past thousand years.

A new stock of words and expressions appeared in Molnár's dictionary, and he encountered great difficulties in translating such words as: *Proletarian*: "Poor people of Rome, who did not do much to serve the state, they just propagated children." or *Dictioniarium*: "Book or register in which every word is written."

That the Hungarian language is not related to any other European language increased Molnár's difficulties.

Molnár's linguistic work had political implications as well for East-Central Europe. There the expression "a nation lives in its language," took on a special meaning early on. The danger of assimilation with the Slavic and German languages created the intolerant concept of linguistic nationalism.*

Molnár dedicated the two-volume *Dictionarium Latino Ungaricum* to the Hungarian King and German Emperor Rudolph, to whom he handed it personally in Prague. The emperor began to read it and rewarded the author with fifty pieces of gold. In the preface of the dictionary the author asked the king to accept this first book from a Hungarian author. He tactfully praised the German creative genius which had given birth to so many works of art. Knowing that Rudolph was a compulsive collector and repairer of clocks, Albert even mentioned what a wonder of the world were "machines built in the belly of towers." Later Molnár confessed that he wrote the dictionary especially because as a child he did not have a reference book in his own language to use in his studies. He concluded his dedication with words befitting a theologian, *"Gloria Deo, Venia Reo"* ("Praise God, pardon the sinner").

---

*The Czech and Polish nations were most exposed to this danger. An awareness of this, among others, stimulated the development of Hussitism.

One of the intriguing stories is how this wandering, unknown writer got into the Prague palace to present his dictionary in person to the melancholy recluse, Emperor Rudolph, who closeted himself with his clocks and astronomy. It was possible because in Heidelberg Molnár had come under the protection of second-generation followers of Martin Luther and Philip Melanchthon. This circle of scholars, influential in literature, politics, and universities, arranged an earlier journey of Molnár to Prague where he stayed some months as guest of the greatest scientist of the age, John Kepler, the emperor's court astronomer.[5] Kepler belonged to the German scientific circle and wanted to repay a personal debt to the Hungarian people who had given him asylum when he was forced to flee from Austria because of his Protestant convictions. So it was Kepler who as court astronomer opened the way for Molnár to present his dictionary to the recluse emperor in the palace in Prague.

Molnár's dictionaries sold quickly, and he also arranged for some to be sent to persons in Prague. The councillor of the royal court recommended him for a post at the University of Vienna on condition that he convert to Catholicism. Though tempted by the offer of prominence, Molnár left Prague and made a detour around Vienna, so that "my faith in Christ would not be shaken."

News of Albert Szenci Molnár's successes in Prague reached intellectual circles in Germany and enhanced his prestige as a scholar. As soon as he had recovered from the fatigue of his return journey from Prague to Heidelberg, he began to write again.

Psalms

First the Hungarian dictionary. Now the Hungarian psalms. For years Molnár had been singing the psalms, morning and evening, in misery or abundance. Sometimes he earned a meager income as singing master or choir director. The psalms in German, Latin, and even Hungarian were an integral part of his life. Already he had translated a few of them in Hungarian. Now he was urged to translate more, for the psalms, along with the sermon, had become the mainstays of the Protestant worship service. At first the Catholics ridiculed the psalms of David as "heretical songs." In 1531 already, long before Molnár was born, the Sorbonne University, as official spokesman of the Roman Catholic Church, had forbidden the use of psalms in Roman Catholic worship.

The sixteenth century was the century of psalm singing. The liturgical needs of the Reformation necessitated translation of the psalms. Luther, Zwingli, and Calvin, themselves famous composers and translators, were the first to provide them. Someone observed that the German people sang themselves into the Lutheran faith. (*das Volk singt sich in Luther's Lehre hinein.*)

The French Huguenots had been the first to develop Protestant church singing. Other nations had soon followed. Thus, the Germans in 1533, the English in 1562, the Dutch in 1567, the Italians in 1578, the Poles in 1580, and the Czechs in 1599 gave this incomparable musical heritage to their people as a profession of faith.*

Clement Marot, the Frenchman, translated thirty psalms, which he dedicated to the Roman Emperor, Charles V, when he visited the court of the French king, Francois I. The emperor encouraged Marot to translate more of them, though this did not prevent Marot from being accused of heresy, thereby forcing him to flee. The rest of his life he lived in obscurity in the Italian city of Turin.**

At Calvin's request, Theodore Beza finished translating the so-called Genevan psalms, which were published in 1543. Louis Bourgeois was one of those who set the Huguenot psalms to music. He collected some of the melodies from Swiss taverns and folk meetings, thereby making the psalms quite popular. For this desecration the town council of Geneva sentenced him to prison.***

Molnár's Hungarian psalm translations were based on the work of the Frenchman Marot and the German Ambrose Lobwasser, whose psalm book was the one generally used in German Protestant church services.

Molnár became the Hungarian interpreter of the psalms. His talent was a fortunate combination of poetic sensitivity and knowledge of theology and languages. In his translations he strove for fidelity of meaning rather than poetic beauty, though this shone clearly also.

---

*The Psalms of David were by that time translated into twenty-five languages.

**Recently a Hungarian scholar discovered in the Library of Munich Marot's first psalm translations of 1529.

***See *Confessio*, Budapest 1980, ch. 4, pg. 30.

He was a deeply religious man, but his life was a ceaseless struggle with fate. No wonder that his translations carried a poignant identification with the heart cries of the Old Testament Jews. Most psalms were once born in suffering, persecution, or other struggles, and Molnár himself had suffered many trials during his wanderings from place to place. Moreover, his countrymen were enduring bitter years under Turkish oppression, and they were in need of consolation. The plaintive spirit of many psalms comforted equally the ancient Israelites and the invaded Hungarians. In a sense, the history of the two merged in Molnár's translation.*

He finished this work too in an astonishingly short time, scarcely four months. In spite of the prohibition against psalm singing by the Roman Catholic Church, Molnár managed to have his translations published in Herborn, Germany, in 1607.

For the second time in his life, the plague came to his aid. It was decimating the European population and a printer in Herborn had made this vow, "If God will spare me, I will spend the rest of my life doing good deeds." It was at the door of this printer, Christopher Corvinus, that Molnár knocked with his completed psalm translation. Thus the new Hungarian psalter was published.

It may be noted that after more than a hundred editions, these Hungarian psalms are sung today by Molnár's countrymen who are suffering trials no less great.

The *Psalterium Ungaricum* of Molnár contained all one hundred fifty psalms. They were republished thirty times in the seventeenth century.

In order to understand the difficulties Molnár faced in translating, it must be noted that the psalms, which had been copied and recopied for centuries, often contained errors in copying which corrupted the meaning beyond comprehension. Therefore, some translators added words to the original text, not always accurate. Further problems arose in matching the concept of a word in one language to a precisely equivalent concept in another. In addition, exegetists of the Old Testament who had forgotten the original meaning of words or their grammatical interpretation, had also often caused obscurities. Furthermore, the Israelites had adopted a new language during their long captivity. And finally, the introduction of punctuation in previously unpunctuated manuscripts had added confusion to

---

*Similarly, the Hussites used the psalms to defend their faith.

original meaning. Sometimes psalms had even been wholly rewritten to make them more comprehensible. Perhaps it had been on this basis that Luther had accused the Hebrew linguists of tampering with the texts. Molnár, who was well-versed in the Old Testament, could see that many of his predecessors had distorted the meaning of some psalms. (One had even gone so far as to weave into the text praise of Martin Luther's personal merits.)*

Recognizing the probable inadequacy of his undertaking, he wrote apologetically, "A translation is never perfect or identical with the original; it is like a rug; if we turn it over, we can see a great difference between one side and the other."

Molnár's concept of God's presence in history he shared with Marot, Beza, and Lobwasser only partially, for their life styles differed to a great extent from his. Yet, it is undeniable that they helped him with his artistic forms. Marot was not a Protestant as might have been expected of a psalm translator, and how could Beza's heavy, scholarly, hand contribute French lyric poetry? Molnár restored to David's psalms what Marot and Beza had taken from them. Marot's psalms were written by a courtier, Molnár's by a prophet, as the Hungarian László Németh has expressed it.

Thus Molnár was not only a translator, but also a poet whose burning and eruptive talent produced an original Hungarian translation and created poetry at the same time. Molnár kept himself in the background and faithfully rendered the psalms according to the spirit of the Bible. As syncretic theologian, he was not willing to use this part of the Old Testament to defend Church dogmas or as a weapon of polemics. He gave the eternal values of the Bible and its revelations to his people. For this reason, the Hungarian Catholic Church was later able to adopt many of his translations.

Molnár dedicated his *Psalterium Ungaricum* to his two German patrons. He personally carried his new work to Prince Elector Frederick IV and to Morits, Landgrave of Hesse. On his mother's side, Morits was a descendant of Saint Elizabeth, daughter of Hungarian King Béla, and he knew the language of his maternal ancestors well. Naturally, the patrons rewarded Molnár financially, and Morits wrote his son, rector of the University of

---

*Presently the Jesuit Michael Dahood has tried to clear up these confusions with his translations and explanations of the psalms in his recently published Ugaritic texts. His work has helped greatly to clarify many corrupted texts.

Marburg, to give Molnár a scholarship. The patrons asked the latter also to write a grammar of the Hungarian language.

When reading Molnár's dedications and comparing them to the humanist's flattering, at times blackmailing style, one feels the stark contrast with the attitude of the Protestants. As an example, Molnár's dedication of the *Psalterium Ungaricum* reads:

> "The saying of Aristides which goes like this sounds wise to me: It is proper to dedicate temples to God, and honor decent people by dedicating books to them. I follow this truth all the more gladly as I know even holy men did so. The Evangelist Luke honored the great Theophilus by dedicating two books to him. I quote the following lines from the writings of the Apostle Peter: 'Silver or gold I do not have, but what I have I give you'. For this reason, I present and dedicate David's Psalms to Your Highness, which I translated into Hungarian at the cost of great labor."

These facts illustrate how, after the Reformation, laymen took over from the church the directing of cultural affairs. They established new universities, installed printing presses, and gave scholarships to poor students.

It also should be noted that the translation of religious and secular literature into national tongues was a result of the humanism of the time. Molnár's literary activities developed under this pervading influence.

It seems incredible that authors of Molnár's day rarely received honoraria. In fact, receiving payment was sometimes viewed as a form of simony, selling the gift of the Holy Spirit, that is, the creations of genius, for money.[6]

What motives kept the geniuses of that age faithful to demanding work they undertook for their entire lives? Only faith, and a commitment to serve the people of whom they were a part, could have sustained them. For Molnár, serving his countrymen also meant raising their cultural level, which he compared to the highly developed life of the Western nations. His obsessions with writing not only satisfied personal goals, but also helped to shape the collective spirit of his countrymen in later centuries. His books also were part of the intellectual and spiritual bridge built between Western and Eastern Europe by religious scholars and authors. He contributed significantly to this synthesis.

Bible Revision

First the dictionary, then the psalm book, and next came a revision of the Bible. Molnár moved to Marburg in 1607. Landgrave Morits had arranged for a scholarship for him there. He received his board at a student Mensa, which freed him from the paralyzing effect of poverty. Fluent in scholarly Latin and German, he worked further to perfect his Hungarian mother tongue. This experience prepared him for his main effort, a revised version of the Hungarian Bible, earlier translated by Gáspár Károlyi in 1590. Because of the danger of confiscation of the Bibles during transportation, the printing had to be done in small format. The casting of Hungarian letter type for a German printing press also presented a problem. Finally in 1608, fifteen hundred copies of Molnár's revision were published by a poor widow working on a German printing press in Hanau. *Finita est impressio Bibliorum*, Molnár wrote in his Journal.[*] A second edition appeared in 1612 in Oppenheim.

Molnár dedicated the revised Bible to his patron, Landgrave Morits.

The revision, including the first printing, had taken him one year. The Biblical poetry he wrote in verse form, as a poet would, basing his verses on two modern translations of his age, John Piscater's Bible and the so-called Geneva Bible. Copyright laws were then unknown. So, in his introduction, Molnár called upon printers of his time not to allow anyone else to publish his revision, because that would hurt the poor widow who had printed the original copies.

Of course Molnár was concerned about the financial aspect of publishing the revised Bible. He was even more concerned about how to get copies into Hungary. The Inquisition and his own king stood in his way. A shrewd merchant advised Molnár to pack the fifteen hundred copies in casks as if they were ordinary merchandise and to wait for a merchant caravan heading for Hungary by way of Vienna. The mercenaries hired by the merchant would protect the casks from Turkish attacks. And if asked, they could always plead the excuse, "How can we assume responsibility for delivery of the Holy Scriptures under such cover of respectability?"

Thus the revised Bibles departed for Hungary. Their delivery was an example of the many ruses which characterized the ongoing battle between

---

[*]Hannoviae, *Journal*, p.48

Protestants and Roman Catholics. The counter-Reformation following the Council of Trent added impetus to the struggle.

Grammar

As soon as the "Bible casks" were on their way, Molnár began a new project. He responded to the earlier request of Landgrave Morits for a Hungarian grammar. Far from the spoken language of his people, from Hungarian libraries and other reference sources, he began the virtually impossible task. There were no Hungarian pioneers in this field. So Molnár turned to European linguistic literature for inspiration. The most accomplished linguist then was the French Huguenot, Petrus Ramus, professor at the College de France. Unfortunately, he had been among the hundred thousand French Protestants killed in the massacre of Saint Bartholomew's Night in 1572.

Using Ramus' grammatical system, Molnár completed his *Novae grammaticus Ungaricae* after two years of research, study, and writing. In the introduction he recounts the difficulties he overcame and compared himself to other writers, such as the German, John Clajus, who took twenty years to finish his *Deutsche Sprachlehre* even though others had worked in that area before him. Molnár's main reference source, besides his knowledge of the language, was the Hungarian Bible which he had revised.

Grammar is the art of expressing oneself well, *Ars bene loquendi*, according to Molnár. With his dictionary and now his grammar, he wanted to give theology a tool with which to drive out pagan philosophical ideas. He attempted to relate the Hungarian language to other European languages, and became the first to determine that his mother tongue was not related to Germanic, nor to Romance, nor to Slavic languages.

Language Research

The work he had done on the dictionary and the grammar inspired Molnár's research into the origins of the Hungarian language. In a short time he refuted the romantic hypothesis of the German Kekkermann, who had claimed that the name "Hungarian" itself came from the Bible and that the language was related to Hebrew. Research in the next generation after Molnár proved that the Hungarian language is a member of the Finno-Ugric language family.*

At the same time that Molnár was busy with his linguistic research, German linguistic studies were emerging. Martin Opitz, a poet and close friend of Molnár, was the leader in this field. He was also instrumental in introducing German into the schools which had been teaching only in Latin. Through men such as these, national languages became literary. Printed literature replaced handwritten pages so that each national language acquired standards of grammar and literary expression.

Institutio

The dictionary, the psalm book, the Bible, the grammar—what else of basic value deserved to be written or translated into Hungarian? Albert found his answer in the *Institutio religionis christianae* of John Calvin, a great classic statement of Reformation theology. He completed the translation in 1620 and dedicated it to Gábor Bethlen, Prince of Transylvania, who had commissioned him to do the work and supported him meanwhile. The translation was published in 1624 in Hanau, Germany, and was intended especially for the Reformed churches of the prince's area.**

The *Institutio* in more than a hundred fifty editions was translated all over Europe by devout Protestants who vied with one another to be the first to publish it in their own languages. For Albert this work was no insignificant accomplishment. It put his command of language to a severe test. Hundreds of new terms had to be invented to express the concepts which thereby entered Hungarian theological nomenclature. No fewer than

---

*The Hungarian attitude toward the discoveries of their own linguist, János Sajnovits, was skeptical. When Sajnovits returned from Scandinavia and presented his observations concerning linguistic affinity between Finnish, Lapp, and Hungarian, the Hungarian experts rejected them. They were not willing to acknowledge a relationship to languages that "smelled of fish". They preferred to identify themselves with classical Hebrew, according to L. Venetianer in *Comparative Linguistics, Hebrew Hungarian*, Budapest, 1898.

**This is demonstrated in the dedication Molnár wrote for the Transylvanian ruler:

"Your Majesty's pastor justifiably calls Your Majesty the second Josiah. King Josiah reformed his temple based on the recently found Book of Laws; now Your Majesty can rebuild the Church of the Bible based on the new book, the *Institutio*. For this reason, it is to you I dedicate this book which I translated at Your Majesty's request.[14]

three hundred such technical expressions can be found in the translation. As a writer on a high intellectual level, Albert carried out his task with philological precision. His so-called Protestant spelling helped standardize Hungarian spelling and spread from his works into the Hungarian language as a whole.

The translation of Calvin's *Institutio* was the crown of Molnár's life work; later his Protestant countrymen drew inspiration from it to practice the principle of *semper reformare*.

Through this effort of Molnár the spiritual integration of the West into the East was accomplished. (In retrospect the contemporary Calvin critics affirm Calvin's impact upon the European religious and social changes which took place. While the secular humanists had undermined the foundation of "thus says the Lord", Calvin had preached it.)

Marriage

Tiring of his solitude, Molnár made up his mind to marry. He must have been nearly forty years old by then. The woman he chose was the abandoned wife of his former Hebrew professor, Cunigonde Gerinari Wildpretert. (Cunigonde was a close relative of Martin Luther.)

The Hebrew professor had become so absorbed in the Old Testament world that he converted to Judaism and deserted to Salonica, which was under Turkish (Moslem) control. (In these days Moslems believing in one God and Jews worshipping Jehovah often collaborated for mutual economic interests, and many Jews fleeing the Spanish Inquisition had settled in Turkish territory.) Molnár married the abandoned wife and took in her and her three daughters. Three more daughters were born to the couple.

In order to support his large family, Molnár was forced to abandon his scholarly attitude. He accepted a position as director of a large press. Nevertheless, his family burdens compelled him to return to Hungary, where he became a teacher and a preacher.

The Prince of Transylvania offered to make him director of the newly established college. After two years, however, the constant threat of war with the Turks so frightened the family that to assure the safety of the "German womenfolk", he returned to Germany with them.

There he became a singing master, later a rector in Oppenheim. He was successful and received adequate salary. This made it possible for him to return to literary life, and he surprised Western readers with a timely historical work, *Idea Christianorum Ungarorum sub tyranide Turcica*, in which he described the problems of Hungarian Christians under Turkish tyranny. He also published a book of sermons, *Postilla Scultetica*, which was soon followed by another collection of sermons.

From time to time, he rested from his feverish activities and reflected upon his experiences. In the introduction of one of his books, he meditated on the meaning of life:

> "Our Lord Christ wandered the face of the earth as an exile. We suffer a similar fate as we are parts of Him."

Continuing, he recalled the wandering Apostles, who wrote their works, the Gospels, in exile, and added that Calvin himself was in exile, suffering for his people, while writing books that could fill a library. He consoled himself with these thoughts in his own exile, and continued to write the Word of God to the oppressed Hungarians.

A persistent traveler, he returned again to the University of Heidelberg for reasons unknown today, but this creative restlessness was a constant stimulant for him. He wrote in his journal that he was perpetually occupied with writing. He kept his eyes riveted on his master Calvin, whose literary output numbered forty volumes. Molnár had time for only twenty works. Historians have observed that Europe was torn both spiritually and morally by the Thirty Years' Religious War in which a third of the male population of Germany lost their lives on the battlefield. Consequently, German women who could no longer count on marriage asked the ruler to introduce temporary marriage, in other words bigamy, the ancient custom of the Old Testament. The Czech people suffered a similar fate. By the time the war abated, two-thirds of the population of East Central Europe had died. For example, the Protestant Church in Czech territory ceased to exist, mainly due to Habsburg-Catholic oppression.[7]

A catastrophic shift in Europe's demography took place; the people, deserting the rural regions, swarmed into the cities for protection. For a century and a half, Hungary defended itself in incessant Turkish wars, and by the time the Moslem invaders were finally routed, the Hungarian population was reduced from about four million to one million.

Working in Heidelberg, Molnár was also affected by these wars. In 1621 Spanish Catholic mercenaries occupied the city of Germany's oldest university, the center of German Calvinism since 1560. The marauding soldiers tied Molnár by the feet to the ceiling of his library and tortured him with burning candles to force him to confess where he had hidden a supposed treasure. Finally, he managed to escape his tormenters and fled with his family to the city of Hanau, where his works had been published. There he lived with his family in abject poverty.

In this destroyed and demoralized Europe, Molnár tried to struggle on and continue his activities as literary reformer. Slowly, however, the European spirit was exhausted and its spiritual life turned into the passive attitude of Catholic restoration. Exhausted men were confronted with the recurring historic dilemma; that is, whether to choose security or freedom, to resign themselves to a Catholicism that promised peace, or to continue suffering for the Protestant faith.

During these trying days, Molnár's friends had either died or fled, and his royal patrons had lost their thrones. In his desperation there was no other way out than to return to Hungary with his family and his worries. Hungary was ravaged by the cruel religious wars, but the ruler of Transylvania, Gábor Bethlen, took Molnár under his wing.

Gábor Bethlen was an extraordinary man who took part in twenty-two wars. When barely fifteen years old, he had been wounded gravely in battle with the Turks; thereafter his body was covered with scars, his limbs paralyzed. His chronicler noted that "He spent half his life on the battlefield, but the other half was left to devote to his country."

He was scarcely twenty years old when he became court councillor and general to the king and emperor's court in Prague. He was thirty years old when he was elected ruler of Transylvania. and he soon realized that the sword alone was not enough to fight off the aggression of Habsburg Catholicism and Turkish Mohammedanism, but that a high standard of cultural life would be needed.

Bethlen had read the Bible thirty times, from beginning to end, and he had found religious-spiritual inspiration for himself and for his subjects in Calvinism. This explained his cultural policy, which bestowed the rank of nobility on graduating students in addition to the diplomas they received from the university that Bethlen had founded.[8] This privilege also endowed the elite of the future with personal immunity in the midst of the barbarism of that age. It was evident that the Biblical warning "My people are destroyed for the lack of knowledge," (Hosea, 4. vs. 6) had made a deep impression on him.

Bethlen was an exceptional individual; remarkably, in an age characterized by religious intolerance, he, as a Protestant ruler, supported the translation of the Catholic Bible.[9]

During his campaign in Moravia, he saved thousands of Anabaptists from the hands of the Spanish inquisitors and settled them in his country, where he gave them thirty-four villages and granted a reduction in taxes.[10] As for the Rumanian Orthodox believers who had escaped to his realm, he instituted priestly missionary education, organized bishoprics, and ordered translation of the Holy Scriptures for them.

Bethlen brought in Jews from territories ruled by the Turks and gave them several privileges; he allowed them, for instance, to dress like Christians, something uncommon at that time in East Central Europe.

In this manner, hoping to bolster the weakened economy, Bethlen tried to replace the merchant class which had been deported by the Turks.

Bethlen extended religious tolerance to nine denominations: Reformed, Lutheran, Roman Catholic, Unitarian, Greek Orthodox, Sabbatarian, Habanian-Baptists, Jews and Moslems. He did this, while the Thirty Years' Religious War was wiping out large numbers of the population, and in neighboring countries rulers could not tolerate even two religious denominations.

When Molnár and his family returned to Transylvania, where he presented the folios of his completed translation of Calvin's *Institutes* to Gábor Bethlen, the latter rewarded him for this literary work and gave him a position as professor.

Very little of Molnár's biographical information has survived from then on, because he stopped keeping a diary. It seems that when his patron died in 1629, Molnár could not continue his literary activity for long. One of the facts we do know is that he married off his six daughters.

Although Molnár had somehow avoided the plague in Germany, he fell victim to it in Kolozsvár. The registers of the college of the Unitarian Church, founded and developed by Francis Dávid, contain information, recently discovered, on Albert Szenci Molnár's death. The registers listed name, circumstances of death, and cost of tolling the bells for plague victims. Calvinist churches did not have bells at that time, and the Unitarian churches performed, therefore, the bell-ringing service at funerals, demonstrating a certain religious tolerance. In 1634 the number of plague victims was so large that for only a third of the twelve hundred dead, bells were rung. Fortunately for historiography, the name of Albert Szenci Molnár was included in this list. The record reads:

> *1634. 18 Januarii pulsatum est Reverendo Albert Molnár Majoribus. 3 Vicibus Facit florenum 1, dinarius 40.* 1634. 18 January died Reverend Albert Molnár Sr.[11]

Thus Molnár's life of wandering scholar came to an end. He belonged to the generation of Biblical seekers of his century. One could virtually draw a map of Europe of the sixteenth century in tracing Molnár's footsteps. He represented the spiritual yearnings of the Hungarian people, who, ever since they reached Europe in the ninth century, had looked to the West, longing to become European.

In summary, one may conclude that Albert Szenci Molnár's literary work was mainly influenced by an historical situation, the Islamic conquest of Hungary, which had broken spiritual-religious continuity in this country. Molnár yearned to restore this lost continuity on a literary level. That is why he spent forty-three of his sixty years abroad, studying and adapting what he learned to the needs of Hungary. In a letter he analogized himself to Jacob:

> "When Pharaoh asked Patriarch Jacob how old he was, Jacob answered that the years of his wanderings were a hundred and thirty. The holy man called his life wandering. I too can call forty-three years of my life wandering, because I spent barely twelve years with my parents. I soon left them to wander the world."[12]

For Albert Molnár, journeying set a task for a man; it was not an end in itself, only a means. He followed the intellectual paths of Europe in order to be able to introduce Western culture to East Central Europe. He gradually insinuated himself into the company of scholars, because for him, as for many others, travel equalled wisdom and knowledge. He always remained a faithful follower of the Dutch-Flemish scholar, Lipsius, until Lipsius wearied of practicing his own principles and returned to the bosom of the Roman Catholic Church.

In most of Molnár's work it becomes clear that the guiding spirit behind his entire cultural philosophy was Petrus Ramus, the French Huguenot, who, as a Christian humanist, first had opposed Aristotelian Scholasticism, and had stressed Calvinist theology, and who also had strongly recommended the use of national language instead of Latin.[13]

Molnár's writings were concerned only with the needs of his country. Like Ramus, he was an advocate for the critical mind, for the creativity of rationalism. He settled only for short periods of time to digest what he had absorbed and to prepare himself for the next step.

Living on the Eastern religious and spiritual frontier of Europe, Molnár worked hard to bring about a synthesis between East and West. He was, as it were, "Janus-faced" in that he had two spiritual homes: the West where he studied and worked, the East where he taught and which he tried to steer to completion of the Reformation.

By temperament, Molnár was not a fighter, but his often miserable circumstances, the alien surroundings in which he wrote and studied, and surrounding social situations forced him to fight. In his journal he wrote once: *"Patria quae me non ornat* (My country did not pamper me.)"

In his last publication, *Discursus de summo bono*, which appeared in 1630, he warned his readers, not without a trace of bitterness, not to build their trust on the constant goodwill of those in power because:

> "God bids us in the First Commandment to put our trust only in Him and not in any of His creatures. Do not trust the princes of this world; they are sons of man and have no power to liberate us."[14]

He concluded that no one can find the ultimate good in the goodwill and favors of great lords. For that reason one should flee as fast as one could the life at the courts. This realistic outlook is the last message which Albert Szenci Molnár, molded by the contradictions of his age, left for his and for the younger generation.

These remarks revealed a new tone in him. One can sense in them that his strength was on the wane. There appeared a tendency to withdraw into a passive, puritan way of life, which isolated him from others. He rather chose to suffer for his moral principles.

Did Albert Molnár, who grew up in the more highly developed West, find it hard in his last years to fit into the lower cultural life of his own country? The tension between East and West had made him the creative artist he was. He was instrumental in the miracle which brought his countrymen to the Reformed religion. This is why history pays tribute to him, the wandering scholar, who, like most of his contemporary reformers was buried in an unmarked grave.

Footnotes

1. Vargha, Anna. *Justus Lipsius és a magyar szellemi élet.* Budapest, 1942.

2. Kovács, Sándor Iván. *Pannoniából Europába.* Budapest, 1975. Gondolat kiadó.

3. Richter, A. *Bilder aus der deutsche Kulturgeschichte.* Vol. II. p. 110. Leipzig, 1893.

4. Dézsi, Lajos. *Szenczi Molnár Albert Naploja.* Budapest, 1898.

5. Turoczi-Trostler, J. *Szenczi Molnár Albert Heidelbergben. Magyar Irodalom Tőrténet Világ Irodalom Tőrténet.* Budapest, 1961. Akadémia Kiadó.

6. Kopp, Fr. *Geschichte des Deutschen Buchhandels.* Vol. I. Leipzig, 1886. pp. 315–316.

7. Gindely, Anton. *Geschichte des dreissigjǎhrigen Krieges.* Vol. I, II. 1878.

8. Zsinka, Ferenc. *Bethlen Gábor cimeres levele papok részére. Nagyenyedi Album.* ed. Imre Lukinics. Budapest, 1936. p. 101.

9. Szekfű, Gyula. *Bethlen Gábor.* in *Magyar Szemle Társaság.* Budapest, 1929. p. 148.

10. Krausz, George. *Siebenbürgische Kronik.* in *Fontes Rerum Austricarum.* Dpl.43.393.

11. *Regestrum Ecclesiae Claudiopoli. Unitaris Kollegium. (Kolozsvár-Cluj.)*

12. Incze, Gábor. *Szenczi Molnár Albert.* Budapest, 1939. p. 57.

13. Moltmann, Jürgen. *Zur Bedeutung der Petrus Ramus für Philosophie und Theologie im Calvinismus. Zeitschrift für Kirchengeschichte.* 1957. Heft 3/4. p. 317.

14. Incze, Gábor. *op. cit.,* p. 259.

Chapter XV

Péter Bornemissza, Lutheran Bishop
± 1535–1584

Péter Bornemissza's life story is in itself typical of the sixteenth century. A tragic sense permeated his activities as a Reformer throughout his life. He could never rest in that noisy God-seeking century. He was a man who burned himself out as a befitting prophet serving a church that had found the Gospel again in the spiritual revolution which was taking place in Europe. He was a man persecuted relentlessly by the Roman Catholic Bishop Telegdi, a man who was frequently forced to change his domicile. Married three times, he fathered six children, all of whom died of the plague which was raging in Europe.

Born perhaps in 1535, (the date of his birth is uncertain), he was a scion of an illustrious aristocratic family. Early in life when he was barely six years old, Bornemissza lost his parents. The Turks beheaded his father in Buda, because he had allegedly supported Habsburg Ferdinand's claim to the Hungarian throne. Young Péter escaped to his relatives who raised him. At the age of 18, he confessed already the Protestant faith. Leonard Cox, the humanist of English descent, who taught first at the university of Cracow, then at a Hungarian college, introduced Bornemissza to the world of new ideas.

At that age, young Péter also learned the prison life style, which taught him not to fear but to endure suffering. As a youthful prank, one night he stole into the bedroom of the Roman Catholic captain of the castle in Kassa, where he was staying, and warned the captain in a voice which seemed to come from another world, not to worship graven images. The captain woke up and, realizing that it was not the voice of an angel but a human one, pulled Bornemissza from behind the stove where he was hiding, thrashed him with his club, and had him thrown in prison. The young man, however, learned with the "help of angels," as he said, to open the lock of the iron door and escaped.

For an unknown reason, he spent three years in another castle prison. He was freed after his innocence finally had been proved.

In 1559 Bornemissza set out with "eight florins" in his pocket to visit Italian and German universities to continue his studies. At that time, probably, he wrote this poem:

Miserable I feel

Miserable I feel thus to depart from thee
My blessed Magyar land, afar to go from thee
When if ever shall I dwell again in Buda?

Highland hills are in the hands of the haughty Germans
Szerémség is in the hands of the Turkish heathen,
When if ever shall I dwell again in Buda?

I was forsaken by the lords of the Magyar race;
Expelled is the true God; who then can hope for grace?
When if ever, shall I dwell again in Buda?

Thus, I say my farewell, blessed Hungary, to thee
Because there is in thee no great nobility.
When if ever shall I dwell again in Buda?

In fair castle of Huszt were these verses writ,
Péter Bornemissza when in his versing wit
When if ever shall I dwell again in Buda?
translation Egon Kunz

The poem is a good illustration of Bornemissza's historical and psychological outlook, and of the yearning of his restless soul for his native land.

He visited the institutions of learning in Rome, Padua, and Venice. The University of Padua had at that time become completely secularized; it represented, among others, Arab philosophy and rabbinical anti-Christian freethinking. From there he went on to Wittenberg, where he studied under Melanchthon. However, he was shocked by the corruption wrought by the

Roman and humanist spirits at all these universities. After a while he left Wittenberg and registered at the University in Vienna. At that time this university was trying to reconcile humanist and Protestant teachings. Two Hungarian professors who taught there had already embraced Protestantism; one of them, John Sylvester, originally sided with the followers of Erasmus, who had advised King Ferdinand to practice religious reconciliation. In his writing entitled *Querele Fidei*, Sylvester, like Erasmus, emphasized that the innate goodness of humanity was the virtue that contributed most to peace. He also felt it necessary to revive Christian theology. The religious conflicts during this time of transition had not yet solidified. Sylvester's disciple, Bornemissza, was one of those who strived for reconciliation between the theologians and humanists. His teachers—Cox, Erasmus, Melanchthon—as well as the spirit of the school of Padua, had advocated inner loftiness, peace and reform.

These idyllic intellectual and religious aspirations,however, changed while Bornemissza was still a student. The Counter-Reformation refused to tolerate the followers of an ambiguous confession. At first the citizens of Vienna resisted firmly the Catholic reforms of the Council of Trent. When, for example, the Jesuit provost and papal nuncio, Peter Canisius, went to preach in the cathedral of St. Stephen, the Habsburg king had to call out special troops to protect him from the attacks of the Lutheran citizens.[1]

As a student of the university, Péter Bornemissza preached Lutheran sermons in his apartment. Apart from fellow students even some citizens of Vienna came to hear him preach. Finally, the bishop of Vienna had him thrown into prison for this provocative behavior. Bornemissza wrote later in his memoirs about this incident: "Three bishops and King Ferdinand himself questioned me; I was afraid, but my heart was burning and perhaps my sides would have split, if I had not opened my mouth and embraced Jesus."[2]

The Apostle Paul once gave in to a similar compulsion when writing to the Corinthians.

But why should three bishops and the king concern themselves with a poor Viennese student? From Bornemissza's narratives we learn that he, as an aristocrat, was a frequent visitor to the royal court. He related, for example, a conversation he had with the king's daughters, who would rather have been born daughters of a cobbler, for then they would not be forced to enter a convent, which to them seemed a living death.

The main reason for Bornemissza's interrogation may well have been his writings; his comrades at the university had asked him to write an entertaining drama for them. As a humanist, he had a thorough grounding in Greek literature, and he had chosen the famous Greek social drama, Sophocles' *Electra*, and adapted it for the age.

In this adaptation, Bornemissza tried to improve the morals of the time by criticizing them. (Similarly, his contemporary in Geneva, John Calvin, tried to evoke Christian ethics by translating the works of the Roman Seneca.) Finally, Bornemissza was banished from Vienna, even though his father several years earlier had shown his loyalty to the Habsburg king, for which he had been beheaded on order of the Turkish Sultan.

He went back to Wittenberg, where he became once again a student of Melanchthon. He lived in Melanchthon's house, and later became his follower and correspondent.

As part of his memories of Wittenberg. Bornemissza described the domestic life of his beloved teacher Melanchthon, whose wife often pounded on her husband's door and with abusive language demanded to be let in, upon which Melanchthon would remark quietly: "This too belongs to the Calvary of marriage." Bornemissza also related how Melanchthon tried to awaken his pupils at seven o'clock in the morning by reading them his famous theological collection *Loci communes*, but at times he would tell them funny and not overly Biblical stories.

Emperor Maximilian was quite contemptuous of this withered little man, who had no peer in the world for his modest dress and physical weakness, and called him "Half a man." Bornemissza would later experience a similar contempt from the same Emperor, whom he described as having "bulging eyes and pouting Habsburg lips."

After eight years of study, doubt, and finally conversion, Bornemissza returned to Hungary with the burning consciousness of a divine mission: He wanted to be the liberator of the Hungarian people, who were suffering under the double oppression of "two pagans"—the Roman Catholic Habsburgs and the Moslem Turks. In spite of this view, he acted as secretary to King Ferdinand until the latter's death in 1564 and then became a pastor in Northwest Hungary. Ten years later he became a Lutheran bishop.

Bornemissza's worst enemy was the erudite and fanatical Catholic Bishop Miklos Telegdi. Telegdi was already a disciple of the reformed Roman

Catholicism of Trent. He dedicated his life to silencing his Lutheran opponent, Péter Bornemissza, and was willing to use any means whatever to attain this end. He invoked every power from the Pope, Gregory XIII, to the King and Emperor Maximilian,[3] who had succeeded Ferdinand I, to attain this "Christian" goal, as he wrote in one of his letters:

> "I understand, my friend, what is eating you . . . I am building a stone wall against you to save Israel . . . I am not running from you wolves and I am not letting you into God's sheepfold to prey on Christ's sheep. I will fight you until you cease to be wolves. Until then, I will not cease to be a pastor. I will ask the king to persecute you until you recant. If you do not do so, I will ask him to kill you and wipe you off the face of the earth."[4]

Eventually the Holy See gave Bishop Telegdi specific authority to take any action he wished. And so, the Emperor and the Pope embarked on a campaign to silence the only Lutheran bishop in Northwest Hungary. Telegdi did not stop inciting against the Lutheran bishop Bornemissza, who had become well-known throughout the country. "If you do not recant, I will smoke you out of your fox-hole," Telegdi admonished.

Bornemissza was dragged off to Vienna by the Inquisition four times during his lifetime, the first time in 1564. Emperor Ferdinand I, before his death, had clearly recognized the Turkish threat to his territory, he had also understood that the religious quarrels that were raging only added to the political problems. Therefore, he had asked the Pope to allow the repeal of celibacy and the practice of Communion in both kinds for Lutheran Hungarians, Czechs, and Austrians. It was fortunate for Bornemissza that at the moment of his interrogation, the papal nuncio arrived in Vienna with a positive answer to the late Emperor's request. He was set free and returned to Hungary after Emperor Maximilian, in spite of the papal permission of the late Ferdinand's request, personally examined him on the following points:

1. As an ordained priest, why did you marry?
2. Why were you ordained in the Lutheran Church?
3. By what right have you administered Holy Communion with leavened bread?

In order to form a clear picture of the situation in 1564 one must realize the incredible fact that the papal nuncio could not find a bishop for Hungary that year, nobody was willing to assume the position because of the low remuneration that could be expected. When Archbishop Olah convoked a council, instead of thousands of priests, only one hundred nineteen came. Of these, sixty-two were married, and forty-four already celebrated Communion in both kinds. There were those who celebrated Mass in Slovak instead of Latin, heard confession in the Protestant manner, but they themselves did not confess their sins.

In 1545 the Hungarian archbishop had already announced at the opening of the Council of Trent that virtually every priest was married and nobody had been surprised when the loss of Hungary to the Roman Catholic Church was announced. Though the church fathers of Trent had mourned this loss, the Protestant revival of faith had established an evangelical renewal in Hungary.

Thus, it was not surprising that Bornemissza, as a successful church organizer, repeatedly clashed with the impoverished Roman Catholic Church leaders, who had been forced into the background. The latter, on the defensive, attempted to enforce the decrees of reform formulated at Trent. Their intolerance was understandable; after all in 1573, there were only two consecrated Roman Catholic bishops left in Hungary. One after the other, former church leaders had married and left their offices. This development is illustrated, for example, by three members of the Thurzo family; all three were once Roman Catholic bishops. They belonged to one of the richest families in East Central Europe; like the German Fugger family, they became proprietors of the mines of three countries. They lived worldly lives in the milieu of Renaissance humanism, which had grown decadent. Finally these men, with their enormous wealth, joined the Lutherans, thereby bringing whole regions into the Protestant Church.

Another example is furnished by András Dudich, the Roman Catholic bishop of Pécs, who represented Hungary at the Council of Trent. He was the Council's most celebrated orator. Returning to Hungary at the close of the Council, he married and continued his life as an Antitrinitarian humanist.

A final illustration shows that the Hungarian Roman Catholic Church was reduced to such desperate conditions that when it came to send its delegate to the Council of Trent, the Holy See had to cover the expenses by pawning church treasures.

The leaders of the Church had ceased to live Christian lives; the demoralizing effect of this reached the lowest priestly orders. A Roman Catholic church historian reported:

". . . monks sold the property, even the books of the monasteries
. . . the prior squandered the wealth of the order so that the monks
had no money for food or clothing . . . the city council guarded the
gold and silver vessels needed in the church service and allowed
members of the order to use them only during worship service."[5]

When the Hungarian Parliament assembled in 1569 in Pozsony to discuss
religious disputes, Bornemissza went to attend and to propagate Lutheran
Protestantism. When the Emperor heard about this, he intervened personally to have Bornemissza stopped, and the reformer was banned from
the city.[6]

In spite of these developments, Bornemissza went also to the next Diet,
where he opposed Emperor Rudolph and called on him to grant freedom
of worship. The Emperor refused, for he had vowed at his coronation to
protect the Roman Catholic religion.

In 1570(?), Bornemissza, like many reformers, went to work under the
patronage and protection of a landowner. His patron was Count Julius
Salm, who himself leaned toward Lutheranism. Bornemissza moved his
family and his servants to the Count's castle and became pastor of the
realm belonging to his patron. There he also established his printing
presses. In the years that followed Bornemissza was able to publish his daily
sermons which eventually formed five volumes. He called them *Postilla*.

His clashes with Roman Catholics continued and in 1573 Bishop Telegdi
once again called Bornemissza in for interrogation. When Bornemissza
refused to appear, he was excommunicated from the Roman Catholic
Church. He reported this in these words: "They excommunicated me, they
cursed me, they blew out all the candles in the church to demonstrate the
darkness which had fallen over me." A warrant was issued for his arrest in
Vienna. In 1574, he was elected Lutheran bishop.

In 1577, Emperor Rudolph forbade the practice of Lutheranism in
Austria. This decree, which expelled all Lutheran pastors under the threat
of the death sentence, was issued in disregard of the Augsburg Declaration
of 1555, which had allowed the Lutheran persuasion for the time being.

This action of the Emperor created an uncomfortable situation for Count
Salm, who owned extensive property in Austria in addition to his Hungarian
realm. From then on, he began to exercise pressure on Bornemissza to
recant.

When Bornemissza published in 1578 *The Temptations of the Devil*, in which he unmasked the nobility for their moral laxity and political corruption, Count Salm convened all other Lutheran pastors in his realm, to discuss the contents of this book. When they unanimously condemned the writing, Count Salm demanded a written recantation from Bornemissza. The latter refused to do so, and was then forced to leave Sempte in the midst of winter: "With my six-month-old twins, my sick wife, and my servants, I was driven out into the cold winter rain from the castle where for six years I had faithfully served the great cause, because I did not close my eyes to the sins of the lords. Ultimately, the blessing of the Lord will be with me."[7]

Before Bornemissza's expulsion, Count Salm had ordered him to write a work in which he would deny his Lutheran faith, confess his error, and return to the Roman Catholic Church. The reformer, however, could not renounce his prophetic mission. Instead he wrote: "I preferred to go out into the unknown, rather than give in to the temptation; my soul was joyful, for my heart could not blame me." Péter Bornemissza would not compromise. On the contrary, he published *From God's Mercy*, which he dedicated to his former patron Count Salm, probably not without a certain smugness.

From Sempte, Bornemissza then moved to Detrekö, the castle of his old friend, Baron Balassa. His family and entourage, and his four printing presses went with him. In the same year, 1579, Emperor Rudolph, informed of Bornemissza's inveterate behavior, ordered all printing presses shut down. Only with his permission could a press function in Hungary. The Protestants could no longer publish the Holy Scriptures or any other religious literature. According to Emperor Rudolph all Protestant preachers ought to be hanged; the late Ferdinand I had already concluded before him that all heretic printers should be drowned!

The aim of the Emperor and the Roman defenders of the faith was to deprive Bornemissza of his mightiest weapon, his printing presses, because they were well aware that the Protestant faith was the product of that special book, the Bible, printed in the vernacular.

In the immunity of Baron Balassa's castle, in which cellars Bornemissza's printing presses had been installed, the reformer began a wideranging correspondence in the interest of his planned translation and publication of the Bible. To print a complete Bible in translation in the sixteenth century imposed an unusually great task on its publisher. It not only necessitated knowledge of theology and linguistics, but also of considerable material resources. Bornemissza needed four thousand florins for such an undertaking, and this at a time when the income of a preacher was approximately seventy florins per year.

Bornemissza's inner compulsion was to devote his life now to the translation of the Bible. He could not realize this task because he died before its completion.

The evangelical Lutheran Church was of course based on the Holy Scriptures and Bornemissza stressed this repeatedly: "We are not living to digest, sleep, and get fat . . . but to make peace with Him, to become new men, thereby escaping the devil's clutches . . . to help each other, to grow in the knowledge of God. That is what preaching of the Gospel and the administration of the sacraments are for. If you do not want them at any price, and prefer Egyptian food to manna from heaven, the Lord will give the task of preaching the Kingdom of God to other nations. Thus, if you pass up God's Word by being absent from a service, consider it a greater sin than if you were to steal or kill."[8]

This estimation of the value of the Scriptures above all else gave the reformers that death-defying courage with which they endured many troubles and indignities in East Central Europe.

Hungarian Protestant preachers intended to fortify their people spiritually, to enable them to endure the misery forced on them by the Catholicism of the Habsburgs and the invading Islamic Turks. And so Bornemissza spread the Word among the people, continually admonishing them not to withdraw from the company of believers, because then their faith would wither and they would run out of prayers; their religion would grow cold, and they would slowly alienate themselves from God Himself. If, on the other hand, they would stay in a congregation, they would be fortified, and they would learn, and would serve as examples to others. Those were trying times and young people's hair would suddenly turn grey. Bornemissza's burdens were heavy; his many spiritual struggles and confrontations with the opposition sorely tempted him.

He subordinated everything to his service of the Church. As a healing physician does, he opened wounds to heal them. He wrote about the ills and sins of his society; he exposed the causes of mistakes; he felt that the nation had to face its sins in order to clear its conscience. In this manner he influenced the reform of an entire nation.

For obscure reasons, not known to historiography, Bornemissza went to Vienna in February 1579, was promptly arrested on order of Gaspar

Neubeck, Bishop of Vienna and thrown in jail. For several weeks he was tortured, but his tormenters could not break his spirit. In fact, he defied the bishop who was torturing him. Citing his aristocratic privilege, he protested his imprisonment and quoted passages from the Bible on Christian love. Finally he escaped. Later he wrote that angels had helped him out of prison. As once St. Paul had been lowered down the city wall in a basket, "I jumped down from the third floor of the bishop's prison." The Roman Catholic authorities, however, chided him saying that St. Paul's escape from prison had not been accomplished by the use of a file, indicating that Bornemissza had done so. Bornemissza sustained a broken arm and leg when he escaped from Vienna in this manner, to "the great humiliation of the Emperor and the Bishop."

In spite of these persecutions, Bornemissza's abilities as a church organizer, his literary achievements, and fearless faith made him a leader in a part of the country. Aristocrats, his own class, began to come to him for consolation, spiritual counsel, and advice. Reformers of neighboring countries such as Austria, Bohemia, and Moravia, also turned to him for help. He maintained a constant contact with his fellow-Lutherans, the Czechs, Moravians, Slovaks, and thus became a pioneer with them in the Protestant Reformation.

He represented and exemplified the century in which he lived. Such was the former student who had set off to see Europe, with eight florins in his pocket and who had returned with new teachings to help the Hungarians join the world in transformation by means of the new faith. As was common in that age, he burned himself out. The constant persecution hounded him to death. In every battle, he had struggled for the spiritual renewal of the nation.* In appearance he resembled his teacher Melanchthon, whom Emperor Maximilian once sneeringly had called "half a man", but Bornemissza's strength was rooted in God, who had enabled him to take on superhuman tasks.

When he died, a chronicler dared to register the event with these words:

"Péter Bornemissza suddenly went to sleep, but I do not know whether he is with the Lord or not, after all he was a Lutheran, poor fellow."

---

*Although they were contemporaries, no evidence exists so far which indicates that Bornemissza and the other reformer Melius, ever met or worked together in the struggle for spiritual renewal.

At his death, his relatives and patrons, converted lords of castles and fortresses, arranged a royal funeral for the persecuted Reformer. A towering tomb was placed above his broken body. The mourning congregation left his grave with the comforting thought that, thanks to Péter Bornemissza, religious reform and spiritual revolution were victorious in their part of Europe.

The next century, however, Habsburg Catholicism gained ground again. As a sign of their victory, the Habsburgs had Bornemissza's tomb destroyed and every trace of its existence was wiped out.

Bornemissza as Author

Few who played a role in Hungarian religious history have felt themselves to be an instrument of God as much as Bornemissza. He was the most prolific writer in sixteenth century Hungary. His contribution surpassed that of all previous religious writers. In barely ten years he published thirteen books, of which eleven composed his own theological writings. These make up fourteen thousand pages. In comparison, about thirty thousand pages left the presses in Hungary between 1558 and 1600. Nearly half of those were written by Péter Bornemissza; he alone wrote more than all Hungarian Lutheran bishops put together in the three hundred years that have passed since then, as Bauhoffer noted.[9]

Bornemissza is generally credited with creating Hungarian prose.

His adaptation of *Electra*, written in his native tongue while still a student in Vienna, directed the attention of Hungarian intellectuals to the issue of social justice. The central idea of his drama was the necessity to resist compromise. Courageous struggle alone could solve the problem of freedom that was the right of the people, he argued. Passivity would only condemn a nation to destruction.

In the drama young Bornemissza rejected the compromise of the middle road. Instead he introduced the question of the people's assumption of social responsibility instead of reliance upon an evil and tyrannical ruler. In this Hungarian *Electra*, Bornemissza asked: "Will Orestes achieve the hopes placed in him, will he become a good ruler?" The reason for doubt was that the entire family of Orestes had perpetrated horrible crimes.

"the great God blinded their hearts . . . who did not want to put a stop to their odious sins?"

The Master feared for Orestes and gave him this advice:

"Be pious and clear in mind, live charitably if you do not want to
suffer the same fate as your predecessors."

Bornemissza remembered all too well the Habsburg policies which had
resulted in feudal anarchy; thus, his suspicions of Orestes seemed justified.
He wondered whether a good ruler could be born who would serve the
people. At that moment Bornemissza could only give an evasive answer to
this question.

When one reads Bornemissza's *Electra* in its adapted version, it becomes
clear that he was not only preaching the Gospel to the students of Vienna.
He was using the classical drama to campaign against Habsburg
Catholicism,* and the Roman Catholic Church which had lost its original
mission. He had no illusion about changing an evil and tyrannical Catholic
ruler. His hopes lay in the people's assumption of responsibility for social
justice in the troubled time when people were deprived of their human
rights, on the one hand by Habsburg Catholicism and, on the other hand
by Turkish Mohammedanism, which were wreaking havoc in the country.

His studies completed and ordained in the ministry, Bornemissza rapidly
developed his talents as author. As a social critic and the most revolutionary church writer of his century, he rigorously exposed the abuses of the
Roman Catholic Church. He became one of those theologians who helped
bring about the social transformation of East Central Europe. Through his
sermons and activities as church leader, he transformed the social consciousness of the until-then anonymous masses. Using new means, "the
beautiful written word", as he called it, he created for himself an audience
of readers. Leaning on the bourgeois order that he had activated, he fought
the feudal aristocracy that could not keep pace with the times; likewise he
pitted his Evangelical Lutheranism against the humanist Catholic leaders
who were following the influence of the "divine" Erasmus. Among them
was Cardinal Bembo, the Pope's secretary, who warned his scholarly colleagues not to read the Vulgate, for fear its "barbarian" language would
ruin the beauty of their Latin style.

A Catholic church historian writing about Bornemissza corroborates the
Reformer's criticism in this way:

---

*The term Habsburg Catholicism is used to indicate that the Habsburgs had replaced
Roman Catholicism with their own version of Catholicism for dynastic purposes of
political interest and Germanization.

"The destructive effect of the activities of Erasmus' followers is incontestable . . . . His selfish tolerance spread like the contagion of religious indifference. Hungarian humanism was almost exclusively limited to high dignitaries of the Hungarian Church. And Mohács, the lost battle against the Turks, brought to ruin many decaying buildings of the Hungarian Catholic Church. The prelates who lost their lives in the battle of Mohács, two archbishops, five bishops, and innumerable monks and priests, thus atoned, to a certain extent, for what they had done during their lives."[10]

Bornemissza, one of the most cultured men of his generation in Hungary, could rival the most outstanding Hungarian humanists in breadth of knowledge.

His chief literary works are the five-volume collection of sermons, *Postilla*,* which provided the pastors of the Luthern church with much needed religious material. In preface Bornemissza wrote:

"I write so that other preachers can hold half-hour sermons, not only on Sunday, but every morning. Thus the community can be consecrated and improved every day by God's Word."[11]

As a pastor Bornemissza preached every morning in his native tongue, and his sermons caught on. When he preached, the people, before going to work in the fields, leaned their tools against the walls of the church building and attended the worship service. The building would be surrounded by a veritable forest of hoes, scythes, and spades.

As a writer his style was simple and direct. Hundreds of ideas and images teemed in his head. He often used vivid colors, displaying his fertile imagination. It is of interest to note that the contents of his sermons changed as society changed. Existential questions, the real problems of the day, were gradually incorporated in his daily Biblical lessons; he did not hesitate to expose both the social and the individual sins of his time.

Sometimes he had to criticize his colleagues harshly:

---

*In the sixteenth century published collections of sermons were known as *Postilla*. The word comes from a combination of the Latin *Post* (after) and *illa* (that). This refers to the fact that the sermons were delivered after the reading of the Gospels. These *Postilla* were published in collections *Regi magyar költök tára*, (Treasury of Old Hungarian Poets) Budapest, 1926.

"When the preachers write or speak to each other, they are without love, humility, and good will. It is not Christ whom they preach, but themselves."[12]

The chief source of conflict among pastors must have been the swarm of theological problems that had not been cleared up at the time. Among Bornemissza's contemporaries, Lutheran, Helvetian, Unitarian, and Baptist theologians constantly were in conflict with each other over principles of their beliefs.

With his publication of *The Temptations of the Devil* in 1578, Bornemissza gained a special place in the Protestant literature of the sixteenth century; even from a European perspective, it made him famous. He divulged in this pioneer work the crimes perpetrated for decades by the aristocracy and high dignitaries of the Church and named explicitly those whom "the devil has on a leash, as his own."

The robber barons of the times characteristically had supported the claims to the Habsburg throne of successively Ferdinand, Maximilian, and Rudolph, who then had closed their eyes to the pillaging of the robber barons, so as not to lose their support.

This unusual work had its source in Bornemissza's spiritual crises and his desire to warn his readers of the path that led to the tragic destruction of the nation and its populace.

His enemies immediately translated his book in several languages. Then they turned to the Emperor and asked that the author be condemned publicly and his book be burned. It was Bornemissza's archenemy Telegdi, who demanded the author's death because "The Lord God ordered that false prophets be killed without mercy."

What caused the Bishop's outrageous demand? First, he was antagonized by the strong vein of social criticism in Bornemissza's writings, starting with his adaptation of *Electra*, in which the author had presented a new type of man, the parasite, or the court bootlicker. It was a pardonable offense in the feudal age, to poke fun at the aristocracy, but when Bornemissza held up the Habsburg dynasty to derision, it was denounced as an act of sacrilege. Second, in his sermons, the preacher readily recognized the feudal crimes as the work of the Devil violating the Command "Thou shalt not steal." Third, he saw clearly, that the aristocrats who at first supported the Reformation did so mainly because it gave them a moral pretext for expropriating church property. The most outstanding example of this had been provided by the neighboring Polish aristocracy. After secularizing the property of the Church, the Polish nobility had returned to the bosom of the Church. Bornemissza exposed their motivations and perhaps to a certain extent, he succeeded in limiting the greed of the nobility.

In the years that followed, Bornemissza translated some parts of the Gospel and Epistles, as well as Psalms. His untimely death prevented completion of a total translation of the Bible.

One month before his death in 1584, he published yet a *pericopa*, intended mainly for his fellow-preachers.

In addition to the works mentioned, Bornemissza published songbooks, calendars, catechisms, textbooks, and others. His books were snapped up as soon as they appeared, and they were read until they were in tatters. Their current rarity attests to his success. Often only less interesting books have survived to this day.

Bornemissza the Printer and Publisher

Bornemissza's activities as a printer show him as a practical man. He worked with at least four presses. As he developed bourgeois virtues and business sense in conformity with the early capitalism of the age, he became a good example of the workings of early capitalism and of the Protestant ethic.

If we compare Bornemissza to his pioneer predecessor, Gutenberg, we find that he differs from him in that the latter often had to appear before a court of law. Gutenberg often used questionable methods and business tricks to extract the necessary capital for his ventures from his contemporaries. He even finished his career before a court of justice. Bornemissza, however, campaigned among high-ranking peers, and rich burghers to persuade them to join his spiritual movement. He created a social background with his literature and won "cheerful contributors" for his enterprise.

Due to the persecution he suffered, he often invented the time and place of publication of a book. Distribution was not accomplished through merchants or fairs disseminating his writings, but rather through his relatives, members of the aristocracy, who took care of this. It was a literary event when a new book of his appeared, and readers living in castles, fortresses and cities were quick in purchasing them. Bornemissza introduced the so-called inexpensive paperback edition, popular in our day.

He conquered the transportation difficulties of his day by packing his works in "book barrels" which were carried by wagons and on horseback. His servants would sell his publications at half price. Bornemissza was thus to a great extent instrumental in shaping Protestant public opinion. Through his writings and teachings, the people became aware of their human dignity and they grew stronger in their religious convictions also.

Bornemissza as Preacher

As Bornemissza had formed a community of readers, he also formed a community of believers, with whom he talked like a prophet, because he believed he was an emissary of God. He could not avoid the fate of prophets and he bore it with dignity, "because through preachers, God shouts His anger, and He scourges sin, thereby frightening the sinners." Perhaps Bornemissza preached thus to his congregation in order to comfort himself:

"My kinsmen, do not think you can be more fortunate than Christ;
as He was hounded to death, you too will be pursued to the ends
of the earth."[13]

The intellectual and literary life of the sixteenth century was an enigma. In spite of the reviving spiritual life and the Enlightenment, the dilemma of witchcraft trials dogged the heels of the spiritual leaders.

Literature about the devil cast a pall over the intellectual life of Europe. What explains these phenomena? Were they the legacy of the late Middle Ages? Or perhaps disillusioned and half-pagan man, no longer trusting the priests, could not confess his sins and searched his overburdened soul for the cause of his troubles? He ascribed his spiritual crises to the influence of a mysterious force, which he called the devil. Luther had confessed throwing ink at the devil; earlier the humanist, Benvenuto Cellini, had already described Satan's following him in the shadows of the Coliseum. The devil also showed up in Melanchthon lectures. How did he appear to Bornemissza, preacher of the Protestant faith? "Such is the power and work of the devil, source of all your troubles," he exclaimed. The tormented people were concerned not with angels, but with devils. Bornemissza touched on the solution of these symptoms on a high theological level. The devil had almost crushed the world with the help of the humanist Popes and the Moslem Turks. To enable the reformers to make God great again in the eyes of the populace, to make Him superior to the Devil, they had to emphasize the omnipotence of God over the force of evil. With this all-powerful God, they set out to do spiritual battle. As a result, man became humbler and smaller, and the image of the state and Church also grew smaller. All glory returned to the Creator. *Soli Deo Gloria.*

Bornemissza over the years reflected in his sermons his awareness of change. The essential virtue of the preachers of the time was that they did not overdo anything, not even their virtues. Their followers were somewhat more pagan and stubborn than those who belonged to the Western churches. The spiritual and intellectual climate of East Central Europe was harsher and the continual warfare stripped its inhabitants naked, even spiritually. Shivering, the exhausted souls awaited the new baptism. The churches attempted to herd the faithful to the worship service with the old methods. If a peasant failed to go to church he was flogged. A nobleman had to propitiate his pastors with the price of a calf.

When Bornemissza preached, he refused to hide behind pious words. He spoke frequently of his own experiences, gave his own opinions. That in itself was quite unusual then, but he did not shy away from sharing his own problems, thereby as it were, including his hearers in the discussion. For example, he would describe in a few sentences the perplexing and distressing temptations of a single day.

"As the Lord acquainted me with my own weakness, the devil fawned on me and tempted me."

"There are days when the devil would have provoked me to anger and lust, he would have maddened me, if the Lord had not been merciful to me."

"One day, for example, my serfs were grumbling against me. Then my wife unfuriated me with insignificant things, and my children disobeyed and irritated me. Then my coachman and my cooks were disloyal to me. In my anger I wanted to exchange blows with all of them, but the Lord gave me another thought."

"This very day, my printers got drunk, then my bookbinders needed a lot of urging. Then my dogs killed my chickens, and I had to throw the carcasses into the river. My horses escaped and kicked and bit each other. The teachers and students in my school complained of the food. When I rushed home to pray, my friends came to me with their troubles. Then the townspeople and the Count sent messages demanding that their affairs be taken care of.

All this happened to me on the same day. I saw that not a single devil could have summoned up this much trouble, but a whole swarm came over me. Finally, with God's help, I calmed down, though I was ready to swear."

"One day my children were taken ill, and were on the verge of dying. I thought then of all my former sins and vowed never to let them near me again. That was how God was strangling me for my many devilish sins. Like Paul, I too say that when the outside man is suffering, the inner man is growing in the Spirit of the Lord."[14]

Thus, without beating about the bush, Bornemissza created a spiritual community with his hearers. The listener could think to himself that similar things had happened or could happen to him, too.

Bornemissza argued that human life is virtually hopeless because of human evil. When we do wrong against our will, the evil has a demonic cause. Against this force he intended to help his neighbor. He knew that no one was free of temptation, and so he consoled his congregation with gentle words. He also bound on his hearers heart to speak softer to their fellow man, "for in the depths of their hearts each is crying."

But there were greater sins, social ones, committed by the oppressive ruling class against the poor. Against these, Bornemissza preached with hard words, for he found them inexcusable.

He did not forget either to attack the sexual temptations of his pastoral colleagues as well as himself, and additionally he named members of aristocratic families. He believed these unusual behaviors to be merely the honest errors of God-fearing men. Far ahead of his time, the preacher called the aberrations he described psychological illnesses. In his pastoral summary, he declared that "only God the great Physician could heal man in his distress." The significance of these pastoral addresses is the realization that one cannot eradicate evil by suppressing it. On the contrary, put it out in the open, was Bornemissza's philosophy. In the language of today one might say that he observed and studied the neuroses of his contemporaries with methods akin to those later used in depth psychology.

When the clergy and the aristocracy raised objection to Bornemissza's statements and challenged this kind of openness, his response was simple and direct. He merely wanted to show the reality of sin and the work of the devil in human life. He added that "if modesty allowed, I could have told much more terrible stories."

In his sermons, Bornemissza acquainted his congregation, to a certain extent, with the situation of the country, even of the world. At times, he entertained his listeners, many of whom travelled great distances to listen to him. He put new life into otherwise long sermons by teaching and entertaining. Sometimes he made his characters, taken from the Bible, speak and carry on entire dialogues.

He preached about the prodigal rich who, instead of feeding the poor, kept ten or twenty dogs, gave their horses, which cost five hundred florins, wine to drink, who gave their guests elaborate feasts, serving as many as fifty courses, and even made their guests wash their hands in wine.

He amused his listeners with stories like that of the king's jester who slipped into a monastery where he asked the provost to tell him a couple of lies with which to entertain his master, whereupon the provost replied: "My son, we cannot tell a lie." The jester reacted, laughing and said: "There, you just told one."

In another sermon Bornemissza told a story about an oligarch named Louis Pekri, who in 1526 started as a simple mercenary soldier. With a band of criminals, he used to rob the inhabitants of the villages, the citizens in the cities, as well as the monks in the monasteries. A contemporary historian observed that he was even better at pillaging the country than the Turks. "Louis Pekri invited a wealthy, respected Canon to dinner. He dined him until he was stuffed like a goose and set him in a comfortable chair. Then Pekri ordered his soldiers to keep the Canon captive in that chair, and not to let him fall asleep. Day and night the soldiers shook the poor captive whenever he closed his eyes. The poor man began to beg them to let him sleep, but they just kept shaking him until he promised them one thousand pieces of gold."[15]

Still another time, Bornemissza described with humor how he lost a member of his church when a princess, reconverted to Roman Catholicism, found his sermons too long and too boring. To this he added that "fortunately we still have some Protestant princesses, because they never go to church." He admitted that he did not mention such incidents to be personal; he simply wanted to protect the next generation by presenting a cross-section of the time with these examples. It was characteristic of his sense of honor that he was not ashamed to reveal his own feelings to his followers, he did not spare his own reputation.

It is clear that Bornemissza abandoned dry scholastic sermons. With his soul filled to bursting with the spiritual and intellectual message of the age, he gave the time new words:

> "No matter how small the shoemaker, the blacksmith, the groom, or the peasant, neither the king or noble can live without them. As we endure the clucking of hens for their eggs or the foolishness of our wives for their many good uses, God has joined us together so that we cannot get along without each other. We are all one in Christ, one in the sacraments and one in eternal life."[16]

As the new breed of preacher, Bornemissza was equal in rank to the contemporary leaders and he was and remained open about his religious principles. For instance, he openly demanded that his contemporaries dedicate their material goods as well as their souls to support his church movement, his writings, and his publistic activities. He moved among rulers and companions of high rank, as their cultured and independent contemporary, campaigning for the Lutheran faith.

When, as a student, he wrote *Electra*, Bornemissza had only given an evasive reply to the question whether a good ruler could be born who would serve his people. After he had been a reformer for some years, Bornemissza dared preach like the prophets and concluded that prophesy cannot change rulers.

In his *Electra* the title character had asked: "Is it permitted to oppose the tyrant while the homeland is languishing in brutal captivity?" This question had become a daily one during the Reformation. The Reformers, including Bornemissza, gave numerous positive answers; the most decisive of them came from Calvin. Hungarian history had already codified the right to resist, *ius resistendi*, in the Golden Bull of 1222.

Bornemissza as Church Organizer

Bornemissza's chief weapon in organizing the Church and defending the faith was the printed word. One can say with confidence that Hungarian Protestantism was the first child of the printed book. With this tool, the author formulated a body of religious conceptions hitherto unshaped in the minds of his followers. He gave his companions basic theological literature as a guidebook. When he preached among and wrote for the upper class, he was aware that a church could not be built without the support of secular power. That was what he must have learned in Italy, where the continual heretical movements exhausted the country and made it incapable of forcefully backing the Protestant faith.

Bornemissza as Reformer

Inspired by God, Bornemissza was the most interesting Reformer who combined Biblicism with humanism. His role in church history was not free of paradox. First, as a Lutheran bishop he held the attention and restrained the forces of the Catholic Church in Hungary, thereby giving his contemporary Péter Somogyi Juhász, called Melius, opportunity to organize the Hungarian Reformed Church. Second, he helped neutralize the Anabaptist and the Antitrinitarian movements, which seriously threatened the Reformed Church. Third, by evangelizing the Hungarian aristocracy, he gained support of the nobility in establishing the at first popular Lutheran Church. As a member of the nobility, Bornemissza was able to persuade the most influential aristocrats of the country to support his Church. This was what differentiated him from the bourgeois reformers of the century. Fourth, he was able to persuade the members of his class to form a united religious front, and he managed even to control their purses. He prevailed on his peers to turn against the "priests of Baal" and become the protectors of the faith, contrary to the decision of the national assembly of the same aristocratic class, which, at the request of the Roman Catholic Church in 1524, had enacted several laws to stamp out the heresy, the *pestifera Lutherana*. Citing the Old Testament, the legislators of then had decided that Lutherans should be burned, *Lutherani comburantur*, and immediately they had put three Lutherans to the stake.

Bornemissza's abundant propaganda material produced by his presses prevailed on Catholic leaders to turn to spiritual weapons rather than resort to the stake. They were persuaded to reply to Bornemissza's sermons with their own sermons, to open Roman Catholic institutions, like the Protestants had done for their believers. The Viennese Jesuits commenced to equip their idle presses and create their own reading public.

Bornemissza the Theologian

One gets to know Bornemissza by reading his abundant volumes of sermons. His strong dogmatic education is characteristic of his times; every article of faith had to be newly conceived in the years of the Reformation. His *Postillae* are veritable theological encyclopedias wherein he demonstrates a cultural, historical, and literary knowledge that would be inconceivable in our times. Bornemissza had an excellent foundation of the Protestant theological literature. Parallel to this, he made use of the Greek and Latin classics, which he had thoroughly absorbed while a student in early humanist Italy. He amply integrated the writings of the Church Fathers in his works when he debated his Catholic opponents. It was only with this thorough European background that he could fight the battles of his new Lutheran Church.

Bornemissza's spiritual fight was carried on first with the Popes and their bishops, but when during the Roman restoration, the worldly powers also intervened, he had to fight even his own rulers, the Habsburg emperor-kings. When he discovered that the ruler and the oligarchy joined the Counter-Reformation and espoused the Roman restoration he spoke up. He could see clearly that the campaign against the Protestant churches would be catastrophic from the standpoint of the historical church in East Central Europe. Roman Catholicism there was replaced by Habsburg Catholicism, making the Church a political body much as Emperor Constantine had made a dynastic religion of the Christian Church. Habsburg Catholicism took its authority from the Reform Council of Trent. In East Central Europe the Habsburgs aimed physically to exterminate the reformers. They succeeded in Austria and Bohemia.

Hungary's western territory was close to Vienna and the Counter-Reformation was soon felt in Bornemissza's bishopric where Hungarian, German, and Slovac Protestant churches thrived, and soon the existential question came up whether the Reformers should seek the martyrdom of the Gospel. The majority of pastors did accept it. There was a period when hundreds of ministers and teachers were brought before bloody courts of justice, and those who kept the faith were sentenced to the galleys.*

Bornemissza, who had already suffered imprisonment several times, was willing to answer "yes" to the question of martyrdom. "Can the pastor flee from merciless wolves?" Pastors should understand that a good shepherd has a greater responsibility to teach his flock than to run from persecution.[17] Bornemissza, protected by the political immunity granted to nobility, refused to compromise. Hungarian church history testifies to his significant contribution to the fight against Roman restoration; at the end of the sixteenth century Hungary's population was ninety percent Hungarian Reformed and Lutheran.

---

*See *A Magyarországi Gályarab Predikátorok Emlézete*, Budapest, Magyar Helikon, 1976.

As theologian, Bornemissza represented the syncretic theology which Luther's heir, Melanchthon, had formulated. It was unusually tolerant. Bornemissza had a horror of the sickness of the age, which had overcome the dogmatists of Luther, which certainly was not always to the glory of Christ. In a bishopric letter Bornemissza told his flocks: "Preachers . . . call each other names; one kind is accused by the other of 'chewing the body of Christ' (at the Lord's Supper); others are ridiculed as followers of Arius and Nestorianus; still others as sacramentarians (Helvetians); finally, still others as twice baptized pagans (Anabaptists)."[18]

Bornemissza judged with virtually ecumenical, irenic tolerance, when he declared: "No matter what his nationality, Hungarian or German, no matter what his Christian name, if he is not compatible with Christ, he cannot find salvation."

The spirit of his teacher, Melanchthon, spoke through Bornemissza to the peoples of East Central Europe; that is why his personal enemy, the Catholic Bishop Telegdi, reprimanded him: "Now you are a Lutheran, the next moment a Calvinist, another moment a Zwinglian, and still another Anabaptist, and who knows what else? Until now I have not got to the bottom of who you are. One moment you support the Lutherans against the Calvinists, another the other way around. More than once you swore that you kept the Augustinian Confession, but if you had kept it, you would not condemn the Mass and the vestments of priests. I would rather say that you confess the *Augustana Confusio*."[19]

Telegdi also censured Bornemissza for quoting the Bible in telling his contemporaries: "All are equal before Christ, be they Jew or Turk, rich or poor, noble or peasant, when they pray to Him." Telegdi retorted: "There was no need to bring up the Jew and Turk because they do not deserve anything, since they are not creatures of God as we are."[20]

Bornemissza often mentioned the Jew's adherence to the letter of the Law, citing one instance of a story about a rabbi: "One Saturday, a rabbi fell down a ramshackle latrine. The townspeople did not dare to pull him out, it being a Sabbath, but put off the rescue to the next day; the Catholic bishop did not allow that the rabbi be pulled out on Sunday; however, if the rabbi should keep the Saturday, he could keep the Sunday too as a holy day."[21]

As theologian, Bornemissza definitely followed the principles of liturgical puritanism. He preached in his everyday clothes, he omitted the altar and the images. Standing by the table, he dispensed Holy Communion using leavened bread. He also heard individual and communal confession.

During the days of the catastrophic fragmentation of Protestantism, Bornemissza was forced to stand up for religious unity. During the 1550's, the communistic anarchy of the increasingly radical Anabaptists found its way into his bishopric via Bohemia. The popular naive Biblicism which the Anabaptists introduced seems to have become popular among the Slovaks who lived in his bishopric. He reported on the Anabaptists in one of his sermons that those who were baptized twice taught that nobody was born in sin; that they called their children "holy", whether they were born Jew or Turk. They reasoned that they would be saved even without the grace of Christ. It was for that reason that they did not even baptize their children. They were not satisfied with God's revelation in His Word, but wanted to support their own pseudo-revelations invented by themselves by means of dreams and visions of angels, though God did not make such special announcements. He also described their customs: "They live apart, looking down on other creatures of God. Outwardly they torment themselves and show off their superiority by the denial of married life. There are countless libertines among them. Under cover of the Gospel, they preach the sinfulness of owning private property; they say they must support neither judge nor king."[22]

In fact, they even taught that after adult baptism they were allowed to do anything, for example, to steal, because through their adult baptism they had been freed from the consequences of sin. It is understandable that as church organizer, Bornemissza criticized the sect's spreading such negativistic principles. Many antisocial teachings spread among the Anabaptists in the neighboring states as well. They withdrew from the state which they considered sinful. They did not always observe their own moral teachings. There was a group, for example, whose prophet admitted female members by sexual initiation which they called baptism.[23]

When the Polish Antitrinitarian leaders visited their Moravian Anabaptist brothers to create an alliance with them, the delegation was disillusioned with what they saw. Some of the delegates, upon returning home, warned their Polish fellow Antitrinitarian brothers of the "Anabaptist plague". They described the glaring inequalities: workers received only "watery soup" without content, while at the same time, the leaders were stuffing themselves and drinking good wine in a separate room. The leaders forbade the reading of the Bible which they claimed God had meant only for superiors. According to the Polish delegation, the members of the Moravian community did not practice a simple, apostolic communism as might have been expected.[24]

In the end Anabaptism became isolated and limited to a few places where secular authority did not reach; the main settlement remained in Moravia. As a whole, Anabaptism failed as a religious movement, mainly because it wanted to eradicate the basic institutions such as family and private property; moreover, it proclaimed that theological principles and Christian dogmas were non-essential parts of Christianity.

Bornemissza was also forced to defend the Lutheran church against the Antitrinitarian teachings. This theological and intellectual movement had grown out of Italian Protestantism, that is, worldly humanism. It was spread by reformers who had escaped from Italian territory and was strongly influenced by the Spanish and Portuguese Marranos[25] who taught that Jesus was not God, but only an exceptional man, Joseph's descendant.

Bornemissza could not tolerate heresy, because it undermined Christ's revived Church and thus obstructed the path leading to God. The God-man nature of Christ was the bridge from man to the Creator; that is why the Messiah had to be human too.

Part of Bornemissza's profile as a theologian was his Biblical-eschatological approach to history. The religious war with Islam must have played a great role in forming his passive-eschatological view. On the one hand, Islam threatened Christ's legacy, but on the other, he reasoned, it could represent Gog and Magog, the approaching final Judgment of God.

Who can imagine today, from the distance of centuries, the kind of cosmic fear that gripped that suffering nation? Those who somehow survived, but whose families were carried off by the Turks, (if they did not massacre an entire village), often confessed apocalyptic beliefs. Was it any wonder that under such inhuman conditions those apocalyptic visions assailed the people? The ceaseless wars, the onslaught of the plague, and the religious persecutions made the anguishing souls credulous.

Bornemissza, who suffered with his congregations, felt that God was compelling him to speak of the coming end of the world, with the devil raging boundlessly, this certainly presaged the end of the world that would go under "like an old man."

Today we find it natural that the Biblical historical philosophy of the Middle Ages, which originated with Saint Augustine, or at least he was the one who gave it its Christian formulation, resurfaced with the Reformation. Bornemissza, however, warned his followers: "It is not necessary to concern ourselves with what hour or year it will come to pass, but we must be ready when the Lord comes."

Church historians believe that this kind of expectant passivity is the explanation for Bornemissza's failure to incorporate the defense of the Lutheran Church into a constitution. The reality, as Hungarian church historian, Hermann, noted was that "there are a thousand heretics to one Catholic, and the soldiers who are sent to fight the heretics are themselves heretics."[26] This was the exact situation in terms of religious history toward the end of the sixteenth century; ninety percent of the Hungarian population was made up by Helvetic, that is, Hungarian Reformed and Lutheran Protestants.

By recatholicizing, they made it their goal to assimilate into the German sphere of influence those nations they had conquered.

The newly appointed archbishop of Hungary, Leopold Kolonitz, summarized his future church policies in his *Einrichtungswerk*, an assimilation plan, that he worked out. The country had first to be beggared, then made Catholic, and finally German. His plan to beggar the country was eventually very nearly realized, because "Among a hundred pastors, there were barely ten who were not living like peasants in wretched poverty. There even were parish priests who could not celebrate Mass because they did not have a chalice to dispense the sacrament."[27]

Footnotes

1. Azbach, J. *Geschichte der Wiener Universität im ersten Jahrhundert ihres Bestrebens.* Vienna, 1888. III. p. 90–91.

2. Végh, F. *Bornemissza Péter ifjusága.* In *Irodalom Történet.* Budapest, 1953.

3. Schmitth, N. *Episcopi Agriensis III*, p. 114 Nagyszombat, 1768.

4. Koltay, K. J. *Bornemissza Péter humánizmusa.* in *Irodalom Történet,* Budapest, 1953.

5. Hermann, E. *A katholikus egyház története.* p. 198–199 München: Aurora Könyvek, 1973.

6. Bornemissza, P. *Postillák,* IV, p.862

7. Bornemissza, P. *Folio Postillák LXXXII*

8. Bornemissza, P. *Postillák V,* p.67

9. Bauhoffer, G. *Geschichte der evangelische Kirche in Ungarn.* Berlin, 1854. p.118

10. Hermann, E. *op. cit.,* p. 202–203

11. Bornemissza, P. *Postillák Előszó*

12. Eckhardt, S. *Bornemissza Péter: Őrdőgi kisértések.* Budapest, 1955. p. 36

13. Bornemissza, P. *Postillák III.* p. 78

14. Bornemissza, P. *Postillák IV.* p. 822b

15. Bornemissza, P. *Postillák IV,* p. 598

16. Bornemissza, P. *Postillák I.XXVII.* 1p.

17. Bornemissza, P. *Postillák V,* p.236

18. Bornemissza, P. *Folio Postillák CCCCXC*

19. Telegdi, M. *Felelet Bornemissza Fejtegetésére.* Budapest, 1898. RMK, p.2

20. Telegdi, M. *ibid.,* p. 72

21. Bornemissza, P. *Postillák IV,* p. 478

22. Bornemissza, P. *Postillák III,* p. 280–290

23. Clasen, P. Anabaptism. Cornell University Press, 1972. p. 138

24. Kot, St. Socianism in Poland. Boston, 1957. p.38

25. Williams, G. H. Two Social Stands in Italian Anabaptism. in: The Social History of the Reformation, Ohio State University, ed. L. P. Buck & Zophy. p. 164.

26. Hermann, E. *op. cit.,* p. 257

27. Ipolyi, A. *Veresmarty Miklos élete és munkái* Budapest, 1857. p. 77

Rural Reformed Church

Chapter XVI

Why the Helvetic and Not the Lutheran Reformation Took Hold in Hungary?

A much discussed question in the history of the Hungarian Reformation is the issue of why Lutheran Protestantism failed to take hold in East Central Europe. Barnabás Nagy, a contemporary Hungarian church historian in his *Wittenberger Vorträge*, could not in concrete form explain why the Helvetic-Calvinist* Reformation was accepted by the Hungarians.[1]

Lutheranism had become very popular during the early years in areas where Hungarian, Czech, and Polish were spoken, and the martyrdom of its propagandists is well known. So why did it fail to appeal permanently? The answers to this question are varied. Some are theological, some socio-linguistic, and some metaphysical, but we may not be far off the mark when we say that Martin Luther himself, the "German prophet" as he called himself, became one of the reasons.

From the very beginning, Luther proclaimed that he wanted to be the redeeming prophet of the German people, and in so proclaiming he immediately narrowed his field of activity and ruled out any possibility of making his efforts universal. At the same time, stepping out from his single-minded path, he remained firmly rooted in the Catholic Middle Ages. With Luther, one age ended, but a new one did not begin as yet. According to the German religious historian von Bellow, "Luther did not bring about a new religiosity, but he rather supplied a new objective to a movement that was already under way."[2]

---

*With Helvetic is meant the Zwinglian-Calvinist Reformation as a common denominator.

The paradox of Luther lies in the fact that, although he demanded recognition as a prophet, he was not prepared to give definite answers to the crises then raging throughout Europe. He offered only contradictions when confronted with critical issues and constantly changed his point of view, invariably feeble in his logic.

Another German commentator, Rustow, concluded that Luther factually represented a late Gothic concept, "totally rooted in a declining, decaying medieval age."[3] Apparently, Luther was a closing stone in the age which taught and shaped him.

A further limitation to Luther's effectiveness was a trait which the Roman historian Tacitus, describing the Germans, almost fifteen hundred years earlier had called the *furor teutonicus.*

When one reads Luther's views on non-German neighboring peoples, one finds that these views are, for the most part, uncharitable. For example, he pictures his nearest neighbors, the Czechs, as *pestilentissimos Pighardorum errores* or "pestilential Pighards steeped in error."[4] Luther said this in spite of the fact that Czech leaders were in contact with him five different times in the interest of a common religious front. In his supreme self-assurance he demanded of them that they abandon their century-old religious teachings of the Unity of the Brethren. Finally Luther dismissed any chance of cooperation saying: "Let us both, you Czechs and we Germans, be apostles. You labor there as conditions demand, and we will strive here as we are impelled."[5]

It is of interest to note that Luther had no Slavic co-reformer, except M. Flacius Illyricus of Dalmatia.

Luther also spoke disparagingly of the Jewish, the Slavic, and Latin peoples, and the Wends were "a vile nation that God has burdened us with."[6] As for the Dutch and Flemish, they were "devils incarnate," the English he compared to wolves, the French were "feeble-minded" and the Italians like "insidious foxes." The Turks, however, were a "true and trustworthy people."[7] Luther's anti-Italian feelings may have stemmed from his animosity toward the Pope.

Due to the influence of conscientious German reformers, Protestantism in Poland was mainly centered in "Lutheran German towns" while the villages remained Roman Catholic. According to historian Stökl, many saw in the fact that Polish as well as Hungarian nobility turned predominantly to Calvinism proof of Polish aversion toward the German form of the Reformation.[8] In other words, only the citizens of towns under German influence remained true to Lutheranism. One could call this ecclesiastical Germanization, and it was to be found among the German settlers of East Central Europe.[9]

Among the Czechs a similar situation was noted,[10] as it was also in Hungary and in those towns where a German-speaking population had lived for generations side by side with Hungarians. Luther's ethno-centric theology ended up greatly reducing the influence of Lutheranism in East Central Europe around the middle of the sixteenth century.[11] It now appears obvious that the German religious movement ended in the German settlements.[12]

Luther and the Turks

Another reason for the failure of Lutheranism in East Central Europe and for the spread of the Helvetic-Calvinist concepts coming out of Switzerland, was Luther's views on the war against the Turks. The Turks, as mentioned, were regarded by him as "true and trustworthy." While the Hungarians struggled against the Islamic Turks for centuries, Luther tended to regard this struggle as a theological one. In his disputes with the Pope, *furor theologicus* that he was, he simply brushed aside the Turkish peril, and as "German prophet," expressed such dubious views as to present Turkish imperialism as something brought down in European Christianity because of the errors of the Pope. He vented his bitter feelings toward the Pope thus: "He who has ears, let him hear and stay away from fighting the Turks as long as the name of the Pope exists under heaven,"[13] or "When in the battlefield I would see a priest's cross I would run as if the devil were at my heels."[14]

When Luther's friend Spalatin asked him in 1518 to justify the fight against the Turks on biblical grounds, Luther swept the question aside saying that according to his speculative theology, to fight the Turks was tantamount to opposing the will of God. God was using the Turks to "punish us."[15]

Luther's thesis regarding the Turks as the instrument of Divine wrath against a sinful Europe was not a new idea. Before Luther's age, Attila the Hun had been called "the scourge of God" and Pope Calixtus III (1458) had advocated repentance and amendment of life as one factor in defense against the Turks.

Luther based his view of the Turkish role on the prophecy of Daniel (Ch. VIII). Calvin, his contemporary reformer, opposed this explanation saying that he did not find the Turks mentioned in Daniel's prophecy.[16]

Modern readers are often confused when they read Luther's one-sided diatribes against the Pope: "The Turks always allow everyone to follow his own faith . . . the power of the Pope over bodies and souls is ten times worse than the power of the Turks."[17] To instruct his colleagues in this sense, Luther proclaimed his view far and wide.

It is not by chance that the papal nuncio Aleander sent the following report to Rome after the imperial gathering in 1521 at the Diet of Worms: "Werböczy, the Hungarian ambassador, asked Luther to suspend his attacks on the Pope because the Turks were endangering Europe in a very terrifying way." Luther, however, held fast to his viewpoint. Werböczy and the humanist Jaromess Balbi informed Emperor Charles of this and added that Luther's views and declarations were encouraging ignorance . . . . The ambassador from Venice, Contarini, who was also present at the Diet, gave a similar evaluation of Luther's views and added that the reformer was "an unwise, particularly undisciplined personage, and unscholarly."[18]

It is important to note that when Luther appeared in Worms in 1521 he overshadowed Werböczy's appeal for help which might have saved Nandorfehérvár (later called Belgrad), then the strongest fortification in southern Hungary.

When in 1526, Louis the Second, king of Hungary and Bohemia, lost not only the battle of Mohács but also his life, and when the Sultan occupied Buda, Luther assuaged his conscience saying, "Five years ago several people asked me to take a stand on the Turkish question; now I do it because the Turks are almost here."[19]

When the Turks finally arrived on German soil, he no longer proclaimed the view that "he who fights against the Turks is fighting against God," but corrected his original stand that the Turks allowed religious freedom. "The Turks do not allow practice of religion or the right to free assembly."[20]

With this, Luther contradicted his earlier attitude and numerous statements on the Turkish question. When the sultan abandoned Vienna, Luther belatedly published his *Campaign Sermon against the Turks,*[21] because the

Turks stood at the door, *Turcas ante portam*! It was in these days too that he wrote, inspired by the threat of siege of Vienna, his famous hymn, "A Mighty Fortress," later called the "Marseillaise of the Reformation" by the German poet Heinrich Heine. In this "Christian Battlesong" according to Friedenburg, "our ancient foe" stood for the Turks, the "earthly powers" for the worldly Roman empire.[22] The hymn was sung even at the Reichstag in 1530, when Charles V asked for 40,000 soldiers to ward off the Turkish invasion. During that time, the Protestants adopted the hymn which was based on the medieval Latin song *Libellus de ritu et moribus Turcarum*.[23]

Later, in letters, Luther attempted to explain his change of mind. "I will fight the Turk and his god till death,"[24] and Luther the theologian concluded, "Let us not worry ourselves if we strangle a Turk."[25]

In 1528–29 Luther also wrote and published *On the War against the Turks* in which he defended himself against the accusation that he had opposed resistance to the Moslems. He criticized his colleagues who, on the basis of his own former teachings, still preached against the possible illegality of opposing the Turkish invasion.

Luther's patron, the Elector of Saxony, requested that Luther continue to deal with the Islamic threat, and in consequence Luther published in 1541 *Exhortation to Prayer against the Turks*, in which document he now urged the "sinful" German people to turn their thoughts to God and pray that the punishing whip of God's hand be stayed.[26]

Finally, the better-informed Luther expressed his sympathy toward Queen Mary, widow of Louis the Second and sister of Emperor Charles V and Ferdinand I of Hungary, by dedicating to her his interpretation of four Psalms. In his consolation Luther encouraged Queen Mary, writing "I dedicate these four Psalms to your Majesty, asking you to stand steadfast and even proudly in the support of God's Word, which is to be spread in Hungary."[27]

Luther published a few more pamphlets and recognized very late the essence of religious teaching of the *Koran* where the extermination of the infidel was proclaimed with fanaticism. It was only in 1542 that Luther finally studied the handbook of the Moslem religion, the *Confutatio Alcorani*, written by the Dominican Ricoldus de Monte Crucis, who had spent twenty years among the Moslems (1280–1300). Luther attempted to translate the book and wrote an introduction to it, in which he explained its significance. It became clear to him that the sins of the Popes had not wrought destruction on Europe via the Asian hordes, but rather admonishments of the author of the *Koran* himself, who had declared a holy war on Europe nine hundred years earlier.

Twenty years earlier the German prophet had written disparagingly regarding Hungary's role as the bastion defending European Christianity: "The Hungarians boast that they are God's defenders, and they even sing about it in their litanies." ("Listen to us, your defenders . . . "). According to Luther, God considered such litanies both harmful and sinful.[28]

Luther's one-sided thinking was corrected by a contemporary theologian, Johannes Cockleus, with regard to the historical role of the Hungarians on behalf of Christianity. Cockleus stressed that the Hungarian nation was not blaspheming but serving God and His Church. At the same time he pointed out no fewer than fifteen contradictions or inconsistencies in Luther's pamphlet on the Hungarians.[29]

Of late, historians of religion have recognized the radical change that came about in Luther's views. They point out how Hungarians, studying at the University of Wittenberg, had informed Luther about the Turkish campaigns in which a hundred thousand Hungarian prisoners were sent off to Asia and how entire towns and cities were wiped off the face of the earth by the invaders.[30]

According to an opinion coming from neighboring Austria, "the Turks were Luther's good fortune." King Ferdinand I actually intervened in Rome to gain official recognition for Lutheranism. He had no alternative, faced as he was with the Turkish peril. This Roman Catholic initiative, however, (*Declaratio Ferdinandes*, 1555) compromised Lutheranism in the eyes of the East Central Europeans. In spite of the recognition given to the Lutherans, Hungarians soon tired of Luther's church politics and turned to Swiss reformers. Calvin, Bullinger (who wrote approximately twelve hundred letters to Protestant church leaders in Europe) and Beza were much more realistic in their grasp of the situation and much less naive with regard to the Turks,[31] and the essence of Luther's "Political Utopia" evaporated into thin air.

Luther, the Peasant War and *ius resistendi*

In the beginning of confessional pluralism, the question arose whether it would be permissible for a suffering people to practice *ius resistendi*, the right to resist the tyrant. This became a difficult question when the German peasants rose against their overlords, producing a dilemma for Luther, who supported the overlords with the dictum "Honor thy father." With this attitude and act, he ceased to be in touch with socio-historical reality.

The basis of the Hungarian Reformation was the total involvement of the peasant population. For the first time different social classes were incorporated as equal in the life of the Church, which explains why at the end of the sixteenth century ninety percent of the population became Protestant. Contrary to this situation, the Hungarian students who returned from Wittenberg as the future elite of their people, brought within themselves the knowledge of Luther's role in connection with the Peasant War. More than a thousand Hungarian students had studied in Wittenberg during those years. They had observed how Luther had sided in the beginning with the peasants and had advocated that they free themselves from subjugation. In *Von Weltlicher Obrigkeit* (1523) he had stressed Christian freedom and had declared that God would finish the nobility because "man will not, man cannot, and man will not further endure the tyranny."[32]

In 1525, however, Luther had turned around and had asked the nobility to destroy the agitated peasants. He had openly declared, "I am and always will be on the side of those against whom insurrection is directed, no matter how unjust their cause."[33]

It is obvious that Luther's socio-political view did not fit into the moving history of Hungary or other neighboring nations. Luther's education as a monk had not prepared him to assess historical events, so he had been forced to improvise. It is no wonder that his contemporary Reformer, Heinrich Bullinger, made the observation that Luther boasted of being the "German prophet and apostle" who needed to learn from no one, but from whom all others had to learn.

To be sure, Luther attempted to shrug off responsibility in connection with the peasant revolt and declared the war to be punishment by God, reasoning that whoever fought against God had to be destroyed. He based this explanation on Deuteronomy 32, v. 35, "Vengeance is mine and retribution." He determined that "the vocation of the Christian in this world is to suffer political violence rather than resist it with force." It was Luther, then, who advocated political Augustinianism and, resigned to it, continued to repeat that the Christian Law was "suffering, suffering, cross, cross."[34]

Theologizing in this manner, Luther modified his Biblicism, and already in 1539 he gave the authorization to resistance, "if one may resist the Pope, one may also resist all those who defend and protect him."[35]

In contrast, Calvin's teaching of constitutional resistance to tyranny was based on the Sovereignty of God. "We ought to obey God rather than man." It was an attempt to transform Luther's attitude of reverence toward the worldly power. Calvin went further: "The absolute supremacy of God and His Word demands not passive but active resistance."*

Ius resistendi became a matter of importance in Hungary when the Habsburgs brought in Spanish mercenaries to convert the Hungarians back to Roman Catholicism through force by billeting them in Hungarian homes. Resistance was unavoidable. In the history of the Hungarian Constitution, the Golden Bull of 1222 gave authority to the subjects of a tyrant to resist by force of arms. The Hungarian nobility represented this tradition, just as the Polish nobility did in neighboring Poland. In consequence they turned away from Luther and adopted the Helvetic ideology.

Luther's reaction showed medieval mentality at work. In his opinion those in revolt were "not worthy of mercy . . . lest their blood be on my head."[37] He could not conceive of resistance on the part of the lower estate. Against this reasoning the Hungarian Protestant leaders found the needed religious and moral basis for the defense of their faith in the religious policies of Calvin and later in those of Beza.

In theological context, there were also divisive forces at work in the matter of celebration of Holy Communion. As a former Roman Catholic priest, Luther did not abolish the Roman mass, but, as Karl Heussi points out, Luther "merely cleansed it."[38]

According to Heussi, only the name was changed, but not the essence. The dogma of mystic transcendentalism did not appeal to the Hungarians who had once been a nomadic people and were accustomed to thinking in global terms, with a synthetic mind, in contrast to the analytic-inductive mind of the Germans. The Lutheran-Teuton, inclined to mysticism, and the Hungarian inclined to rationalism, were unable to blend. The historical realism of the Helvetic Confession assured on the one hand the concept of

---

*Theodore Beza published later, after the St. Bartholomew holocaust of 1572, two books in which he advocated even more radical theories than those of Calvin. "Tyrants are not legitimate kings and therefore should be opposed."[36]

freedom of the individual, and on the other simplified the doctrine of Holy Communion through a diverging theological interpretation.

Luther's Stand on Language

Luther's influence on future religious leaders of Hungary was further weakened because of his stand on language. In the sixteenth century no less than 1200 students from Hungary alone were studying in Wittenberg, the largest group of foreign students who attended Luther's university.[39] Although in the universities of Europe lectures were held in Latin, Greek, and Hebrew, and although the Hungarian students had been well prepared at home for this, Luther introduced lectures in German and church services in German as well. With few exceptions, Hungarians did not take easily to the German language.[40] Luther brought up this topic in one of his Table Talks, when he mentioned the fact that his students had requested that he re-establish Latin as the language of instruction, but he had rejected it out of hand.[41] This refusal resulted in students, who could not understand his theological arguments in the German language, gradually drifting away from Wittenberg and Lutheran teachings.

At the same time in Switzerland, Latin retained its universal character and students gravitated there.

Furthermore, the post Lutheran generation of reformers went far beyond mere political patriotism and language loyalty, and engaged in hairsplitting dogmatism; e.g., does repentance come before faith or *vice versa*? (dispute between Melanchthon and Agricola).

In contrast, the Helvetic trend embodied a universal concept that was above nations and therefore made Helvetic Calvinism attractive to Hungarians. When John Calvin had escaped from France, his outlook became more universal. His internationalism did not antagonize national feelings. The church-government he built up from the grassroots, a self-government, called *Consistorium*, secured autonomy for the congregations. Not only was the whole church community involved, but also a self-reforming idea, *Ecclesia semper est reformanda* was built in as well.[42]

After Luther's death, Melanchthon reinstated the tradition of Latin as the language of instruction and, unlike Luther, held special lectures for the Hungarian students, first in his home, later at the university itself. Out of these lectures grew a volume titled *Postilla Melanchthonia*, which was published in Heidelberg in 1594. Perhaps Melanchthon gave special attention to Hungarian students in order to show gratitude to his former teacher, the Hungarian Johannes Hungaricus, who had introduced him to the mysteries of knowledge. Speaking of his Hungarian teacher, Melanchthon remarked, "He used words, the rod, and good grammar." Interestingly, Melanchthon was the only Wittenbergian theologian who visited Hungary to help establish a Lutheran church.[43]

Melanchthon was more patient and conciliatory than Luther had been; he also was more open-minded to the Helvetic point of view. Perhaps one can attribute to his crypto-Calvinism, which gave the Hungarian students an alternative, the fact that the Helvetic trend was gaining ground among Hungarian students.

Lutheran leaders were instigating special investigations among these students, punishing them for their "sectarianism." The harassed students finally left Wittenberg under the leadership of András Ungváry,[44] among them the later Bishop János Ungvary.

Differences in Church Discipline

Certain differences were apparent between the Lutheran and Calvinistic concepts of church discipline. While Luther was satisfied with leaving ethical procedures up to the believer, saying "The Word must do it," the Helvetic-Calvinists held that the "Church is responsible for community life and discipline."

In Hungary, the break-up of the social order made the latter concept necessary, and Calvinist teaching emphasized that religion was not only a personal matter but also a most important public matter as well. Thus the most unbending ethno-social practice spread into every aspect of life and led to a kind of theocratic totalitarianism. At the same time, this principle developed a new work ethic according to which work itself was a way of life and worthy of respect. Thus no one could stand idly by and watch the passing of God-given days without having a guilty conscience and feeling himself a parasite. Helvetic teachings formulated in Hungarian society a Puritan morality which laid the foundation in the city of Debrecen for an early capitalistic work ethic. The representatives of this ethic were the citizens, the *Civis*, of Debrecen, on whom it was incumbent to create and defend the Protestant faith.

Luther's anti-Judaism

Luther's anti-Judaism also became a factor in the alienation of the Hungarian reformers who returned from Wittenberg. Luther had, as in other issues, several times changed his mind about the Jewish people. As long as he had been a monk, he had kept the century-long Church tradition that the Jews were "lost"; "they were murderous people." (His lecture on the Psalms in 1516.)

Later in his most optimistic outlook, when he had succeeded in converting a single Hebrew to the Protestant faith, he aimed with confidence and optimism to convert them all (1521). In that period, he wrote a famous book *That Jesus Was a Jew* (1523). Parallel with this writing, he accused the Roman Catholic hierarchy for their mishandling of the people of the Old Testament.[45] He went so far in his accusations as to say, "I would rather be a swine than a 'Christian' because of the humiliation of the Jews by the Papacy."[46]

With this book, Luther intended to please the Jewish leaders, since its aim was a missionary undertaking. *That Jesus Was a Jew* soon became a bestseller; wherever Jewish people lived it was sponsored, and the Spanish Marranos even sent the book to the Holy Land.

When Luther's efforts were rejected by the Jewish people, he, in return, indignantly condemned them. This led then to Luther's third cycle in which he, rather fatalistically, gave up any further attempt at proselytizing, his ultimate conclusion being that to speak to the Jews was like preaching the Gospel to swine.[47]

After his failure to win the Jews for the Protestant cause, Luther published more books and pamphlets against the obstinate Rabbis. He became even more indignant when he learned about the Jewish success of proselytizing Christians in Bohemia and Moravia. His writings included *Concerning the Jews and Their Lies*, *Concerning the Ineffable Name*, and *Against the Sabbatarians*.

He also demanded openly to destroy all synagogues, to burn Hebrew literature, and to expel all Jews from Germany and deport them to Asia.

In his *Table Talk* he admitted that he intended to write against the Jews once again, saying, "I will advise them [i.e., the Princes] to chase all the

Jews out of their land."[48] He admitted, "I cannot convert the Jews, even as our Lord Jesus could not, but I can stop up their mouth."[49]

Luther's animosity against the Jews may have been motivated, apart from theological considerations, by the fact that during the reformational struggle, the Hebrew leaders had supported Charles V, Roman Emperor, who by his military actions had planned to destroy his Protestant opponents. The Emperor had made German Jewry his personal political tool at the expense of Protestantism. Not only had he accepted all binding privileges of his predecessors, but also he had issued new protections of Jewish privileges in 1544. Consequently, the reformers viewed the Jews as fifth-columnists, who were working against them.[50] Jews supplied the Spanish mercenaries with bread and wine when they went against the Lutherans.[51] There is reason to believe that Jews created an information and espionage network for imperial military planners.[52]

The Hungarian students returning home from Wittenberg were perplexed by all this and could not reconcile Luther's ambiguities. On the one hand, he used the Old Testament as absolute truth, and on the other he regarded the people of the Old Testament as good for nothing.

In contrast to this, the Hungarian reformers had great sympathy and respect toward the suffering people of the Old Testament. Their identification with Jewish fate was rooted in the historical situation of the Hungarian people. The downfall of their nation after the Turkish conquest was compared to the fate of the Hebrews. The enormous suffering of the Hungarians needed interpretation and comfort; hence they identified with the ancient tragedy of Jerusalem. The result was that Hungarian reform theologians developed the so-called Theodicy of Mohács, in which an act of God was included to explain the tragedy of the Hungarian nation as well as that of the Jews. The Protestant historical-theological answer was that as once the Jewish people had been punished for their sins, now the same punishment was measured out to the unfaithful Hungarians. "Our fathers sinned and we bear their iniquities" was quoted endlessly by reform preachers. Among them was the Bible translator Gáspar Károlyi, a former student of Wittenberg, who published this explanation in his *Two Books* in 1563. According to Károlyi's concept, God used the cruel Turks to punish the Hungarian people because the leading oligarchy transgressed His laws, oppressed the poor, robbed each other's properties, and were unfaithful to the Church. As God had used Syrian and Roman pagans to punish the

Jews, He now in a similar manner used other pagans, the Turks, to warn the Hungarian nation to turn back to Him. The Turkish occupation was likened to another Babylonian captivity.

In 1538, another author, András Farkas, had written a book, *From Jewish and Hungarian Nations*, in which he had made a comparison of how God through the Romans had once deported his unfaithful chosen people and how now Buda was destroyed through other barbarians by the same Almighty to teach Hungarians, once children of Western Christendom, to repent.

Several so-called Jeremiads were published in the sixteenth century, literature which presented similar historical explanations, and all authors concurred with Farkas, who had stated that the new reformers were but successors of the ancient Biblical prophets, who asked their people to repent.

It was also popular to identify the Hungarian language with the *lingua primigenia*, that is *sancta hebraica*, because Hebrew literature meant also literary culture. As long as the linguistic science had not established relationship between Hungarian and Finn-Ugor languages, this was a favorite ploy.

Because (in contrast to Luther's attitude) the Hungarian reformers highly respected the heritage of the Old Testament, they welcomed with open arms the persecuted Jews from Austria, Bohemia, Moravia, and Germany. Even the Spanish Marranos reached the country.[53]

Sixteenth century Hungary was the first nation in Europe to recognize by constitutional law, first the Unitarian (1571), and later the Sabbatarian, both Judaizing religions. This act in itself is unique in the history of religious tolerance.

In the end, the Hungarian reformers, though they had received spiritual inspiration from Wittenberg, were forced to revise the Lutheran theological and ecclesiastical influence. They separated themselves from the German national-religious movement in accordance with Hungarian national character and historical realism. The different historical and sociological situations in East Central Europe demanded different solutions. The Slavic peoples–Polish, Bohemian, Croat, Slovak, and Slovenian–responded to the Lutheran Reformation in different ways as well.

Luther and the confusing concept of conscience

Since St. Paul incorporated in his Christology the concept of conscience, it has been used and misused to legitimize many actions or statements. The most quoted example is probably Luther's stand at the Diet of Worms, when he refused to recant his innovative theses. At that moment he used the word conscience as an absolute and infallible guide for human action. Later, in his maturing years, he more or less refrained from using that over-stressed idea as definitive.

When he and his co-workers introduced and practiced the principle of *cuius regio eius religio*, (he who holds the worldly power has the right to dictate the religion), as a compromise solution concerning church authority, Luther contradicted his earlier concept of freedom of conscience. It is worth mentioning that when Luther discussed the problem of freedom of will with Erasmus, his conclusion was that man's will was in bondage.

He later abandoned the concept of infallible conscience and introduced the principle of Biblical authority. This gave him plenty of room to maneuver when he commenced practicing religious intolerance toward other Protestant reformers.

In his final development, conscience became a subjective norm of moral action also in religious matters. Conscience was conditioned by reason and emotions, and it was also a warning signal when making decisions. Thus agreeing with St. Paul that conscience is fallible (I Cor. 8, v. 9–13) and therefore could not pronounce a final judgment in an absolute sense, Luther still saw some spiritual capacity in man to judge human conscience, whether it served the case of Christ in man's life or not.

Luther admitted that from his own experience "The conscience is an evil beast which makes a man take a stand against himself."[54]

Somehow Luther remained until the end ambivalent about the freedom or bondage of man's conscience. If on the one hand man were free in the interacting process of human will and conscience, there would not be room for Providence; on the other hand God's omnipotence would exclude all choices on man's part. Still, in Luther's confession of the "unfree will," that is his certainty of justification by faith, he had found freedom and courage to defy an entire world.

In conclusion, Martin Luther as a reformer temporarily succeeded in integrating the German people; finally, however, after the Thirty Years' War, his beloved people found themselves divided and the territory broken up into more than a hundred parts. It is sad to observe that sometimes prophet and historical conclusion do not agree with each other.

Because Luther could not think in terms of global Christendom, he excluded two basic components: Roman latinity and Judaic messianism. In consequence he reduced his religious reform to a tribal entity. Unintentionally, he once more pushed back the Germans behind the ancient Roman borders (*Limes*).

Socio-political changes as factor

Socio-political changes also helped in the strengthening of the Helvetic Reformation. Just as the Turks had spread their dominion over Hungarian territory, the Magyar land-owning nobility, after having fled from the occupied territories, gathered together, mainly in the vicinity of Debrecen. In the course of two decades, thirty percent of the Hungarian noblesse had settled on the Hungarian plains. Simultaneously the fast growing middle class made common cause with the nobility with whom they shared common cultural and historical traditions. The concept of individual freedom, a common point of view, and a common metaphysical experience influenced deeply the new religious ethos of the rising middle class.[55]

The citizens of Debrecen introduced this newly forming tradition into the framework of their own self-government, but neither the nobleman, the burger, nor the peasant was locked into a single social formula by these continually developing forces. Parallel, they developed in Helvetic fashion self-government in their democratic Reformed Church.

In the course of this historical development, we are faced again with the question whether it was Helvetic-Calvinist metaphysics which formed the spirituality of the Hungarian Reformation, or whether it was the already existing religious and psychological urgent need of the Hungarian soul. It seems hard to believe that in the course of only a few decades a new exposure would have been enough to bring about the formation of a modified "Magyar religion." One would rather have expected the adoption of a ready-made spirituality whereas in fact, a popular metaphysical experience out of their past predestined the formerly mounted nomads to bring into sharp focus Helvetic transcendentalism.

What has been gathered together to this point with regard to Lutheranism versus Helvetic-Calvinism in Hungary, are facts which also show how European church life of the time was filled with contradictions. Facing a complex world after his departure from a secure monk's cell and being unaccustomed to thinking in universal terms, may have been determining factors in Luther's reducing Christianity to a national, that is, German level, thus locking himself into a limited role.

In contrast to Luther, the Magyar religious soul had the yearning to be an integrated part of the total Christian tradition. To verify such spiritual inclination, the cosmic background of the Magyars as a determining factor, must now be explored.

Cosmic background as determining factor

The Magyars had lived for centuries in Europe at the crossroads of four spiritual influences: Slavic melancholy, German mysticism, Latin rationalism, and Islamic fanaticism. These four currents faced each other or mixed together in those border zones, which used to be called "*Zwischen-Europa*."* Living as they were in constant contact with all four currents, the Magyars had to build up a relationship with at least one of them. By way of ecclesiastical affiliation, they finally made Latinity their own. This Latin ethos prevented the Magyar mentality from feeling attracted either by Slavic nihilism or Islamic fatalism.

In the era of religious disputes, however, the Magyar psyche was awakened to its own existential consciousness. In the tumult of men seeking God, which was overwhelming in the sixteenth century, that metaphysical product of Magyar mentality, their literary language, was born, and on its wings, faith rooted in the Bible found its way into the consciousness of the people, an existential reality.

Within its new European frontiers, however, the nomadic horseman's soul became that of the "spiritually homeless." Without relatives and friends, the Magyar psyche went on its pilgrimage to Helvetic Protestantism and so became conscious of its European mission and national vocation. They could acknowledge that they had sinned, and when they were vouchsafed the privilege of becoming Europe's bulwark against the encroaching

---

*Borderline between West and East Europe.

Turks, they made the sacrifice of fighting the East for the West's sake, causing them to be accepted by the Christian church in Europe.

In this consciousness of a mission, the whole cosmic orientation took a turn toward the moral sphere, and the Magyar was prepared for Helvetic Puritanism. By the same token, he avoided the temptations posed by Slavic Messianic pretensions. The basic element of German mentality in Lutheranism was a burden to him, and for this reason he preferred to orient himself toward Helvetic Calvinism.

This expressed for the Magyar soul the grave truth of the Old Testament, which coincided entirely with its spirit of self-accusation. The only acceptable explanation of Hungary's suffering lay in the exclusive sovereignty of the Almighty, an explanation that saved the Magyar soul from accepting authority from whatever worldly source it might come, in the realm of religious freedom. Neither Ottoman nor Habsburg authorities could win the Magyar's basic humility or servile subjection.

Magyar mentality was by now prepared to accept the idea of predestination, because nowhere but on this transcendental level was it able to explain its new historical role and new human conditions. Its role was now no longer determined by human will but was shaped by a higher Force. The Magyars, acquiescing to the change in their human lot, hastened unreservedly to defend their neighbors.

When representatives of the Lutheran faith in Hungary wanted to enforce the principle of *cuius regio eius religio*, the Magyars refused with incredible courage, an act which made their shift to the Helvetic theology more determined.

In conclusion, it appears obvious that in Protestantism the revolution of the Magyar soul went through a specific European evolution. It was the European Church which had brought about its conversion in the first place; now the changes in European metaphysics made it more productive again, and from the deep recesses thereof brought to light elements which belonged to its oldest heritage. As Magyar mentality became profoundly European-Christian in Helvetic-Calvinism, it was to become deeper in its Magyar essence and definitely reached maturity in its faith.

The sixteenth century added autonomy, and thanks to this, admirable theological creativity. This is the metaphysical background of what is called the "Magyar religion," an epithet given by neighboring nations, meaning a variant of the Helvetic theology.

The depicted process is analogous to the processes in other European nations which succeeded in keeping their intellectual autonomy and in expressing it in the religious field. Thus Hungary appears as an organically integrated part of a European process. In the last stage of his development in the sixteenth century, the nomadic horseman of the steppe reached the loftiest expression of Christian faith.

Only a pre-eminent man could cope with the tired souls, bogged down in sixteenth century chaos; he appeared in Péter Melius Juház, whose roots went deep down into that metaphysical heritage, who gave the Helvetic theology its prophetic character in Hungary, and in the God-searching tumult of men, characteristic of the age, sent his flock to the silent recesses of their inmost selves.

Church historian Imre Révész analyzed the merit of these measures:

"As a standard of doctrines and the norm of religious education, the Second Helvetic Confession and the Heidelberg Cathechism came to be accepted. It was mainly through these documents that the spirit of the Swiss Reformation cast its spell over the Hungarian soul . . . . In the atmosphere of this spirit, the fundamental quality of that soul found its full development and sanctification, that natural bent for practical morality, especially its capacity for obedience in many freedoms, which it had brought with itself from the distant steppes of Asia."[56]

Footnotes

1. Nagy, Barnabás. *Wittenberger Vorträge, Reformation 1517–1967. Berlin: Evangelische Verlaganstalt.* p.253.
   "*Die eigentliche Beweggründe aus denen die Madjaren das lutherische Bekenntnis bald mit dem kalvinistischen vertauschten, bleiben im Dunkel.*"

2. von Bellow, G. *Die Ursachen der Reformation. München,* 1917, p. 94.
   "*. . . er hat die Religösitat seiner Zeit nicht geschaffen . . . er gibt dieser Frommigkeit ein neues Ziel.*"

3. Rustow, Alexander. *Ortsbestimmung der Gegenwart. Band II Erlenbach,* Zch.: *Eugen Rentsch Verlag,* 1952, p. 270.
"*Tatsachlich war Luther ein durchaus spätgotischer Geist . . . durchaus dem Mittelalter angehörig, einem herbstlichen, verfallenden, sich auflösenden Mittelalter.*"

4. Luther, Martin. *Werke, 7. 425.f. Weimar. (W.A.)*

5. Lösche, G. *Luther, Melanchton und Kalvin in Österreich-Ungarn.* Tübingen, *1909. p.51.*

6. Luther, Martin. *Tischreden, IV. 606. No. 4997 Weimar, 1916.*

7. Steinlein, H. *Luther und der Krieg. Nurnberg, 1916.*

8. Stökl, Gónther. *Osteuropa und die Deutschen. Hamburg: Stalling Verlag,* 1967.

9. Thulin, Oskar. "*Volkstum und Völker in Luther's Reformation*" *Archiv für Reformations Geschichte, Jahrgang 40.1943. p.26.*

10. Winter, Edward. *Tausend Jahre Geisteskampf im Sudetenland. O. Müller Verlag,* 1938, p. 193.

11. Stökl, Günther. *op. cit.,* p. 42:
"*Man hat zwar in der Tatsache, dass sich der polnische Adel, ebenso wie übrigens auch der ungarische, überwiegend dem Kalvinismus zuwandte, den Beweis für eine polnische Aversion gegen die deutsche Form der Reformation sehen wollen.*"

12. Gause, Fritz. *Deutsch-Sklavische Schicksalgemeinschaft. Würzburg:* 1967. p. 128.

13. Luther, Martin. *Werke, 7.141.24.,*
"Qui habert aures auendi, audiat et a Bello Turco abstineat, donec Papae nomen sub caelo valet."

14. Luther, Martin. *Ibid.,* Bd. 30.2. 113.5.

15. *Magnum Bullarium Romanus, Tomas primas,* 661. Luxemburg, 1742.

16. Panier, Jacques. "*Calvin et les Turcs.*" *Revue Historique,* 1937. p. 283.

17. Luther, Martin. *op. cit.,* 8.708.207.

18. Kalkhoff, P. '
'*Diepeschen des Nuncius Aleander*" *Die Diepeschen und Berichte über Luther vom Wormser Reichstag, 1521. Halle, 1898. 'Aus diesen seiner Irrlehren erfuhr ich dass er sehr unklug, überaus unmässig und in den wissenschaften unwissend ist.'*

19. Luther, Martin. *op. cit.*, 19.662.9
" . . . *weil er (Turk) uns so nahe kommen war.*"

20. Luther, Martin. *op. cit.*, 30.II.120.29.

21. Luther, Martin. *op. cit.*, XXX2, 141–97. *Eine Heerpredigt wider den Türken.*"

22. Friedensburg, Walter. *"Der Türken Einbruch von 1529 und die Erstehung des Luther's Lied."*
*Luther Vierteljahreschrift.Luthergeselschaft.*1937. p 4–15.

23. Wolfram, G. *Ein' feste Burg ist unser Gott.* Berlin: W. de Gruyter Co. 1936. p. 29.

24. Luther. Martin. *op. cit.*, 30.II. p. 149–150.

25. Luther, Martin. *ibid.*, II.173.11.
"Also daas er sich nicht besorgen darf ob er etwa einen Türcken erwurgt."

26. Luther, Martin. *ibid.*, 541.51.585. *"Vermahnung zum Gebet wider den Türcken."*

27. Solyom, Jenö. *Luther és Magyarország.* Budapest: Lutheránus Társaság, 1933. p. 70.

28. Luther, Martin. *op. cit.*, 15.277.21.
" . . . *ut nos defensors tuos exaudire digneris."*
'*Ja die Ungarn rhumen sich Gottes Beschirmer und singen ynn der Litania.*'

29. Cockleus, Johannes. *"Dialogus de Bello Contra Turcas,"* *Antilogias Lutheri.* Leipzig, 1529.
"Hungari, qui pro Gloria Christi et cultu Dei supra C.C. annos contra Turcos punaverunt pia simplicitate passunt Christi Deique defensos dici . . . ."

30. Elert, W. *Morphologie des Luthertums.* München, 1952. I, p. 336, 344.

31. Panier, Jacques. *op. cit.*,

32. Luther, Martin. *Werke.* XXIII.89. *Erlangen*, 1532.

33. Todd, J. M. Luther. New York: Crossroad, 1982. p. 226.

34. Luther, Martin. Luther's Works. vol. 46. Philadelphia, 1955.

35. Luther. Martin. *Werke* XXXIX.II. p. 55–56.

36. Beza, Theodore. *Droits des Magistrats.* Genève, 1573.

37. Luther, Martin. *op. cit.*. XLVI, p. 17–43. Admonition to Peace. 1525.

38. Heussi, Karl. *Compendium der Kirchengeschichte.* Tübingen, 1919. p. e65.

39. Thulin, Oskar. *op. cit.*, p. 28.

40. Asztalos, Miklos. *"Wittenbergi magyar tanulók."* Budapest: *A bécsi magyar történeti intézet. Évkönyv.* 1932. p. 9.

41. Luther, Martin. Luther's Works, Vol. 54. Table Talk. no. 4020. Fortress Press, Philadelphia, 1967.

42. Zeeden, E. W. *Die Erstehung der Konfessionen. München:* Oldenburg Co. p. 178.

43. Thulin, Oskar. *op. cit.,* p.20.

44. Szabo, Géza. *Geschichte des Ungarischen Coetus an der Wittenberger Universität. Halle,* 1941. p. 109.

45. Luther, Martin. *Werke.* 11.336.

46. Luther, Martin. *ibid.,* 11.315.

47. Luther, Martin. WA 53, 417–552.

48. Luther, Martin. Luther's Works, vol. 54. Table Talk. no. 5462.

49. Newman, I. L. Jewish Influence on Christian Reform Movements. New York: AMS Press Inc., 1966. Columbia Univ. Press. Vol. 23.

50. Friedman, Jerome. "The Reformation in Alien Eyes" Jewish Perceptions of Christian Troubles. The Sixteenth Century Journal XIV, No. 1, p. 35. The Sixteenth Century Journal Publ. Inc. NMSU Lb. Kirksville, Missouri.

51. Friedman, Jerome. *ibid.,* p. 35.

52. Friedman, Jerome. *ibid.,* p. 37.

53. Schreiber, Alexander. *Judentum und Christen in Ungarn bis 1526 A.D." Kirche und Synagoge, II. Stuttgart,* 1970. p. 562.

54. Luther, Martin. *op. cit.,* No. 5513.

55. Benda, Kálmán. *A késö Renaszánz politikai összetevöi Magyarországon." Adattár a XVII. sz.szellemi mozgalmanak történetéhez. Szeged:* 1978. No. 4. p. 96.

56. Révész, Imre. *Protestántizmus.* Budapest, 1927. p 5.

Péter Somogyi Juhász (Melius)

Chapter XVII

Péter Somogyi Juhász (Melius), His Importance in the History of the Hungarian Reformed Church 1536–1572

Péter Somogyi Juhász, called Melius, founded the second largest Reformed Church in Europe, and his career is in itself a church history. For one crisis-filled decade and a half, he wrote over fifty books, numerous articles, attended stormy sessions of the church synod, and organized the Reformed Church of Hungary.

His literary activity shows his continuous struggle with various religious groups, with Rome, with the Lutherans and the Unitarians, even with the Anabaptists, and finally shows his persistent opposition to the spiritual encroachments of the Moslem Turks. We may justly call Melius a "front-theologian", because Roman Catholicism, Eastern Orthodoxy, Protestant Christianity, and Oriental Mohammedanism confronted each other, first in Debrecen where he became a pastor and bishop, and later in Hungary at large. Melius had been well conditioned for this unique role during the religious confrontations that were then taking place in East Central Europe.

Melius was not only a theologian, but also a first-rate church politician and church organizer. He was iron-willed, unyielding, and prophetic. He was a true representative of the sixteenthth century, created by the Reform Movement, and like many other figures in the history of his church, he was forced to follow an exceptional calling. Among his opponents was his country's King and Emperor, Maximilian, whose prisons he had to endure twice. He was threatened and humiliated by the Unitarian ruler of Transylvania and, on the third front, narrowly escaped the prisons of the powerful sultan, who wanted him because of his excellent knowledge of the Turkish language to translate into Hungarian the unwelcome message of the Koran. Melius refused. This was a matter of defending the autonomy of European Christianity against the sword and Moslem faith of the sultan, who was then on Europe's eastern border. Buda had already fallen and the Padishah was brandishing the holy sword of Mohammed before the gates of Vienna under siege.

In the outbursts of his volcanic personality and his rebellious subjectiveness, but as the protector and organizer of his church, he followed more in the footsteps of Heinrich Bullinger of Zurich, and he brought forth a new order. With his exceptional genius and almost super-human energy he reshaped the spiritual and social structures of the Magyardom of the sixteenthth century. At the same time he brought his people into the Helvetic Movement and gave them a Calvinistic Weltanschauung. It was not a vain question when later generations asked in grateful wonderment whether the Magyar ethos could have survived without the help of Helvetic Calvinism. It stopped the spread of Antitrinitarianism and, sitting on firm foundations, it was able to withstand the onslaught of a renewed Roman Catholicism after the Council of Trent.

Mark Pattison of Oxford asked a similar question when, in his studies, he pondered whether a recumbent Europe could have survived without Calvinism. Between sectarianism and Jesuit totalitarianism, Calvin offered an alternative, a third way. This third way was theocracy. Here the new criterium could only be the Word of God. According to Calvin, Christ did not bestow His power on the acts of men but kept it for the Word. As long as the pastor, the proclaimer of the Word, served It, he was capable of all things. Speak out! Pass judgment! Act without fear!

It was in such an age that Melius brought all this to the Protestant leaders in Hungary by means of spiritual armament and the faith of the Bible, not by Spanish mercenaries or the sultan's janissaries.

Melius' Beginnings

The biography of Péter Somogyi* Juhász, known as Melius, began before his birth. The county of his family came under Turkish occupation, and his birthplace disappeared from the map. What family records there were,

_____

*meaning of Somogy county

were destroyed because the war, which lasted a century and a half, demolished the very sources of history, its records. In those days, records and chronicles were kept in the monasteries and churches. These all fell victim to the Turkish invasion in the first onslaught, because they represented historical continuity. As for the monasteries, the most widespread were those of the Franciscan order, which worked diligently among the people. Thirty-four percent of Franciscan monasteries, and thirty percent of the Franciscan monks, seventeen hundred of them, were active in that part of Europe under the authority of the Hungarian bishops, the *Vicaria hungariae*. The monks were relatively more numerous here than in other European ecclesiastical territories, and their main task was to carry on the spiritual struggle against heretics pouring in from the Balkans, and to wage the spiritual war against the Moslem Turks.[1]

It is worthwhile to note that it was among these well-prepared Franciscan monks that the propagators of Protestantism sprang at the beginning of the Reformation. Maybe this is one explanation of the fact that the so-called People's Reformation spread so rapidly over the territories served.

Exact information on the birth of Péter Somogyi Juhász (Melius) is lacking due to the burning of the family records, but he was probably born in 1536, descending from a noble family, *natus ex nobili et praeclara familia.*[2]

The original family name Somogyi Juhász was, as with other humanists, hellenized and became Melius, Péter's pen name.

In recent times church historian István Botta in his book *The Youth of Péter Juhász* has attempted to identify Melius with a contemporary Hungarian, whose name and fate allegedly are identical with those of Melius. Botta's theory is based upon prison memoirs in which a Péter Somogyi described two imprisonments and ruthless torture by the Habsburg Catholic Archbishop Miklos Olah. The identification, however, is lacking one important proof, that is to compare this particular manuscript with that of Péter Somogyi Juhász called Melius. A document concerning Péter Melius' family origin is in the archives of Zurich, Switzerland.*

He probably completed his early studies at an institution located somewhere in Turkish occupied territory, because he knew the Turkish language

---

Miscellanea Tigurina II, Th. II, A. Zurich 1723 VIII, let. 222–227 according to this document Melius was of a prominent, noble family.

well. In any case, the precocious and talented youth adopted the Helvetic faith early on and, with this religious background, set out for the University of Wittenberg in the year 1556.[3]

Among Melius' professors were Bugenhagen, Maior, Brenz, Flacius Illyricus, Forster and Philip Melanchthon, who was to become the best known, and they attracted the outstanding students of Europe.

After Luther's death, it was Melanchthon who became the "unifier" who worked for theological unity and toward reconciliation between Geneva and Wittenberg. For this he suffered many fierce attacks. Melanchthon's ideas on cultural humanism made a deep impression on Melius and they influenced his spiritual development considerably. Apart from the theological system, Melius adopted the scholastic methodology. He further perfected the Latin, Greek, and Hebrew which he had learned at home and, because he had special linguistic talents, he became adept in Turkish, Arabic, and German. He could thus increase his knowledge through the medium of seven languages.

Many pages in the story of Melius' life remain blank. We know little about his foreign travels. He was elected rector of the independent *Coetus* of the large Hungarian student body at Wittenberg. This would seem to testify to his exceptional talents and to the scholarly achievements valued by his contemporaries. At the university he earned the degree of Magister.

The next information we have tells us that the 22-year-old Melius was urgently called back to Hungary to become a pastor and a teacher in the city of Debrecen, the Geneva of Hungary. There was a particular reason for this urgent call, and it was closely related to the very history of the church. Melius was given the task of taking up the struggle against the fast-spreading Antitrinitarian Movement.[4]

This assignment in 1558 displays to future generations the beginnings of an extraordinary human destiny. Melius' work was limited to a mere fifteen years due to his early death, but he accomplished his task and stopped the spread of Unitarianism. This historic role raised him up above his contemporaries.

When he began his career in Debrecen, the city was rapidly taking on bourgeois customs and had already surpassed in population the Protestant Swiss cities of Zurich and Basel. In 1551 the citizens of Debrecen had diverted the spiritual direction of their community away from Lutheranism, which had begun there in 1549, and had turned to Helvetic Protestantism. The Helvetic *Consensus Tigurinus* (1549) which constituted an agreement between Calvin and Bullinger on the concept of the Lord's Supper, served as basis for this change. So in the organization of Debrecen great similarity was to be found with the organization of the Reformed Church of Geneva. Here too city autonomy operated under the protection and leadership of the city council, and the council organized the restructured church. When decisions were being made on church matters in Debrecen, Melius presided over the city council.

The most urgent matter for the leadership of the Reformed Church in Debrecen was to halt the spread of sectarianism and to reestablish order and authority. During these troubled times of change, the apparent quiescence of the Roman Church encouraged the rise of numerous sects such as the Fanatics, the Baptists, and the Antitrinitarians. The history of religion pretty well proves that sectarianism was a reaction against the shortcomings of organized religion and a protest of souls thirsting for spiritual solace. At the same time the sects themselves fell prey to similar deficiencies and they soon lost the role they had wished to play. Weary souls were inclined to give up the much desired freedom of religion in the interest of peace and order.

Debrecen, The Calvinist Rome

What was the city to which Melius had been called like? Debrecen became known as the "Calvinist Rome." It had come to be the spiritual center of the Hungarian Reformation and Melius soon received the uncharitable title of "Pope of Debrecen" given to him by his enemies because of his combative and dominating nature. Since this independent city was located in a very exposed position geographically, its religious and political attitude was already determined to a great degree. As the Reformed *Respublica* it tried to maintain itself as the meeting place of a nation divided into three parts. The western part was vegetating under the yoke of the Catholic Habsburgs. In the south the neighbor was the Turkish sultan, and to the east the voivode of Transylvania claimed sovereignty for himself. So Debrecen, lying at the crossroads of three powers, defended itself as best it could over a period of one century and a half, facing yearly onslaughts from Turks, Germans, and Tartar hordes. The key word for its survival was the Hungarian word: *Megadom* "I will pay." They paid taxes to the Turks, to the Habsburg kings, and to the voivod of Transylvania just so that "we can keep our heads on our shoulders."

Melius lived in a century of continuous war. There was not a day without its struggle, not an hour without its danger, but in spite of this, the city of Debrecen had neither the security of walls nor a moat nor the protection of mountains. Out of this continuous state of peril, there developed the so-called "Debrecen resourcefulness", the *debreceni politika*. It was at the price of this that daily bread and even daily life was bought. The resourcefulness did not always work, and the two "pagan" powers, the Turks and the Germans, burned and plundered in turn, and carried off its citizens as prisoners. During Melius' pastorship the enemy burned the city to the ground three times and plundered it twice.

From the fifteenth century on Debrecen had already amassed wealth and, thanks to the prerogative granted it by the king, it could hold fairs seven times a year. The fairs lasted two weeks, and merchants came to display their wares from Russia, from Turkey, Poland and the Balkan states. From the West almost every merchant town of note was represented, and because of the number of days taken up by the seven fairs, one third of the year was given over to buying and selling. Of course an international fair is not puritanical in all things, and it is not surprising that at fair-time the doors of the Reformed College remained closed for the protection of the students' morals. In all events, this roving commerce made Debrecen rich. Seventeen businesses were engaged in producing goods, the main commodity being cattle on the hoof. Sometimes merchants from the West drove herds back home numbering more than ten thousand head. This meant that somewhere war was in the offing and that the "*gulyás* (beef) on the hoof" was destined to feed fighting mercenaries. For the security of their goods, the merchants engaged their own soldiers to protect their property from well-informed enemies. One chronicler named the city of Debrecen the "town with the feet of gold."

In connection with the fairs, we might add that in Turkish occupied territory, fairs were permitted though under Turkish rules, and participants made their own arrangements for protection. Along the line separating Turkish from Hungarian territory, special protecting walls were thrown up by the Hungarian authorities, forming a chain of border fortresses, manned and maintained by the impoverished Hungarian nobility. On their side of the line the Turks threw up their own fortresses and between these two fronts the Magyars carried on continuous guerilla warfare.

One activity developed by these hostilities was fair-raiding by which the Magyars attempted to break up and plunder the fairs held in Turkish occupied territory. With the income derived from fair-raiding, the Magyars were able to supply themselves. One group of Czech Hussites (*Bratske*) received their income from similar plundering. After decades of this activity, however, the military tactics of fair-raiding became more refined. Spies were employed, and in conformity with the information received, the various plans were laid. The expeditions were set up according to the number of Turkish soldiers that had to be taken into account. The first part of the raid was carried out by a small number of men mounted on the fastest horses. They rode onto the fairgrounds making great noise, thus attracting the Turkish defending troops whom they then decoyed into the countryside. Then the real raiders came in and made off with what treasures they could find. When the weary outwitted Turkish soldiers returned, they found that the fair was over, and that the Magyar partisans had taken away many of the rich merchants as prisoners. To get these merchants back, huge ransoms had to be paid.

If a fair-raid was successful, the leader sold the plunder, and one third of the proceeds was given to the school in Debrecen where their own impoverished children were studying. The rest was divided up into equal parts including the part for the families of soldiers killed in battle. This kind of life went on for one hundred and fifty years during which time a homeless nobility, having lost country and fortune, had nothing left but its swords.

The merchants of Debrecen carried on their own danger-ridden commerce in circumstances similar to the ones described. During Melius' tenure as bishop (beginning in 1561), the city was deprived of almost everything, because more than once the armies of the reigning Habsburgs pounced down on the town and stripped its inhabitants bare. It is significant that Melius was unable to write down the church canons that he was preparing, because there was not enough paper in the whole city to finish his task.*

---

*A contemporary of Melius, the Roman Catholic bishop Paul Bornemissza, because of similar Turkish depredations, was also unable to obtain paper and ended his writing with these words:

"I should have written more, but there is no paper. This evening I took this piece of parchment out of a window where it served as glass." (Takáts, Sándor. *Rajzok a törökvilágból.* Vol. I, p. 59. Budapest 1915)

But the wonder of it is that the citizens saw to it that this great work of the Reformation was completed later. The merchants not only kept their doors open to Western goods, but to Western thought as well.

How did Melius justify to the puritanical society in formation this unusual source of material goods gained through fair-raiding? He put it thus: "God gives victory, gentlemen, so that you will acknowledge His assistance. From the gains, in the manner of King David, churches will be built to the Lord, and school and students will be provided for, and schoolbooks printed."

The strong desire of Debrecen to live and survive had predestined it, through its suffering and its cultural role, to become a center of the Reformation.

With the Roman Catholic Church expiring in Eastern Hungary and a society of free citizens emerging from feudalism, the way was open for the completion of Melius' task. The young bishop, still in his twenties, was developing step by step the historical consciousness of his fellow citizens. At the same time he was organizing a church, composing a literature, developing a university, and making the citizens stand taller. Debrecen, this City of God, *Civitas Dei*, as it was called, then set out to win over the people of Eastern Hungary to its religion and draw them to the Word. Starting out from this spiritual center, like the long-suffering Jews whose "movable state" saved their lives, Melius was able to offer the Word of God as the unique remedy.

To help make his people stand tall and be conscientious Christians, Melius laid down hard and sometimes impatient rules of moral conduct at a time when everything–spiritual, moral, and even worldly–was faced with destruction. Furthermore, people arriving from distant parts of the country often brought with them loose moral habits. The problem of moral laxity and the question of free will in the population of Debrecen often produced contradictions and undermined the theocratic order. There were worldly powers, under God, however, who saw to it that good was preserved and evil punished. The preacher living among his people knew very well why the citizens carried the soft inside of a salted loaf of bread in the pocket, "because in the tavern they beat each other over the head . . . " and the salted bread was a prescribed remedy against wounds incurred. Looking back over the centuries, the historian is inclined to condemn the heavy-handed dictator-like bishop whose duty it was to bring the members of a disintegrated society into a new moral way of living.

The other center of the Reformation, Kolozsvár, was in a state similar to that of Debrecen. There, however, the city's population was split up by bizarre religious renovators with extreme views. Finally, the city council of Kolozsvár had to step in and order the sectarian agitators to mount to the pulpit and defend their views on the basis of the Bible. If they failed to do this, they were dressed in a night-shirt, soundly thrashed, and thrown out of town. A similar procedure was followed in Geneva where, after the church service, the culprit had to ask for forgiveness for his actions. Failing to do this, he too was driven out of town.

In Melius' time certain preachers were put into stocks on the town square; others, caught in adultery, were condemned to death by the council. These extreme cases indicate some of the depravity of people in that unsettled age. Debrecen was given a special role in the history of the church: it was to serve as an example for other towns by its exemplary way of life.

Melius, the Church Organizer

The type of church organization and church government set forth by Melius was strictly of an ecclesiastical nature. He described this in one of his writings saying, "It is not the sheep that rule the shepherd, but the shepherd the sheep." He hurriedly threw up a protective wall of strict church laws around his church because, after the disaster of Mohács in 1526 at which the Roman Catholic hierarchy had dug its own grave, a greedy class had sprung up that began to appropriate for themselves the property of the Roman Church and, at the same time had tried to make their influence felt as "Protestants" in the Reformed Church. Luther's example had served them in this type of action, because the Wittenberg Reformer had been forced to call such people to his aid, and the dukes themselves had appointed leaders of Luther's Reformed churches. In Hungary Melius forestalled this development. Every year he called together his ever-growing clergy to a meeting of the church synod. The moderators of the Hungarian church, the *superintendens*, were chosen only from among the clergy at these synodical meetings. The elected church leaders were therefore simply equals among equals.

In this way Melius built the new church as a protection against worldly ambitions when he introduced into the Church constitution the concept of government by the clergy. The Constitution also insured the participation of the temporal powers in the synod, but only as observers. When they took part in the synod, a distinguishing term was used, namely *Conventus Solemnis*. Thus, Melius came near to Melanchthon's formula that "the public authority was an order of God for the defense of good and the extermination of evil."

Melius' *Book of Canon Law* was published in Debrecen in 1567 for the maintenance of church organization and the governance of everyday life. In it the duties of the ministers were strictly set forth as well as the formula according to which the church should be governed. There was great need for this because, at the beginning, the autonomous congregations led a disorganized existence. In the various parts of the country, congregations had organized themselves and had taught according to their own lights.

The *Book of Canon Law* had as it theological basis the Word of God, (*sola scriptura*), and every declaration a minister made had to conform to that. The Synod, already mentioned, was the ruling body of the new Church and, according to the nature of the business at hand, could call a general or a local meeting. The duty of the bishop or moderator, as head of the church district, was to call together the annual meeting of the Synod where decisions were jointly arrived at on any question that happened to come up. The lay-members attending could not direct but only support. With this kind of constitution, the reformers arrived at the complete independence of the post-Constantinian church. It must be borne in mind that the rulers of Hungary were the Roman Catholic Habsburgs, who never had accepted the Reformation and now could exercise no control over it. Of course, in a modern context many laws of former times have lost their meaning and their timeliness. There was, for example, the question of the legal status of a marriage partner taken captive by the Turks. It had often happened that the wife of such a man remarried. The first husband, once freed and returning home, expected to resume his married status with his wife. A law had to be formulated to establish the legal position of the wife. This became a serious question in Canon Law because of the frequency of the situation, resulting in an appeal to the Swiss Bullinger for advice. The natural situation prevailed, and the first husband had the right to resume marital status with his wife.

The citizens of Debrecen had asked for a new interpretation of the Ten Commandments and received from Melius a new view of morality. For instance, refusing to pay back a debt was declared a sinful act. Likewise, deceit in commercial dealings, falsifying measures, selling unfit animals, all required a very serious administration of clerical justice. To refuse to pay a worker his wages counted as a capital sin.

The Church was further influenced by the introduction in 1563 of Melius' *Book on the Order of Service*, the *Agendás könyve*, in which he gave final form to the order of the church service.

Today we do not know what his liturgical order was like, but we do know that the Roman Catholic tradition of the time often tried his patience. In the memory of the people, the ceremony itself was the dominant factor, and little understanding was given to dogma. Melius slowly transformed the tradition of the Roman Mass and in a forceful voice proclaimed to his hearers: "Having faith in man's worthiness and in the Mass is a far greater sin than murder." He described the Mass as "Resplendent on the outside, but on the inside like a dead animal . . . . Beautiful are the priest's robes, but the Mass is an invention of man and therefore a human falsehood." In that time rich and splendid priestly garments were given away to the beggars in poorhouses. Melius emphasized that, although whatever had a Biblical basis (and some practices of the Roman Catholic Church clearly had such a foundation), still it was imperative to remember that "in stinking old barrels the new wine can go bad."

In keeping with the *Book on the Order of Service* immersion was practiced for baptism at first, only later modified when sprinkling was introduced. Melius held that it was not necessary to use salt water in the baptismal service because John the Baptist had not used it either, neither had he taken water from the rock. He allowed baptism taking place outside of the church building, as long as it was not done in a tavern or a bathhouse, but he warned that the baby should not be "slobbered over in popish manner."[5]

In regard to membership, the constitution of the new Church was very clear in holding that all who openly confessed their faith would be received as members.

Melius also had to bring some order to congregational singing, as well as to take a position in the use of musical instruments in the church service. There were those who, following the example of Zwingli, wanted to ban all music, not only musical instruments such as organs. Melius, however, remembered his experience abroad and recalled that "Lutherans had sung themselves into the Lutheran faith." It seemed that singing was maybe even more important than dogma: "At such times God converts through song." Even the Roman Catholics recognized the success the Protestants were having in the field of religious conversion. Early on, the *Debrecen Confession* had also admitted that "We can teach no one through silence." It was for this reason that Melius kept his congregation singing, which aimed at building up the church. It was out of this development that the Debrecen *Hymnal* came into being, in which some hymns composed by Melius were incorporated.

Although the decree *scriptura scripturam interpretatur*, "the Gospel has to be explained through the Gospel", a church service could only last one hour, to avoid the "danger of soporific boredom."

In questions of church government, it was not the Presbyterian form of Geneva that Melius considered the most suitable, but rather the Episcopalian one. One reason for this may be that, Western citizenry of East Central Europe had not yet developed far enough to attain the West European level. Therefore only the clergy had the privilege of deciding on dogma, on teaching, and on who could render accounts to the "Judge of Life and Death." It was only after several centuries that the Presbyterian system was introduced.

The matter of theocratic order was dealt with by the Senate and the High Council (*civitas et ecclesia*) together and free from aristocratic interference. The cultural and religious problems to be found in Melius' *Debrecen Confession* faithfully reflect the spiritual turmoil of Debrecen in that time. Unorthodox views were rampant among the people who clung to their altars, their candles, and the wafers, and even to the custom of going to confession.[6] The Reformation continued to weed out the monolithic traditions of the Church, so that in 1567 the *Second Helvetic Confession* was introduced at the Synod meeting in Debrecen. This was the Confession drawn up by Bullinger. The document received final acceptance only in the late seventeenth century when, through united action by both Geneva and Zurich, final form was given to its contents. With the *Second Helvetic Confession* Hungarian church-life was brought closer to the Western and more dynamic Helvetic model. The Moravian Brethren, who were refugees in Hungary, also adopted it, and on this basis Johann Amos Comenius became bishop of their congregations, which had been organized in Hungary.

In similar fashion, the Polish reformers had accepted the Helvetic Confession in 1566, and with these developments the cause of the Reformation could develop simultaneously throughout East Central Europe.[7]

The second important decision of the Hungarian Reformed Church was the introduction in 1577 of the Heidelberg Catechism, which had been published in 1563 by Heidelberg theologians at the request of Frederick III, ruler of the Palatinate. In many ways this Catechism brought the Hungarian Church even closer to the Helvetic Confession.

In 1563 Theodore Beza had already put his stamp of approval on the Heidelberg Catechism with his *Short Confession*, which also had appeared in Heidelberg. From this, one can easily see how Calvin's former collaborator and follower, Beza, exercised a wide influence on the Helvetic Reformation, not only in Switzerland, but in Holland, Germany, Poland, and Hungary as well.[8]

The new economic way of life also expected recognition in the teachings of the Church. For example, the question of an economy based on money had to be cleared up. Luther had taught that dealing in money was not a clean occupation, because money did not create money. Those citizens of Geneva who carried on commerce and depended on a lively turnover of money, however, were allowed by Calvin to charge interest, and this formula suited those inhabitants of Debrecen who were engaged in commerce.

A final note may make clear some of the difficulties Melius had to deal with. Because of religious persecution, pestilence, and the abduction of men during wartime, the subsequent shortage of ministers of the Gospel made it necessary at times for one pastor to serve as many as three congregations. It occasionally happened that in the course of a visit of inspection by the bishop or his aid, they found a complaisant minister who, besides serving his Reformed congregation, also served a Roman Catholic one, in order to supplement his rather low income.

Melius Preaches the Gospel

In the *Debrecen Confession*, which Melius edited and helped formulate in 1562, his prescription in regard to sermons stated that a preacher must practice his homily and not his rhetoric; God's Word was to be the essential element of a sermon. Only the Gospel could explain the Gospel, and hence the sermon could be nothing more than an exposition and an application through which the writings of the Prophets and the Apostles were to be explained. After reading aloud his Biblical text, the preacher should explain it first and then apply it by summing up the moral lesson, making it relevant to life.

During the period of religious renovation, a solid theological basis was very important. One might say that the history of preaching is identical with the history of theological comprehension. When the different Protestant movements were drawing away from one another, precepts had to be hurriedly drawn up regarding preaching, based on differing dogmas. The *pericopa* which had formerly been practiced by the Roman Catholics, and which meant that each Sunday a prescribed Biblical text was given on which the sermon was to be built, was abolished by Melius. Instead, and in agreement with Calvin, Melius preached and taught the books of the Bible one at a time and in succession. He had a good knowledge of Hebrew, Latin, and German, and could refer to original texts in carrying on his teaching. In doing so, he always got his message across, and for that reason his sermons have stood the test of time. He never orated in empty phrases that tickled the ear, but proclaimed the Glory of God and armed his congregation for the daily struggle for existence. He often repeated: "Where the Word of God is not heard, the living Christ is not present; and a country which does not acknowledge a redeeming Christ is not yet a nation, just a populated land with neither purpose not destiny."

Melius' church service was so conducted as to erase all remnants of the Roman Catholic Mass which he disparaged thus: "To worship human values in the Mass is a greater sin than murder, because it is an act of transgression against the first commandment of Moses."

Of the thousands of sermons Melius preached, only two hundred remain. He put the Bible at the center of his sermons, the Bible which up until then had been in little use in church services, and he carried on a continuing commentary on its text. He often used commentaries written by the Church Fathers. When he dealt with the Apostle Paul's epistle to the Romans, he analyzed it in seventy-six continuing sermons. Everyone of them was built on his Christology, on which he laid great stress. The central thought of every one of his messages was the substitutional atonement. The godliness of Christ restored the mercy of the Father, and through this act restored the lost image of God in His chosen ones. Since Melius dealt with all books of the Bible, he later assembled and published these discourses. (One can experience even today the particular strength of the living Word and its immediacy in his sermons.)

After explaining the essential points of his sermons, Melius would read appropriate Bible passages to justify what he had said. Often personal feelings shone through, and he attacked his adversaries angrily and loudly. Melius was well aware of the intellectual level of his congregation and timed his sermons accordingly. In unheated churches, in the cold of winter, his listeners must have awaited the final "Amen" shivering, but as a practical minister Melius knew that if a sermon was good and interesting, it could be long and still seem short. If the sermon was not good, it would appear long even though it were short. (One of Melius' contemporaries and former professors, the Lutheran Johann Bugenhagen from Wittenberg, is known to have preached seven hours at a stretch!)

It was Melius' opinion that he was not so much speaking at an individual in his sermons, but to the very soul of the community. The spiritual emanation from the pulpit would bring about a fusing together of the entire congregation. According to Melius an essential element of a sermon was the wonder which could be felt surrounding it. This wonderment could only be brought into touch with the souls in the congregation by another soul, but a prophetic one. Prophets are seldom surrounded by crowds and so Melius often felt lonely.

Melius was constantly faced with that thousand-year-old question: "Why and what should I preach?" To many pastors preaching was merely teaching, but to Melius teaching without a prophetic element in it, was not complete preaching. Melius, the prophet, indicated to his followers the life they should lead, and so he was carrying a mortal responsibility on his shoulders. His word was therefore hazardous, because it did not fit into the petrified forms of church-life. If he would let himself drift, he would bury the prophetic Christ. He might practice an exegesis with which he wanted to prove the truth of his dogmas on a Biblical basis and demonstrate their absolute truth, but he knew from his own experience as a preacher that a newly born faith formed its own dogmas, and if faith flickered and went out, dogma simply became an unnecessary burden on the church. Melius was later unable to avoid these pitfalls, and because of the many attacks against the militant Reformation, he got stuck in a tangle of orthodoxy trying to defend its precepts. Before this happened, however, he managed to bring into being a church and a congregation. So the essence of Melius' life work was "to awaken souls with the Word of God." As he often wrote: "I am the trumpet, the spoken word, and I speak not from myself, but from God."

One can notice in the second phase of his work that Melius gave too much effort to an intellectualism that theologized and polemicized to excess.[9] He was often too unbending and would openly castigate those of his colleagues who remained silent about the sins of the temporal powers, and called them "dumb dogs" because, according to him the life of a good clergyman was like a living Bible displayed before the people, "Let the good minister study until he dies."

The Eclectic Theology of Melius

Among Hungarian church historians, there were some who called Melius the Magyar Calvin. Modern research in comparative dogma has modified this view. Melius' strong personality guarded him from becoming an imitator. His extensive knowledge of European theology made him eclectic. As a reformer, organizer, and writer, Melius always kept sight of the whole, and with a global view of things, he only accepted from other theologians the impulses that set him in motion. In final analysis, he brought into being a synthesis of European Protestantism. When he took elements from the West, he used only those that suited the spiritual climate of East Central Europe. Although in Wittenberg he had listened to the dignitaries of the Lutheran Church, he became a follower of the Helvetic Movement, but, unlike the Swiss, Melius gave preference to the writings of the Church Fathers. Thus he shaped his own tradition, which in the history of the Church has been called the Debrecen model, and it was according to this model of theology and church organization that the Hungarian Church developed its historic role. The continuous struggle carried on by Melius' generation centered on and stabilized the theological system of Helvetic theology. From this struggle for reform emerged, from the union of Aristotelianism and Calvinism, a distinct new orthodoxy. Melius also struggled to narrow down dogmatic contradictions coming from Western Europe, which were dangerous elements for his church. The danger manifested itself in Hungary in the Antitrinitarian movement, which checked Melius in his endeavors and forced him into a decade of negative struggle. A similar danger was also manifest in Poland where sectarianism flourished.

Melius wanted to bring into reality and by peaceful means a closed spiritual authority based on the Word of God. He needed to develop such a church quickly and, because it was surrounded by enemies, make his flock obedient in the service of God and able to defend itself. Melius' theology must therefore be judged not only from the point of view of religion, but also in the light of church politics. As a front-line theologian, he could not take his eyes off temporal dangers that were threatening his followers.

The first decade of his activity can be called his theological period and, approaching him on this terrain, we can find a spiritual kinship in theology between Melius and Calvin. Calvin was not just a theoretical theologian either, but one whose practical theology spread through the entire fabric of life in Geneva. The connections, relationships and dissimilarities between the theology of these two men are clearly seen in the following points: Predestination, the Doctrine of the Lord's Supper, and the question of the Trinity.

Predestination

Melius adhered to the infralapsarian point of view that God brought about a double predestination: There was first the Fall through sin, followed by the justice of predestination. In this manner Melius voided the view of Calvin's successor, Theodore Beza, who held that: Adam of necessity fell from grace, that is from happiness, through God's decree. Melius offered the opinion that God punished man because of his disobedience, therefore he had fallen from grace. Here he agreed with Bullinger that God only allows sin, but that He did not create it. The Fall was therefore not sin, but punishment. On this question Melius disagreed with Calvin's supralapsarian position. For Melius man retained some part of independence and Adam was seen as the victim of his own action. According to Melius' thoughts on the matter, the chosen could not totally fall from grace, because they contained within themselves the "seed of faith."

Calvin held that the remission of sin, mercy, was the act of the sovereign God; Melius maintained that mercy was like the act of the father of the prodigal son. In the spirit of the Gospel, there was great consolation. Although through sin man had lost his likeness to God, and had taken on that of the devil, through which he was lost and spiritually died, man could be born again in the spirit of God's mercy through Jesus Christ. Hence man was saved from damnation through the offering up by Christ of Himself.

The deep meaning of this explanation of predestination is that the believer himself is not capable of appropriating for himself his own faith, but that faith is a merciful gift of God. This belief became a great comfort for the Hungarians during the trials and tribulations of the sixteenth century.

Melius could be called the theologian of mercy.[10]

Melius' Theology of the Lord's Supper

The Protestant doctrine of the Lord's Supper became a very divisive matter during the first half of the Reformation because no unanimity could be found in the Gospel on the subject. Therefore reformers attempted to explain it through exegesis and speculation. Luther, for example, would allow only those of his congregation to partake of Communion who were ready to accept his views on dogma and his interpretation of it. In fact he merely changed the name of the doctrine of the medieval Eucharist, not its essence.[11] Calvin and Melanchthon were more flexible but radically changed the understanding of the Lord's Supper, and could be more forebearing on less important details.

It is characteristic of the age that Melius argued over every shade of meaning in the doctrine, and it became such a dominant theme in his writings that, outside of ethnical and linguistic questions, his argumentations did much to bring about an alienation from the Lutheran followers in Hungary. For Melius the question of transubstantiation did not exist, and token bread and token wine were simply the names of token things, namely flesh and blood, but not their essence. However, the body and blood of Christ were present in spirit by virtue of the Promise and through faith were given to the chosen faithful. As for those who were without faith, they received only the token. For Melius the question of the Lord's Supper was not only one of theology but also of a practicality as well. According to him, the sacrament consisted of worldly and heavenly elements, the first being the bread and wine, the second the holy body and blood of Christ. The human body would take in the corporal food of bread and wine, while the human spirit would feed on the holy body and blood through faith. Melius argued that Christ could not possibly be bodily present at the Lord's Supper because his body was in heaven, sitting at the right hand of God, but His Spirit was present everywhere. (He explained this in *Debrecen Confession*.) Besides, he argued, since the apostles did not eat Christ's body at the first

Lord's Supper, the people could much less eat it now that He was departed. The human spirit could be united with Christ's spiritual body, as bread becomes part of the human body after being eaten, turning into blood. The Holy Spirit brings so to human souls the very presence of Christ.[12]

Melius always emphasized that only the Holy Spirit could make the Redeemer present in the human spirit, because man could not gain conversion through his own will, because conversion was "the most difficult mission at man's creation and at his resurrection."

Of less importance to Melius was whether leavened or unleavened bread was used at the celebration, or whether the communicant had fasted or not. "Veneration does not go to the tokens, but to God. Christ himself did not bless the bread, His blessing was for God, his heavenly Father." [13] Another leniency was shown when he advised that abstainers from wine should be given beer or water.

In the beginning of his work Melius considered it correct to permit group confession of sin, which in practice was simply a confession of faith. Later he became more restrictive and individualism was stressed.

The most important role of the early Reformed Church was teaching those who had renewed their faith. To bring an illiterate people to an understanding of Christ's Word was a matter of teaching, using any means available. For that reason Melius urged impatiently that the ruling class "make schools out of the churches," because it was the teacher who had to establish and preserve the militant Reformation. Melius early recognized the approaching danger from a rejuvenated Roman Catholicism.[14] As a genuine dialectician, he tried to avoid disputes by putting the basic doctrine of the Church into well chosen words, in a period which was characterized by the resistance to the Roman Catholic doctrines and during which the Protestant dogmas were being drawn up. These doctrines may truly be called doctrines of protest.

Melius' irenic theology proved applicable to the whole of Europe. His literary preparation made it possible for him to play a unifying role among the students who before returning to Hungary had been influenced by Luther, Melanchthon, Zwingli, and Calvin. In spite of the extremely strained theological arguments that were then current, he could offer these young men a more healthy view. In the congregation he posed theological questions which were not over the heads of simple believers, and in this way he approached social questions as well. "I write and teach so that, after I have departed from this life, preaching and teaching will go on." Through Melius the Hungarian Reformed Church was influenced by Zwingli's practical theology, by Luther's and Melanchthon's subjective approach, and by the Biblical and theological elements of John Calvin. In other words, it was the emotion of Luther, the will of Calvin, and the humanistic concepts of Zwingli that shaped the Hungarian Reformed Church.

Melius and the Struggles Against Antitrinitarianism

While Calvin's followers in Geneva were trying to put an end to Antitrinitarianism with the burning of Servetus, in East-Central Europe Melius attempted to neutralize the sect's influence through the writing of books and through discussions in the synod. He and his followers did not erect stakes or light fires, but he did angrily attack the Italian humanists on the question of the Trinity. Those humanists, Ferenc Dávid and the Antitrinitarians in Hungary, enjoyed complete freedom and mounted to the attack. When, however, the Antitrinitarians in Transylvania became ever more radical in their religious teachings, the Roman Catholic voivod,* with the collaboration of Giorgio Blandrata and the help of an intriguing Jesuit court councillor, deprived Ferenc Dávid of his freedom. One might add that Ferenc Dávid contributed to his own downfall by a desire for martyrdom.[15]

Unlike the policy of Dávid, that of Melius can be characterized by the policy of trying to create a spiritual union of all Hungarians, and of declaring war on anything that threatened this purpose. That is why he engaged half of his literary works, numbering over fifty volumes, in the struggle against Antitrinitarianism. For a long time Melius was regarded as the theologian of the Holy Trinity, and Trinitarianism was indeed the central theme of his theology. Melius' approach to the problem was more dogmatic and much more complicated than that of his Swiss counterparts. The fact is that he founded his entire life's work on the Word. For that reason it was impossible for him to compromise with Rome or to remain silent in the face of Antitrinitarianism. With the biting ridicule of his thundering pen, he used every means at his disposal to silence his enemies. He heaped ridicule on the Franciscan brothers, calling them "the keepers of the tail of the Pope's horse" and he called the Pope "the monkey of

---

*voivod = ruler.

Moses" because of the seemingly empty ceremonies in which he was involved. He further declared that "man can no more gain salvation through merit than a gypsy on a lame horse can catch a Turk, or a turtle can catch a hare."

As bishop, Melius had begun to organize the Reformed Church in territories outside his own bishopric, namely in Transylvania. At that time, another Reformer, Ferenc Dávid, still belonged to the Helvetic movement and he had given Melius his full support. But when Dávid began to preach Antitrinitarianism, Melius hurriedly prevailed on the voivode of Transylvania to call together a synod. He thus hoped to defeat his extremist opponents. He also began a bitter dialogue on a literary level with the movement now led by Dávid. One might call this writing campaign a kind of "linguistic neurosis", because his attacks were vitriolic in the extreme. The central theme of his bitter diatribes was how long the activity of these impatient sects and religious nihilists would be tolerated. In his age religion was something definite, as definite as any other manifestation of life, and the fate of the church determined the fate of all things political, cultural, social, and of life itself. For that reason Melius went into battle against Reformers of another ilk who threatened to destroy his church. To be sure, he left to the Creator that power which soars above the spirit of men, but feeling the message of the Redeemer, he went into battle for his flock, and encountering resistance, he became what his opponents called, the "Pope of Debrecen." In this, he fell into line with Calvin, the "Pope of Geneva", and feeling God's mercy he said, "It is not I who live, but Christ within me."

In those days, religious love meant not merely the care for one's soul; it was seen as a social act as well. It was the social love for one's fellow man which caused the chosen of the new church to embark on an apostolic mission to save souls. From this came the fundamental cause of their impatience. The German theologian Tröltsch pointed out the necessity of this kind of impatience, saying, "To build a society and keep it up cannot be done without forceful means; this is a fact of life and history . . . ."[16] In another writing he stated, "Freedom for true faith, and oppression of unbelievers, was the basic concept of those who thought that they possessed an absolute truth."[17] The Church could be tolerant only when it possessed absolute security, a condition absent in the sixteenth century.

When Antitrinitarian radicalism gained a dominant role in Transylvania, the great prestige that Luther had enjoyed until then went into eclipse. Therefore the task of neutralizing the movement fell on the shoulders of the Helvetic Reformers in Hungary and, among them, of course, Melius. This religious radicalism also appeared in the church in Debrecen and its representative, Tamás Arany, spread the views of the Hebraist, Stancaro. According to the latter: "If the part of intervention is attributed to the Son, it means that He is not equal in rank to the Father. If He were equal there would be no reason for Him to supplicate." This reasoning brought Stancaro and Dávid later to the doctrine of non-worship of Christ, the *non adoramus* thesis. It is interesting to note that the first diatribe of Dávid was directed against the same Stancaro against whom Melius was then waging a literary battle. Among these writings, the most significant is "Sermon on the Intervention of Jesus Christ,"[18] (to be found in his collection of sermons), in which he defended Christ's intervention with these words:

> "It was necessary to create a new heart and a new soul in man. This was possible only through the power of God, the Creator. God so moved that He chose an eternal person as Redeemer, His own Holy Son. Cursed be he who gives the task of intervention to mere man . . . . The Gospel nowhere says that Christ could only intervene as a man. Mad are those who aver that supplication and kneeling before Christ are of no avail.

> "Holy Scripture calls this Jacob's ladder. This ladder is Christ, and one end of it touches Heaven. This is the Divinity of Christ, because He is God in God's realm. The other end of the ladder touches the earth because Christ is a man among men.

> "The Holy Spirit also supplicates, (Romans 8, vs. 14–16), but this does not make Him less than the Father. In power Christ is one with the Godhead of His Father, and He does not supplicate, but gives."

Melius explained that Christ took part in the creation and later in the redemption as a divine mediator. Tamás Arany argued that He could not be the mediator in both forms, but only in the human one. In the beginning

Erasmus, with his Biblical criticism, was the source and authority of the Antitrinitarian, later called Unitarian, movement.*

For instance, Erasmus had in his Bible translation omitted the so-called *Comma Johanneum*, (I John 5:7), which would have supported the dogma of the Trinity. At the same time he had introduced a part of the Gospel of Saint Matthew which had been left out of the translation of the Vulgate, (Matthew 24:36), according to which the Son could not know when the End Time would come. It was this very verse that could have served the earlier Arians in the discussion about the divinity of Christ, and in the sixteenth century the Antitrinitarians identified themselves with the Arians.

Melius' knowledge of Hebrew, Greek, Latin, and Arabic served him well in his diatribes with the Unitarians.[19] He was able to show that the original literary sources which inspired Servetus, Dávid, Blandrata, and Socinus in their attacks on the Trinity were mainly of Hebrew origin. In a letter written to Bullinger in 1569,[20] he expressed that "rabbinical literature was the principal source of the internal contradictions in the Reformation." He referred to the well-known Parisian rabbi Joseph Albo, whose arguments against the possibility of the doctrine of omnipresence he found in the writings of Ferenc Dávid and his followers; Albo had written, "It is logically impossible that one object, namely Christ's body, could be in two places at once, and therefore this doctrine is not credible." Thus Luther's thesis, which claimed the corporal presence of Christ at the Lord's Supper was considered not acceptable by Albo and those who quoted him.

Theodore Beza had great respect for Melius' knowledge of Hebrew; Melius wrote him, among other things, "I am enclosing a refutation of the heresy of Servetus, Blandrata, and the Jewish rabbi Joseph, and other Godless people. These people lie most abominably, like Julius the Apostate, against the Holy Trinity, against all the articles of our faith, and against the Bible, and about the eternal nature of the Son's origin, (*Fillii generationem*), and mock these things. These are the foundation of the Servetus-Blandrata heresy."[21]

Melius' principal accusation against the innovations of Dávid were that they were a menace that could wipe out religion and were capable of

---

*The word Unitarian was introduced by Francis (Ferenc) Dávid in referring to the Antitrinitarian movement. It also soon replaced the word Socianism for the same movement in Poland.

weakening the very historical position of the nation itself, because of their sympathy with the Turkish Moslem religion. He wrote:

> "Dávid simply degrades Christ to the status of a common man, who is in no way different from the Christ of the Turks . . . . Christ a poor man stripped of his godliness, and in this way he continues his propaganda."[22]

With this statement, Melius attacked Dávid and his Christology at its most vulnerable point: collaboration with the Turks. Perhaps there was a serious basis for this accusation, because Dávid's one-time close collaborator, István Bazilius-Balázs, later charged the Unitarian movement with being a "disgusting business" and accused it of siding with the Koran and the Turkish religion. At one Synod Melius stated it thus:

> "And this Church of ours, (Helvetic Reformed), is simple and universal, and may God preserve us in it and free us from the claws of the mad friends of the Turks."[23]

Ferenc Dávid always denied that he made frequent use of Koran and Talmudic sources, or that they influenced the doctrines of the Unitarian faith. Nevertheless, a thorough examination shows only that many thoughts were taken over from Servetus and from the Koran as well. When Socinus was arguing with Dávid, he charged Dávid with messianological and eschatological Judaism. When Dávid adduced the criticism in the Koran that Christians err in praying to Christ as God, Socinus retorted that Dávid truly drew his blasphemy against Christ from the Koran and the books of the Talmud.[24]

Historical realism proves that a feeling of danger leads people to compromise. Melius had only to look toward the South, toward the Balkans, to see how the downtrodden people of the region melted into their surroundings, first in religion and then ethnically, to become part of the Moslem world of the Turks. Thus the question of one God in three Persons was not only a matter of religion to Melius but a political one as well. The collision of the two cultures, the Christian one and the Turkish Moslem one, meant just that. It was easy to see how the military might of the Turks, pushing into Hungarian territory, encouraged the spread of Islam.[25] Melius had to arrive at the conclusion that Unitarianism, sympathizing as it did with Mohammedanism, almost conquered Transylvania. As a reaction to this development, which meant the presence of a "foreign religion by foreign people", Melius offered as an alternative a third way – the Helvetic Reformed religion, at the time called Magyar religion. For that reason one must not regard the bitter debate between Melius and Dávid as simply the result of theological aberrations, or as mere hairsplitting. The very fate of the Hungarian nation depended on it. In the historical framework of the sixteenth century, the dilemma of the Protestant reformer was whether the people should be Christian or Moslem. To resolve this, a politico-religious war had to be fought, a war of the greatest significance for Europe, of which there are few parallels in the pages of religious history.

Melius carried on his literary battle for years and often in great bitterness. He finally was successful and brought an end to Antitrinitarianism on his own territory of Debrecen, later in its very heartland, Transylvania. This was one of the really significant roles of the "Pope of Debrecen" in the history of the Hungarian Reformed Church.

Against the expression Unitarian, introduced by Dávid, meaning a monotheistic God, Melius introduced the expression *orthodox fides* and later *Deus est trinitarius*, (God in three Persons).

The radical theology of Dávid slowly would have deprived Christianity of its religious character. His one-time supporter, Giorgio Blandrata, also recognized this and denounced it to Stephan Báthory, who was then voivod of Transylvania and King of Poland. Blandrata cautioned the voivod and asked that he protect religion, because, "If the continuous advance of Dávid's Unitarianism is not halted, we will sink lower than if Mohammedanism were to triumph."[26]

An investigation was ordered and Blandrata proven right, but the investigation was such that it threw into dismay even the wily Italian humanist because of what it uncovered. Among others, such religious ideas came to light from Unitarian circles as:

> "Christ is a man like any other man, and therefore it is not
>   necessary to worship him."
> "Christ's sermons are no different from the sermons of any other
>   prophet."
> "He is just as much a sinful man as we are."
> "Christ did not come to redeem us but to rule."
> "There is no difference between Him and Moses."

Public opinion sympathized with the charges brought by the government and the synod. The practice of innovations by Dávid was forbidden. Transylvania did not run out of sects until the end of the sixteenth century, but Melius' accusations had won the day and were proven correct. It is not surprising that writers of the Western church dealt so extensively with the Antitrinitarian movement that spread from Rome to Wittenberg and further.

Research in church history and in the history of art shows it influenced the Dutch Rembrandt, for example. Rembrandt, a painter of Biblical scenes modified the idea of Christ in his later paintings. At first they had shown a super-natural inspiration in the presence of an angel whose heavenly hands, reaching out of a cloud, illustrated divine revelation. Later on, this apparition disappeared from his canvasses, and the idea of Christ, the Redeemer, was transformed into a human Christ, a change which his admirers hardly noticed.[27]

Melius the writer, preacher, and apologist ended his vocal arguments with Dávid and his followers only when he was able to continue them in his writings. Largely through him, and during his own time, the literary language became one with the language of theology. Melius' rough use of words and his biting style were merely the reflection of the neurotic way of life of the sixteenth century.

In his twenty-sixth year John Calvin had written the *Institutes*; Melius at the same age fulfilled a task of equal magnitude. If we add one of the very few details known about his private life, namely, that, like Saint Paul, he accomplished his task carrying a thorn in his flesh, one can follow his accomplishments with added respect. Moravian Brethren who once visited Melius in Debrecen reported that Melius was suffering from "the affliction of the gods," epilepsy, that sometimes even attacked him in the pulpit.

The role played by Melius in the history of the church shows that Unitarianism did not coincide with the needed spiritual evolution which was taking place in Europe. Dávid's religious movement rather isolated his followers and his nation in an age that demanded integration with the West. In contrast, the Debrecen Reformation attempted to integrate the nation into the way of life then evolving from Western Christendom while at the same time defending Europe and Christian autonomy.

The Writings of Melius

In the course of fifteen years Péter Somogyi Juhász, Melius, wrote some fifty volumes, unfortunately much of his work lies hidden in unknown places, or is lost entirely, or exists only in fragments. What remains of his literary work lies scattered in far-flung libraries in London, Vienna, Munich, Geneva, and in the countries of northern Europe. Often his work can be reconstructed through the writings of his adversaries. Many works dealing with church history have come to light, for instance:

> The very first Confession of Faith in the Hungarian language
> The Debrecen Confession
> The first Hungarian Hymnal
> The most original contemporary Bible translation
> The Constitution of the Hungarian Church
> The first Hungarian Herbarium

In Melius' writings one finds the motto of his faith: "God sees that I cannot remain like a speechless dog. I am the trumpet, the spoken word, but I do not speak from myself but from God." As in the case of other reformers of the time, his vocation echoes forth for all to hear. The effect of this is seen in the constant wandering hither and yon by fellow ministers of the Gospel who refused to compromise and, living by the word of the prophet, were persecuted by the powerful of the land. Puritanical preachers, driven from their churches and prevented from studying, had to plough fields and hoe gardens just to keep from starving. Melius had to promulgate a new law for the benefit of the developing citizenry in that post-feudal period. The papal church and its priests, who supported the old feudal order, served the people badly, and according to Melius, for that reason God condemned them. In a similar medieval feudalism the nobility was to rule, the priests were to pray, and the peasants to work. But when the nobles did not perform their duty by defending the people, and the priests forgot to pray and only meditated, the peasants were not inclined to work. Therefore the peasants throughout the whole of Europe attacked with insurrections the feudal order at its very basis. The peasant revolt in Hungary in the year 1514 preceded that of the Germans. In the Hungarian revolt almost one hundred thousand peasants lost their lives, but out of this happening emerged the preacher-reformer, who tried to establish a Christian brotherhood among his fellow men, first in the Church itself and then

in a society corrupted by a debased Roman Catholic Church. This led
Melius to embark on social criticism in which his angry pen cut into the
very flesh of a corrupt society. Criticizing his age he wrote: "See you lords
and kings how God is tearing our country apart because of your idols."[28]
"Princes are merely servants and mercenaries. They receive their pay so
they can serve God and protect the people. Like servants they can work
for their pay, whosoever does not serve is a thief. If the princes do not
serve in return for their payments, they are thieves and God will punish
them."[29] "Every man, no matter what his station in life, is allowed by Holy
Scripture and by Law of Nature to own property . . . to be worked by his
own hands. Let the people eat their own bread!"[30] He described the
prevailing lawlessness openly: "Read this, you murderers who kill the
innocent like pagans do, you who hang them, you who rob the poor . . . ."[31]
He also accused the leaders of the Roman Catholic Church of worshipping
idols.

The second greatest sin for him was the Antitrinitarian movement which
was causing society to disintegrate.

A new social order was being born with a new outlook on the morality
of labor, the prince was no longer regarded as the owner of the country
but merely as its first working citizen. To this was added what Calvin and
Beza had already propounded, that if the ruler was to break God's law, his
subjects had the right to protest (*ius resistendi*).[32]

In the beginning of the Reformation in Hungary, during the Lutheran
period, obedience to the princes had been preached, but, with the growing
strength of the Helvetic movement, the doctrine of resistance became
dominant. Melius too supported it: "Let the laws of the land be only those
decreed by God."[33] He particularly backed the merchants of Debrecen,
whom he almost considered God's chosen servants, saying that according
to God's law, commerce and saving were good and proper in the eyes of
the Lord. He meant that they ought to put their purses at the disposal of
God, the fortunes they earned in the service of the Church.

From the foregoing we know about Melius' activities in church organization and about his participation in synod meetings as well as in other
religious discussions. These activities occupied half of his time; the rest was
devoted to preaching and the writing of religious literature. The medium
for informing the public was the printing press, which Melius had founded
with the help of a refugee clergyman. This press printed Melius' writings

over a period of fifteen years. A special literary genre developed in these years, to explain the Gospel in spoken words of sermons.

One early publication was a book which Melius wrote especially for the many traveling Hungarian merchants who visited various European countries. In *Sermons on Christ's Intervention, (A Krisztus közbenjárásáról való predikációban)*, which appeared in Debrecen in 1561, he instructed them on how to spread the Gospel on these voyages, and encouraged them saying that God had entrusted them with the great affair of spreading the Reformation, because the ruling class had refused to undertake this task, being more interested in their bellies and therefore impotent and miserly. This book was to serve the new society as a leading light. An interesting note about this book is, that the people of Debrecen, during a fair, took up a collection to cover the printing costs of this book. The sermons which it contained had been written and preached during the time of a debate between Melius and Stancaro in which Melius had demonstrated that Christ in His two forms, human and godly, was intervening for His faithful with His Father.

In that manner, Melius led the citizens of Debrecen, as conscientious believers, into the battles of church and civil life. It was not in Melius' nature to be accommodating and to bargain. His collaborators remarked that there was no rest either in his writing, in his discussions, or in the meetings of the synod. In his writings as well as in his preaching, his voice kept thundering over the heads of his often drowsy followers: "Do not go to sleep, for the devil is sitting on your back. The Queen of Sheba did not guffaw during King Solomon's sermon as the bored people of today are doing. As for you, lazy people in your gay clothes, you do not even want to take the few steps that it takes to bring you to your church."

In 1561 Melius prepared and published a very extensive and detailed collection of articles of faith, which is known in the history of the Hungarian Reformed Church as the *Debrecen Confession (Debreceni Hitvallás)*, or the *Religious Systematization of the Debrecen Reformed Church*. It was the first formulation of a Confession of Faith of the Hungarian Reformed Church, unique in the history of dogma because of the extent of its coverage and its thoroughness. The *Debrecen Confession* included practically all questions related to the many aspects of church life, and it gave a detailed examination of the concept of the Holy Trinity as well as of the divinity of Jesus Christ. It also embraced the spiritual, cultural, and material aspects of everyday life within the framework of religion. As in every Confession of Faith, without exception, the confession of sin was stressed. The real title of Melius' Confession could have been *Confessio Pecatorum*.

The *Debrecen Confession* tried to establish order out of the decisions made in the numerous Confessions scattered far and wide and to unify them. Melius' synthesis shows the effect of haste, because, outside of the theological principles involved, it was also necessary to prescribe immediate solutions to problems of everyday living. Therefore, latter-day readers often find repetitions and numerous contradictions in his work. These may well be due to the unsettled times. While Melius was working on the Confession, the Turks were occupying Debrecen and there was little time for re-editing. Besides this turmoil, the city ran out of paper, and the author had to omit the refutation directed at the heretics.[34]

The Synod of Debrecen had the *Debrecen Confession* published in both Hungarian and Latin.

In its main theological precepts, the *Debrecen Confession* belonged within the family of the Helvetic faith as proclaimed by Calvin, Bullinger, and Beza.

Melius' writings served to build and organize congregations between the years 1561 and 1566. His *Catechism* served as a basis for the terse formulation of the Articles of Faith.[35] Published in 1562, it was much more detailed than either Melanchthon's or that of Heidelberg, because it had to reflect the teaching of the new dogmas and at the same time guide the entire spiritual life of his followers. The first question was: "Who are you?" Answer: "I am a spiritual being created by God in His own likeness."

The *Cathechism* explained why man lost his awareness of being created in God's image, and why he took on the likeness of the Devil. Melius explicated the Fall of Man and his Death, and elucidated how the Creator, the personification of love, had made it possible for man to turn to acts of goodness through the Redeemer, the Son of God. He explained the ways by which this could be realized through the intervention of the Holy Spirit. Melius dealt with each part of the Catechism, the Ten Commandments, the Apostle's Creed, the Communion of Saints, the Lord's Prayer, and finally, with the preparation of souls seeking renewal in the knowledge of faith.

For Melius, the theologian, the Old Covenant, based on the Law, was superceded by the New Covenant based on mercy. From this, his concrete optimistic view of life drew its sustenance, because the God of the Trinity created faith and love in the believer and so restored him to life. Keeping the Ten Commandments was not unconditionally a precondition, rather a reward.

In *The Book of the Soul (Lélek Könyve)*,[36] published in Debrecen in 1563, he affirmed the immortality of the soul. Melius held that the soul could go to heaven only after the resurrection of the body and the Last Judgment. In the intervening time, it would sleep in Paradise. In a later book dealing with a similar subject, he devoted much space to the numerous explanations of the soul and of death. He especially refuted the doctrine of the Anabaptists regarding the human soul.

In 1565, Melius had already translated the books of *Samuel II* and *Kings II* from Greek and Hebrew sources. "I translated them," he wrote in his introduction, "without changing either the text or the meaning." For Melius translation was not a matter of slavish faithfulness to the words but an attempt to give the meaning in the true sense; this was his goal. With that in view, he compared several contemporary translations and stated: "You see, my dear brethren, the translations of even wise translators all differ from each other, so how can you determine which is the original one?"

When the Synod of 1567 decreed that every minister of the Gospel had to have a Bible both in Latin and in Hungarian, Melius undertook further translations into the vernacular. He translated many parts of the Old and the New Testaments, but here again the Turkish war prevented him from completing the entire translation. He was only able to complete the translation of the New Testament, but, as in the case of so many of his writings, this work was also lost without a trace.*

In his translations, Melius often brought the content up to date by relating them to existing times. He was not afraid either to use his work in his arguments against the Unitarians.

---

*An unfortunate phenomenon is observable in Hungarian Bible translations; there were in the early period some good translations, of which the author is now unknown, or, as in the case of Lászlo Báthory, a Paulinian monk, his good translation is lost. Melius' translations suffered this fate also.

After finishing the translation of the *Book of Job*, he introduced it with surprising frankness: "The translation of this book is most useful, but at the same time it is exceedingly difficult. You will not find a more difficult text in the whole Bible with regard to meaning than in this book. I translated it not only word for word, but I brought the words into harmony with the meaning. Do not translate from the old Vulgate but from the original Hebrew. If you do not know Hebrew, do not attempt to translate, because a blind man does not recognize colors."

Meanwhile, Melius stubbornly translated the word *Elohim* as if it were identical in meaning with the word Trinity. Because of this he was subjected to much biting scorn from the Unitarians, who characterized his exegetic procedure as something that belonged in a museum of exotica.

In 1568, Melius completed the Book of *Revelation*. He compiled fifty-eight sermons on the topic in book form. In this exegesis were many subjective elements with which he hoped to "modernize" the revelation of the mystic hermit of Patmos. "Where Christ is not, the Devil is the judge. It is not enough to fight like a hero for the Christians, you have to win. Christ broke the power of the serpent, it is now our task to bash in the Turk's head." He continued to explain: "You rule over sin, sin does not rule over you. Since Christ is the only teacher, every other teacher is speechless without the Holy Spirit. The reason I take you to task is because you only seem to be a teacher, in reality you are but a delusion."

The explanation of Melius' translations and their applications reflect the serious political situation in which they found themselves. When we compare this, for example, with Heinrich Bullinger's explanation of John's visions, which he spread over a hundred sermons, one can understand the intention of Melius working away in East Central Europe. His declarations had to be made timely and applicable to daily life in order to encourage the souls struggling on in strife and despair. He had to scold, for instance, the Hungarian civil leaders who destroyed each other, plundering like enfuriated lions, and tearing the people apart. Melius often complained about his own brethren who, according to him, were enjoying worldly delights and forgot what holy knowledge they possessed.

Of the two beasts of the Apocalypse, he explained, one was the antiChrist incarnate, the Holy Roman Empire, and the other, the spiritual one, was the Roman Pope, killing Christ's followers by means of Spanish mercenaries. Neither did he forget the Unitarians, who had gone astray and for whom he prayed: "May God free them from their spiritual darkness." He urged his fellow ministers not to proclaim God's Word in a whisper, nor in secret, but openly. "You are teachers, so shout like trumpets."

In an explanation of the letter written to the *Colossians*, he urged his colleagues, who could do so, to write books for posterity. "Let those who come after us reap some of the harvest, because only our contemporaries can hear our sermons." He also asked them to fulfill their pledge as ministers of the Gospel and to work toward improvement of moral standards.

Reading the rough language of the time, one can understand why the secular leaders issued several laws in civil parliament against blasphemy. They justified their actions saying: "Taking the Lord's name in vain draws down His anger on the whole nation." This neurotic language, however, stuck to the very soul of the people, and the ministers continued to reprimand and punish the blasphemers. One sees too that the urgency of the time did not permit Melius to live the life of an abstract analytical theologian, and that he developed into a church politician, one moment defending, the next moment attacking.

In 1567 Melius also published a *Short Confession (Rövid Hitvallás)*, also known as *Brevis Confessio pastorum ad Synodum Debrecii celebratum*, which he dedicated to John Sigismund, then voivod of Transylvania. He drew the voivode's attention to the fact that Christ was the King of kings to whom all earthly rulers owed allegiance. They would be judged on the basis of the Word, whether they used their power to serve God or the devil. Therefore the first duty of the rulers should be to punish heretics such as Servetus and Gentillis who had revived the Arian heresy which still was infecting the country. "Do not forget that the Reformation and the dogma of Christ's godhead are inseparable from each other, and whoever maintains that Christ is only a man cannot be called a Christian, for without Him there is no redemption. The doctrine of the Holy Trinity is not polytheistic, but proof that there is one God in three Persons." Melius indignantly rejected the widely held concept of the time, that women had no soul and therefore they could not be included in the resurrection, which was the teaching of the Anabaptists.

If Melius found that the ruler was not faithful to the Gospel, he painted him in appropriate colors. In the *Short Confession*, and on behalf of the Hungarian Reformed Church, he also declared war on the antitrinitarianism of Dávid and Blandrata.

The Bible translations and the *Short Confession* were not enough work for one year apparently, because in the same year 1567 Melius published a *Book of Canon Law*, also named *Articles which were created from the Word of God and the Laws of Nature (Articuli ex Verbo Dei et Lege Naturae compositi)*. It dealt with the maintenance of church organization and the governance of everyday Christian life. The duties of the ministers were strictly set forth as well as the formula according to which the Church would be governed. There was a great need for such guidelines because, in the beginning, the autonomous congregations led a disorganized existence. In the various parts of the country, congregations had organized themselves and taught entirely according to their own light.

Melius composed the canon on the basis of the Word and according to the necessities of the time. He quoted almost four hundred thirty texts from the Bible, mainly from the Old Testament, and this led eventually to a rigid traditionalism. At the same time, he drew also on the laws of nature, because only in that way could he justify the laws that were necessary for society. This is dominant in his canon on marital law. Often his inexorable temper tried to make puritanical family morals the basis for all society. For instance, a girl from a minister's family had committed an immoral act and was condemned to death by fire. The *Book of Canon Law*, which touched every aspect of living, directed the life functions of the Reformed Church for centuries. With it, Melius also helped form a new civil society.

Another of Melius' writings, important to his doctrine of Christology, was *Propositions of Jah and Jehovah or Unity and Trinity in the Living God*, published in 1568. It undertook to show, somewhat artificially and with an exegesis from the Old Testament, the truth of the doctrine of the Trinity. Jah, meaning God, in essence stood for the singleness of the Holy Name, he reasoned, while Jehovah, also meaning God, by virtue of the change to more syllables stood for the Trinity, that is the Unity of God.

Melius hoped to convince Dávid and Blandrata and other like-minded, that the Son and the Holy Spirit were to be worshipped along with the Father, because they were Three in One.

One cannot help but marvel at Melius' thorough knowledge of foreign languages when reading this book, and be fascinated by his many-faceted scholarship as well as by his tendency to rabid gymnastics with the language.

In 1568 appeared his most radical writing, *Contradictions between the true Christ and the Christ of the Turks (Antithesis veri et Turcici Christi)*. This diatribe was directed against the Unitarians and was published in Debrecen. This work was also lost, but somehow the content of the work can be reconstructed out of the answers of Dávid and Blandrata, still in existence. The writing was apparently in defense of the Trinity.

Dávid and Blandrata defended their theses by basing them on an antithesis dealing with the essence of the one true God. With arguments both scholarly and orthodox, Melius must have attempted to show that Christ existed before time, and that God the Father could never have been a Father if he had never had a Son from time eternal. Therefore, Christ is equal to God. Christ was the creator of heaven and earth and the maker of the second creation.

Against this reasoning Dávid used the argument of Socinus who held that Christ would have been the maker of the second creation only, which is to say of Redemption. To this Melius must have reiterated that God became man in Christ and that their two natures could not be separated from each other. Melius apparently made the sweeping accusation that Dávid presented Christ simply as a man, identical to the prophet of the Turks, who did not recognize the divinity of Christ because, since God had no wife, He could not have a son.

Melius had a good knowledge of the Turkish and Arabic languages, and it was easy for him to point out that Dávid and his associates had drawn on the *Koran* when they called Christianity polytheistic. It is mentioned in the *Koran* that it goes against the dignity of Allah to take himself a son and to share with him. Mary had shared meals with Jesus, so it is impossible to say that Christ is equal to Allah.[37]

Modern researchers have come down on the side of Melius and accuse Dávid and his collaborators of drawing close to the Moslem faith on the basis of their Christology. One former associate of Dávid, István Bazilius Balázs, accused Dávid of being in debt to the *Koran*; even Socinus, whom Dávid had quoted, accused him of an exaggerated sympathy for the Moslem faith. Dávid never hesitated to quote the *Koran* in order to support his doctrine of the non-worship of Christ. Melius was inclined to confess that the birth of the Son and the reality of the Holy Spirit would remain an eternal mystery. "I would rather stammer together with the prophets and the apostles and meditate on the wisdom literature than arrogantly philosophize and follow fabrications of heretics."

From all these writings one can surmise that Melius' literary activity in those years dealt mainly with the formulation of dogma. His role in this field was dominant among the Reformers of the sixteenth century. From Debrecen, which Melius called the seed-plot of the Word, the city that listened to the Word of God, went forth the reform that was to touch the faithful in all parts of the territory. For that reason Melius' literary work is so worthy of note; it was the only means by which he could gather the Hungarians into the Hungarian Reformed Church.

It is impossible to deal with every single work he produced, even if we would devote only a few lines to each one of them, because his writing includes over five thousand pages. Outside of his theological writing, special attention should be given to his last book, *Herbarium*, which was published after his death, in 1578 in Kolozsvár.

At that time it was the custom for ministers of the Gospel to devote themselves to healing, following the example of Jesus. As already mentioned, Melius himself carried a thorn in his flesh in the form of epilepsy, which supposedly caused his death at the age of forty. Maybe his own state of health caused him to write this work on the widely used medicinal herbs; on the healing effect of trees, grasses, and plants in general, all presented together in the form of a lexicon. It is more than a mere handbook on botany; it is a medical book which represents a whole collection of recipes for healing.

In *Herbarium* he appears as a teaching physician because the age was rampant with unimaginable superstitions concerning the practice of witchcraft, which was deemed the cause of sickness and suffering. For Melius the preparation of remedies was a simple procedure; he used the juices of herbs and grasses. There were remedies that consisted of more than a hundred components. According to the prevailing beliefs, the more elements that were mixed into a potion, the more ailments it could cure. Already in Melius' time there were medications with a chemical base, along with the homeopathic ones. The author sounded like a good diagnostician. For example, he pointed out that over-eating could result in the ailment called "gout", which frequently occurred, and bile, kidneys, etc. were all involved in the chemistry of the body.

From a technical point of view *Herbarium* was modern for the time. The names of all plants appeared in the index in three languages–Latin, Hungarian, and German. Melius listed more than two thousand plants. Botanists can be grateful for this work because Melius supplied them, in the sixteenth the sixteenth century, with a botanical nomenclature. He described the characteristics of the plants and their healing powers. Interestingly, ninety percent of the medicinal herbs listed are still used today in homeopathic medicine. Melius also listed the names of illnesses and their symptoms. It is no wonder that *Herbarium* became very popular, because the century was epidemic-ridden, and it was on the basis of Melius' work that household dispensaries could be set up.

If one compares *Herbarium* with the medical knowledge of the Age of Enlightenment and its recorded therapies, one finds that Melius was far superior in efficacy and in the soundness of his recommendations. The therapies of the Enlightenment were generally not far removed from the fanaticism of witchcraft, and incorporated popular superstitions such as maintaining that herbs, to be efficacious, had to be gathered before dawn. The herb Alexus, for example, could be picked only during certain ceremonies, had to be dug with a bone at eleven o'clock in the morning on the fifteenth of March. One gets a picture that, although the Reformation meant progress in many things, in the minds of the people witchcraft and superstition lived on, in spite of scolding and punishment meted out by their ministers.

In conclusion it should be pointed out as a significant case-history of a front-theologian that Melius produced more than twenty volumes of polemic literature. He wrote in his final will and testament that, although many would attack him after his death saying that he did not proclaim the knowledge of the true God, "Nevertheless I am going before God in the true religion which I taught to all."

In fact, all the adversaries who attacked him and argued with him during his lifetime, stated that this preacher of the Gospel and steadfast bishop-reformer, was like a block of solid granite. Once he had developed a definite opinion, he did not easily change it. Melius might have appeared to those who followed him, like the statue of Jeremiah in the Geneva of today, who, fearing for his Jewish people and therefore admonishing them, raised his fist toward Heaven. Jeremiah's quarreling would have been quite understandable to Melius' contemporaries, because the sixteenth century was an apocalyptic age for them.

The leaders of various churches had either died on the battlefield or had become victims of the humanistic paganism. It was an age in which people yearned for a serving, teaching church and for preachers proclaiming Biblical truth, which would expose the very nature of sin, and cover the nudity of Renaissance humanism with a hair shirt. Though Rome could excommunicate preachers, Jesus Christ reinstalled and authorized them; Jesus Christ never stopped preaching.

Melius came very close to John Calvin in the qualities portrayed in the phrase *corpore fractus, anima potens, fide victor*; he may have been weak in body, but he was powerful in spirit and indeed victorious in faith.

Footnotes

1. Toldy, Ferenc. *Analecta Monumentorum Hungariae*. Vol. 1, p. 271.

2. Veszprémi, István. *Succinta Medicorum Hungariae et Transylvaniae Bibliographia. Centuria prima*. Lipsiae, 1774. p. 104.

3. Kathona, Géza. *"Juhász Péter és életműve"*, *Studia et Acta Ecclesiastica*, Vol. II, p. 114. Budapest, 1967.

4. Laskoi, Csokás P. *De homine magne illo in rerum natura miraculo.*Wittenberg, 1585. RMK 744.

5. Melius, J.P. *Articuli ex Verbo Dei et Lege naturae compositi. Kanonos Könyv*. Debrecen, 1567.

6. Zoványi, Jenö. *Magyar reformácio története 1565–1600*. Budapest: Akadémia Kiadó. p. 292.

7. Wotschke, Th. *Geschichte der Reformation in Poland*. Leipzig, 1911. p. 218.

8. Nagy, Barnabás. *"A Heidelbergi Káté jelentkezése."* *Studia et Acta Ecclesiastica,* Vol. I, p. 20. Budapest, 1965.

9. Czeglédi, Sándor. *"Melius Agendája és hymnologiai tevékenysége."* *Studia et Acta Ecclesias tica,* Vol. II, p. 350.

10. Bucsay, Mihály. *"Melius theologiája."* *Studia et Acta Ecclesiastica,* Vol. II, p. 1318.

11. Heussi, Karl. *Kompendium*. Tübingen 1919. 4th ed. p. 365.

12. Melius, J.P. *"Debreceni Hitvallás."* *Studia et Acta Ecclesiastica,* Vol. II, p. 331.

13. Melius, J.P. *Válogatott Predikációk*. Debrecen. p. 251.

14. Czeglédi, Sándor. *op. cit.,* p. 390.

15. Veress, Endre. *Fontes Rerum Transylvanicarum, I-III*. Budapest, 1911–1913, Vol. III, p. 235.

16. Tröltsch, E. *Sociallehren der Christlichen Kirchen und Gruppen*. Tübingen, 1912. p. 471.

17. Tröltsch, E. *"Protestant Christentum und Kirche in der Neuzeit."* Die *Kultur der Gegenwart.1 Abt1.IV.* Leipzig, 1906, p. 294.

18. Melius, J.P. *Krisztus közbenjárásárol szoló predikáciok.* Debrecen, 1561.

19. Melius, J.P. *Antithesis veri et Turcici Christi.* Debrecen 1568. RMK.II.109 a; also in *Studia et Acta Ecclesiastica,* Vol. II. p. 246.

20. Dán, Robert *Humanizsmus, Reformácio, antitrinitárizmus és a héber nyelv Magyarorzzságon.* Budapest: Akadémia Kiadó, 1973, pp. 73,74,80,82.

21. Melius, J.P. *op. cit.,* p. 246.

22. Melius, J.P. *ibid.,* p. 244.

23. Ember-Lampe, *Historia ecclesiae reformatae in Hungaria et Transylvania.* Utrecht, 1728.

24. Williams, George H. "The Christological issues between Francis Dávid and Faustus Socinus during the Disputation on the invocation of Christ, 1578–79." *Antitrinitarianism in the Second Half of the 16th Century.* Akadémia Kiadó. Budapest, 1982. p. 302.

25. Nagy, Barnabás. *Antithesis veri et Turcici Christi.* in: *Studia et Acta Ecclesiasticae,* Vol. II. p. 259. Budapest 1967.

26. Zoványi, J. *Magyar protestántizmus története. 1565–1600.* Budapest, Akadémia Kiadó. 1977. p. 124.

27. van de Waal, H. *Steps Toward Rembrandt.* North Holland Or. Amsterdam, 1974.

28. Melius, Péter. *A Két Sámuel könyveinek és a Két Királyi Könyveknek a zsido nyelvnek Igazságából..,* Debrecen, 1565. RMK.I. p. 55.

29. Melius, Péter. *ibid.* p.48.

30. Melius, Péter. *Confessio Ecclesiae Debreciensis. Kiss Áron forditása.* p. 262. Debrecen, 1562.

31. Melius, Péter. *A Két Sámuel könyveinek és a Két Királyi könyveknek a zsido nyelvnek Igazságábol . . ,* Debrecen, 1565. RMK.I. p. 48.

32. Gritsch, Eric. *Martin Luther and Violence.* In The Sixteenth Century Journal. St. Louis, Missouri. Forum Press. April 1983. p. 37.

33. Melius, Péter. *Magyar Prédikáciok, kit Postillaciónak neveznek.* Debrecen, 1563. RMK.I. p. 53.

34. Melius, Péter. *Antithesis veri et Turcici Christi.* Debrecen, 1568. RMK.II. p. 109 a.

35. Melius, Péter. *Kathekizmusz.* Debrecen, 1562.

36. Melius, Péter. *Lélek könyve.* Debrecen 1563. RMK I 53 a.

37. Ab al Fadi. *The person of Christ in the Gospel and the Koran.*

The Wandering Student

Chapter XVIII

The Reformed College of Debrecen, Developed by Melius

Among Melius' enduring creations belong the educational system he organized and the new pedagogical theories he introduced to the youth of his time. One of the most well-known institutions to grow out of this was the Reformed College (*Reformatus Kollegium*). This was later to become the University of Debrecen which recently celebrated its four hundred and fiftieth anniversary. Soon after its foundation students from all over East Central Europe–Magyars, Slavs, Rumanians, Germans–were all studying there, having been brought together by the Reformation.

Students returning home from the universities of Wittenberg, Padua, and Cracow helped lay the foundations of this institution. One special contribution these returning students made was to bring back with them the significant books of Western literature which they presented to the library of the College. It is easy to imagine the enrichment that these brought, since the young Hungarian pilgrims had gone abroad by the thousands. In addition, Melius exhorted the wealthy, the cities, and towns to support their institutions, and once in an angry outburst he said:

> "Princes of today are not very willing to spend one hundred florins in the service of God, on schools, on teachers, or on the publication of books. God does not help them either, because it is not in Heaven but in Hell that they will end . . . . Though you rob the vineyards of the Church, you pay for neither schools nor teachers from your booty."[1]

So a new nobility developed in the College of Debrecen. It was a spiritual nobility for sure, and it prepared itself for its new calling in keeping with the tenets of the Reformation.

Between the years 1588 and 1896, twenty-five thousand students studied within the College walls. There this new nobility developed an ideology that grew out of the Protestant faith. The degree to which Hungarian Protestant leaders were aware of the existence of the new nobility and the importance of a Protestant elite was adequately demonstrated by the action of Gábor Bethlen, Prince of Transylvania, who took it upon himself to grant letters of nobility to pastors at their ordination. In this way he attempted to assure beforehand their immunity from religious persecution of the times.

As in the case of the German and French universities, the students who attended the College in Debrecen were for the most part poor young men from noble families prepared mainly for military careers. A minority of them would aim for high positions in the Reformed Church, but few of these young noblemen ever completed their theological studies, and so the College, which originally had been a small parochial school, remained for a long time to come the school of the poor.

The continuing conflict with the Turks and Germans bled the country dry, and the youth who escaped captivity sought refuge within the walls of the College. There were other towns, too, which, in similar circumstances, helped the students. One of these was Bártfa where every morning at ten the students set out to collect offerings which were used for their daily sustenance.[2]

Debrecen had set aside two days each week during which meals were prepared for the students. Victuals and bread were gathered in turn by the students themselves, and the meals were eaten in a common dining hall.

Students with good singing voices had access to a special source of income by taking part in funerals, for which service they received a fixed fee. Another source of income for the youths was the rounding up of stray cattle. An unusual fact pertaining to this story of education is that a certain share of the fines paid into the treasury of Debrecen by people so condemned, was turned over to the students.

During the early years of the College, students had to bake their own bread in ovens built especially for them, and, as fuel was often difficult to come by, the fences of citizens sometimes disappeared overnight, ending up heating the students' ovens.

Throughout the summer vacations, they traveled the roads and byways as supplicants of alms. The territory was divided into districts, and the students called on the inhabitants to pledge donations. In the fall when the hills resounded from the activities of the grape harvest, students appeared and collected the wine-alms, *boralamizsna*. The wine thus collected was stored in the cellars of the College, and once a week the students were given their share. This was due to the fact that it was forbidden for the College to sell this wine in town, and the authorities kept a strict control in this matter. It may sound like a paradox, but the law of the College decreed that anyone who dared to drink coffee would be punished. Coffee was popularly called "Turkish poison".

The College, which had been in operation as a parochial school from 1549 on as an institution of the Reformed Church, aimed, as earlier the school had done, at training church leaders for the Reformed Church. It enjoyed an autonomous life from the very beginning. Students managed their own affairs according to their own laws. The scholastic community, called *Bursa*, drew up its own laws, developed the foundations of its economy, and carried out its own disciplinary measures; remarkably few breaches of discipline appear in its history. Perhaps the reason for this was that the students arose at three o'clock every morning and had to put out the lights at nine in the evening. Their youthful energies were consumed in continuous activity, and little time was left for mischief. Another reason may have been psychological. The grim situation prevailing then, with wars, poverty, and constant danger, increased the need for self-discipline.

As in the history of other European universities, in Debrecen too conflicts arose between town and College, between town and gown. In Paris open hostilities had broken out between the City of Paris and the Sorbonne and they lasted until the king granted extraterritoriality to the University, thus attempting to separate the two factions. In Debrecen the student body withdrew from the town because the town fathers wanted to limit the autonomy of the scholastic community. The town council objected, among other things, to the fact that students were wearing their hair too long or too short, because, while some were wearing it down to the shoulders, others were shaving their heads *a la turque*, in Turkish fashion.

Very strict dress-codes prevailed; a long gown or toga had to be worn even when students were fighting fires, which happened frequently. Students could not set foot outside the College without wearing black boots and a black necktie. Gloves could be either black or white. In Debrecen the English mode of wearing wigs was not allowed, because "the dress of the prophets, and of the apostles and disciples, had been simple ones."

The leader of the scholastic community was the *senior* who was chosen yearly by the students. He represented the student body before the town council and before the College faculty. It was his task to manage business, disciplinary and legislative matters, and for this he received commensurate remuneration. On the completion of his studies he was given a scholarship of one thousand florins, to enable him to continue his studies abroad at a foreign university. It is worthy to note that for centuries church leaders and leading educators in Hungary had all, without exception, studied abroad and with their up-to-date preparedness formed a continuing spiritual and cultural link with developments in Europe.

The installation of the new *senior* was always a special event. The town council and the faculty of the College installed the new student leader with pomp and ceremony. This new leader was always the most outstanding student. If, however, the *senior* was found to abuse his power, he was turned out of office, and was whipped out of town as punishment. His successor who carried on the administration would be the *contrascriba*.

In addition to the mentioned functions, the *senior* also kept an eye on the students to see that they attended the lectures. It was he who had to lock the College doors at night and who had to put out the lights. He would send out students to sing at funerals and distribute among them the money they had thus earned. It was the *senior* also who watched over the regular religious services at the College, and who placed *janitores* at the two College doors to make sure that no student would escape from these services. It was also his task to see to it that the students took part in the singing during the church service. He also counted the money on the collection plate, separated the good money from the false, and then turned it in to the treasurer.

A special student secretary made sure that forgetful professors held their classes. Every lecture began with prayer and ended with a song. However, strange things did happen. There was one professor who, in twenty-five years of teaching never finished a history course because of his meandering through irrelevant details. (Such things happened abroad as well; in Leipzig a certain professor could only complete teaching eight chapters of the Book of Jeremiah in twenty-four years of teaching!) Generally, though, the professors all showed a high level of preparedness, and it was mandatory for them to master at least four foreign languages before they could enter upon their careers. A professor was obligated to hold a lecture only once every two weeks; the rest of the time he devoted to studies, according to Church Records of Debrecen.[3]

One encounters some interesting lines on discipline when reading the history of the College. For instance, a student could find himself in the College jail for mocking or criticizing other religious opinions. Because of their tightly packed daily schedule, it was decreed that students could serve their sentences just before bed time, in the evening. Before "serving their time," they took part in the common prayer and, after serving their sentence, they sang a psalm of repentance. Punishment apparently was also frequently meted out to those students who were found conversing in their mother-tongue, thereby neglecting the official Latin. When a student missed too many classes he had to memorize thirty chapters of the Bible. In another instance, a professor accused a student of "ploughing with other people's oxen" (plagiarism).

If one compares the life of the students of Debrecen with that of the students in Cambridge, for instance, one finds not only the luxury of one room assigned to two students, but also, regarding discipline, Cambridge students were told that they should henceforth refrain from making indecent noises during religious services; they should not lie down during lectures, nor allow cows to enter the chapel . . . . In Debrecen, a student was punished when he so much as yawned in classroom or church.

Strict discipline, serious studying, and the poverty of the young students were reasons why the song "Let us be merry" (*Gaudeamus igitur*), a song that had come down from the Middle Ages, was seldom heard in the College. These young men who had been forced to mature before their time and who carried a heavy burden of responsibility, also had to do their duty by the community.

In times of plague and pestilence, the students were active in town helping the sick and burying the dead. During the wars the town was sometimes burned and plundered either by Turks or by the armies of the Habsburgs, and according to one chronicler, students were then sometimes bereft of their beds and had to sleep on donated straw, spread on the bare ground. The frequent fire alarms in town also kept the students awake, because they would have to get up and hurriedly gather together their firefighting equipment at the firehouse. Each student had two water buckets with his name on them, and these he would hand down the line to help quench the fire. It was customary for the two most stalwart students to run ahead, in the direction of the fire, and with stout clubs knock down any obstacle that stood in their way such as fences and the like. This was done so that the fire-wagon could reach the fire as quickly as possible. Usually the thatched roofs were pulled off the dwellings near the fire, thus isolating it and preventing further spread. This did not always work, and during Melius' time in Debrecen, the city burned down three times, either partially or completely.

Another special duty incumbent on the begowned students was, in case of war, fire or epidemic, to hold public prayer in the streets and to comfort the city's terrified populace. According to a chronicler, this was "within living memory" the custom and the rule. That these services now and then touched the heart of a citizen was reported in the chronicles of the College: "A man deeply touched by the visit of a student, gave the latter fifty gold florins, four hundred kilograms of wheat, twenty buckets of wine, two fat hogs, a tub of curds, ten cheeses, six measures of butter, and three measures of honey."[4]

Students wearing their togas as full-fledged theologians entered into their functions early, serving rural congregations as assistants of the pastor. These young delegates served two hundred and forty country churches. When they returned to the College after serving in the capacity of assistants, they would bring back the pastor's letter of recommendation and the alms gathered on their behalf.

In spite of their busy lives, they apparently had time for some tricks. In the official report containing a record of misbehaviors, one finds examples of mischief like "visiting" outlying orchards and helping themselves to fruit, (apparently they were suffering from a lack of vitamins), and there was a misdemeanor which involved a honey barrel.

In this instance, the ever-hungry student had first bought a loaf of bread on the market. He had proceeded to remove the soft inner part of the bread and ate it, then he had gone to the honey merchant and had asked that his hollow loaf of bread be filled with honey. When he was asked to pay, however, he had claimed that the price was too high and had poured the honey back into the barrel. Of course, by then the honey had soaked into the bread and the inventive student departed with his treasure. A contemporary observer came to the conclusion that "there are no limits to God's mercy, nor to the tricks that students play."

In spite of all the extra-curricular activities, the students studied hard. The test came for the theological students when they had to prepare for the defense of their faith which was their final examination, the so-called *Polemica Disputatio*. If the student was successful, the *Disputatio* would conclude his studies.

To this end the students organized each year a *Disputatio*, which had a two-fold goal: to develop and test a future preacher's oratory skills, important in those times of constant religious disputes, and secondly to provide a process of selection among the preachers-to-be. In order to be qualified as a preacher, the student simply had to pass the test which the *Disputatio* offered.

The yearly event was organized by the students themselves, and both faculty and students acted as judges. The student had to defend his thesis, while his student opponent (*opponens*) critiqued his presentation. If the defense was not well prepared the defender not only flunked his final examination, but he also had to pay a fine of twenty-five dinars as well into the students' treasury. His opponent had to pay twelve dinars if his critique had not been well prepared.

The Reformed College played quite a special role in the so-called particularist school network. This consisted of sending headmasters (*rectors*) out into the towns and villages of the countryside. No less than two hundred of them came under the jurisdiction of the mother-institution, and in each of these a rector would organize the necessary elementary and secondary schools. It was out of these branch schools that the most talented students eventually came to continue further studies at the College. In this manner a selection was made of the most promising students, and so the supply of future pastors and teachers was assured. The most exceptional from among these students received further training abroad, and thanks to this system, no church leader or any leading educator in Hungary up to the nineteenth century failed to study abroad. It was the instruction in Latin that did much to facilitate this process. Latin was the universal language of instruction, and the schools prepared the students early in it, even seven- and eight-year-old children could already handle Latin. The second required language was Greek, the third Hebrew. Greek and Aramaic were required of theologians.

It was Melius who master-minded the totally new educational system, in which the lower class was pulled, to prepare and select a new elite, which was to replace the former elite of the nobility. The latter had for a greater part lost their lives on the battlefields. This new elite was to become a serving elite, taking the place of the former ruling one. It was a totally new concept that a man of the lower estate not only could be prepared for studies at the College, but also that he could even go abroad for further study with the help of a stipend.

Bishop Melius, with historical impact, had recognized that the Hungarian nation could not defend itself with only a sword; it needed highly developed cultural minds to avoid a melting into the Asiatic Moslem world. The continuous state of war made it necessary for the students that they carry swords if they stepped outside of the College walls, but they faced the conflicts on their path of life not only with the sword, but also with the Book. *Arte et Marte.*

These were the things on which education in and around Debrecen was based, and only that learned activity was deemed blessed that served to glorify God, and only that knowledge was considered blessed which practiced piety.

Footnotes

1. Melius, Péter. *A Két Sámuel könyveinek és a Két Királyi könyveknek a zsido nyelvnek Igazságábol* . . . Debrecen, 1565. RMK.I.
2. Fraknoi, Vilmos. *A Hazai és kűlföldi iskolázás a XVI-ik században.* Budapest, Akadémia Kiadó, 1882. p. 53.
3. Church Records, 1792. Debrecen, *Református Kollegium.*
4. Balogh, F.A. *Debreceni akadémia alapitványai törzskönyv.* Debrecen, 1911. p. 317.

Chapter XIX

Francis Dávid
The Apostle Of Unitarianism
1510?-1579

Introduction

In the religious history of East Central Europe two Church founders come to mind. One is John Huss (1369–1415), the Czech reformer, and the other is Francis Dávid (1510?-1579), the Unitarian theologian of Hungary. Their roles were similar on many points, and the lives of both reformers ended in martyrdom.

John Huss

John Huss originally wanted to bring about a religious reform for his people such as had been accomplished in England by John Wycliffe (1328–1384). However, Huss' reform activity challenged the predominant political and religious supremacy of the ruling German stratum of society. This made the church renovator both the adversary of the Germans and a Czech national hero.[1] Thus, very early on as spokesman in the ethnic and linguistic antagonism that divided Slavs and Germans, he became, among others, the creator of nationalism based on language, a significant historical phenomenon appearing in East Central Europe where Poles and Hungarians were defending themselves against Germanization as had happened in Czech territory.

Hussitism, emerging from ethnic and linguistic consciousness, became a religious movement which had a profound influence on the life of neighboring peoples with similar problems in similar historical settings. This religious development and the ensuing socio-political one that grew out of it absorbed the strength of the Czech people for centuries and ended with negative results. Hussitism broke up into factions, became radical, and a religious communism took over which was completely destroyed by the Habsburg rulers.

Many Czech historians have condemned the extremist Hussite movement, and among those who thus evaluate its historical significance is Rudolf Rican who wrote: "Zizka and the Taborites as fanatical warriors took delight in the shedding of blood. It was through them that the Czech nation suffered heavy damage and was torn into two parts which bled in fratricide . . . For two hundred years the majority of the people were seduced into heresy."[2]

Joseph Pekar, on the other hand, judged the events differently and stressed that the continuous war isolated the nation from its South European culture. When the nation became involved in the Thirty Years' War, it entirely sapped its strength.[3] He searched for a deeper cause of Hussitism and found it in the Slavic-German conflicts of interests: "One is in the habit of saying that the Hussite movement and especially their wars can be seen as proof of Czech force against German elements in Bohemia and against their German neighbors."[4]

Ernest Denis summarized "The historians of that age agree that the fanatic sectarians inflicted deadly wounds on their own people. The Hussites overestimated their power and fought a vain battle which exhausted the strength of the nation."[5]

Although the depleted popular church of the Czechs comforted itself with the thought that through suffering the primitive church of the first century could be recreated, their church almost disappeared from the pages of history, and it was only during the Enlightenment that it was reorganized and, with the help of the neighboring Hungarian Reformed Churches, rebuilt.[6] Thus, John Huss, as a politico-religious martyr, contributed indirectly to the social and religious development of East Central Europe.

Francis Dávid

Francis Dávid, the second founder, labored along with the reformers of the sixteenth century on the renewal of the Church in Hungary. Unlike

Huss, he was interested only in theological questions, and in the course of his activity as a reformer he founded the Unitarian Church.*

In his struggle for religious change he, acting like a *furor theologicus*, burned out his whole life in order to destroy the old dogmas and to replace them with his new ones. In the meantime he almost argued to death the spiritual, cultural, and political forces of his country. He was doing this when the country itself was engaged in a life and death struggle against the attacks of the Islamic Turks.

Those who have appraised Francis Dávid up until now have tended to elevate him into a transcendental world and have almost forgotten to fit him into his own age. It is necessary to relate him to the actual history of the sixteenth century in the course of surveying his life's work. His role is very complex, and all four church denominations of his time eventually excommunicated Dávid, even though he played a leading role in each of them for a short while. To this very day it is a matter open to discussion which confession will claim him as its own; Catholic, Lutheran, Reformed or Unitarian. To which one was he true to himself?

The historical dilemma of his day was this: How could the atomized Hungarian society survive when the Muslim Turks were set on destroying it biologically, and to what degree could the Unitarian Church fulfill the historical task that fell to it to spiritually integrate the nation and strengthen its national consciousness?

In relation to this question Francis Dávid is a paradox in that he did not feel responsibility for political questions. In the end it was his apolitical behavior that sealed his fate. Unlike Dávid, Melius, the theologian of Debrecen, and the Catholic ruler Báthory, represented the tragic awareness of national danger. Both accused Dávid and his followers of being pro-Turkish, and in this condemnation of the Unitarian faith, political reasons

---

*The name *Unitarian* instead of Arinarian appeared first in 1568 and was used to distinguish the Antitrinitarian sect. It was only in 1600 that this word was entered into official documents in an act asking for religious freedom. "The National Diet has demanded from King Rudolph that religious freedom be assured and that four established denominations be allowed to live in complete freedom. These are the Roman Catholic, the Calvinist, the Lutheran, and the Unitarian Confessions." *Magyar emlékek*, IV, p. 551, Budapest, 1860.

In British ecclesiastical literature, the word Unitarian was first used in 1687 in a dispute between the Quaker William Penn and Henry Hedworth who was a disciple of Socinus. Hedworth had learned the word in Holland from a Hungarian student.

played a role. In 1594 the Voivod Sigismund Báthory settled an account with his Turcophile opponents, who were radical Antitrinitarians as well as supporters of union with the Turks.[7]

So the existential question of the nation made urgent the cessation of all activity that would tend to bring about a religious and social break-up. For the same reason the doors of Déva castle finally closed upon Dávid in 1579.

The historical background of this development points to the fact that Dávid lost his freedom not only for religious reasons but for political ones as well. Thus, while the anti-German political and religious stance brought John Huss to the stake, it was the apolitical-theological attitude of Francis Dávid that destroyed him.

The events of that age prove that history does not recognize the possibility of separating Church from society. The society of the state defends freedom of religion. Religion, on the other hand, is a force that inspires history and whose *raison d'être* is to hold together the culture of the nation. This is particularly true in the history of East Central Europe, where Church and state were divided only after the Second World War. An important task of church history is to show the very considerable influence that the leader of a non-conformist religion can exercise on the social life of the age. Where one sectarian leader with anti-social asceticism undermines the established society when he idealizes a former church as a religious utopia, another discovers the cause of all ills in the past of the established church and gives out "prophetic judgments." In this way a religious movement can become a destructive force that only criticizes and destroys itself and society.

During the sixteenth and seventeenth centuries, Hungarian Christianity was in constant tension because of the danger represented by the Islamic Turks. That is why religion became especially important. While the Protestant Church was trying to establish itself amid dangers, Francis Dávid tied down for decades with his radicalism the country's spiritual and political energy. Cultural and spiritual activity of the state were paralyzed and reduced to religious issues exclusively. A laming effect on political life resulted. The fact that over a period of thirty-one years (1545–1576) some thirty meetings of the National Diet took place to deal with religious questions illustrates this clearly. Finally a compromise was reached in the

Pax Dissidentium, out of which the free practice of four confessions was born.

Usually what took place at the meetings of the National Diet was a "dialogue of the deaf." Religious leaders proclaimed their *a priori* principles for weeks on end and described the horrors that lurked in the dogmas of their adversaries. At such times there were voices that asserted ever more loudly, "Whosoever says 'yes' to Christ will have to say 'no' to religious division." Dávid could not bear the thought of competitive church authorities living together in one country. So when Péter Melius Juhász became bishop of Debrecen, he became a counteractive force in Dávid's path. It may be true that in order to rise to great heights in one's own age and become a decisive leader, one must have an opponent of equal metal. The history of the Hungarian Reformed Church gives account of Melius' role as Dávid's opponent. For decades the attention of the country was held by these two exceptionally gifted personalities, and in the shadow of the Islamic peril they finally agreed in an Edict of Tolerance (1568), which was the first to be introduced into European church history. It involved the official recognition of four confessions. Dávid played an eminent role in this development, because having been a leading bishop in the Lutheran as well as the Reformed Church before, and now being a Unitarian bishop, he fought for and won acceptance of all four.

Francis Dávid, the Beginnings

Dávid was born in Kolozsvár between 1510 and 1520. The city, founded by the Romans, was once known as Claudipolia. His parents were of Saxon origin and, as was the humanistic custom of the time, Francis latinized his name to Franciscus Davidis on the basis of his father's Christian name. In his literary activities he used the Hungarian form of his name, Dávid Ferenc.

With the help of two Hungarian patrons, he set out early for foreign universities, first to the Lutheran Wittenberg University, where he enrolled at two different times, and then to Frankfurt am Main. He ended up studying at the Roman Catholic Academy of Padua in Italy.[8] He spent almost six years abroad. It is true that family data are scarce, but this much is certain: the epidemics of the time did not spare his family. Three marriages produced four children, of whom two were boys, two were girls. It is assumed that one daughter became the wife of the famous theologian

Johann Sommer, who was of German descent and who himself later became victim of the plague.[9] Dávid's second wife divorced him under scandalous circumstances, and the ensuing trial cast an unpleasant light on Dávid, condemning him as being the cause of the family trouble.

For a short time after his return from abroad, Dávid served as a Catholic priest. But, in 1555, he was a Lutheran minister and in time became a bishop and leader of the Lutheran Evangelical Church in Transylvania for four years. He soon adopted the much more radical precepts of the Helvetic confession and, in his capacity, first as pastor for five years, then as Reformed bishop, he brought these new teachings to his people.

From the year 1566, following newer developments in the field of faith and dogma, he wrote his name on the pages of church history as the founder of the Unitarian Church. In his last period, he became remarkably active in writing, growing always more radical in his religious precepts. Perhaps it was only through death that he was prevented from becoming a theologian of the Sabbatarians, who had strong Judaic tendencies.

These changes in direction show Dávid setting off four times down his "road to Damascus." While St. Paul was able to find his Redeemer after one sudden conversion, Dávid, as will appear later, never met his Christ, but only Jesus the Man to whom he was unable as a believer to say a prayer. With the final precept of *non adoramus*, he ended his efforts as a reformer.

First Public Appearance, Dávid contra Stancaro

Francis Dávid first demonstrated his thorough grounding in theology and his debating ability in a theological dispute with the Italian Jewish humanist Francis (Francisco) Stancaro. At the time of this debate, Dávid faced Stancaro as a Lutheran. Francis Stancaro came from the University of Padua, where he taught Hebrew in the 1540's and, as was the case of most humanist reformers of the time, proclaimed the new Mediterranean paganism. Stancaro was such a wild *furor theologicus* that once, meeting a humanist colleague, Andreas Osiander, for a debate, the followers of both appeared in the lecture hall fully armed.[10]

Stancaro, as a well-versed Hebraist, debated at synods all over Europe, succeeding in causing scandals wherever he went, and for that reason was driven out of every country he visited. According to his rabbinical logic, Christ could only intervene as a human being. If Christ were equal to God, in what manner could one God appeal to another? He who appealed had to be below the one to whom he appealed. Therefore, if Christ were really God, he could not appeal to himself, and because of His divinity he could not be an intercessor. He could only intercede in his human capacity.

After another escape, Stancaro arrived in Hungary around 1549. Here too he was condemned by the synods of the Church, but he did not back down. Among his enemies he especially slandered Phillip Melanchthon who, according to him, was a pseudo-Lutheran. In a petition he sent to the government of Transylvania, he demanded that his mendacious opponents be persecuted with the most ferocious mercilessness and be burned at the stake along with Francis Dávid, because they were all Arians.[11]

Dávid reacted in writing, using a remarkably calm tone and pointing out Stancaro's errors.[12] Altogether he devoted six theses to this, Stancaro dismissed them all as laughable aberrations. Dávid answered with an even more detailed documentation and summarized the arguments pro and contra[13], according to which, Christ could act as intercessor and Redeemer in both natures, human and godly. Dávid summarized his theological views, which were Lutheran at the time, in sixteen themes; then he strongly attacked Stancaro personally, referring to him as Jew or Muslim and adding the term "deformer."

Dávid warned Stancaro with the words of St. Paul: "Let us hold back our judgment in our obedience toward God!" He advised him to accept the Nicene Creed, which spoke both of the single substance and of the Holy Trinity. He added, "The Word is the Son of God. . . who is both human and godly and true God and true Man." Then, with a concept which he later denied, he admonished Stancaro saying, "We must believe God's Word even if our understanding is unable to grasp it or indeed advises the opposite." Finally he asked Stancaro to see in the formula of the creed mysteries which pass human understanding. "So leave your mad, fierce, arguments." When Stancaro was finally expelled from the country, the main accusation against him was that "he carved a man out of Christ." Not much time elapsed before Dávid himself faced the same accusation.

Stancaro had built his entire case on I Timothy 2:5 which he had interpreted wrongly: "For there is one God and one mediator between God and men, the man Christ Jesus." Stancaro, and later Dávid also, had borrowed this idea from the famous *Liber Sententiarum* of Pier Lombardo. Stancaro's expulsion came in 1558, after his teaching had been discussed at the Diet of Torda and Dávid had advised his removal. After his departure Stancaro settled in Poland. John Calvin warned the leaders of Polish Protestantism against the propaganda of this "mad dog." In the end Stancaro appealed to the archbishop of Cracow saying that he wished to change from Judaism to Roman Catholicism, but his request was refused. The main reason for the misfortunes that befell his career was that, although he could have been a professor of the Hebrew language, he persisted in proclaiming his fantastic theological views instead. In these tormented years, signs of mental disorder began to appear.

Stancaro jeered at the Catholic priests of Transylvania, called them "wine jugs," and demoted the earlier fathers of the Church to the rank of "beer barrels." At the same time in a request written to the ruling Queen Isabella, he mentioned "God's rights" and advocated the confiscation of priests' property and the burning of priests at the stake.[14] It would be appropriate, in connection with Stancaro, to point to the insincerity of the humanists with regard to tolerance while allegedly they were the representatives of God's tolerance, because many humanists advocated the most merciless punishments and Sebastien Castellio, in his *Traité des herétiques*,[15] as a great defender of heretics, wrote in support of the death sentence for all those who blasphemed the Lord. His subjective "truth" sounds like this: *Veritas est dicere quae sentias, etiam si erres*, or: the truth is what you proclaim, even if you know it is not true.

Dávid himself was unable to avoid the religious impatience of the neophyte. As Lutheran bishop, during the Synod of 1557, he wrote the *Consensus doctrinae de sacramentis* which in its summary dismissed, with curt impatience, the Helvetic creed, then known as the *Sacramentalis*,[16] which theology, according to him, was built on impossibilities of common sense. At the same time Dávid strongly emphasized that "only the Word of God must be believed and followed,"[17] as this was the key to salvation.

Dávid was successful at the Synod in excluding ministers of the Helvetic persuasion "because they are rotten parts," saying that if they did not change their views they would end up in prison. After this he requested and received police support from the City Council in the name of the Lutheran faithful of Kolozsvár, so that they could jail those of the Helvetic faith.

It is a commonly occurring historical phenomenon that as long as a political or religious group is in the minority, it loudly proclaims tolerance. However, as soon as it finds itself in a position of power, it becomes impatient and bigoted. Stoeckel, a Lutheran colleague of Dávid's, was just as contemptuous of the views of the Helvetic believers: "If the Helvetic dogma consists of that, it is fit not only to greet the Turks and the Jews, but the devil himself."

Francis Dávid's Roads to Damascus

After his Roman Catholic beginnings as priest, Dávid had become a Lutheran pastor and bishop in his search for truth. It is possible that Melanchthon's deep influence accompanied the sensitive Dávid back from Germany to Transylvania. However, according to the inner logic of things intellectual, the orthodoxy that was developing within Lutheran circles ended up enclosing its followers in an already obsolete scholastic inflexibility which infected Dávid himself. The Helvetic concept promised to dispel this theological tension, this dogmatism, and in his spiritual homelessness Dávid set out on his third road leading to Damascus.

In 1559 Dávid had scarcely finished his successful debate with the radical Stancaro, when he continued into theological crossroads. He adopted the rapidly spreading Helvetic dogma whose followers, the Sacramentalists, he had attacked two years earlier. It would be difficult today to determine the exact reason for his decision. His Lutheran opponents, German Saxons, accused him of being a disturber of religious peace, and they did not even reply to the new principles of faith which Dávid published under the title: *In Defense of Orthodoxy in the Lord's Supper*. This was his first Helvetic work and he justified with rationalistic methods the Helvetic teaching of the doctrine of the Lord's Supper which he had previously strongly condemned. He now stated that outside of the Lord's Supper there was no real sacrament.

One can observe the impact of the history of reformed religious interaction on Dávid's theological development and its constantly changing pattern. Several times he proved the thesis of the nihilist of Greek philosophy, "The one thing that is constant is change."

Hardly had Dávid's conversion to the Helvetic confession become known when he influenced the ruler of Transylvania to call together a Synod for the defense of the Helvetic faith, and he was even able to formulate the topics for debate at the Synod:

Defensio Orthodoxiae Claudipolitanae et Religiorum Recte Docentium in Ecclesiis Transylvanicis.

So in the defense of the Lord's Supper, Dávid endeavored to bring together the conflicting ideas of Saxons and Magyars on the subject, but on the basis of Helvetic teaching. When this undertaking did not succeed, he resigned from the episcopacy of the Lutheran Church. In one of his later writings, the *Short Explanation*,* which appeared in 1567, he mentioned in retrospect his reason for turning away from the Lutheran Church. It was because the mystic presence of Christ was too speculative for him. As justification he then published Heinrich Bullinger's pertinent article, written in 1551, the *Libellus Epistolari*, which was of a syncretic character and reconciled the various Helvetic opinions.

On this third stumbling down the "road to Damascus" Dávid started out with Péter Melius Juhász, the Helvetic Reformed bishop, who was active in Debrecen. They went to Transylvania together to organize a Reformed Church. In this capacity Dávid was elected bishop at the Diet of Torda in 1564, and he was even successful in obtaining legal and official freedom for the Reformed Church.

Fairly soon he lost his way. He could not escape from Calvinist syllogisms and the rationalism that went with them nor from his own humanistic inclinations. Neither could he harmonize the radical Biblical anthropology of humanism and the Biblical relativism of Erasmus. Later, however, Erasmus' Biblical relativism accompanied Dávid in his thinking to the very end. Perhaps he did not do it consciously, but Dávid was soon introducing interconfessional relativism into the religious life of the churches he had reformed. He developed thus step by step his own subjective concept of salvation, imagining that in this way he could find an absolute and objective truth. For him as for all latter-day Faustinian men, the struggle was for complete knowledge, without recognizing that man's understanding of God was and must always be incomplete. Naturally his pseudo-religious idea placed all emphasis on reason only.** This rationalism formed a new dogma and attempted to explain in theory the living God who is both immanent and transcendant, both in the universe and in history. In other

---

**Rövid Magyarázat.*

**Not long before Dávid had taken Stancaro to task for proclaiming the exclusivity of the human mind in matters of faith, saying, "Do not follow the philosophers who encourage turning away from God and who lead us to paganism."

words, Dávid was incapable of experiencing through faith alone the reality of the eternal Christ. Religious rationalism undermined his faith and he became a religious-philosophical skeptic. In clearer moments he still could express an unconscious knowledge of Christ, "Christ is not there where truth is absent" (*Christus non est, ubi veritas absens*). Later uncertainty again pursued his soul when he determined that it was certain that the Bible contained God's truth, "but how can I arrive there when the Synods and the contradictory decrees of the Church Fathers stand in my way?"

What had brought about Dávid's odyssey? Maybe the years spent abroad studying had encouraged him to search for new ways? Was it in part the Biblical criticism that fed on Melanchthon's humanism in Wittenberg that shook up the young candidate for the Catholic priesthood? Was it Melanchthon, the crypto-Calvinist of the *Praeceptor Germaniae* and his conciliatory theology that had loosened Dávid's closed system of dogma, or was it his sojourn at the University of Padua, where the religious influences of Judaism and Islam then reigned supreme and consequently created doubt in him? In the end, did the ceaseless dynamism of the mind predominate? A further influence could have occurred during his student years at Wittenberg where there had been Magyar students at the university who sympathized with Antitrinitarianism. The large number of Hungarian students there had their own organization, which they called *Bursa* and whose members, during the time that Mihály (Michael) Ungvári was the rector, had drawn up rules of behavior, the *Regula Vitae* (1568). According to these rules, any student sympathizing with Antitrinitarianism was excluded from the organization. This would indicate that Antitrinitarianism already existed among the students, a fact borne out by our knowledge of Socinus' presence at that time in Wittenberg.[18]

As stated, for Dávid fidelity of faith comes exclusively from knowledge, and it took only a short time for him to no longer be able through reason alone to pray to Christ (*non adoramus*); he could only meditate on Him. While Dávid was unable to compose a new Christology, which was a task that far surpassed his human capabilities, he turned to other sources of theology. This eventually led to his fourth beginning, Unitarianism. It is nigh to impossible to draw a spiritual and intellectual picture of him. Among the dogmas of the four confessions he chose, who can say at what period he was true to himself?

The Radical Influence of Servetus and Blandrata
on the Theology of Francis Dávid

Giorgio Blandrata was among the Italian humanists who represented new Mediterranean paganism in the spiritual life of Europe. When Blandrata, after successfully bringing about the disintegration of the Protestant Church in Poland, left for Transylvania, he needed a well-prepared theologian through whom he could spread his theological views. As physician and as amateur theologian he found a position at the voivod's court which also assured his authority. He was successful in winning over the dynamic preacher, Francis Dávid, around 1564 and 1565. One of Dávid's faithful apologists, Lászlo Iván, registered this important moment in the history of religion:

> "The single decisive turn in the life of Francis Dávid took place in 1565. We can thank the coming of this turn in Dávid's life to God's Providence which brought him the works of the Spanish renewer of faith, Michael Servetus. While reading these works, Dávid experienced that great adventure through which he was actually born again to the world . . . Servetus became the guide who was to lead Dávid to salvation. Sometime after the Diet of Nagyenyed in 1564, Blandrata gave the books written by Servetus to Dávid. The reading of the *Restitutio Christianismi* released in Dávid the triumphant feeling of having hit upon the road leading to truth."[19]

So it was Blandrata, the "beloved doctor" as he was generally called, who established his influence on Dávid, then proceeded to use his genius, and later debated him until he was imprisoned at Déva. Actually Dávid became more the victim of Blandrata's intrigue than just the martyr of his own faith.

With *Restitutio Christianisimi* Servetus had hoped to reform the Christian Church by connecting Islamic and rabbinical literature. He had known the Koran well and had used it copiously as a source. Many times he had shown preference for the teaching of Mohammed over the Bible.[20] Theodore Bibliander and his coworkers had translated the Koran in 1543, and Servetus had amply used the translation when he attacked the Trinitarian dogma. Newman states: "Servetus also is quick to indicate that the Mohammedans and the Jews are justified in their mockery of the Trinity . . . and in the truth of the Unitarian view of God."[21] At the same time Servetus had borrowed many elements from the Aristotelian writings of the Averroes, which were built on pantheism. It seems probable that this Arabic material came into Spanish spiritual life through the intermediary of Hebrew literature translated into Latin. As Hebrew historian Graetz pointed out: "Michael Servetus . . . instructed by Marranos in Spain, wrote a pamphlet on the errors of the Trinity."[22] (Marranos were those Spanish Jews who, under duress, had changed their faith to Roman Catholicism but who remained in essence faithful to Judaism.) With excellent theological preparedness, they cast doubts on certain points of theology, among them the doctrine of the Trinity. The Hebrew language nowhere played a larger role in theological literature than in that of the Antitrinitarians. Robert Dán, historian and Hebraist, gave an excellent insight into this when he disclosed the sixteenth century sources of the Unitarian and Sabbatarian religions.[23] Christian Hebraists analyzing the Bible could be regarded as the followers of Erasmus from the point of view of their methods. Erasmus, with exaggerated humanistic approach, undermined the basic tenets of Christology in many ways. It is true that he later admitted that the philological works which he had promoted had prepared the way for Hebraic influences. In a letter written to Wolfgang Capito in 1516, he said that he was afraid that outside of Judaism a new paganism could develop.[24]

According to historian and Hebraist Newman, Servetus' theological system contains more elements from the Old Testament than from any other literature, whether Neo-Platonic, Greek, Mohammedan, Patristic, or early heretical such as Sabellian, Pelagian, Manichean, or Arian.[25]

What Erasmus could do in his latter years, that is, avoid rabbinical literature, Servetus could not do. His tragedy was a paradox. He became the victim of that religious legalism which he himself generously had propagated. In fact, it was the Law of Moses which was carried out on him (Exodus 22:20, Leviticus 24:16). The Koran also prescribed a punishment similar to the one Servetus advocated.*

The Biblical literature of the humanists no doubt attempted to perfect the text of the Bible, but in so doing it introduced Biblical relativism, which one medieval theologian characterized thus:

"The Vulgate was stretched out between two thieves. One was Hebrew, the other Greek."[27]

---

*Melanchthon also maintained that the "Mosaic Law against idolatry and blasphemy was binding on Christian states and was applicable to heresies as well."[26]

When Dávid adopted the theological innovations of Servetus, he attempted to integrate them entirely with his own ideas. Today, it is possible, using philological means, to show exactly how much he relied on the literature of the Spanish humanist. For instance, in 1569 Dávid published two learned essays, *De Regno Christi liber primus* and *De Regno Antichristi liber secundus*, which were actually transcriptions of Servetus' famous *Restitutio* in abbreviated form.[28] From these copious adaptations, it is apparent that between the years 1565 and 1571 Dávid drew on foreign sources but was unable to form his own theological system. It is also true that due to numerous plagiarisms his dogmas were filled with contradictions. One contemporary monographer recognized that when Dávid characterized something as original it could not be called a religious innovation of his own. "That is to say that the thoughts and ideas which he spread about were without exception taken from others."[29] In fact, one can observe in these two essays that thoughts were introduced by Dávid from the works of Servetus.

When Dávid and Blandrata finally managed in 1571 to gain official recognition for Unitarianism, Dávid still considered the worship of Christ as necessary. He expressed it for his followers thus: "I do not hold Christ to be the prime creator of the world, but I consider it necessary to worship him . . . To be sure God's firstborn is to be worshipped."[30] When, however, the Reformed theologians of Debrecen accused him of being the imitator of Servetus, he vehemently denied it. Bishop Melius of Debrecen was a good Hebraist and also knew Arabic; already in 1567 he had exposed Dávid's sources. For example, Servetus had stated at the beginning that Christ is God (*Christus est Deus*); Dávid also repeated "I will say that anyone who does not acknowledge that Christ is the true God, let him be cursed."[31] As Dávid penetrated further into the complicated disorderliness of Servetus' religious thoughts and recognized his contradictions, he turned to newer theological sources. This was circa 1571. In contrast he remained under the influence of Erasmus right to the end.

Influence of Erasmus

According to papal nuncio Antonio Possevino, Erasmus was the representative of the *sceptica doctrina*. When Dávid omitted the text of the *comma Johanneum* (I John 5:7) which taught the Trinity, he referred openly to Erasmus who had done the same in his *Novum Testamentum.** According to Possevino, "Erasmus wiped his feet, dirty with the filth of arrogance, on the holy books, and the best proof of this is the *Ministri Transylvani*" [Dávid].[32]

Erasmus' contemporaries named him, perhaps not without reason, the *homo pro se* or "the most selfish person." It was he who made his own Roman Catholic Church a laughingstock and simultaneously demanded tolerance for it. His pacifism was out of touch with all reality. At a time when the Turks were continually attacking Europe, he regarded this peril as simply an opportunity for converting them. He forgot how St. Francis had once arrived at the court of the sultan with similar missionary zeal, and how when he had begun to preach to the sultan about love with his Bible in his hand, the Padishah had him thrown into the sea. Likewise, he also forgot the Hungarian missionary Bálint Ujlaki, who among other things had translated the Hussite Bible into Hungarian and afterwards preached with such success in Constantinople that the sultan had him flayed alive. With such missionary utopianism, Erasmus contributed largely to the neutralist attitude of the Unitarians in the face of the hazard coming from the Islamic Turks. Those Unitarians whose radicalism led them into trouble simply went over to Turkish occupied territory, and some even became Turkish soldiers supporting Turkish imperialism.

Influence of Sommer

Dávid's son-in-law, Johann Sommer, who had fled from Germany to Transylvania with the so-called Heidelberg Group, became famous for the funeral oration[33] which he wrote on the death of the Voivod, John Sigismund (1571). In this discourse he insinuated that the pro-Turkish movement which John Sigismund had supported had lost its patron, thus using this opportunity to make political propaganda. He hoped to gain a supporter like Gáspár Békés, who was an Antitrinitarian and a Turkish sympathizer. This indifferent attitude of Sommer toward the catastrophic holocaust brought about by the policy of Islam was indeed tragic. The conqueror decreased the country's population by one-third. Sommer in his propaganda reflected the indifferent attitude expressed by Dávid and his

---

*Erasmus' *Novum Testamentum* had been published in translation in 1577 in Transylvania and the Unitarian exegesis drew from it arguments in profusion.

circle and thus invited accusations from the opposition, both at home and in parts of Europe, where the voivod and the Unitarians had been criticized because of their Eastern orientation, which isolated Hungarian Christians from their brethren in the West.[34]

Influence of Neuser

Adam Neuser was a German Turcophile, who had written to the sultan, advocating the conquest of Germany by the Turks, with the assurance that they could count on the support of the Unitarians. According to Neuser, the concept of Jehovah and Allah as one common God would wipe out all differences and bring about the union of mankind.[35]

In a letter to Blandrata, Neuser described how he planned to set up a free press on Turkish territory, in order to produce anti-Christian literature aiming to destroy the Trinity concept, and to spread this throughout Germany. However, the Turks forbade the use of a printing press because, according to them, one book was enough for salvation, and that book was the Koran.

When Neuser, as one of the Heidelberg Group of Turkish sympathizers, fled to Transylvania with Sommer, the latter helped him obtain, under a false name, a Saxon church in Kolozsvár, from Bishop Dávid, who also shared the knowledge of his true identity. Neuser continued to propagate his beliefs here. His congregation inevitably discovered the deception, and Neuser had to flee once more. In his attempt to reach the sultan in person, he chose a road leading across Hungary. Twice imprisoned by Habsburg authorities, he finally escaped by bribing a merchant whose boat plied the Danube, and had himself smuggled aboard in a wine barrel. Unfortunately, when the thirsty boat captain tried to draw wine from the barrel with his siphon, he drew instead an Antitrinitarian agitator. Thus Neuser's attempt to flee was thwarted and he was sent back to Germany.

From several more imprisonments in western Europe, he described in letters to the sultan how he wished to continue a literary struggle against the concept of the Trinity and against what he called false Christians on Turkish occupied soil. Then with a very original Biblical exegesis based on the second and seventh chapter of the Book of Daniel, he encouraged the sultan to go forth to conquer the world and rule over kings and emperors. He believed that the sultan would have to obey the predictions of Daniel.[36] He anticipated that under Turkish protection his life would be safe.[37]

Neuser finally drifted to Constantinople and ended his days as a mercenary of the sultan.[38]

The Christian solidarity of the humanists was unravelled by ill-founded notions. Because they were convinced that if they cast aside the dogmas of Christianity, the Mohammedan conquerors would mercilessly put an end to all religious fanaticism; they were ready to exchange the God of the Trinity for Jehovah and Allah, thus blending two worlds into one. They forgot, however, to clarify which God concept they adhered to–the fatalistic enforcer who paralyzes the will, Allah; or the angry one, Jehovah; or the loving, pardoning Christ.

Not surprisingly, Melius, Bishop of Debrecen, accused his former fellow-bishop Dávid and his Christology of being pro-Turkish. This touched the Unitarians on their most sensitive point, because at that time sympathy with the Turks was part and parcel of Antitrinitarian beliefs, as illustrated in the case of Neuser. At a meeting of the Synod Melius begged that they be spared the blasphemy of the fanatical Turkish sympathizers. Unfortunately, his pertinent article, *Antithesis veri et Turcici Christi* (the Antithesis between the true and the Turkish Christ) was lost, and it is only thanks to the preserved answer to it that reconstruction has been possible. In short, Melius stated in his accusation that the Antitrinitarians and Dávid's supporters daily degraded Christ to the status of man and in this showed Him to be no different from the Christ of the Turks.[39] In this view, Melius was supported by one of Francis Dávid's erstwhile faithful collaborators, Stephan Bazilius-Balázs, who also accused Dávid of being a Turkish sympathizer.[40] Possevino, the papal nuncius, described how much this religious argument occupied the ruling class, and how nobles and commoners took part en masse as if they were all born theologians. According to him, Blandrata and company were "steeping the poor voivod in Turkish godlessness." The court's right hand man, Gáspár Békés, who later made a bid for kingship, did not fear the Turks, because he himself was a believer in Antitrinitarianism. At the same time, however, the court chancellor Kovácsozy-Farkas, seeing the sad state that Transylvania was in, complained that if Western Christianity did not help, Transylvania would be lost to the Turks and would just melt away. The troubled Possevino asked why the Unitarians could not see that they had no right to reap where they did not sow.[41]

Perhaps the most serious accusation against Turcophile Antitrinitarians came later from the ruler Stephan Báthory who succeeded John (János) Sigismund. Bringing a bill before the Diet, he asked that the numerous heretical movements, including Mohammedanism, be outlawed throughout the country, because, as pointed out by the Saxon historian Teutsch, they wanted to wipe out the true Christian faith.[42] These examples show how Francis Dávid and Unitarianism that had developed in Transylvania were compromised by the humanistic reformers and political adventurers who had sought refuge there.

Francis Dávid and Giorgio Blandrata succeeded in making Unitarianism the "court religion". With the support of John Sigismund an important number of the population of Transylvania were converted to the new Unitarian teachings and many modern dialecticians of historical materialism would like to consider this as a plebeian progressive movement and the Reformed Church of Debrecen as the reactionary antithesis. They regarded Melius' church as arrested in its development and rigid orthodoxy.

In fact, this is a rash and hasty evaluation, because in Transylvania, from the ruling class down, the aristocracy and most of the lesser nobles were united in the so-called plebeian church. As historian Antal Pirnát determined in a most impartial way, there is no proof that the Antitrinitarian movement developed from the bottom up and that the working class became its living testimony.[43]

One of the Marxist apologists of Dávid, Tibor Klaniczay, relates that the plebeian element in the end excommunicated Dávid and his followers rather than the practice of a progressive (radical) theology. To present this movement as that of a radical religious leader or that of various ideologies engaged in a class struggle seems a somewhat far-fetched evaluation.[44]

Thanks to the chronicle of Sebastian Boross, a contemporary of Dávid, there is a much more credible observation as to how the working class, which has been described as radical, behaved:

> "The common people are ignorant and confused, because they are all Calvinists of the Melius ilk or Unitarians of the Dávid persuasion, who propagate the tenets of their beliefs, with great energy. In the end, however, the people draw closer to the Unitarians because *Mobile mutatur semper cum Principe vulgus Regis ad exem plus totus componitur orbis*, or The common people

undecided always follow the prince. The world accommodates itself to the head that wears the crown."[45]

Another contemporary observer, the historian Istvánfy, evaluated the massive Unitarian conversion similarly, and pointed out that only Unitarians obtained worthwhile work, so that people simply went over to a better-paying religion.[46]

The present author therefore draws the attention of modern Dávidists to the fact that the dialectical and confessional duel did not take place in the spirit of class struggle, nor in the intransigence of the plebeians against the feudal class. He believes that since Adam lost his privileged "class," his descendants are continuously looking for the burning bush by which they can somehow come again into the presence of God. Men hope thus to end self-alienation, which stems from a spiritual and not from a materialistic longing.

Francis Dávid did open a path with his ideological and religious radicalism to outside foreign spiritual and religious influences that served the interests neither of his church nor of his people, which showed that he did not devote much attention to the social and political questions of the day.

Dávid in his method of religious criticism did not emphasize faith in search of truth, but rather spiritual wisdom or understanding. Thus rationalism became a bridge over which Greek, Italian, German, and other humanists poured into Transylvania with their own adventuresome theological notions. They wished to help Dávid gain recognition for his endeavors, which aimed at reconciling faith, reason, and transcendental metaphysics with earthly immanence, in this way drafting a new Christology. He could imagine that God in His transcendental nature could find the path into the souls of men, therefore He could become immanent in men. Thus through faith, the pure experience of God could be transcendental but at the same time immanent as well. The danger naturally is that, if balance tilts in the direction of immanence, this could result in pantheism. Although this came about in later centuries in the period of theism and deism, in the author's judgment Dávid cannot be regarded as a pre-deist.

In these decisive years for the churches of European Protestantism, there was a desire to stabilize the revolutionary results under the direction of Luther and Calvin. They considered religious renewal as complete, and this view was shared by their Hungarian followers as well. The church leaders built up authority which banished doubt and feverish searching. That is why Luther, Calvin, and Melius organized their churches as "strong castles." Dávid borrowed a slogan from St. Augustine: "It is necessary to speak the truth even if the world falls apart." (*Fuit veritas pereat mundus*) as opposed to Melius' "On earth peace among all men!", (*In terra pax hominibus*).

Melius critics condemned him for his search for peace and claimed that Debrecen had become the center for compromise of the Hungarian Reformation, and Melius was that Reformation's chief ideologist. The citizenry was no longer interested in renewal but in consolation.

To just what degree the citizens of Kolozsvár were supposedly inclined to accept dialectical materialism and join the battles of the working class is demonstrated by an Antitrinitarian-Anabaptist minister, Elias, according to whom the true Christian way of life could only be built on communal property, and no Christian should be able to say "This penny is mine." (This is like the communal way of life among Moravian Brethren.) Nor could one justify marital fidelity or the oath of fealty, because Jesus had abolished oaths, and in order to give heart to criminals, Elias maintained that it was God who had caused crime and not man himself. Besides all this, the pastor advised that no one should fight against the conquering Turks, because they were the greatest power on earth and therefore the authority. The Anabaptists hoped that the Turks would conquer Germany, and then they would be free of persecution.[47]

After all these utterances, Pastor Elias fled from Kolozsvár under cover of darkness and did not stop until he reached Poland. He was apparently afraid to wait for the plebeians to express their opinions on his ideas.

Later Dávid himself stated in an article, *"The Reign of Christ"*, that the millenium would not be brought about by a revolution of the people, but by God.

It seems clear that the theological nihilism of Elias would have led to social anarchy. Perhaps this contributed to the subsequent action taken by the civil government, which put a ban on religious innovations and that at the very time when Dávid proclaimed that the millenium would soon arrive in Kolozsvár, in 1570 to be precise.

Church Synods of the Diet of Transylvania

The revived battles of the confessions of Transylvania took place at the religious Synods (*vallási zsinatok*) under the leadership of Dávid and Blandrata. Since the entire political and religious energy of Transylvania was being absorbed by the Protestant Reformation, the Diet of the temporal powers organized and directed these Synods on the basis of *ius reformandi*. It was at these frequently held meetings that the nation's elite gave full vent to their intellectual energy. Finally these Synods became forums for the discovery of talent that often lay hidden until it was brought to the surface and enriched the society with its genius. The life stories of Francis Dávid and of Péter Melius-Juhász illustrate this. Later, at these same Synods, the intelligentsia of Europe's generation of humanists and reformers met.

Toward the end of the sixteenth century, it was at these Synods that the Hungarian people were being educated, and the result was that ninety percent of them became Protestants, so that after an overwhelming percentage of the nation converted to a new faith, there was no need to grapple with a Roman Catholic minority. The dogmatic struggles of the new confessions consumed each other's energies, however, within the churches themselves. The Protestant leaders, fighting each other, confirmed the saying of St. Augustine, that "as long as heretics destroy each other, the Mother Church can enjoy peace." (*Bellum hereticorum pax est Ecclesiae.*)

Francis Dávid was the hero of these Synods. He lived in a dramatic age and was himself a dramatic personality, driven by Protestantism and by his limitless demands for freedom. Dávid's sustaining strength came from the interpretation of the Holy Scriptures. The idea of *semper reformare* determined and captivated him, made him the slave of his arguments.

In his favor it can be said that he would not proclaim a word which, according to his own judgment, was not blessed by the Lord. Later, at his final trial, his last act was in defense of freedom of thought and conscience, just as had been that of John Huss, his spiritual brother.

Transylvania was an independent province of the Kingdom of Hungary, and its political legacy included three different national groups. These were the Hungarians, the Székler (Székely or Siculi), and the German-Saxons, who constituted a confederation not unlike the later Swiss Confederation, for in Transylvania too a political symbiosis of three ethnic groups existed which developed a tolerant coexistence of various confessions. At the time of the Reformation, the three national groups represented four officially recognized religious denominations and drew up an edict (previously referred to) on religious freedom based on the Bible. It stated: "Faith is a gift of God. Secular powers cannot give it nor can they take it away; they are only obliged to serve it."[48] At the meeting of the Diet the theologians of all three ethnic groups founded their own organizations, discussed dogma, and if the case arose, turned to foreign theologians for advice.

At a meeting of the Synod, authorized by the political Diet, in 1568, for example, the Unitarian voivod strengthened the Synod's decision on unlimited freedom of religion:

> "According to this, preachers can preach the Gospel everywhere, some according to their own interpretation if this has been accepted by the congregation. No one can be forced to accept it, but let each congregation keep the kind of preacher it likes . . . It is not permitted to mock anyone for his religious convictions. It is not permitted to punish anyone with imprisonment for his teaching, or to deprive him of his livelihood, because faith is a gift of God and comes from a sense of hearing, and hearing is the treasure that comes from God's Word."[49]

At this Synod of 1568, we note that it was the first time in Europe that unlimited freedom was sanctioned, and with it a new confession came officially in existence, Unitarianism. (In contrast, the Diet of the western part of the Hungarian kingdom, ruled by the Habsburg Maximilian, declared that "all Antitrinitarians ought to be burned and their books with them!" (1572)

Francis Dávid, the Voivod John Sigismund, and Blandrata were the founders of this confession, but they were not ready yet to detach themselves as an independent church organization. Maybe therefore the bishop of the Helvetic Church, Melius, asked that the voivod call a second meeting of the Synod; he wished to prevent the absorption of the Unitarians into his own Church. From the very beginning, Melius fought with the confession that denied the existence of the Holy Trinity, and in the letter he sent out to his adversaries inviting them to the Synod he used the words: "The pestridden descendants of scorpions, the offspring of vipers are going to meet a tragic death according to God's decree." He lumped together the theological works of Arius, Servetus, and Dávid, forecasting for Dávid the same tragic end that befell the others, and declared war on their theology.

It is easy to understand why Dávid, Blandrata, and their Unitarian followers were not inclined to appear at the Synod to be held in Debrecen. They could well remember that Latin phrase about footprints all leading into the bear's den (*Vestigia terrent*). Perhaps that is why the voivod called the Synod together in 1568 first in Torda, then in Alba Julia, instead of Debrecen, and Transylvania became the general headquarters of the Unitarians. The voivod warned Melius not to overstep the bounds of Christian forebearance, not to dismiss his brother ministers, and not to dare set himself up as a pope "with raised eyebrows like a confessor at the Sorbonne."

The agenda of the meeting of the general Synod was drawn up by Dávid and Blandrata, not by Melius, and the following line was added to the invitation: "We admonish our colleagues to avoid wherever possible the doctrine of the Trinity, which is mixed with Melius' poison and black bile." This text could not be classified as particularly inviting.

The order of the debate was:

I. Everything outside of what is written and taught by the Prophets, Christ, and the Apostles, must be omitted during the discussions because those who wish to speak on the Trinity are nothing but sophists, uttering human speculation only.

II. The question of Infant Baptism must be put aside and the explanation and cause of it will be dealt with later.

III. The elected judges will direct the order of debate, and they will be chosen from among the Hungarians, including Székler, and German-Saxons.

IV. Only the words of the Holy Scripture will be used in the arguments, and the decisions of the Church Fathers and Church Synods are to be disregarded.

V. Do not aggravate each other.

VI. Those who are declared losers, let them be silenced.

VII. Foreign theologians may be consulted in connection with questions discussed. [50]

The participants of this arduous Synod must have been in excellent condition of mind and body. Debate began at five o'clock in the morning. Dávid started things off with his view against the Trinity. Melius immediately requested that the loquacious Dávid present his theses briefly and in more concrete form, since he had already strayed away from his topic . . . Blandrata intervened and asked Melius to use only words of the Bible when giving his views in the defense of the Trinity.

Francis Dávid:

"I find nowhere in the Bible the term *Deus Trinitas*. Therefore there is no God in three persons. 'Because I and the Father are One' can only be a human speculation which does not prove the truth of God in three persons."

Melius:

"Christianity was born in the name of the Trinity and through the Trinity, God in three persons, which is to say Christ's grace, the Father's love, and the Communion of the Holy Spirit. These three are one God. This proves the truth of the worship of the Trinity in Isaiah 6.

Francis Dávid:

"These are only logical inferences . . . "

After the debaters had completely exhausted themselves pro and contra on the subject of the Holy Trinity, the voivod, who was presiding over the meeting and who was ailing, closed the assembly for that day.

The theme for the second day was: Did Christ exist from all eternity or was He born?

Melius opened the program of the Synod with quotations from the Bible, "I was appointed from eternity, from the beginning, before the world began." (Proverbs 8:23) "Thus says the Lord: 'You are my Son, today I have begotten you'." (Psalm 2:7) "For God was pleased to have all his fullness dwell in him." (Col. 1:19)

Finally, on the ninth day everybody was exhausted in mind and body because of the highly charged debate. Therefore, the Lutheran bishop, the Saxon Hebler, asked the voivod to let them leave, since he felt absolutely no spiritual value in Dávid's innovations.

Voivod John Sigismund:

"I authorized this meeting of the Synod because I wanted to hear
Dávid's theological teaching. We will stay."

Melius then summed up his opinion saying: "You, Francis Dávid, are
simply repeating the innovations of Socinus, but you cannot give anything
new of your own. You knew him in Wittenberg, and he was an ignorant
fool there. How, therefore, can you subordinate Christ's Church, which has
lived and taught for one thousand five hundred years, to his ideas? I would
rather babble like an infant with the Holy Ghost and the Fathers of the
Church than to reason with Laelius Socinus."

On the tenth day, the voivod asked the participants to pray for unity; he
then stated that everyone in the country should be able to proclaim his
religious opinions, and declared the meeting closed. Reading the prayers of
an age born in the shadow of such theological arguments, one can imagine
how they tried the patience of a merciful God. They always asked for
enlightenment from above for the souls of their adversaries. As Dávid said;
"I ask the eternal God to bring them out of their eternal darkness and
expose their souls to the light of knowledge . . . and protect us from the
darkness that Melius represents. Amen."

Melius recognized the importance of the theological questions in the
European framework and as their sources were from the West, he did not
want to isolate the Transylvanian controversy. That is why half of his
writing, about twenty volumes, were devoted to the bitter religious argument. For instance, he informed the leaders of the neighboring Reformed
Church of Poland of the ongoing religious struggle and through his colleague, Christopher Thretius, with whom he had studied in Wittenberg, he
carried on a correspondence with the West, because Thretius maintained
close ties with the Swiss Reformers. The influence of numerous rabbis on
Antitrinitarianism became known to Melius, and he mentioned this in a
letter to Bullinger to whom he sent a refutation of the propaganda of
Servetus, Blandrata, and Dávid, for publication in Zurich. He listed among
other things all the arguments which Dávid had brought forth and their
rabbinical sources such as the books of Albo and Kimhi.[51]

Melius fully recognized the sources of religious radicalism that were
developing in the church literature of Europe, and he pointed to the
radicalization caused by the introduction of the Hebrew language and the
exegeses of the Hebraists, who cast doubt on the traditional dogmas of

Christianity. That is why Melius fought so determinedly. He also saw and recognized the logic of sectarianism according to which a sect could prepare the way for more radical heresy, and that Antitrinitarian road building opened the gate to Islam.

After the dispute Francis Dávid mobilized all his spiritual energy and with the printing press he received from the voivod, (confiscated from his opponents), he duplicated for an entire year the literature of the debate. Of this the most significant was perhaps *On the Divinity of Jesus Christ*, in which he presented his new Christology.

His opponents challenged Dávid:

I. If God exists alone, as claimed by Dávid, Christ can not be a true God.

II. On the other hand, if Christ is God, then God cannot be alone.

Dávid then studied his spiritual predecessors, Sabellius and Arianus, and their reasoning, and answered his opponents thus:

> "In the Old Testament Christ was a promise of God, but in the New Testament the promise verified by the evangelists and the apostles came into fulfillment. Christ was called the Son of Man because of his mother, Mary, and because he resembles us. Because of Father, we can call him Son of God since he received everything from God."[52]

Recognizing the many foreign and conflicting ideologies which he could not reconcile, Dávid deplored the limited nature of his understanding, as he wished to believe with reason alone. "My intellect is not capable of understanding the Trinity. Logic weakens faith. I cannot pray to such an uncertain plural God . . . three Gods cannot sit on one heavenly throne . . . It is strange, because one God carries out the command of another God and a third intervenes while the First is sitting in Heaven."[53]

The Synod at Alba Julia (Gyulafehérvár) had broken up without achieving any concrete result. The increasingly radically orientated Unitarians continued along their dialectical way. Nevertheless, there was still an impact on history, because the Helvetic Reformers proceeded to organize their church separately under the leadership of Melius, drew up their own eclectic theological propositions, and removed themselves from the Unitarian movement. The influence of Dávid and Blandrata was apparent when Voivod John Sigismund openly announced his Unitarian convictions.

The result was that most of his subjects were converted to the Antitrinitarian God concept (God is one).

The theologians of Western Europe also entered into the Transylvanian religious controversy, and among them was Georg Maior, professor at Wittenberg. He forced Dávid into a vigorous debate, even condemning him in books.[54] The ever "patient" Dávid replied, "You can return to the Masses of the Popes, to their seven sacraments, and descend with them to hell."

Maior then asked Dávid: "Do you believe in the Christian who has been faithful and who has suffered for a thousand years, in his churches, in his Church Fathers, in his martyrs or in the devilish monsters of Francis Dávid, Blandrata, and Samoseta-Arianus?"[55]

Dávid did not want to be defeated, and losing his alleged patience, he exclaimed in indignation, "Maior betrays the confusion of his sick soul. The devil leads him, and he rolls about in the swamp of his sinful impulses; he is a liar and a murderer."[56]

Dávid and Stephan Bazilius, who was still his faithful companion, answered Maior's writings together in their book *Refutatio Scripti Gregorii Maioris*, which appeared in 1569.[57] Dávid propounded his stand dressed in Christian garb. His followers received the self-revealing document as if it came from someone "who had taken Christ from the tomb after he had been buried by the Popes."[58]

Among the never-ending Synods, that of Alba Julia (Gyulafehérvár) was important for three reasons: first, it was there that the doctrine of the Trinity was debated in all its essentials; second, since the comparative history of the time had established the spiritual connection between Dávid and Servetus, the ideas of Servetus were thoroughly debated there; third, since the debaters did not find a substantiating text, they called Erasmus' writings as witness and his prestige was placed above the Holy Scriptures. "See Erasmus and you will understand."[59]

When Beza wrote with indignation from Geneva that Transylvania had become a hotbed of sects, these were not empty words. Lecler, a modern Jesuit scholar affirms Beza's statement, saying, "Transylvania was a Babel of religious confessions."

A contemporary of Dávid who knew him well characterized him thus: "Every new idea seizes him and goads him into abandoning a former standpoint. He is the kind of man who favors ambitious and theatrical arguments, so much so that he has never settled down and can never stand having anyone who is equal to himself."[60]

The instinct to argue drove Dávid on continuously, compelling him to attack even what he had defended previously. His knowledge of the Bible was unsurpassed; he could not be beaten in this. His quotations and proofs were such that he always escaped when attacked from any angle. In this too he was like Erasmus, "who was like an eel that only the devil could catch."

The Second Decisive Discussion on Faith in Nagyvárad, 1569

The second decisive discussion on faith took place in Nagyvárad.[61] As Dávid and Blandrata were unable to decisively influence the life of the churches in Transylvania at the Alba Julia Synod, they convinced the voivod to call together another Synod. Permission obtained, the voivod called the meeting which was to take place in Nagyvárad, a city not far from Calvinist Debrecen. The voivod appeared at the Synod with his entire court. From Debrecen came the most outstanding theologians, among them the translator of the Bible, Gáspár Károlyi. They were led by Bishop Melius. The voivod appointed Gáspár Békés to preside over the Synod, and a contemporary of Békés thought it important to note: "He [Békés] studied in Padua where he adopted the Arab-Hebrew theology; he did not believe in an after-life; he did not fear hell, nor had he hope of going to Heaven. He was Unitarian or at least showed himself as such."[62]

The Synod was opened with prayers by Melius and Dávid beseeching the Creator to help bring peace among them.

Each side appointed nine debaters from among their theologians to be directed by Melius and Dávid. Melius wanted to put the religious questions into a European framework and repeatedly asked the voivod to invite theologians from Wittenberg and Geneva as arbiters. This request was opposed by the wily Blandrata, understandably from his point of view, because there was not a single theologian in Western Europe who would be inclined to support the Antitrinitarians. It was at this Synod that a Jesuit priest, John Leleszi, was allowed to take part; later, in collaboration with Blandrata, he brought about Dávid's downfall.

That the Calvinist Gáspár Károlyi served on the Synod was a surprise. Requesting the floor in the name of the Helvetists of Hungary, he asked that Voivod John Sigismund play a role similar to that of an early Byzantine emperor, Constantine the Great, who at the Council of Nicea in 321, took to task those Arian theologians who denied Christ. He suggested that the voivod should act similarly: "Stop the mouths of the new heretics."[63] Then Melius took advantage of freedom of speech and warned John Sigismund: "Do not allow God's honor to be insulted; protect the truth and those who defend it. If you do that, your name will live forever, but if you do not, eternal shame and damnation will fall on your Majesty."[64]

After this unusual outspokenness, Melius appealed to Francis Dávid, saying, "You are turning our Christian society upside down. Think it over! We ask you to abandon your destructive work. If you were the pastor of a church, you would have to render accounts for your behavior. If you have done this until now out of ignorance, mend your ways. If on the other hand you have been doing it out of selfishness," (Melius reproved him here for occupying three bishoprics), "well, then may the Lord punish you."

After these hard words, John Sigismund took Francis Dávid under his protection and, turning Melius' admonition around, threatened him.

This over-heated atmosphere exemplified the controversial situation in East Central Europe.

Melius' aggressiveness was not surprising. He was, after all, not only a church leader, but also a statesman, fighting against the Islamic Turks and the Counter-Reformation of the Habsburgs. The people's church was his defending bastion, and the prevention of the developing religious tradition had become a question of life and death. During the church-building period, Melius became a theologian fighting on three fronts: against Habsburg Catholicism, against Islam, and against the danger coming from Unitarianism. The state, split into three parts, could not protect the people when Roman Catholic mercenaries or Turkish janissaries burned, deported, or massacred them. When the Tridentine popes legalized the Jesuit order, which was ready to do anything asked, and the sultan occupied Buda with a ruse, only Melius' church was able to keep the people organized.

Blandrata was quite influential at the voivod's court and directed the Unitarian delegates to the Synod behind the scenes. As he had earlier divided the just developing Reformed church in Poland, he now used the same atomizing tactics in Transylvania. He also influenced Gáspár Békés, the presiding chairman of the Synod, to put the following items on the agenda:

1. Who is God?
2. Who is the Son of the Father, God?
3. What is the role of the Holy Ghost?
4. The question of the deity of Christ.

As in Alba Julia, the debates began at five o'clock in the morning, and the important opening topic was: Who led the Jews out of Egypt?

Melius:

> "It was an angel, who in reality could have been Jesus Christ."
> (Cor. I, 10:9)
> (In his book *Christus Mediator* he had given a detailed proof of this topic)

Francis Dávid:

> "It was God Himself who took the Jews out of the claypit."

Here the Voivod John Sigismund, intervened, reprimanding Melius:

> "How dare you state such things?"

He then put the riddle before Melius:

> "Was the angel in the burning bush God?"

Melius:

> "No, but it could have been Jesus Christ."

This disputed question, in itself ridiculous, caused a fierce argument that lasted for four days. Then, referring to the essence of Christ, John Sigismund asked the question: "Who can God's Son be?"

Melius:

> "He, Christ, who created all, and existed before the world existed
> . . . is from the essence of God. In other words, He is the eternal
> Son of God."

Dávid:

> "John's writings express only the future, the second coming of
> Christ and therefore it deals with the Second Creation."

John Sigismund:

"Prove from the Bible and use no sophistry."

Melius:

"The Bible contains two tenets. One points to the divinity, and the other to the humanity of Christ."

John Sigismund:

"So that is the basis for your two Christs? A complete God and a complete man in one person? According to you, your Christ has existed from all eternity, but at the same time your other Christ lives in time, born of Mary, and each has two kinds of authority?"

In the meantime, Dávid had annoyed the Melius camp by using a popular saying: "You cannot say anything new; you just go around in circles, skinning the same ram and trying to shear him at the same time."

Voivod John Sigismund abandoned again the agenda and commanded: "Prove that your Christ is the visible and invisible God in one person."

As Melius was not prepared for this question, because it was not on the agenda, he merely quoted Zechariah in the Biblical text referring to Jehovah: "On that day his feet shall stand on the Mount of Olives east of Jerusalem . . . ." (Zech. 14:4).

Dávid:

"In this quotation Zechariah does not make clear that Christ is in himself the living God; it speaks rather of what is yet to come."

Melius:

"It certainly speaks of Christ, because it shows that the Creator has feet." (the feet being the issue.)

The voivod goaded Melius:

"Peter, tell me. Did the Son of God, who exists from all eternity, really have feet, too?"

On the third day, the work was still centered around "shearing of the ram" which Dávid had brought up in jest. Then the ailing voivod gathered what strength he could and continued to goad Melius and his followers.

"Was Christ a second person in God, or did the Father only make him up later?"

Melius:

"Fatherhood is one thing, and Godhood is something else. The first he kept to Himself but he gave complete Godhood to His Son."

Dávid:

"But that is not a satisfactory answer, because the question is: Is the Godhood of Christ the Son from all eternity, and is He equal to His Father?"

When the voivod continued to mock Melius, the latter began to read passages from a piece of parchment from the Bible. In the meantime the voivod, who was not too well versed in theology, asked Melius to put his paper aside and give verbatim an explanation of his Christology, adding that if Melius would be capable of doing that, he would send him a barrel of old wine.

A member of the Debrecen group, George Czeglédi, asked Dávid why he was not inclined to expose his own ideas about Christ's role and told him to stop his whispering with Blandrata. This angered Dávid, who replied that he always fought for truth and that his opponents were those who hid truth in a sack.

It was Blandrata's strategy to divide the participants of the Synod by throwing to them such theological questions as would foil any possibility of coming to an understanding. He did this with an innocent face as if he were an ignorant outsider who only wanted to dispel "dialectical" doubts. Some examples:

"Who made Christ out of bread?
At the Lord's Supper, does one feel the warmth of the Body of Christ that is present?
Is the conversion effective if a non-believer wanders in at the Lord's Supper and, while partaking, is converted?"

While the arguments were going on about questions which were frivolous in themselves, the opposing sides were tearing at each other's beards. Blandrata hurriedly informed the voivod that there was no way of coming to agreement. He then advised him to announce that the Helvetic and Lutheran churches needed to be separate institutions.*

---

*Later he used the same strategy of divide and conquer to prevent reconciliation between the Helvetic and Unitarian churches, when he complained to the new voivod, Stephan Báthory, about the animosity between the two.

On the fifth day of the debate, the argument was still going on about the alleged numbers of Persons involved in the Trinity, and Dávid and his followers continually stated that Melius and his followers taught "four Gods", which they called *Quaternity*. This meant one substance and three Persons. Why did Melius and his people make three out of one? Then out of Christ came a double Christ, divine and human. They also kneaded the multiple God into One, but He would never become One. As long as man had a thinking mind, he could never make one out of two.

On the tenth day, the voivod was tired out, and he closed the proceedings. This was the last occasion on which Melius and Dávid, the two outstanding and talented church leaders, met. After this unsuccessful debate, the "dialogue of the deaf" continued by other means. They turned to literature in order to clarify their ideas, and in this way the entire nation became involved in the discussion of religious questions.

There was an echo in Western Europe on the debate in Nagyvárad, when in 1569 the Hungarian students in Wittenberg published the *Trinitarius Confessio*, which dealt with sixteen points rejecting the Unitarian doctrine.[65]

Dávid soon published his *Confession of Faith*, which set forth a very moderate theology. He even proclaimed the worship of God and Son. "The home of God on earth is Jesus Christ."[66] It was followed by his *Prédikacios Könyv*, which contained sixty sermons, aimed at reeducating the "uneducated" Helvetic ministers and students. The list of on-going arguments proves too numerous to include in this study.

In what follows, facts of decisive importance and pertinent cases of foreign influence on Dávid will be pointed out, in order to illustrate his further and final developments.

Francis Dávid and the Non Adoramus Controversy

Already mentioned is the invasion of Transylvania by foreign humanists of Italian, Greek, German and other nationalities. This invasion had a decisive and fatal influence on the ideology of Dávid, radicalizing it. This was his final start down his "road to Damascus," and it ended in the prison of Déva. He spoke of the objective of this last journey, saying, "We are going to chase the three Gods out of Transylvania by hook and crook. Then we will make the Lord our Father one God."[67]

On this last journey, Dávid cast aside every Credo except the Apostle's Creed. For a while he still recognized the verbal inspiration of the Bible, but at the same time he mixed it up with allegorical interpretations and finally replaced it with the rational exegesis. Although he emphasized the exclusivity of the *Sola Scriptura* practiced by John Calvin, his philosophical dialetics disturbed his opponents. On the basis of his new theology, there is one God and he called the three Gods in One Person a three-headed Cerberus. This too he had borrowed from Servetus. He called his two unequal doctrines of God monotheism and declared that Christ was not divine from birth, but only later was adopted by the Father.

The idea that his opponents were defenders of the faith and of the Church, was brushed aside as so much importunate bigotry; his own new dogmas he regarded as the Word of God.

Swept onward on sometimes mystical, sometimes irrational thinking, he introduced the truth of a continuous and personal revelation that would not suffer contradiction, because in his prophetic role he could not resist proclaiming the final truth. Although he professed and practiced the principle of free examination, he was quick at judging anyone who arrived at another conclusion to be a heretic. Like his humanistic companions, he was deeply convinced that they and only they could reach out without prejudice for an explanation of the Holy Scripture.

As long as Dávid was Servetus' spokesman, he could innovate with Blandrata, but from 1570 on, this collaboration did not satisfy him. All through his latest writings, we can observe his rejection of Blandrata's policy of compromise in church matters and his application of the more radical religious teachings of Sommer, Paleologus, and Glirius. From the point of view of theology, this meant that the pivotal question for Dávid and his Transylvanian associates concerned the Lord's Supper. They tried to gain insight as to how Christ was present at Holy Communion. However, this unclear doctrine raised in Dávid's mind the question of the uncertain role of Christ in the Doctrine of the Trinity.

At the Synod of Alba Julia (Gyulafehérvár) he had introduced a new aspect in his Biblical exegesis. He was inclined to recognize only that tenet of faith that could be verified in the Scriptures. With this method he examined the entire teaching of the Church and arrived at his final conclusion of one God in one Person. He tried to prove this with some words of Christ, and explained that, because Christ was born in time, he could not be the equal of the Almighty God, nor could he be eternal. With this new interpretation he introduced two contradictory lines into his church policy, bringing about a decrease in Blandrata's influence and an increase in that of John Sommer, Jacob Paleologus, and Matthias Glirius, who became the dominant triumvirate. Thanks to the influence of these men, Dávid was brought face to face with the new voivod, Stephan Báthory, who was a Roman Catholic. Blandrata, positioning himself cleverly during the change in rule, joined the new Catholic entourage at court.

Báthory, although a Roman Catholic, proved to be very patient, and among other things proclaimed the following:

"God reserved for Himself three tasks: creating something from nothing, knowing the future, and ruling over conscience."[68]

Blandrata had a new partner in the Jesuit Leleszi for whom the Unitarians were indeed dangerous people, not only because they could deprive the faithful of their religion on earth, but also of their place in Heaven as well. They deprived Christ of His eternal godliness, the Holy Ghost of His essence, and children of their baptism.[69] Nevertheless, the free-spirited generation, under the rule of the new voivod, reaffirmed at the Diet of Torda in 1572 that the laws pertaining to the freedom of religion were still valid. They added to this that, if anyone introduced innovations in the four official recognized confessions, his Majesty, with the cooperation of Bishop Dávid, would excommunicate him.[70] With this modification the voivod ruled out the possibility of any religious innovation, because he made Dávid responsible, and no one among the Unitarians could push radicalization further. Another step led to censorship in publishing. An agreement was reached by Stephen [István] Báthory, ruler of Transylvania and king of Poland, and Péter Melius Juhász to abolish the aimless, public religious disputes. This meant the end of the "dialogue of the deaf". In spite of these regulations, religious innovation could not be stopped in its development. The Unitarians continued their theological propaganda, and with the help of emigrant theologians, they produced the most fantastic religious writings. The Greek Jacob Paleologus influenced Dávid to go further with his theological revisions and declared that the Lord's Supper and Baptism could be dispensed with for salvation.

The question of worship or non-adoration of Christ came up also. Against this extreme religious revisionism, Melius hastily published an article to oppose the Non Adoramus concept.*

Dávid tried to extricate himself from the numerous contradictions that had developed out of his many adaptations from other sources by new explanations that came out in the 1570's. He published two booklets, *On the one majestic God and his true Son*, and *On the divinity of the One God and Father and of His blessed Son, Jesus Christ*. With the publication of these booklets, Dávid apparently forgot about the law promulgated at the Synod of Kolozsvár in 1565, which stated that no one could proclaim anything that was not identical with the teaching of the Bible. In these new articles he continued to work on the reform of theology and the Church. He must have remembered the lurking prediction that the world would come to an end, and the Kingdom of Christ would come into fulfillment, which he had expected to come in 1570. In spite of this statement, he strongly denied that he had added anything that was not Biblical. He repeated that the doctrine of the Trinity was introduced by fraud into the life of the Church. This conclusion was self-evident. God did not become a man in Jesus, but the man Jesus took on the name of God after his birth. He proceeded to discuss the question of worship and found that a distinction ought to be made between the worship of God and the worship of Christ. Great respect was due only to the father because Christ himself had said: "My Father is greater than I am." Similarly only with an exegesis agreeing with the Bible could it be proved that there was any basis for calling on Christ for help. God had never commanded this. Christ simply acted as Messiah in the manner of Moses, thus carrying out a command and having completed his task, his work was ended. Palaeologus, Glirius, and Sommer had already come out with this theological sleight-of-hand. On the way to revising all these dogmas, Dávid borrowed another new idea from the Italian humanist Jacob Acontius and introduced the practice of *Communis prophetia*. According to Acontius, a decision made on faith could not be the task of one person but must be the common task of the whole congregation. Johann Sommer introduced this new idea to his father-in-law, and Dávid adopted it. With the acceptance of this concept, Dávid aban-

---

*From a letter written by Dávid which was only recently discovered and brought to light by the Unitarian historian Louis Kelemen, it is apparent that already in 1566 Dávid was leaning toward an Antitrinitarian theology.[71]

doned his previous fight for unlimited individual freedom and now stressed the importance of the community.[72]

Johann Sommer documented in one of his books Dávid's early ideas on the non-worship of Christ (1566), which the Reformer now openly embraced. Since according to His nature Christ was not God, worshipping Him meant nothing. When St. Paul quoted, "Every knee will bow before me" (Romans 14:11) he did not refer to worship, but only to the respect owed to the judicial office of Jesus. Jesus was first man, the son of Mary, before he was God's adopted son. By identifying with the Old Testament, Dávid and Sommer did not work ahead but rather backwards and drew closer to Judaic concepts.

When the Poles elected Stephan Báthory as their king, he had to leave Transylvania. Therefore he had put Blandrata in charge of religious affairs of the Hungarians. He, with his Jesuit friend Leleszi, quickly set about reorganizing the church of the Unitarians. One of his first acts was the summoning to Kolozsvár of Faustus Socinus, the Antitrinitarian who was the exalted leader of the much more moderate Polish Antitrinitarian Church. There was in fact a period in the Polish Antitrinitarian Church when a movement initiated by Socinus was called Socianism. Blandrata's reason for summoning Socinus and settling him in Dávid's house was that he should have a moderating effect on Dávid's innovating ambitions. What was Dávid thinking in that year, 1578, in the private theological debate lasting for months between himself and Socinus? The latter published an account of this after Dávid's death under the title *Disputatio-Refutatio*.[73]

Dávid had been ready to summarize under four headings[74] his arguments dealing with the teaching for his own Christology:

1. God's strict order is that outside of God the Father, Creator of Heaven and Earth, it is not necessary to worship anyone. (This was the basis of the teaching of *non adoramus*.)

2. Christ also taught that apart from the Heavenly Father no one was to be worshipped.

3. True worship is directed to God in spirit and in truth. (John 4:23)

4. The worship of the Lord speaks to the Lord and not to the Son.

Dávid and Socinus agreed that Jesus was only a man. But the latter persisted in the teaching of the Immaculate Conception. Dávid, however, stubbornly insisted on his principle that Jesus Christ was not God, because he found "nowhere in the Bible the worship of Jesus Christ." To do so, he regarded as the wounding and blaspheming of God. When Socinus informed Blandrata of the result of their arguments, he admitted that although he was attached to the worship of Christ, he could not find a Biblical basis for it. The only discoverable reference was: "At the birth of Jesus the angels themselves sang."

Dávid depended to a very large degree on the Old Testament, quoting Jehovah, who, according to him, was "jealous and not inclined to share His glory. 'I am the Lord; that is my name, I will not give my glory to another' (Isaiah 42:8)." (Although it is true that at the time of the text, foreign gods were infiltrating Judaism and were competing with Jehovah, this would hardly apply to the time of the New Testament.) It is not surprising then that Socinus accused Dávid, in the midst of a bitter argument, of being an "eschatological Judaizer" when Dávid quoted from the Koran and the Talmud to support his arguments against the divinity of Jesus. Dávid retaliated that Christ could not even hear the pleas addressed to Him, because like the other prophets, He was dead.[75]

Later, in his prison cell Dávid modified his views "because you can nevertheless worship Christ, not as a born God, but on the basis of his mission."

Dávid soon understood why Socinus was living in his house, with Blandrata paying the expenses. For that reason, Dávid, foreseeing what might come, turned to Blandrata one day saying: "I cannot presume that you will be less merciless to me than Calvin was to Servetus."

In order to create a new forum for himself, (for Báthory, now king of Poland, had taken away his printing press), Dávid called together a Synod in Torda, although he was not empowered to do so. On his agenda he informed his fellow pastors, among other things, that "on inspiration from God we have examined the concept of the Trinity and concluded that it does not agree with the Word of God which we now can prove. We openly teach that the true God is not three persons in one, Father, Son, and Holy Ghost. We have been proclaiming this for a long time, and the word innovation cannot be applied to us."

His contemporaries agreed that Dávid had fallen deeply into the temptation of regarding his own affairs as the affairs of God. He declared his own enemies to be the enemies of God, in such an extreme interpretation of the truth excluding all objective understanding, and in the end making subjective the absolute nature of the Word itself. This could bring about religious anarchy, from cosmos to chaos, even though unintentionally.

The best known Unitarian of our time, Wilbur, writes:

> "By temperament, however, he seems to have been less interested in the organization and administration of churches than in further reforms of their doctrine."[76]

Blandrata soon realized that his former influence was on the wane and that if Dávid's followers accepted the new teaching at the announced Synod meeting, he would fall out of grace with everyone. As a counter-action, he gathered together a few of the more moderate Unitarian leaders and with their help was able to prevent the legal introduction of the *non adoramus* doctrine at the meeting in Torda in 1579. He managed also to have Dávid's evil spirit, Matthias Vehe-Glirius, the German humanist, expelled from the country, since apparently it was Glirius who had composed the thesis Blandrata wanted to impute to Dávid, namely: Jesus, son of Joseph, *ex eiusdem Josephi semine conceptus*, who was born of the seed of Joseph.[77]

Among the most moderate Unitarian leaders, who in the interest of church policy supported Blandrata, was Stephan Bazilius who explained in six points why he had turned away from Dávid:

1. Francis Dávid's complete rejection of the New Testament and his misinterpretation of it.
2. The abolition of redemption through the blood of Christ.
3. Repudiation of redemption built on Christ.
4. In the future there is no resurrection through Christ's mercy.
5. Abandoning of Christ's love deprives us of hope.
6. Dávid abolished Christ's seat at the right hand of God.[78]

He concluded: "Because of this nullification of our Christology, our Christian heritage is corrupted." He topped this off with a special and strongly worded accusation charging Dávid with propagating Mohammedanism. Finally, there was an attempt to send out a committee of ten to bring about unity. This did not bring peace.

Jealous for his future, Blandrata continued his campaign mercilessly and sent around among Unitarian leaders a circular letter of accusation, stressing sixteen points. In this letter he disclosed the theological formulas which were supposed to have come from Dávid. This very fact leads us to believe that they did not originate with Dávid but were formulated by Blandrata himself. The man who is best acquainted with church history of Dávid's age, Pirnát, gives this opinion: "The sixteen theses that were distributed by Blandrata as Dávid's own have to be read with great reservation."[79]

In this confused situation, the Catholic voivod ordered Dávid's arrest by the city council of Kolozsvár. Dávid mounted the pulpit nevertheless in defiance of the ruler's decree forbidding him to preach. In this, his last appearance in the pulpit, he upheld his principles, among them the concept of *non adoramus*, which was the most radical, and stressed that Christ was not to be worshipped.

Then on the advice of Blandrata, the voivod appointed Demetrius Hunyadi bishop of the Unitarians. He called together the Synod, and the majority of the participants repudiated Dávid's theological innovations, reestablishing the more moderate dogmas. We again can quote Pirnát's criticism in tracing the history of Dávid's fall. "The most radical of the Unitarian spokesmen in Transylvania were from foreign countries."[80] Nowhere else in Europe were there such religious extremes.

Soon after this, it became obvious that the movement did not have as wide a popular base as had been assumed in the propaganda.

Meanwhile, Dávid was struggling with ill health, and because he had temporarily lost his voice, his son-in-law, Trauzner, had to answer for him at the meeting of the Diet in Alba Julia (Gyulafehérvár). At this session the voivod himself was present, and the prosecuting attorney was regarded as a Unitarian. Blandrata summed up the charges against Dávid and emphasized how many times he had warned his erstwhile friend not to fall into excesses.

After discussions which lasted three days, the crown prosecutor read to Dávid the accusation and sentence:

> "You, Francis Dávid, following your own advice and without the agreement of the Church, have committed blasphemy by denying God.* Against the laws of the land, you have proclaimed innovations.
>
> His Majesty therefore punishes you in exemplary fashion and according to what you deserve; so as to discourage others from

---

*Author's comment: Dávid never denied the divinity of God.

similar innovations, you are to be held in prison until further notice."[81]

After the show-trial, everybody went home except Francis Dávid, who was locked up in Déva castle, and there, after an illness that lasted several months, he died in November 1579.

This trial was not at all as simple as the cold chronicle would have us believe. A court intrigue was in the background of Blandrata's maneuvers. A report found in the archives of the Vatican, written by the father-confessor, Leleszi, of the Voivod Báthory, gives some insight into it. The document, which had been gathering dust for centuries, contains data that cast a bad light on the leaders of the Roman Catholic Church, revealing the intrigues that were going on behind the scenes of the trial and, as already surmised, not essentially of religious origin, but chiefly political.* Against the ruler Stephan Báthory was Gáspár Békés who, supported by the Unitarians, set up a party which was pro-Turkish. This was what compromised Francis Dávid. At the same time he was surrounded by foreign immigrants who wanted to promote Mohammedanism in the interest of their own fantastic, world-wide, religious peace movement.

Leleszi described in detail how in conversation with the voivod they prepared the trial. He advised Báthory that a religious argument should not be allowed because one could never know what kind of result would come out of such a debate. Only one question should be raised: "Did Francis Dávid innovate or did he not?" Leleszi had organized the Catholic nobles and thus, with the backing of the German-Saxon Lutherans, he had been assured a majority against Dávid's people. Luther's followers in Transylvania had never forgiven Dávid for his desertion of their Church, and at this time they had a chance to get even, an outcome which Leleszi had counted on as certain.

His report included a list of those who voted for the condemnation of Dávid. When the Unitarian nobles came to vote, their perfidy was quite amazing. They were unanimous in declaring Dávid's theology a blasphemy of God. Only his second son-in-law, Lukas Trauzner, remained faithful to him and organized his defense. (Later he too returned to the Roman Catholic fold and occupied a high position.)

---

*See *Keresztény Magvető*, 77 *Évfolyam* 1–2 *Szám* p. 52. *Kolozsvár 1971.*

Leleszi dared to invoke God Himself to enter into his conniving manipulations. He even ended his report to the Pope with these words: "Praised be God and our Lord, the Father of Jesus Christ, who said there is no peace for the godless. That is why Blandrata, Dávid's erstwhile master, armed himself against Dávid as an enemy." One doubts that Leleszi showed this letter to Blandrata!

Dávid left behind him a religious and spiritual legacy which, because of its contradictions, continued to occupy the pages of church history for centuries. Great men generally influence posterity rather than their own generation.

Dávid faced his destiny with the knowledge that with his revision he completed the spiritual revolution of the sixteenth century and its Reformation. According to the view of a more balanced church history, Dávid did not work towards the coming age of Enlightenment, but rather backwards in the direction of Old Testament Judaism.

On the occasion of the 400th anniversary of Dávid's death, which was celebrated in Hungary in 1979, the historian of the radical Reformation, G. H. Willliams of Harvard University, eulogized the religious ideas of Dávid before the experts who had gathered there from around the world:

"Dávid was not really an innovator but the restorationist of Jewish Christianity . . . ."[82]

For those who still treasure the Judeo-Christian tradition, the above formula can have an appeasing effect and point to the end of bitter contradictions.

Blandrata's fight could have ended with Dávid's trial. But he who himself was once a heretic now entered his name in the history of Unitarianism as the persecutor of heretics. Among those who collaborated with him was the ominous General of the Jesuits, stationed in Vienna, who compared Blandrata's proceedings to those of Calvin, whom the badly informed still make exclusively responsible for the condemnation of Servetus.

It is apparent that the religious life of the sixteenth century was new because it placed the Bible in the forefront. Francis Dávid in his own way joined the new development because he wanted to make the Bible the central point in the lives of his people. He became the hero of a new confession, but not of the new paganism of the later Enlightenment which was a science of sophists. The man of the Enlightenment was, in a sense, only half a man, because the metaphysical instinct was lacking, as has been pointed out by one of Dávid's apologists, Lászlo Iván.

After the trial a great uncertainty overtook the Unitarians. Dávid's conviction sent fear into those of the Transylvanian *non adoramus* camp. According to Lech Szczucki, modern Polish church historian, many fled and took refuge among the like-minded as in Poland, others, Turcophile collaborators, fled to Turkish occupied territory.[83]

Footnotes

1. Kaminsky, Howard. A History of the Hussite Reformation. Berkeley University Press, California. 1967, p. 59.

2. Rican, Rudolf. *Das Reich Gottes in den Böhmischen Ländern*. Stuttgart, Evagelischer Verlag, p. 59.

3. Rican, Rudolf. *ibid.*, p. 60.

4. Rican, Rudolf. *ibid.*, p. 62.

5. Rican, Rudolf. *ibid.*, p. 124.

6. Prazek, Richard. *Madarska reformovana intelligence v ceskem obrazeni Magyar reformatus értelmiség a cseh nemzeti ébredésben*. Prague, 1962. Opera Univ. Purkynaianae Brunensis. Fak. Phil. Ser. 83

7. Szabo, Géza. A Hungarian Antitrinitarian poet and theologian, Miklos Bogáti Fazakas. Budapest, 1982. Studia Humanitatis. Vol. V, p. 230.

8. Székely, Sándor. *Unitárius vallástörténet*. Kolozsvár, 1839. p. 78.

9. Pirnát, Antal. *Der Antitrinitarischer Humanist Johann Sommer, etc. Eine Samlung von Materialen. Besorgt von J. Gruscher*. Berlin, 1962, vol. II, p. 50.

10. Church, F. C. The Italian Reformers, 1534–1564. New York, 1923. p. 263.

11. Magyar Református Adattár. Budapest, 1906. p. 150–151.

12. Dávid, Ferenc. *Dualysis scripti Stancari contra primum articulum Synodi Szekiensis*. Kolozsvár, 1555.

13. Dávid, Ferenc. *Apologia Adversus Maledicentiam at Calumnias Francisci Stancari*. Kolozsvár, 1557.

14. Sigler, M. *Adparatus ad Historiam Hung*. Decas. I. Mon. II. G. Haner: Hit. Ecc. p. 245–46.

15. Castellio, Sebestyen *Traite des heretiques* alias Bellius, M. Protestans. Szemle, 1915.

16. Pokoly, József. *Erdélyi Református egyház története.* Budapest, 1905. Vol. I, pp. 14, 117, 118.

17. Dávid, Ferenc. *Predikacioknak elsö része. Krisztus. ik predikacioja.* Kolozsvár.

18. Szabo, Géza. *Geschichte des Ungarischen Coetus (Bursa) an der Universität Wittenberg, 1555–1613.* Halle, 1941. Akademischer Verlag.

19. Iván, Lászlo. *Dávid Ferenc szellemi arca a szellemtudományi lélektan történetében,* Kolozsvár, 1936. Magvetö. p. 122.

20. Wilbur, E. H. A History of Unitarianism. Boston, 1945. Beacon Press, p. 45.

21. Newman, L. I. Jewish Influence in Christian Reform Movements. New York, 1966. AMS Press. pp. 577, 579.

22. Graetz, H. History of Jews. Philadelphia, 1894. Vol. IV. p. 541.

23. Dán, Robert. *Humanizmus, reformácio, Antitrinitárizmus és héber nyelv Magyarországon.* Budapest, 1973. Akadémia Kiadó, pp. 71 73.

24. Erasmus of Rotterdam. *Opus Epistolorum.* II. p. 491.

25. Newman, L. I. *op. cit.,* p. 595.

26. Melanchthon, Philip. *In Corpus reformatorum.* VIII. 520.

27. Lathomas, B. *De trium linguarum et studii theol. ratione dialogus.* Paris, 1519.

28. Borbély, István. *A Magyar unitárizmus története.* Kolozsvár, 1914. p. 43.

29. Iván, Lászlo. *op. cit.,* p. 31.

30. Dávid, Ferenc. *Az egy Atya Istennek és áldott szent Fiának* . . . . Kolozsvár, BB b.i.j.CC.

31. Dávid, Ferenc. *A prédikácioknak elsö része* . . . . Gyulafehervar, 1569. p. 23.

32. Possevino, Antonio *Judicium de Confessione* . . . . Posnaniae, 1586. p. 78–79.

33. Sommer, Johann. *Oratio funebris.* Budapest, Régi magyar könyvtar. Vol. II. art. 129.

34. Pirnát, Antal. *Die Ideologie der Siebenbürger Antitrinitarier in den 1570er Jahren.* Budapest, 1961. Akadémia Kiádo, p. 118.

35. Pirnát, Antal. *ibid.,* p. 37.

36. Wild, K. *Adam Neuser, oder Leben und Ende eines Lichtfreundes aus früherer Zeit.* Schaffhausen, 1878, 2er Auflage, p. 8.

37. Wild, K. *ibid.,* p. 31–33.

38. Pirnát, Antal. *op. cit.,* p. 126.

39. Melius Juhász, Péter. *Anti-thesis veri Turcici Christi.* Debrecen, 1568.

40. Bazilius, István. *Unitárius Egyháztörténete.* Kolozsvári példány. Vol. I. p. 253.

41. Possevino, Antonio. *Transylvania. 1584 Fontes Rerum Trans. Tomus III.* Budapest, 1913. Stephanum Kiádo, pp. 231, 251.

42. Teutsch, G. D. *Urkundenbuch der evangelische Landeskirche in Siebenbürgen.* Hermanstadt, 1862.
   "*Qui de Jesus Christo et de Spiritu Sancto ab ecclesia catholica dissentiunt, Mahometismum aut quemcuque atheismum volnetes inferre.*"

43. Pirnát, Antal. *op cit.,* p. 165.

44. Klaniczay, Tibor. *Reneszánc és Barokk.* Budapest, 1961. Szépirodalmi Kiadó. p. 115.

45. Mikó, Imre. *Erdély Történeti Adattár.* 1855. Vol. I. p. 337.

46. Istvánfius, Nicolaus. *Regni Hungarici Historia.* Colonniae, 1685. p. 337.

47. Pál, Ferenc. *Über die sozialen und religiösen Auseinandersetzungen in (Kolozsvár) Klausenburg.* Budapest, 1963. Studia Historia. Akadémia Kiadó. p. 313.

48. Szilágyi, Sándor. *Erdély Története. Vol. I. Nationalem Sinodeum Institutere.* Budapest, 1857.

49. Erdély Országgyűlési Emlékek, Vol. II. Budapest, 1877. p. 343.

50. Gyulafehérvár zsinat forrása, R.M.K. Vol. II. p. 117.

51. Dán, Robert. *op. cit.,* p. 80.

52. Dávid, Ferenc. *Antitheses Doctrinae Ministrorum Christi Crucifixi.* Egyháztörténeti Emlékek, XXI.

53. Dávid, Ferenc. *Három személyü Isten Leirása.* Egyháztörténeti Emlékek II. Dávid Irodalma. XXIII.

54. Maior, Georg. *De Uno et Tribus Personis Divinitatis.* Wittenberg, 1569.

55. Maior, Georg. *Commone factio ad Ecclesiam Catholicam orthodoxam ... contra Blandratum.* Wittenberg, 1569. also in Herzog, Hauch, Realencyklopedie III.

368 The Hungarian Protestant Reformation . . .

56. Jakab Elek. *Dávid Ferenc Emléke*, Budapest, 1879. Egyetemi Nyomda Történet. p. 1331.

57. Dávid & Bazilius. *Refutatio scripti Gregorii Maioris*. RMK II, p. 121.

58. Heltai, Gáspár. *Disputatio in causa sacrosanctae Trinitatis*. Kolozsvár, 1568.

59. Mátrai, Lászlo. *Régi magyar filozofusok XV-XVII századokban*. Budapest, 1961. Vol. VIII, p. 16.

60. Schesaeus, K. in G. D. Teutsch: *Urkundenbuch*. Vol. II. p. 241.

61. Zoványi, Jenö. *A magyarországi protestántizmus 1569-tol 1600 ig*. Budapest, 1977. Akadémia Kiadó. pp. 39,40.

62. Possevino, Antonio. *op. cit.*, p. 231.

63. Jakab, Elek. *Egyháztörténeti Emlékek*. Vol. II. XVII. GIV. G. pp. 2, 3.

64. Jakab, Elek. *ibid.*, p. 148.

65. Lampe, F.A.-Ember, Pál Debreceni. *Confessio heareticis*. *In Historia ecclesiae reformatae in Hungaria et Transylvania*. Trajecti ad Rhenum (Utrecht) 1728. p. 267.

66. Jakab, Elek. *op. cit.*, p. 147.

67. Pokoly, József. *Erdélyi Református Egyház Története*. Vol. I. p. 234.

68. Haner, Georg. *Historia ecclesianm Transylvani carum*. Frankfurt/Leipzig. 1694. ed. Friedrich A. Lampe. in Historia Ecclesiae Reformatae in Hungaria et Transylvania. Trajecti ad Rhenum (Utrecht) 1728. p. 295.

69. *Erdély Országgyülesi Emlékek*, Vol. II. p. 526.

70. *ibid.*, p. 528

71. Dávid, Ferenc. Letter known as Filptch letter. Anno 1566. 20 Januarii. *"coepit Fr. Davidis primum dogma Trinitatis negare, eidem que contradicere."* published by Lajos Kelemen in Kolozsvár.

72. Sommer, Johann. *Refutatio Petri Carolii editii Wittenbergae Scripta a Johanne Sommero Pirnensi; Rectore Scholae, Claudiopolitanae Transylvania*. Ingolstadii. Postmortem, 1582.

73. Socinus, Faustus. *Opera Omnia. Bibliotheca Fratrum Polonorum, Amsterdam ab anno. 1566–92*. Vol. II. see Disputatio-Refutatio.

74. Egyház történeti Emlékek. Vol. II, D. F. Irodalmi emlékek. XLI.

75. William, G. H. Antitrinitarianism in the second half of the 16th century. Budapest, 1982. Akademia Kiadó. p. 302.

76. Wilbur, Earl M. History of Unitarianism. Boston, Beacon Press, 1969. p. 63.

77. Pirnát, Antal. *op. cit.*, p. 178.

78. Pirnát, Antal. *ibid.*, p. 183.

79. Pirnát, Antal. *ibid.*, p. 178.

80. Pirnát, Antal. *ibid.*, p. 180.

81. *Magyar Történeti Emlékek*, Budapest. 1860. Vol. III. pp. 22–29. also: *Documenta Romana Historiae Societatis Jesu in regnis elim corona Hungarica unitis.* Romae, 1965. Vol. II, pp. 353–357. ed. Lukácz Lászlo és Polgár Lászlo.

82. Williams, G. H. *op. cit.*, p. 321.

83. Szczucki, Lech. *Két XVI századi eretnek gondolkozó.* Budapest, 1980. Akadémia Kiadó. p. 49.

Chapter XX

Foreign Literary Elements in Dávid's Theological Writings

In the foregoing, Ferenc Dávid's personal struggles and his relationships to foreign theological visitors have been discussed. The focus, although it be sketchy, now is on Dávid's literary works. It is quite impossible to review in logical order his many writings. Growing foreign influences on Dávid as well as his many adoptions from a variety of theological works will demand much attention from interested readers.

This author has documented how Hungary did become a kind of promised land for the European Antitrinitarian radicals in the sixteenth century. These sectarian immigrants did not recognize the religious dogmas of any established Church. It is obvious to assume that Dávid was deeply influenced by several of these foreigners when he formulated his views and so came to stimulate the emergence of the Unitarian movement.

Parallel with the disputes in which he was engaged, Dávid also published literary works which presented his constantly changing intellectual map. Such an intellectual change could be observed for instance when Dávid challenged the notorious dialectician, Francesco Stancaro. One should remember that when Dávid confronted Stancaro for the first time, he was still a Lutheran priest. Dávid's first writing, *Dialysis scripti Stancari contra primum articulum synodi Szekensis*, published in 1555 in Kolozsvár, was the result of his first dispute with Stancaro. Dávid's second confrontation with Stancaro resulted in *Apologia adversus maledicentiam et calumnias Francisco Stancari*, which also was published in Kolozsvár, in 1558, when Dávid was Lutheran bishop.

The essence of these bitter disputes was the question of Christ's redemptive work: Was it in his human or in his divine nature that he was the Mediator? Stancaro insisted that Christ could mediate only in his human capacity, because in his divine nature he could not appeal to One with whom he was equal; only subordinates could.

When Dávid accepted the more progressive Helvetic ideology, in a short time he was able to formulate a new theological outlook. In *Defensio orthodoxae sententiae de coena Domini*, which was published in Kolozsvár in 1559, he joined with Bishop Melius to defend the most controversial theology of the Lord's Supper under the heading: *Simple Christian Teaching of the Lord's Supper*, (*Az Urnak vacsorájáról való közönséges keresztyéni tanitás*). It was also Dávid's first *Confession*, based upon the teachings of Bullinger and Calvin, which he published in the German language also. With the same eagerness he published Beza's *Confessio* under the title *Compendium doctrinae christianae* in 1563 in Kolozsvár. A year later, in 1564, the Helvetic religion was declared lawful with the help of Melius, Dávid, and Blandrata, at the Synod of Torda.

How quickly Dávid could adapt himself to other religious views showed in the jointly (with Melius) formulated *Cathechism* of 1566. In this *Cathechism* Dávid was already leaning toward the oblique direction of "God is One." He intended to get rid of all theological phraseology formulated by Hellenistic philosophy like *trinitas, persona, essentia*, etc. His argument was simple: These terms were not to be found in the Scriptures, and therefore he insisted upon eliminating them all from Reformed theology. In reality, Dávid pointed toward his other notion Tritheism. Tritheism obviously was not identical with the concept of Trinity, and it easily could melt into Antitrinitarianism. This tactical phase, used by Dávid and behind him by Blandrata, was soon recognized by Melius, who then refused this kind of cooperation with Dávid, even though at this time Dávid still appeared loyal and stated that in the Trinity the Holy Spirit was equal to the Father and the Son.[1] A year later Dávid openly denied the divinity of Christ. Then, under Blandrata's tutorship commenced Dávid's acceptance of Servetus' ideology as can be seen in his further theological developments. In 1567 Dávid published a new book, *Refutatio scripti Petri Melii, quo nomine synodi Debrecinae docet Jehovalitatem et Trinitarium Deum . . . .*, which appeared in Gyulafehérvár, in which he presented his changed

Christological views and fervently dismissed any orthodox dogmas which only recently he had defended with the same vigor.

The introduction of his new exegetical method, called Biblical criticism, was another innovation intended to replace scholastic Biblical dogmatism. The *Refutatio* also contained his modified *Credo* in which he gainsayed Christ's preexistence and who now was declared to be only the adopted son of God. It is interesting to note Dávid's short memory: Only a few years earlier he had denounced Stancaro and had called him a Jewish doctor who dissolved the unity of the Trinity. Now he attacked Stancaro from another side, because Stancaro still partially held onto the Trinitarian tradition.[2]

In his new position as bishop, Dávid advocated the absolute freedom of religious inquiry, which was recently granted by the Synod of Torda. In the famous declaration, unparalleled in the history of creedal freedom, limitless liberty in confessional matters was proclaimed. As it later turned out, religious anarchy soon established itself in Transylvania, which was unanimously condemned by Western theologians. Dávid's *Creed* was directed toward simple laymen, and he with pride declared his *Credo* equal to the Bible. Later it became clear that Dávid had translated this *Credo* from Laelius Socinus' book, *Brevis explicatio in primus Joannis caput*, and had given it a new title, *Confessio vera de Triade Ecclesia Dei in Transylvania consentientium*. Dávid had ended his translation with the advice that in the realm of faith one should not fight with the sword of the authorities but with divine truth. It took many years before this advice could be realized.

In general, all Dávid's writings created controversy due to his constant ideological innovations. Temporarily Dávid defended his publications with a new theological orientation, but very soon he would abandon his previous writings for another viewpoint.

Unitarianism, inaugurated by Dávid, had a special tradition, namely no Synod ever adopted officially Dávid's theological ideas and dogmas. As a theological gladiator Dávid superseded his contemporary rivals; it was his own failure, however, that he did not stop his disputations to issue a final theological *loci communes* as Melanchthon had done. Dávid did not have the peace or the time to formulate his constantly changing dogmas into a system. Was it because he wrote under the pressure of circumstances, or was it possible that he had no basic convictions to stand by?

According to Béla Varga, contemporary apologist of Dávid, "Throughout his lifetime, Dávid did nothing but dispute . . . . It was true for him that the search itself was more important than the findings . . . ., His theology was never finished, as had happened to other reformers. Even when he formulated a final statement it was possible for him to change it quickly afterward."[3]

The main part of Dávid's literary work was issued during his Unitarian period. His was a remarkably productive theological literature. In 1568 he published several books, explaining his new orientation, among them *De falsa et vera unius Dei Patris, Filii et Spiritum Sancti cognitione libri duo*, which contained many studies by Hungarian, Polish, and Italian authors. The main ideological line pointed toward revisions of traditional Christology, that is open Antitrinitarian tendencies, proposed by Erasmus and Servetus. The sectarian excesses were obvious. The foreign authors claimed that only the Arian-Antitrinitarian Biblical exegesis was valid.

Dávid published also in the Hungarian language a study, *Rövid Magyarázat, (Short Explanation)*, which basically was a transposition of one of Servetus' writings. Dávid narrated the development of Trinitarian dogmatism as had been propounded by Servetus and Socinus. He treated with great sympathy the struggles of Arian sectarians in 325 A.D. with Bishop Athanasius, who defended the official Christology. Among those Church Fathers, Dávid did not spare St. Augustine, "because he mixed up heaven with earth"; he also accused him of frequently changing his theological views. Dávid's dialectics are of interest here, because he himself followed this example of St. Augustine. He accepted without criticism the misguided explanation of Servetus concerning Mohammed's turning away from Christianity, allegedly because of the Trinitarian teaching of the Church Fathers. It would be interesting to know whether Servetus also explained why Mohammed turned away from early Judaism also, where the only God, Jehovah, was worshipped.

It was in the *Short Explanation* that Dávid explained his own chiliastic statement. How had he reached this conclusion? Contrary to the more cautious dating of Servetus, Dávid definitely assigned the year 1570 as the year of the fulfillment of the Parousia. The humanist vision of the golden age, the *aurum seculum*, obviously had made an impact on Dávid, who also was inspired by Martin Cellarius, another millenarian prophet. One may note the historical return of the Parousia expectation among those sectarians who lost their role in the established society in that age and therefore escaped to an unrealistic utopian world. At this point Dávid and his pupils almost waited at the gate of the Promised Land of Canaan for it to be opened for them.

In neighboring Poland, the Anabaptists, like Dávid, organized themselves into a New Jerusalem, imitating the Moravian Brethren, and established themselves waiting for the last days. After two years of idling, the Polish Anabaptists ended their unrealistic flight from the world.

Dávid's reasoning went like this: The End Time is near because, first, Luther has already partially reformed Christianity; second, Calvin has purified the false Roman Catholic dogma of the Lord's Supper; and third, when we shall have abolished the concept of the Trinity, in which process of purification Christ will defeat the Anti-Christ, the Parousia will be at hand.

By what exegesis did Dávid verify this interpretation? When a particular Bible text did not yield the prophesy he required, he just omitted the locus saying that it had to be interpreted only symbolically. The *Short Explanation* contained furthermore the Lord's Prayer and the Creed; all other liturgical doctrines were omitted.

In his next publication, *Demonstratio falsitatis doctrinae Petri Melii*, Dávid turned against his former co-reformer, Bishop Melius. In this book Dávid still refused any Mohammedan sympathy or Turcophile involvement, although it was public knowledge that many foreigners with Paduan-Turcophile sympathies were among his closest friends. Several of them openly praised the alleged Turkish tolerance and later emigrated to the sultan's empire. Dávid denied that he himself had Turkish associations and tried to find a way to disaffiliate himself from these friends, and in a way acted again as before, when he had been accused of propagating Servetus' teachings, by calling the accusation of his Turcophile sympathies a slanderous lie. The latest philological identification, however, has proved the validity of the allegations. Was it fear and memory of Servetus' fate that forced Dávid to behave in this manner? This vacillation was the most vulnerable part of Dávid's apolitical position, because the Islamic Turks, obeying Koranic law, had for centuries attempted to destroy Hungarian Christianity.

Later another threat came up when Dávid was blamed for his innovations. In order to defend himself against the charges, he appealed to earlier theological authors as John Gerson (1429) and Martin Cellarius (1564), who allegedly had held similar principles.

Naturally, the Protestant church leaders in the West were alarmed by this religious radicalism in Hungary. Reform leaders in Switzerland and Wittenberg expressed their disapproval in a large number of publications. Among them was Georg Maior in Wittenberg, who attacked Dávid's excessive criticism and theological distortions. Dávid rebuked Maior in good dialectical phraseology, and in a temperate reply suggested that he remain silent. In his book *Refutatio scripti Georgii Maiores* Dávid continued his rebuke and denounced not only Maior but all Church Fathers and the Synodical resolutions as well, and he forsook the pre-Constantine teachings of Christianity. In the end, Dávid lost once again his tolerance and accused Maior of a low standard of dialogue and wished him to hell . . . . In the same year, 1569, Maior published a second book, *Commone factio ad Ecclesiam Catholicam orthodoxam . . . contra Blandratum* in which he asked all Protestant church leaders to eliminate all of Dávid's heresy from the earth.[4]

The never-wearied Dávid continued to write and discuss the true meaning of the Word. With moderation he explained the relationship between the Old and the New Testament and concluded that the Old Testament could not be understood as long as it was not interpreted from Christ's point of view. He also adopted another unorthodox idea of creation according to which there were two creations: the first one, revealed through Moses, and the second one, revealed by Christ. The first one was visible, the second one was spiritual, inward and metaphysically oriented. Although Christ could never have created *ex nihilo*, he still ruled over heaven and earth. To this explanation Dávid added: "If you do not understand it, just believe it."

This speculation of Dávid's was rooted in the writings of Laelius Socinus, who had stressed that the first creation took place before Christ's arrival, and hence Christ could only be involved in spiritual matters. Laelius Socinus had also explained Christ's nature in this manner; Because He was conceived of the Holy Spirit and born of Mary, he could be human only, and therefore the second person of the Trinity was a mortal being.

Basically, Dávid's Biblicism and his new exegetical method formed the foundation of his innovative theology. He used specific quotations from the

Bible to prove and justify his theological declarations. He frequently inter-
changed the doctrines of Servetus and Socinus. A few years earlier Dávid
had still agreed with Servetus when he had declared, "Even now I say: if
somebody denies the divinity of Christ, let him be cursed." In this later
development, however, Dávid concluded: "Out of Jesus, God's human son,
theologians have carved a divine God."[5]

When Dávid exhausted all his own arguments, he simply turned to
foreign sources and borrowed heavily. In his time this kind of borrowing
was characterized in Hungary as "plowing too much with someone else's
oxen." And yet, Dávid solemnly vowed that he never used another person's
writings as his own. "I relied upon the righteous and revenging Jehovah as
well as upon my word and I did not borrow either from the Koran, nor
from Servetus; I learned it from the Gospel of the living God, and I taught
it constantly."[6]

The two publications, *De Regno Christi* and *De Regno Antichristi et eius
mysteris*, both of 1569, illustrate how often Dávid did borrow from foreign
authors. The original author of both was nobody else than the Spanish
humanist Servetus, whose theological writings were a combination of
Hebrew and Aristotelian-Arab ideologies in behalf of the re-reform of
Christianity which he regarded as outdated. The title of Servetus' work was
Restitutio Christianismi . . . . It was from this work that Dávid rearranged
and published about 280 pages of the 350 page original script. When
Servetus depended on Hebrew and Islam God concepts because of the
influence of the Marranos, he logically refused the doctrine of the Holy
Trinity. He also had made ample use of Hebrew exegeses. From Antitrinitarian literature, it is obvious that the Hebrew language never played
so important a role in Christian theological controversies as in the Sixteenth
Century Reformation. This observation has been stressed by the well-
known historians L. J. Newman, G. H. Williams, and Robert Dán. It is
noteworthy that German church historians, who dominated the field for a
long time, have neglected to see this fact, maybe because of Luther's
unfortunate attitude against Hebrew scholars. It has been proved that the
whole Antitrinitarian ideology, from Servetus onward, has been rooted in
post-Biblical rabbinical writings, mainly of the Marranos.

When Dávid selected from Servetus' *Restitutio* certain parts, he omitted
some too radical concepts, and he reformulated others according to his own
current dogmatic considerations. He was quite selective and kept his intel-

lectual independence. In some parts, however, he was not able to harmonize his own ideas with those of the original *Restitutio*, and thus it was unavoidable that he could not escape from contradictions. Basically, he did agree with Servetus' teaching that God is One and that Jesus was a human only.

In the question of baptism, Dávid kept his options open when he accepted the teaching of John the Baptist; however, he also granted freedom of choice in the forms and timing of baptism. Later he drastically changed his position as we will see.

Dávid also accepted from Servetus the priority of love over against faith, and good works were seen as more important than the *Sola fides* concept of Luther (Romans 3:28). Like Servetus, Dávid relied exclusively upon reason when it came to Biblical interpretation: "Only reason leads to eternal truth" and "A man must be his own redeemer". Critics naturally asked Dávid: If man by nature inclines to goodness, why does he need to be saved? Apparently, Dávid indeed identified with Mohammed, who had declared that the gracious Allah abolished sin when He forgave Adam.

In his borrowing of the *Restitutio*, Dávid also incorporated some ethical questions to which he had not paid much attention before. He gave a role to Christ, saying that the Father transferred some power to His adopted son, to rule on earth as well as in heaven. Dávid also incorporated some teachings of Laelius Socinus in his concepts, but when he proclaimed his chiliastic prognosis, Dávid relied on Servetus rather than on Socinus, as has been shown in the elaboration on the *Short Explanation*.

The most controversial theological topic during the sixteenth century was the meaning of the sacrament of Holy Communion. Dávid was for a time not ready either to take a definite position. Historians have called the decade in which Dávid struggled with the formulation of his dogma the decade of his theological radicalism. He validated Christ's teachings only when they fitted into the utterances of the Old Testament. For him the Mosaic law still remained dominant in spite of the New Revelation, and so Dávid concluded that Christ was unable to save anyone who did not hold on to the Old Testament traditions. In 1571 he formulated his final stand on Holy Communion. In his booklet *Az Ő magától való feleséges Istenről*, published in that year in Kolozsvár, he declared "Christ does no longer dwell in the bread", and from then on he omitted the sacrament from the worship service.

In his view on baptism, Dávid still insisted on the necessity of faith, and hence he only recognized adult baptism. His simple argument was that Jesus himself had been baptized when he was thirty years old, and that Abraham was one hundred years old when he was circumcized. For Dávid it did not matter whether one was baptized or not.

In the intellectual history of Dávid began a new epoch with the arrival of his son-in-law Johann Sommer, who was among the German-Arian refugee immigrants who settled down in Hungary. Sommer was first appointed as preacher to the German-Saxons in Kolozsvár, and later became a teacher at the Unitarian College there. Sommer had a very creative mind, and he became a prolific writer. His first literary effort was the translation of a pamphlet by the former Italian humanist and escaped Catholic priest, Jacob Acontius. The pamphlet, *Satanae Strategema*, had been published in Basel in 1565, and when Acontius had settled in England, he had dedicated it to Queen Elizabeth I. The central problem discussed was an eternal theological question: What was the source of Satan? Acontius had stated that man by nature was the source and so indirectly was the Creator himself. The only remedy for eliminating satanic influence would be, according to Acontius, to abolish all religious controversies and disputes, to abolish all religious dogmas, and a born-in tolerance would result. His conclusion was that the Protestant Reformation as well as Roman Catholicism had become bankrupt, and that human immorality would never be lessened by any religion. (In retrospect it seems naive and ironic that Acontius dedicated this pamphlet to Queen Elizabeth I who, as head of the Anglican Church, treated her bishops so cruelly, that she had them beheaded, burned, imprisoned, or exiled, to the extent that hardly any bishops were left in England.)

The sceptic Acontius had warned against any religious controversy and disputes because he wondered who possessed the truth, *Quid est veritas*? The obvious result of his propositions would be that doubt would become the measuring-stick of intellectual endeavor; that no one would be able to believe in an absolute truth. Another aspect of his proposition would be not to judge, which logically would lead to moral indifference, even more so because absolute truth would be impossible and each man's opinion would be free from restrictions; Acontius assumed that this would result in the abolition of agnostic disputes, because he had based his reasoning on the second chapter of the Acts of the Apostles in which the congregation together made decisions and not a theologian or the clergy. He called such forums *communis prophetia*.

It was on Sommer's suggestion that Dávid commenced to introduce a similar forum to proclaim his more radical utterances. Contrary to the practice suggested by Acontius, it was, however, the clergy and not the laymen who used the forum to legalize their innovations, so that instead of the expected forbearance and indifference, the assembly produced the most controversial disputes.

Dávid's last abominable attack against Christology was the *non adoramus* doctrine, in which he refused to direct prayers to Jesus Christ. This extraordinary innovation was condemned even by Faustus Socinus as "a very wicked and detestable view that Christ should not be adored or involved in prayer."[7]

With the *communis prophetia* and his *non adoramus* practice began Dávid's downfall.

Another contribution which Sommer made to Dávid was his introduction of a rational exegetical method; the scholastic exegetical procedure was always the result of theological consideration, and now Sommer and Dávid reversed this practice and the exegetical result determined the future nature of Dávid's theology. In connection with this critical exegesis, Sommer wanted to prove that the Trinitarian dogmas by origin belonged to pre-Christian time; they existed in the third century before Christ in the Hellenistic cosmology, and later two Church Fathers, Origenes and Clement of Alexandria, had, according to Sommer, interwoven the Hellenistic elements into the Trinitarian dogmas.

In the beginning Dávid refused to accept this Sommerian explanation and he called his son-in-law a troublemaker of the Church, *turbator ecclesiae*. When the Synod finally brought an end to Sommer's attack, the latter, in order to divert attention, began to select carefully a topic like predestination, and denouncing it he pleased the Catholic king, the Jesuits, and the Lutheran clergy. The influential roles played by Servetus and Faustus Socinus diminished when Sommer and later the Greek Palaeologus began their dominating influence on Dávid and led him to post-Biblical rabbinical sources. That period has been characterized by Robert Dán, Hungarian Hebraist, who has clarified several Antitrinitarian problems, as follows: In 1577 the Transylvanian Unitarians had already left behind themselves the primary problem of *unitas* and *trinitas* and had developed new religious theories, built upon a thesis of the Hebraist Albo. Sommer just reaffirmed Albo's thesis that "man's God concept must agree with reason."[8]

After the death of Sommer and his family in an epidemic in 1574, his former influence was soon taken over by Palaeologus, the most notorious imposter of the century, who soon guided Dávid even further on his seemingly endless road to Damascus. Slowly more and more negative elements made their way into Unitarian religious history.

Another successor of Sommer was the Hebraist Matthias Vehe-Glirius, who was for a time a houseguest of Dávid. Faustus Socinus had introduced him to Dávid as the "Jewish doctor", and he very soon became another teacher of the always open-for-new-ideas Dávid. The immigrant in hiding, Vehe-Glirius, translated Albo's *Ikkarion* in 1577, and he concluded that not only the concept of Trinity but also the idea of predestination was nonsensical, illogical, and contrary to human reason. In the same vein Christ's messianic role was seen as an absurd illusion and original sin was pronounced to be an aberration. The foreign immigrants, by and by, brought all kinds of radical and sometimes bizarre literature into Hungarian ecclesiastical territory. Robert Dán recently located in a library in the Netherlands, a long-lost document written by Vehe-Glirius, titled *Mattanjah*, and published it in Budapest. Vehe-Glirius had escaped from Germany where he had been persecuted for his radical teachings, and now continued his colorful pilgrimage under several pseudo names. His biographer characterized him as a "scandalous Arian and follower of Servetus". Among other aberrations, Vehe-Glirius declared that the New Testament could not be a new Covenant between God and man. Maybe Jesus could be the Messiah, but he could not be divine, and hence he did not deserve any prayers, and it would be absolute nonsense to treat him as One who had pre-existed. Vehe-Glirius easily convinced Dávid of the exclusiveness of the Old Testament, and of the fact that the writings of the Apostles were only valid as long as they agreed with Mosaic teachings. He regarded baptism as an illogical act because original sin did not exist. That the Old Testament remained valid was due to the fact that Jesus had failed as Messiah, and that therefore the New Testament lost its validity. Vehe-Glirius agreed with Albo in his denial of God's omnipotence; at the same time, however, he declared that only those people would be resurrected who kept the Mosaic law, that is, exclusively the people of the Old Testament. No wonder that his contemporaries called him "Jewish doctor."[9]

The more balanced Hungarian Christian citizens were shocked when day after day these heretics offended the century-old church traditions, and abolished all sacraments, which opened the way for Turkish Mohammedanism. During Vehe-Glirius' stay in Dávid's house, Dávid more openly proclaimed his *non adoramus* concept, and this resulted in the expulsion of Vehe-Glirius from Transylvania. The city council of Kolozsvár accused him of misleading the Unitarian theologian Dávid. After his expulsion, Vehe-Glirius returned to Poland in 1579 where under another alias he continued his colorful propaganda.

After his departure Dávid once again revised his *Credo* and introduced it at the next controversial Synod of Torda in 1579. He stated that: "With the help of God we have rebuked the validity of the concept of Trinity, and we have proved that this concept does not agree with His own words." The central theme at the Synod became naturally the *non adoramus* of Christ. Dávid's argument was, "Because the omnipresent Jehovah sees and hears everything, there is no longer need for an Advocate Mediator."

During the Reformation the Gospel had brought an end to the religion of the Mosaic law, and Dávid now attempted to expel all orthodox dogmas in his Unitarian crusade. He definitely misunderstood the ecclesiastical significance of these dogmas. During the period in which Christianity had established the Church, the latter had been attacked and had been forced to formulate her dogmas in self-defense. In that early period, the rabbinical persecution of Christians had forced St. Paul to make dogmatic assessments, and later the Roman and early agnostic Christian controversies had demanded an awareness of Christological definitions. The history of dogma-development can be illustrated in a nutshell by narration of the formulation of the Apostles' Creed. During the second and third centuries the Trinitarian elements were formulated by the Church Fathers. During the Gallian period the content of the Creed was clarified, but, when the Church was extended, more sectarian theological questions were raised which needed explanations. For instance:

1. To explain the essence of the Father, the elucidation "creator of heaven and earth" was added as defense against the dualistic teaching of the Manichaeans.

2. The clarification "his only begotten Son" was necessary because the Sabellians decreed that Jesus was born in time and not in eternity.

3. The addition "conceived of the Holy Spirit" was necessary to rebuke Abonite teaching.

4. "He suffered" was added because docetism regarded Christ's divinity made it impossible for Him to suffer.

5. The additions, "he died, descended into hell", "catholic", "almighty" were all needed to counteract the confusions created by gnostics.

Among the dangerous attacks, the Antitrinitarian, (Unitarian), sectarian subversion was most challenging, because it involved rabbinical as well as Islamic theological assertions.

One more source should perhaps be added to illustrate Dávid's debts to Hebrew authors, namely that of Jichak ben Avraham Troky (1533–1594). Although Dávid attempted to reconcile Troky's radical ideas with the more moderate teachings of Christian reformers, unfortunately he failed. Melius, the guardian of a more balanced Reformation, had time and again exposed Dávid's theological sources, and it was he who pointed to Troky's work *Strengthening of Faith* which Dávid had translated and published in 1571 under another title: *Az Ő egy magától való felséges Jehováról és az ö igaz fiárol*. Troky had written "Even human reason proves that the true God is One, in whom we believe, and it refuses any multiplication of the Divine. This is true even when there are those who believe that One equals Three, and Three equals One. Such faith is a lie, and it contradicts human reason; therefore Three can never be One, because Jesus is only the son of man and not of God."[10]

It is possible that Paruta told Dávid about this argument called *"rabbinorum sententia"*.

Dávid the unbelieving believer came under several more similar influences and headed toward an intellectual crisis. Contrary to all human efforts, Dávid failed to organize his Church with a solid doctrine, and when he was eliminated from the Unitarian realm, an age of epigones followed and compromise became a virtue. Even today Dávid's successors, the Unitarian-Universalists, rebuke his tradition and propose to delete the name of God the Father from its founding statement of principles. After the first discriminating step in the sixteenth century was made to eliminate the divinity of Christ, the next logical step is to ask whether there is a God anywhere.

A brief discussion of Dávid's selected sermons, published in 1569 under the title *The First Part of the Holy Scripture*, which still reflect his more moderate theological views, close this arduous presentation. In sixty sermons Dávid preached about God, the Father, the promised Messiah, and the Holy Spirit. With his genius spirit, he became the father-preacher not only of his own congregation, but also of the whole denomination. With his intellectual richness, he could mobilize his own generation, and when he succeeded in renovating his followers spiritually, he kept them under his control. In the dim-lighted Gothic cathedral, his pale face became radiant when he pronounced his convictions from the pulpit.

Dávid's spoken and written sermons were highly controversial, yet at that time he still formulated his message on the basis of Scripture only. Some of his sermons concerned the abolishment of dogmatic theological controversies from the inherited traditional church life. Since his main pastoral goal was to refute the "erroneous doctrines", all the Roman Catholics and Lutherans were blamed. As preacher, Dávid assumed, as it were, a role like Elijah's, and his pulpit became Mount Carmel where he declared judgment between Jehovah and the new priests of Baal. When rational enlightenment became involved in his sermons, the result was that the mystical union with Christ, which should be the basis of his sermons, was lost.

The construction of his sermons was simple and lucid in order to reach out toward the uneducated laymen. With one eye held toward the ruling and supporting classes, he also included now and then in his sermons the suggestion that it would be advantageous for society if the lower classes were religious, because they would sooner abide with secular law.

In contradiction to his later teachings, Dávid still stressed that only by faith and not by good works salvation could be received. He also proclaimed a degree of free choice concerning belief, because God had not closed himself into a tiny catechism.

In conclusion: On his final etappe to Damascus, Dávid reached the following conclusions:

1. God is One.
2. Christ is human, in consequence praying to him is in vain.
3. The concept of Trinity is of Hellenistic origin and unbiblical.
4. The Lord's Supper as a sacrament is no longer valid because "we took Christ's presence out of the bread."

5. Baptism is no longer necessary because God has forgiven all sins via Adam.

6. Love and good works are more important than faith to obtain salvation.

7. By nature man is good and able to work out his own salvation.

In one thing Dávid remained constant: he was faithful to St. Paul's advice to the Thessalonians, Test everything, *Omnia probate.*

Footnotes

1. Wotschke, Theodore. *Zur Geschichte des Antitrinitarianismus.* In: *Archiv für Religionsgeschichte,* Jhrg. 1926, Band XXIII, p. 88.

2. Zoványi, Jenö. *Magyarországi protestántizmus 1565–1600.* Akadémia Kiadó, Budapest, 1977. p. 19.

3. Varga, Béla. *Dávid Ferenc és az Unitárius vallás.* Budapest, 1979. p. 16.

4. Herzog, Hauck. *Realencyklopedie, III.* ed. on Dávid.

5. Dávid, Ferenc. *De dualite, tractatus az az értekezés a Kettös istenségröl.*

6. Dávid, Ference. *Az Ő magától való felséges Istenröl.* Letter A. Kolozsvár, 1571.

7. Socinus, Faustus. *Opera Omnia.* In: *Bibliotheca Fratrum Polonorum,* Vol. II, p. 359. Posthumous edition, 1656, Irenopoli.

8. Dán, Robert. *Humánizmus, reformáció, Antitrinitáriánizmus és a héber nyelv Magyarországon.* Budapest, Akadémia Kiadó, pp. 80, 82.

9. Pirnát, Antal. *Die Ideologie der Siebenbürger Antitrinitarier in den 1570 er Jahren.* Budapest, 1961. Akadémia Kiadó, p. 23.

10. Dán, Robert. *op. cit.,* p. 117.

Chapter XXI

Synopsis of Pax Transylvania

The careful reader may have observed that the Hungarian Reformed Church was a Cross-bearing Church from its very beginning. First, the Ottoman Islam attempted to dissolve her as a Christian organization. Second, later Habsburg Catholicism, with the help of German and Spanish armies, undertook to eliminate the reforming Church of Christ. It was under sufferings such as these that the Hungarian Reformed Church, as the only Reformed Church in East Central Europe, was built up. Until the present time she remains the second largest Reformed Church in Europe even though her congregations since World War I are dispersed in Czechoslovakia, Rumania, Yugoslavia, and Austria.

After the Roman and Lutheran Confessions, the sixteenth century Hungarian Reformation completed with the third Confession, that is HelveticCalvinist, the "Second Reformation" as it is called. Thus, the Hungarians realized the revolution which Luther had inaugurated but had not been able to bring to completion. It has been pointed out that the Wittenberg Reformers delimitated their innovations to the Teutonic realm and even declared that the Geneva Confession appeared to be worse than the papacy. Herings stated that many Lutherans seriously discussed as thesis that it would be better to be Papist than Calvinist.[1]

The "Second Reformation" was proof of the creativeness of the reformers in East Central Europe who built upon the principle of *semper reformanda* in a unique historical situation. That principle, however, was more than sheer religious dogmatism; it rather meant a collective transformation of life which included a new socio-economic dimension. One can characterize those reformers as eclectic, irenic theologians, working far removed from Wittenberg and Geneva, freeing themselves from exclusive dogmatism. The distance had a calming effect and so they were able to build a Reformed Church in which they tried to integrate the atomized society and divided nation through the authority of the Gospel.

As reforming elite they represented for the first time in the existence of Hungarian Christianity a new social consciousness. They not only incorporated into the life of the struggling nation the neglected lower classes which had played no part until then, but also succeeded in formulating a defensive ideology with profound religio-ethical content. As once the Hebrew elite in Babylonian captivity had done, now the pastors, as a new elite, assumed the leadership which formerly had belonged to the nobility who had perished during the century-long battles. Parallel with this religio-ethical ideology, these preachers secured not only national survival, but also the loyalty of the Hungarian Christians as well, as they defended Western Christendom against the threat of Asiatic Mohammedanism.

Because the Reformed generation lived between "two pagans", that is Islam and Habsburg Catholicism, the oppressions by the latter caused these central problems to dominate the ecclesiastical and national life of the Hungarians: The doctrinal problems of freedom of thought, freedom in social life, (that is equality), freedom of religious practice. In final analysis, these problems led to the thousand-year-old Christian dilemma: The quest for tolerance.

The sixteenth century generation of Reformers, facing the question of religious tolerance, incorporated into their struggle for political freedom the solution for religious coexistence. They tried to establish an authority with which they could realize order in the society and that would guarantee religious as well as political equality. Protestantism, originally a freedom movement for universal political and religious freedom, saw its aspiration thus intensified in East Central Europe in the very shadow of Asiatic despotism. Although the Reformers did not totally reach their goal, they did obtain guaranteed freedom of conscience; this freedom was to make the individual morally responsible, to guarantee political and religious equality to his fellow man. The Biblical foundation of the Reformers' historical ambition for religious tolerance and social equality was found in II Corinthians 3:17: "Now the Lord is the Spirit, and where the Spirit of the Lord is, there is freedom." The unique result of their efforts was the *Pax Transylvania*.

The sociological characteristic of the Hungarian ethos was that it did not know subordination, only coordinate human relationship. Its root may go back to the Asiatic period, when in the Khazar Empire the ancestors of the Magyars practiced a coordinate socio-religious way of life. This heritage was manifested in the practice of religious tolerance during the Sixteenth Century Reformation among the Hungarian Protestant leaders and reaffirmed by the Helvetic-Calvinist theological explanation that the authority and sovereignty of the Gospel were never transferred to anyone, not even to the Church, but remained with God. The immediate result of this was that the superintendent as Church leader was only *primus inter pares*, first among equals.

The Hungarian "Second Reformation" [that is Helvetic], basically did nothing else than return the believers to the Holy Scriptures. From the process of *semper reformanda* the redeemed soul was reborn for freedom in order to become the servant of his fellow man. The Reformation had to become prophetic in order to produce a constant self-revision and to lead the faithful out of the fatalistic attitude toward their suffering, an attitude so characteristic of sixteenth century society. To work out this solution the preachers had to replace the humanistic historical concept with a Biblical one to reach down to the people, incorporating them into the national life.

The Lutheran Reformation had re-established the dominating role of religion. Its dominance became twice more obvious in Hungary where the Church was challenged by the Islamic threat.

Religious exclusiveness, however, had and still has the dilemma that it cannot solve the problem of tolerance.

Ever since being in the center of religious history, the Cross was erected by the bigotry of hatred, the spiritual wound of intolerance has never been healed on the body of Christianity; however, an effort in this direction was inaugurated by the Protestant reformers in Transylvania, where, in order to secure political stability in the midst of religious controversies, the political Diet established a church Synod, constituted of Church leaders and representatives of the three ethnical "nations"–Magyar, Székely, and Saxon. The positive result was that this political and ecclesiastical leadership worked out a *modus vivendi*, according to which for the first time in European religious history equality and freedom of religion was granted by constitution to the members of the four denominations: Roman Catholic, Lutheran,

Helvetic-Calvinist, and Unitarian. From 1545 until 1576, twenty-eight Synods and political Diets were dealing with this religious question.

Until recently nobody had recognized this unique religious legislation in history, which declared that: Preachers may proclaim the Gospel everywhere, each after his own understanding. If a congregation decides to accept their pastor's viewpoint, good; but when not, no preacher may force it to accept what would make its soul restless. Nobody may attack the preachers. Nobody shall be ridiculed because of his religious beliefs, neither may he be persecuted, because faith, which one learns by hearing, is given by God, and hearing occurs through the Gospel of God.[2]

Karl Heussi, in his often quoted text, *Kompendium der Kirchengeschichte*, showed his ignorance when he stated that in England under Cromwell religious freedom had ruled for the first time in Europe.[3]

Fortunately, the former Transylvanian of Saxon origin, Paul Philippi, teaching at the University of Heidelberg, has corrected this viewpoint, stating that the alleged religious freedom [under Cromwell] was aborted twice; first, when the Irish priests were massacred and the Catholics as well as the Antitrinitarians were excluded; second, when the Episcopalians were left out from the so-called tolerance, which ended completely after less than twenty years upon the installation of the Stuart dynasty.

Already in 1557 the Lutheran religion in Transylvania was granted that everyone could practice his religion as he wished.[4]

Philippi's conclusion in connection with the first legislated religious freedom was that Transylvania was the first state within Europe to give an example of reconciliation between religious differences built on state legislation and the possibility of incorporating the different confessions into the totality of the state.[5]

Erick Hassinger, researcher of the problem of religious tolerance, concluded that in Transylvania in the late 1600's a maximum of religious tolerance had been realized.[6]

One has to admit that the legislation of tolerance always will remain a relative task because absolute tolerance is a utopia, like the "samaritan tolerance".

It was exactly one hundred years before the disputed Cromwellian religious legislation took place, that Transylvanian confessional freedom was issued and practiced, beginning in 1557 with the Lutherans, in 1564 also with the Reformed, and finally in 1571 with the Unitarians. The latter were still threatened with the death penalty in England until 1813. Philippi's statement that Transylvania was the first Christian country with universal freedom of religion is thus convincing.[7]

How far the Transylvanian leaders and legislators distanced themselves from the age of the *Codex Justiniani* which declared death to those who questioned the dogma of the Holy Trinity! During the discussed religious development of *Pax Transylvania*, an uncommon process took place in the National Diet in the presence of the ruler, when Francis Dávid, Unitarian Bishop, was accused and tried for the shattering of the established religious coexistence. He was given the opportunity to defend himself, after which he was incarcerated *pro tempore*. He never was condemned under the law, and after a show imprisonment died a natural death, as has been explained by contemporary Unitarian Bishop Sándor Szent-Iványi.[8]

Dávid's trial took place at a time when in Western Christendom–in Switzerland, the Republic of Venice, France, and England–intolerance was common practice resulting in a death penalty. In Hungary and Transylvania, no one was burned at the stake, because its spiritual-religious climate was different. The following event may illustrate the difference. A self-confident Roman Catholic prelate challenged a Reformed preacher to a religious dispute. The prelate set a condition like that of Valentine Gentilis in Berne, namely that the loser should be beheaded. In the end, however, the victorious Reformed preacher asked from his opponent only one of his teeth as a remembrance.

***

In the preceding chapters many interrelated problems within the Hungarian Reformation have been presented in order to demonstrate its uniqueness, which was that toward the end of the sixteenth century ninety percent of the surviving Hungarian people had accepted the Protestant Reformation in Hungary and that the Lutheran policy of *cuius regio eius religio* which granted religious freedom exclusively to the ruling nobility in Germany, was not endorsed in Hungary.

In the framework of comparative church history, it is clear that the early Lutheran domination in East Central European countries such as Poland, Bohemia, Hungary, and Croatia, was arrested in the middle of the sixteenth century. From that time on, the Helvetic-Calvinist Reformation began to develop in those countries; however, only the Hungarian people remained faithful to its teaching.

Footnotes

1. Herings, D. H. *Historische Nachricht von dem ersten Anfang der Evangelisch-Reformierten Kirche in Brandenburg.* In: *Ecclesia Reformata.* ed. Gassmann. Wien, 1968. Benno Herder, p. 96.
" . . . *schlimmer erschien als das Papstum: das Sprichwort 'lieber papstisch als Kalvinisch' wurde von vielen Lutheranen ernsthaft als These verfochten.*"

2. Erdélyi Országgyűllési Emlékek. Ed. Magyar Tudományos Akadémia Történeti Bizottsága.
see also: *Moumenta Comitalia Regni Transylvaniae.* Vol. TT. Budapest, 1875, p. 343.

3. Heussi, Karl. *Kompendium der Kirchengeschichte. 4e Auflage.* Tübingen, 1919. J.C.B. Mohr, p. 453.
"*Unter Cromwell hat in England wenn auch mit gewissen Einschränkungen, für die christliche Denominationen Religionsfreiheit geherrscht zum ersten Male in Europa.*"

4. *Urkundenbuch der Evangelische Landeskirche.* A.B. 1 1862, p. 85.

5. Philippi, Paul. *Grundsatzliches und historisches über die Anfänge der religiösen Freiheit in England und Siebenbürgen.* In: *Evangelische Diaspora. Zeitschrift des Gustav Adolf Werkes.* Franz Lau, 1955, 26 Jhg. p. 118.

6. Hassinger, Erick H. *Toleranz im 16en Jahrhundert.* Basel, 1966. Vlg. Helbing und Lichtenhahn. p. 24.

7. Philippi, Paul. *Reformation in Türkennot.* In: *Evangelische Diaspora.* Franz Lau, 1954, 25 Jhg. p. 98.

8. Szent-Iványi, Sándor. *A Magyar Vallásszabadság.* American Library and Historical Society. New York, 1964. p. 69.

Index

TEXTS AND STUDIES IN RELIGION